The Gurkhas

The Gurkhas

Special Force

CHRIS BELLAMY

JOHN MURRAY

First published in Great Britain in 2011 by John Murray (Publishers)
An Hachette UK Company

1

© Chris Bellamy 2011

The right of Chris Bellamy to be identified as the Author of the Work has been asserted by him in accordance with the Copyright, Designs and Patents Act 1988.

Maps drawn by Rodney Paull

A CIP catalogue record for this title is available from the British Library

Hardback ISBN 978-1-84854-342-3
Trade paperback ISBN 978-1-84854-343-0

Typeset in 11.5/14 Bembo
by Servis Filmsetting Ltd, Stockport, Cheshire

Printed and bound by Clays Ltd, St Ives plc

John Murray policy is to use papers that are natural, renewable and recyclable products and made from wood grown in sustainable forests. The logging and manufacturing processes are expected to conform to the environmental regulations of the country of origin.

John Murray (Publishers)
338 Euston Road
London NW1 3BH

www.johnmurray.co.uk

For my sister, Kate, and her husband, Lieutenant Commander Paul Gray, Fleet Air Arm, serving in our fourth Afghan War as I write.

That we may learn something from history. . .

Contents

List of Plates

twenty-six assaults by mutineers, 1857. They are standing in front of Hindoo Rao's house on the Badle-ki-Serai ridge, north of Delhi, looking to the south.

14. A British officer – seemingly called Alex – and Gurkhas at the time of the Mutiny, or just after; one of very few contemporary photographs. An Indian Army List for 1858 lists a Major A. Bagot as commandant of the New Nasiri (Rifle) Battalion, but it is not certain that 'Alex' is him

15. British officers of the 4th Gurkhas, Second Afghan War, Captain C. A. Mercer standing left, Lieutenant Colonel Rowcroft, CO, third from right

16. British officers of the 5th Gurkhas, Second Afghan War, Lieutenant W. Yielding standing behind Lieutenant Colonel Fitzherbert, CO

17. Bayonet team of the 5th Gurkhas, Second Afghan War

18. Mercer and Mainwaring's tent, 4th Gurkhas, Jellalabad, March 1879, painted by a press correspondent

19. Gurkhas, possibly Gurkha Scouts, 1897 or later. The men appear to be from 5th Gurkhas. The unidentified officer is also from 5th Gurkhas, possibly Lieutenant Tillard

20. Afridi or Orakzai tribesman, probably a sniper, captured by the Gurkha Scouts, 1897. They are wearing shorts, which were first worn by the 5th Gurkhas in the Tirah campaign in 1897

21. The assault on Dargai, 1897. Contemporary photograph and annotation showing the flank attack of 18 October and the approach to the summit

22. The assault on Dargai, 1897. Contemporary photograph and annotation showing the key positions of Chagru Kotal, the object of the frontal attack, and Samana Suk, the commanding height above it, seized by the flanking force

23. Early Gurkha parachutist. The helmet is of the type first issued to British paratroops after 1942

24. Brigadier Michael Calvert (left front) with Lieutenant Colonel Shaw and, just visible, left rear, Major Lumley

25. Surrender, 1945: Japanese surrender to Gurkhas

26. Anti-riot drills, 10th Gurkha Rifles, Malaya

List of Figures and Tables

List of Figures

List of Tables

Glossary and Guide to Military Terms

This book is for the general reader as well as the military professional and enthusiast. Given that National Service ended fifty years ago, no great familiarity with military organisation, structures, terminology or sociology is assumed.

1/1st, etc. Regiments (see below)   Regiments may comprise a number of **battalions.** Where isolated references appear, these are written in full – 1st Battalion, 1st Gurkha Rifles. However, where a number of units are referred to together, the numbering is abbreviated: 1/1st, 2/6th for example, refers to 1st Battalion, 1st Gurkha Rifles, 2nd Battalion, 6th Gurkha Rifles, and so on.

Army   This refers to the whole of a nation's land forces ('the British Army'), or a major administrative subdivision of the same. Thus, the British-Indian Army comprised three separate armies, one for each of the principalities – those of Bengal (the largest, in which the Gurkhas were formed), Madras and Bombay. Finally, an 'army' can be the largest-but-one fighting formation on land, such as the 8th Army in North Africa in the Second World War. In the Second World War, however, armies, which could reach 100,000 strong, were linked together in 'army groups' (British and American) or 'fronts' (Russian), or 'area armies' (Japanese).

Battalion   The basic tactical unit of infantry, very roughly 1,000 strong, give or take a few hundred either way. It is the principal administrative unit in most armies and has a long history, being very much like a Roman cohort. In the modern British Army, a battalion is commanded by a lieutenant colonel, although the first Gurkha battalions were commanded by lieutenants, then captains, then majors and so forth.

Brevet Effectively a local or acting rank, in order to make officers more senior without waiting for promotion, which depended on seniority and, in the case of British officers before 1871, purchase. East India Company officers were jealous of the fact that officers of the King's or (from 1837) the Queen's Regiments, based in the UK, were eligible for promotion by brevet, while they were not. The facility was later extended to them.

Brigade The lowest formation comprising all arms and services necessary to sustain a major force in the field, typically 5,000 strong, give or take a thousand or so. Usually commanded by a brigadier (general), but sometimes by a colonel.

Brigade of Gurkhas The combined body of UK Gurkha forces, currently about 3,000 strong. It currently comprises the two infantry battalions (see above) of the 1st and 2nd Battalions, the Royal Gurkha Rifles (RGR), the Queen's Gurkha Engineers, the Queen's Gurkha Signals and the Queen's Own Gurkha Logistic Regiment (see below).

Carbine A shorter-barrelled firearm, still fired from the shoulder, carried by cavalry, artillery or police.

Commanding officer The head of a major unit (battalion; see above).

Commission A letter from the head of state appointing an officer in the armed forces. The fact that officers hold their appointment from the sovereign personally imbues them with special authority. Traditionally, commissions were signed by the head of state in person – the king or queen in the UK, the president in the United States, and so on. At the time of writing, however, commissions are signed by the Secretary of State for Defence and the Secretary of Defense, respectively.

Company The basic subdivision of a battalion, very roughly 100 strong. As such, it equates to a Roman century. Companies are commanded by a major in the modern British Army or a captain in the American. In the Gurkhas, companies were traditionally commanded by non-British Gurkha officers, but by the twentieth century the officer commanding and his second-in-command were usually British.

Corps Like **regiment** (see below), corps has more than one meaning. The first Gurkha **regiments**, that 'newly formed and so peculiar a corps',

were called 'corps'. The term therefore refers to a coherent body of people, whether intended for armed combat or other onerous service – the 'Peace Corps', for example. In military terminology nowadays it is used to denote either a specialised arm of the armed forces, such as the Corps of Royal Engineers or the Royal Corps of Signals, or a major formation comprising more than one **division** (see below). The latter would typically be commanded by a lieutenant general. Finally, in the Gurkha context, British and other officers and other ranks attached to the Brigade of Gurkhas (see below) from the supporting arms of the British Army are referred to by the Royal Gurkha Rifles as 'Corps' people. These include officers, warrant officers and NCOs of the Royal Engineers posted to the Queen's Gurkha Engineers, the Royal Signals posted to the Queen's Gurkha Signals, and the Royal Logistic Corps posted to the Queen's Own Gurkha Logistic Regiment.

Desant   Russian term for a surprise attack in the enemy rear, whether delivered by parachute, helicopter, amphibious or rapid ground movement. Adopted by British and US forces in the 1980s.

Division   A formation comprising all arms and services necessary to undertake independent action. Typically commanded by a major general and in the order of 10,000 strong. In 1814–15, David Ochterlony, unusually, commanded a division as a colonel.

DSO   Distinguished Service Order. Award for gallantry and/or outstanding competence in command.

Fusil   A short, smooth-bore firearm, often carried by cavalry until the mid-nineteenth century. Effectively a **carbine**.

GCO   Gurkha Commissioned Officer (1957–2007). A Gurkha holding the Queen's Commission, and therefore part of the same career structure as British officers. Until the Gurkha Terms and Conditions of Service (GTACOS) review published on 8 March 2007, such appointments were quite rare.

Governor-General   The East India Company's top man in India, before 1857.

Gurkha, Gorkha, Goorkha   See Chapter 1. Most narrowly, a member of 'Gurkha' designated units of the British, Indian, Nepalese, Singapore or Brunei security forces. More widely, Tibeto-Burman *jats* (tribes) from the 'hills' of Nepal.

Havildar   An Indian Army or Gurkha sergeant.

Havildar major   An Indian Army or Gurkha sergeant major.

Infantry   Soldiers who usually fight on their feet, although they may be carried in armoured vehicles, whose job is to close with and destroy the enemy. In the nineteenth century, the term was used of line troops, as distinct from the elite riflemen.

IOM   Indian Order of Merit. The first award for gallantry in British military service to be created, in 1837.

Jat   A Nepalese 'tribe', including the *jats* such as the Magars and Gurungs from which the Gurkhas have traditionally been recruited to the British and Indian armies.

JCO   Junior Commissioned Officer, Indian Army, post-1947. Three ranks – jemadar (from 1965, naib subedar); subedar; and subedar major (see below) – for officers promoted from the ranks, equivalent to QGOs and VCOs. See Table 2.

Jemadar   (later **naib subedar** in the post-1947 Indian Army). Lieutenant in the East India Company and British-Indian armies, and a JCO (see above) in the post-1947 Indian Army. See Table 2.

KCIO   King's Commissioned Indian Officer. After the First World War, the British made tentative steps to start the process of 'Indianisation' under which Indians could be promoted into higher officer ranks. A very few Indian cadets were sent to study at the Royal Military College, Sandhurst (it did not become the 'Academy' until after the Second World War), and were given full commissions as KCIOs. These were equivalent in every way to British commissioned officers and had full authority over British troops (unlike VCOs).

Khaki   From the Hindi and Urdu word for 'earth' or 'dust-coloured', and deriving from the Persian noun *khāk*, meaning 'earth' or 'dust'. It entered the English language in 1857 as a descriptive word for the covert uniforms first worn by Harry Lumsden's Corps of Guides in 1848, and khaki uniforms were certainly in use during the 1857 Indian Mutiny. Although now associated with a light olive drab or sandy colour, and also used to describe the darker brown of British uniforms in both world wars, the original khaki was very grey, like the landscape on the North-West Frontier and in Afghanistan, akin to the shade we now call taupe.

KGO   King's Gurkha Officer (1947–53). Holding a rank and responsibilities equivalent to a fully commissioned officer, a member of an intermediate or 'sandwich' band between fully commissioned officers and warrant officers (see Table 2).

Kotal   (Mountain) pass in Iranian and other related languages.

Lance naik   Lance corporal. See Table 2.

Line, infantry of the   Soldiers whose job was originally mainly to fight in close order and deliver volleys of massed but relatively inaccurate musket fire. The Indian Army's line infantry was better paid than 'irregulars' and light troops, which included the Gurkhas. As weapons became more lethal, all infantry had to disperse, and the distinction between 'line infantry' and 'rifles' (see below) became blurred.

Mutiny   The great Indian Mutiny, 1857–8.

Musket   A long, smooth-bore firearm. From the sixteenth-century Spanish word *mosquete*, originally a heavy firearm fired from a rest, which rapidly supplanted the smaller arquebus. The armament of most infantry until the 1850s.

Naib subedar   The equivalent of a lieutenant, promoted from the ranks, in the modern Indian Army. See Table 2.

Naik   Indian Army or Gurkha corporal.

NCO   Non-commissioned officer. A person in the armed forces exercising authority but not holding a commission from the head of state (see

above). Usually NCOs are appointed from the ranks, although some armed forces have a distinct NCO intake. In practice, senior NCOs exist in a parallel hierarchy with junior officers and often do the same jobs, for example, platoon commanders. NCOs can be promoted and demoted at the behest of their commander, without the lengthy selection processes, courses and procedures that attend officer promotions.

Officer   A responsible person in the armed forces holding a **commission**, usually from the sovereign (see above).

Officer commanding   The head of a minor unit, below a **battalion** (see above).

Picquet (also picket, piquet)   To temporarily occupy high ground to secure the passage of a column below, a necessary technique in mountainous terrain such as the North-West Frontier.

Platoon   The basic subdivision of a **company** (see above). Roughly thirty or so strong. In the modern British Army it is the lowest sub-unit commanded by a commissioned officer, but in the Gurkhas it was traditionally commanded by a Viceroy's Commissioned Officer (VCO) or a Queen's Gurkha Officer (QGO). See below and Table 2.

PVC   Param Vir Chakra ('Bravest of the Brave circle'). Post-1947, the Indian equivalent of the VC. Normally only awarded posthumously. Two of the three awarded have been posthumous (see Chapters 9 and 10).

QGE   Queen's Gurkha Engineers. A **regiment** (see below) of the Royal Engineers designated as part of the **Brigade of Gurkhas** (see above).

QGO(1953–2007)   Queen's Gurkha Officer. Holding a rank and responsibilities broadly equivalent to a fully commissioned officer, but a member of an intermediate or 'sandwich' band between fully commissioned officers and warrant officers (see Table 2). The title was abolished after the publication of the Gurkha Terms and Conditions of Service (GTACOS) review on 8 March 2007 (see Table 2).

QGS   Queen's Gurkha Signals. A **regiment** (see below) of the Royal Signals designated as part of the **Brigade of Gurkhas** (see above).

QOGLR   Queen's Own Gurkha Logistics Regiment. A **regiment** (see below) of the Royal Logistic Corps designated as part of the **Brigade of Gurkhas** (see above).

Regiment   The regiment, in the British armed forces and those of the British Commonwealth, is the 'family' organisation to which a soldier belongs. It is also used, however, to refer to a **battalion** (see above) – equivalent in arms other than the **infantry** – as in 'regiments' of artillery, engineers, signals and so on. In this book, Gurkha regiments often comprise several battalions, a **battalion** (see above) being a tactical unit of several hundred men. In continental armies – the German and Russian included – however, a regiment may be a tactical unit, comprising, typically, three battalions and supporting arms. Thus, a Russian motor-rifle regiment, around 1,500 strong, is a miniature **brigade** (see above). In the modern British and Indian armies, regiments may each comprise several battalions, from the two of the British Royal Gurkha Rifles, to five or six battalions for some of the seven Indian Gurkha regiments (see Figure 4).

Rifle   A long firearm with spiralling grooves down the barrel to impart spin to the bullet and make it travel further and more accurately. First introduced in the sixteenth century, they were adopted by rich landowners and huntsmen, but were rare on the battlefield until the eighteenth century because they were slow to load. At the end of the eighteenth century specialist rifle units were introduced.

Rifleman   A soldier (lowest grade) in a rifle unit, including the British Rifles (Greenjackets and Light Infantry) and the Gurkha Rifles.

Rifles   Originally units armed with **rifles** (see above). After rifles became pretty much universal as infantry small-arms, the name was retained, like many designations of specialist troops, as a mark of elite status.

Sangar   The word derives from the Afghan term for a tiny fort, originally built of rocks, for one or a handful of soldiers. A sangar is a fortified observation post, from which fire can be delivered. Sangars can also be prefabricated from concrete.

Sappers Military engineers responsible for constructing bridges, fortifications and the like, and for demolishing those of the enemy by placing explosive charges (mines) and other means.

Section The smallest military grouping, typically eight to ten men, equating with the American squad, commanded in the Indian and British armies by a naik or corporal. Smaller groups of four soldiers have, however, been found convenient and used – known in the British Army as a 'brick' or (in the Special Forces), as a 'sabre'.

Sepoy An Indian Army soldier, equivalent to a private. Technically the Gurkhas were 'sepoys', until they became riflemen, but they and their British officers hated the term. Sepoy is still the term for a modern Indian Army infantryman.

Sowar An Indian Army cavalry or (now) armoured soldier, equivalent to a trooper.

Subedar A captain equivalent, in the East India Company and British-Indian armies, and a captain equivalent promoted from the ranks in the modern (post-1947) Indian Army.

Subedar major A major equivalent, in the East India Company and British-Indian armies, and promoted from the ranks in the modern (post-1947) Indian Army.

VC Victoria Cross. Supreme award for gallantry, instituted in 1856, backdated to 1854. Open to Gurkhas and Indian soldiers from 1911.

VCO Viceroy's Commissioned Officer. An officer in the pre-1947 Indian Army holding 'commissioned' rank (lieutenant up to major), but whose commission was signed by the **Viceroy** (see below) and not by the sovereign. After 1947 they were redesignated King's Gurkha Officers (KGO) or, from 1953, Queen's Gurkha Officers (QGO; see above).

Viceroy Literally 'Vice-King', from the French. The British rulers of India from 1858 to 1947. They were all male, and their wives were called the Vicereine.

WO   Warrant officer. A senior soldier holding important administrative and command responsibilities but not a full **commission** (see above). Instead, they hold a [Royal] Warrant, which is fairly close. Sergeant majors or, in the case of the Indian army and the Gurkhas, havildar majors, were and are warrant officers.

Preface and Acknowledgements

O N THE MORNING of 21 May 2009, the then Home Secretary, Jacqui Smith, conceded a massive defeat for the British government. Men born in Nepal who had served in the British Army's Brigade of Gurkhas for more than four years, and their dependants, would finally be allowed to settle in the United Kingdom. Just under a month earlier, on 23 April, there had been outrage when the British government had imposed stringent criteria for ex-Gurkhas wishing to settle in the UK. Many people felt these criteria were unreasonably demanding for a group of men who had served so loyally and prominently throughout nearly 200 years of British military history. In the 153 years that the Victoria Cross had been given as the supreme award for gallantry in the face of the enemy, the Gurkhas had won no fewer than twenty-six. Thirteen were won by Nepali or Sikkim Gurkhas and thirteen by their British officers. Nepalese Gurkhas, as opposed to their British officers, were not eligible for the VC until 1911, before which date they won many Indian Orders of Merit (IOM), many of which were the equivalent of the VC. Since 1947 three Gorkhas, as they are known in India, have also won India's highest gallantry award, the Param Vir Chakra (PVC).

After an energetic and hard-fought campaign led by the popular British actress Joanna Lumley, whose father had served in the Gurkhas (see plate 24), the British government finally gave way. Many in the British Brigade of Gurkhas had advised against acceding on this issue, warning of the potential liabilities for the UK and the cost to Nepal in both money and talent. The British had traditionally 'taken the best and sent them back better' – and with pensions that were a big contribution to the Nepalese economy.

However, there were other arguments, including the political and social situation in Nepal, and changes in the way ex-Gurkhas were regarded there. The Justice for Gurkhas campaign won. Brandishing the distinctive Gurkha kukri, the curved knife, with its 10-inch blade, the iconic emblem, weapon and tool of the Gurkha, Joanna Lumley uttered the war cry that had terrified the Queen's enemies for nearly two centuries. '*Ayo Gurkhali*' – 'We are the Gurkhas'.[1]

This book examines who the Gurkhas are, the story of their 200 years as instruments of Indian and British security policy, and in so doing will help show why they have inspired such affection and found such a place in the British heart. The Gurkhas are professional soldiers, subject to probably the most rigorous and exclusive selection procedure in the world, which the author has witnessed. They are then deployed in isolation from their home and native culture, on behalf of a foreign state. That makes them perfect for the security requirements of the twenty-first century, as we leave the citizen armies of the twentieth century far behind. In a way, they epitomise a return to the era before the British started recruiting them in 1815 – in which highly disciplined professional armies were recruited to fight limited wars.

Does that mean that the Gurkhas are, as many critics have alleged, mercenaries? Technically, no.[2] They may have started out that way, but very soon became members of the armed forces, first of the East India Company, and then, after 1857, of British India. Members of the armed forces of a party to a conflict are specifically excluded from the definition of 'mercenary' in the 1977 Protocol to the 1949 Geneva Conventions.

Another myth is that the kukri must draw blood every time it is drawn. That idea has been very effective in honing the Gurkhas' image as formidable fighters, but is untrue. Gurkhas draw their kukris to chop firewood, build fences – just about anything. As a result, they have never carried the British Army-issue machete.

The British Army is not the only force that employs these tough, resilient men from the mountains of Nepal as soldiers. The Gurkhas were a natural part of the British-Indian Army, and when it became the army of the new Republic of India in 1947, four regiments were transferred to the British Army. Before 1947 the Gurkha regiments

had certain distinctive characteristics and formed 'a separate Gurkha line within the Indian Army'.[3] Nevertheless, the way they were organised and officered was much the same as the rest of the British-Indian Army. After 1947, six regiments remained with the Indian Army, their natural home, and their name was changed back to Gorkha in 1949. The four that were transferred to the British Army found themselves in a strange, aberrant position, which has continued until the present day.

At the time of writing, there are about 40,000 Gorkhas serving in the Indian Army. One of India's two field marshals since independence in 1947, Sam Manekshaw, was a Gorkha. A chapter in this book covers the very substantial Indian Gorkha force – now nearly half the size of the entire British Army – since 1947, and their role in India's wars against China in 1962, and against Pakistan in 1965, 1971 and 1999. In 1971, the 4th Battalion, 5th Gorkha Rifles was the first Indian Army regiment to be used in a heliborne attack. Indian Army Gorkhas have also been deployed extensively in peacekeeping operations, from the Congo to Kosovo. The sultan of Brunei has his own Gurkha Reserve Unit, an internal security force, as well as a British Gurkha battalion based in his sultanate, while the Singapore Police has an elite Gurkha contingent. And there are also Gurkha contingents in the Malaysian armed forces. Finally, the US Navy employs Gurkha guards in Bahrain, and for security at certain other foreign ports and consulates. And if you cross the Atlantic on an ocean liner belonging to a certain well-known British shipping line, you may feel comfortably secure when you notice that many of the smartly turned-out waiters have the distinctive, though varied, build and features of 'Gurkhas'.[4]

Why a new book when no other part of the former British-Indian Army, or of the British Army since 1947, has 'received more printer's ink than the Gurkhas'?[5] Field Marshal Sir John Chapple's 1980 *Bibliography*, now thirty years old, identified 320 such works, of which about half are substantial.[6] There have been many more since then. The British popular view of the Gurkhas was formed in the colonial period and, in its most popular form, has changed relatively little since. Sometimes this has embarrassed serving Gurkhas, whether British or Nepalese. Sometimes descriptions, like the one

from *Navy and Army Illustrated* in 1900, highlight a combination of the sometimes contradictory qualities that make the Gurkhas special: 'As fighters . . . [Gurkhas] possess not only the dash which determines the fortunes of the attack, but the stubborn pluck which knows how to endure punishment without becoming demoralised.'[7] Since then, however, the constant emphasis on Gurkhas' loyalty and blind obedience has often been condescending, hackneyed and inaccurate, and is certainly out of date. Lionel Caplan's outstanding book, *Warrior Gentlemen*, is one of a few scholarly anthropological treatments of the 'Gurkhas', whom he quickly identifies as 'a fiction'.[8] In his book, Caplan highlighted *The Empire Annual for Boys* for 1917, which portrayed the Gurkhas as being perfect doubles of the ideal public schoolboy:

> 'Gurkhas are brave to reckless . . . faithful to their officers . . . terrible little fighters . . . fearsome national weapon, the kukri . . . The Nepalese are proud and independent maintaining their political freedom through long centuries . . . While fighting fiercely, Gurkhas showed a most generous spirit of courtesy, worthy of a more enlightened people . . . they despise the natives of India, but have a great admiration for the British . . . faithfulness, high spirits, and love of humour . . . fond of sports.[9]

Much of the literature about the 'Gurkhas' mirrors this patronising tone. The Gurkhas' utter loyalty to their British officers is a recurring theme, reinforced by thirteen examples of Gurkhas who did not know what they were fighting for.[10] Even those who knew better and who spoke the truth about the Gurkhas might sometimes find it twisted to support this view. The great scholar Sir Ralph Turner, who served with the 3rd Queen Alexandra's Own Gurkha Rifles in the First World War, dedicated his 1931 *Dictionary of the Nepali Language* to them.

> As I write these words my thoughts return to those who were my comrades, the stubborn and indomitable peasants of Nepal. Once more I hear the laughter with which you greeted every hardship. Once more I see you in your bivouacs or about your fires, on forced march or in the trenches, now shivering with wet and cold, now scorched by a pitiless and burning sun. Uncomplaining you endure

hunger and thirst and wounds; and at the last your wavering lines disappear into the smoke and wrath of battle. Bravest of the brave, most generous of the generous, never had country more faithful friends than you.[11]

Sir Ralph, the great authority on Sanskrit, was one of a remarkable generation of scholars formed before the First World War, who then served in it and were catalysed and hardened by it. The last sentence, which appears on the Gurkha memorial in London, is true enough, but the tone is open to misinterpretation. *Bravest of the Brave* was a possible title for the present book, but a serving Gurkha officer told the author he thought it was 'hackneyed'. One useful characteristic of modern Gurkha soldiers, which has attracted comment in the context of peace-support operations, is their inventiveness and the way they quickly make friends with local people:

> 'They're good at using local stuff. How many British soldiers would kill a chicken and eat it? Our boys do. They are quite inventive. When I was in Sarajevo [in 1994], we arrived at the camp and after about half an hour the officer commanding, the second-in-command and I went out to survey the area. Then we saw two of our boys playing chess with one of the local shopkeepers. Half an hour!'[12]

The praise lavished on the Gurkhas in British folklore, and the general awareness of their history and identity among educated elements of British society, are not replicated in their native Nepal. A British radio programme could refer to 'the Gurkhas' as a respected institution and elite military force, without having to explain who they were.[13] However, in Nepal, outside the main 'Gurkha' recruiting areas the response is likely to be: '*Gorkha*. That's a town . . .'[14] As we shall see in Chapter 1, the 'Gurkhas' are not generally recruited from the highest-caste *jats*, and high-caste Nepalis may look down on them, especially the Brahmans, many of whom have espoused the Maoist movement in Nepali politics. After a few drinks, they may also refer to those who serve in foreign armies as little better than traitors. John Cross is a retired Gurkha lieutenant colonel who left the UK in 1944. He commanded the Gurkha Parachute Company and the UK's Jungle Warfare School.[15] A distinguished scholar who speaks nine oriental languages, he has settled

in Nepal and is now regarded as a guru by the Pokhara community where he lives. He explained that the massive esteem in which British hold the Gurkhas is not shared by many Nepalis.

> This country is the only country in the world that does not hold the military in any regard. [Being a Gurkha] is a bit like being a mason. If you're a mason, the lodge means everything to you. If you're not a mason, it means bugger all. They [high-caste Nepalis] regard 'Gurkhas' as knuckle-headed, second-class citizens with no proper religious background. They regard them as a vociferous, overpaid and spoiled minority'.[16]

The economic and political situation in Nepal shaped the emergence of the 'Gurkha' as a professional soldier in foreign service 200 years ago, and is shaping his fate today. Brutally put, if Gurkhas are not respected and welcomed back in the country whence they came, they have more incentive to settle in UK.

The changed political climate in Nepal since 2001, when the Crown Prince killed himself and there was a Maoist insurrection, makes a new book timely. So does the deployment of Gurkhas to Iraq and Afghanistan, both areas where they have served before. A new official history of the British 'Gurkhas', and Indian Gurkhas before 1947, *Britain's Gurkhas*, by Brigadier Christopher Bullock, was published in October 2009.[17] The present book does not seek to compete with or replicate Christopher's splendid volume, which was completed with the support of the Brigade of Gurkhas UK and the Ministry of Defence. This one was not supported by the MoD, being completed at the author's own expense. However, it is hoped that it will complement the other Christopher's work, and highlight other areas, particularly India's Gorkhas since 1947.

The view of the Gurkhas in English-language writing is almost invariably positive. In 165 years of publications, Byron Farwell, the writer of an excellent book in 1984, found only one disparaging word about the Gurkhas, and that by the 'eccentric' Orde Wingate, who said they were 'mentally unsuited' for the role given to them in the first Chindit operation in Burma in the Second World War. This remark immediately attracted refutation by the Gurkha community. Wingate, an artilleryman, was, of course, an outsider.[18]

There are four main kinds of book about the Gurkhas. The first are regimental histories of the eleven Gurkha regiments raised at various times by the British-Indian Army and regimental histories of the Indian Gurkha regiments after 1947. The second are personal memoirs and diaries by British officers who served with the Gurkhas. The third are 'coffee table picture books with splendid photographs of Gurkhas in various settings. These books always include a commentary or introductory text on the Gurkhas, their history and exploits, by an officer with the appropriate Gurkha experience.'[19] Finally there are books 'which attempt to tell the Gurkha story in a general and popular way'.

Of the latter, Tony Gould's *Imperial Warriors* (1999)[20] is, in the author's view, probably the best. Clearly there have been major developments since it was published and the present book, which probably also falls into the same genre, will underline those. As a work of scholarship, A. P. Coleman's *A Special Corps*, the authoritative study of the beginnings of Gurkha service with the British, stands apart and also deserves special recommendation.[21] The definitive account of how the Gurkha regiments evolved, including masses of detail about organisation and recruiting, is *The Lineages and Composition of Gurkha Regiments in British Service*, the latest edition of which was published as a limited edition by the Gurkha Museum in March 2010.[22] However, the present volume differs from most others in the genre because I am, emphatically, an *outsider*. Tony Gould describes himself as an 'inside outsider', but served as a National Service officer with the Gurkhas. Most books about the 'Gurkhas' emphasise the author's credentials by stressing that he (they are almost universally male) has 'been there, done that' – and got the T-shirt. Usually the authors get a more senior officer writing a foreword to underline the credentials.[23]

This book is a bit different. I attempted to buy the T-shirt at the headquarters of British Gurkhas Nepal in Kathmandu, but Gurkhas are generally of small stature and, unfortunately, even the *Gurkha* size 'extra large' was not big enough. I might have found a candidate to write a foreword in Lieutenant General Sir Philip Trousdell, who began his career as a Royal Irish Ranger but commanded 48 Gurkha Brigade in Hong Kong and was then colonel commandant

of the Brigade of Gurkhas and chair of the Gurkha Welfare Trust. It was good to meet again, by chance, in Pokhara. Sir Philip and Diana Donovan were there to open the first ever retirement home for Gurkhas. That, in itself was significant, as well as a slightly sad indicator of changed social circumstances, and the breakdown of traditional reliance on the extended family in Nepal. However, instead of delaying the story of the Gurkhas with Sir Philip's observations, they are cited in the appropriate place in the book.

I am grateful to Sir Philip, to Colonel Andrew Mills, the Defence Attaché in Kathmandu, and to 'MB', for all their help in Nepal, and to numerous others, serving and retired, who spoke on condition of anonymity. I thank Lieutenant Colonel (retired) John Cross, one of the greatest authorities on the Gurkhas and also on Nepal, who gave his time in Pokhara, and who provided additional comment and correction. I also thank Gavin Edgerley-Harris, the archivist at the Gurkha Museum in Winchester, who worked long and hard to help me; Carl Schultze, who kindly gave permission to allow the use of a poignant and particularly relevant photograph of his, obtained through the Gurkha Museum; the staff at the Templer Study Centre, the National Army Museum, and, in particular, Emma Lefley of the Photographic Department; the staff of the British Library, and the National Archives at Kew for all their help. My thanks also to the National Galleries of Scotland for the picture of General Ochterlony, and to Sandeep Khanal of the National Museum of Nepal for permission to take and use my photograph of the intimidating portrait of Prithwi Narayan Shah, 'the Great', the unifier of Nepal.

Finally, my thanks to my superb representatives at PFD (Peters, Fraser and Dunlop), Michael Sissons and Annabel Merullo, and to my publishers, John Murray of London, especially Roland Philipps and Victoria Murray-Browne, my editors. When I encountered one of the first lithographs of a Gurkha soldier, from the 1830s (Plate 8), in the Gurkha Museum, I noticed that the copyright was held by John Murray of Albemarle Street, who at the time specialised in publishing books about the subcontinent, as they still do. As always, my agents and publishers have been wondrously patient. Thank you. And thank you, too, to all the contacts in Nepal, who helped,

but asked for no acknowledgement. Professor sahib thanks you, from the bottom of his heart.

As always my wonderful wife Heather, who uses her maiden name of Kerr for her professional work in places where even the bravest of the brave hesitate to go, has been essential. Thank you, memsahib. Responsibility for any errors or misinterpretations is mine alone.

So, without further ado, the command the Gurkhas await to launch an attack, with courage *tempered by cunning*: – '*jañ!*' – 'go!'

Prologue

AFGHANISTAN, 4 NOVEMBER 2008. Musah Qaleh is a town in northern Helmand province with a population of about 20,000. It has been held by Afghan security forces since December 2007, but Taliban insurgents have gained the area south of the town. They have occupied several compounds surrounded by mud-brick walls and laced the area with home-made bombs – improvised explosive devices (IEDs). These threaten local civilians and Afghan and foreign security forces alike.

Major Ross Daines, the British officer commanding B Company, 2nd Royal Gurkha Rifles, said his mission was to clear a swathe of compounds that had previously been used by the insurgents as out-posts. This would push the insurgents to the south and enable the Afghan National Army to operate freely in the area. When the Gurkhas had cleared it, B Company, 1st Princess of Wales's Royal Regiment, would remain in place to ensure that the insurgents could not return to the area.

After a five-hour move from the patrol base, which took so long because every move had to be covered by someone else and the enemy could be anywhere, the Gurkhas positioned themselves overlooking the first compound. Huge Mastiff armoured vehicles, surrounded by cages to protect them against anti-tank weapons and manned by the Queen's Dragoon Guards, watched over the Gurkha riflemen as they prepared to attack.

They started moving over a piece of open ground – a field about 250 metres across – but came under fire from one of the compounds to the west. Caught in the open, they dived to the ground but no one could see where the fire was coming from.

Then, No. 1 Section under Lance Corporal Gajendra attempted

to 'hard target' – to reach cover – ducking, bobbing and weaving to make themselves as difficult to hit as possible. Rifleman Yubraj Rai was shot and went down. After a moment Lance Corporal Gajendra and Riflemen Manju and Dhan sprinted across 100 metres of open ground towards the wounded man, with complete disregard for their own safety, with bullets landing around their feet, while the rest of the platoon gave covering fire. The three Gurkhas pulled their fallen comrade into cover. According to Rifleman Dhan:

> Rifleman Yubraj dropped to the ground and I did the same. I thought he was taking cover. He didn't move for a while and suddenly shouted. I noticed he was hit by an enemy bullet. I crawled to Yubraj and tried to calm him down. I concentrated on giving first aid to Yub and tried to find the gunshot wound.
>
> I gave him some water to drink and poured some on his head. Lance Corporal Gajendra and Rifleman Manju came crawling towards us. They pulled him to a safer compound and I was responding to enemy fire using both mine and Yub's weapon. We managed to evacuate him to a compound where the medical evacuation team arrived later. *I never noticed the bullets landing around me, but I was shocked when I heard from other members of the section and the platoon how close the rounds had been* [emphasis added].
>
> At the time it seemed impossible to evacuate Rifleman Yubraj, though we managed to do it. I thought he would not leave us this soon. While in the open field I thought we would not come back alive, thank God we are here. I felt helpless not being able to save Yubraj. I am so sad to lose Yubraj.[1]

The platoon had called the Gurkhas' Reconnaissance Platoon to say that a soldier had been wounded. They sent four Jackals – 4x4 all-terrain vehicles – across rough country and under fire to pick up the wounded Gurkha. But they were too late to save him.

'*I never noticed the bullets landing around me, but I was shocked when I heard from other members of the section and the platoon how close the rounds had been* . . .' Rifleman Dhan's description mirrors countless citations for gallantry throughout the 200 years that the Gurkhas – the wiry, tough, cunning, practical Hillmen from Nepal – have been serving in the British and Indian armies. So do the words of the platoon commander, Second Lieutenant Oli Cochrane, a young

British officer in command of more than thirty of these Himalayan soldiers: 'Rounds were dropping at our feet, but no one could identify the firing point.' For 150 years, accounts of fighting in Afghanistan and on the North-West Frontier, that permeable border along a meaningless line drawn by a British colonel, Durand, in 1893, constantly tell of an enemy who cannot be seen.

Rifleman Yubraj was the second member of the British Brigade of Gurkhas to die in the present Afghan war. The first had been a British Gurkha officer, Major Alexis (Lex) Roberts, on 4 October 2007. He was killed by an improvised explosive device (IED). Riffleman Yubraj was killed on 4 November 2008. Soon afterwards, on 15 November, Colour Sergeant Krishnabahadur Dura, also of 2nd Battalion the Royal Gurkha Rifles was killed when his Warrior infantry fighting vehicle was hit by an IED. He had joined in 1982 and had been part of the Gurkha reinforcement company with 2nd Battalion the Parachute Regiment. His company commander, Major Toby Jackman, said he 'epitomised Gurkha infantry professionalism and delivered consistently excellent results'.[2] Two more British officers, Lieutenant Neal Turkington and Major James (Josh) Bowman, and a Gurkha corporal, Arjun Purja Pun, died on 13 July 2010 when an Afghan soldier they had been training turned on them. Again, the Gurkhas have been training Afghan security forces for a long time. In 1840, Gurkha volunteers were sought to officer the bodyguard of Shah Shuja, whom the British had selected as their preferred candidate to run Afghanistan.

The Afghan War that is under way today has seen the most protracted, savage and highest-intensity fighting, apart from some in Iraq, for the British Army since the Second World War. For the British Army, and the Gurkhas, whose evolution was heavily influenced by the situation there, it is the *fourth* Afghan War. This is the story of how the Gurkhas from Nepal came to be in Afghanistan, fighting as part of the British Army to preserve a government acceptable to the West. It also explains how more than 40,000 Gurkhas came to be serving in the Indian Army, the biggest all-volunteer army of the world's most populous democracy. It is the story of 200 years of courage, cunning, military professionalism, diplomacy and intrigue.

I

Whence 'The Gurkhas'?

THE WORD GURKHA, or Gorkha, or Goorkha, in modern usage, originates from the name of a district and town, Gorkhā (गोरखा). The town itself lies about 50 miles (80 kilometres) west of the Nepali capital of Kathmandu. Today, Gorkha, clinging to the side of a crag, is picturesque and sleepy. If it were tidier and white-washed, it might almost be one of the White Villages on *la Frontera* in Spain. Appropriately enough, the name probably comes from the eighth-century warrior-saint, Guru Gorakṣanāth or Gorakhnāth. His name in turn comes from the Sikh *gorakṣakah*, which means tending or protection of cattle – *gorakṣā* in Nepali.[1] Warrior peoples whose lifestyle revolved around herding cattle often gained the wary respect of the British, like the Zulus they encountered in southern Africa. By an interesting coincidence, British soldiers are referred to as *gorā*, from the same word in Hindustani meaning 'fair complexioned'.[2]

'Gurkhas' do not exist as an agreed or identifiable racial or ethnic group. In the 200 years that they have been recruited to serve in foreign security forces, the idea of who, exactly, is a 'Gurkha' or 'Gorkha' has changed. The British identified certain 'martial tribes' or *jats*, on whom they concentrated their recruiting efforts. However, today the British Army and the Singapore Police are ad-amant that all potential recruits – roughly 11,000 annually in recent years – who apply for the 170-odd places in the British Gurkhas and the 80 places in the Singapore Police have an equal chance, what-ever their *jat*. Selection, as the sign in Plate 1 proclaims, is 'free, fair and transparent'.

Significantly, the general term in Nepal for a 'Gurkha' serving in foreign forces is *lahuré*, from Lahore, in Punjab (now in Pakistan),

where Indian princes and then the British recruited their 'Gurkhas'. If you say 'Gurkha' or Gorkha' in Nepal, people will most likely think of the place. The different kinds of *lahuré* are often differentiated by referring to the place where Gurkhas are deployed – 'India *lahuré*', 'Malaya *lahuré*', 'Hong Kong *lahuré*' and now, 'UK *lahuré*'.[3]

'Goorkha' best evokes the true sound of the Nepali word, with a trilled Scottish-type 'r'. In 1891 the British-Indian Army made an attempt to standardise the spelling as Gurkha, generally pronounced 'Gerker'. When India became independent in 1947, the new Indian Army retained most of the Gurkha regiments of the British-Indian Army, and also revived one (the 11th) that had been created in the last year of the Great War but subsequently disbanded. Four of the ten regiments – the 2nd, 6th, 7th and 10th – were transferred to the British Army. The remainder stayed with India. In 1949 the Indians changed the name of all their regiments back to Gorkha.[4] Gorkha is the spelling used in all Indian literature published in English.[5]

The eighth-century guru Gorakhnāth had a high-born disciple, Bappa Rawal, who allegedly founded the Gorkha or Gurkha dynasty and is said to be the ancestor of the modern royal family of Nepal. There is a legend that Bappa Rawal found Gorakhnāth meditating and stopped to guard him while he was so preoccupied. When the guru emerged from his meditation, he was pleased at Bappa's devotion and gave him a kukri (*kukuri*), the traditional distinctive curved Gurkha knife. He supposedly said that the disciples of the Guru Gorakhnāth would be called Gorkhas – or Gurkhas – and that their bravery would become world famous. It is a good story, but could well have been concocted with the benefit of hindsight a thousand years or so later.

However, we know that in the sixteenth century in the modern (Christian) calendar, the Gurkhas conquered the district that now bears their name, one of the seventy-five districts of modern Nepal. The timing is significant because after about 1500 the Rajput nobles of northern India, who were Hindus, began moving north to escape the Mughals (Moguls) who had invaded India from Central Asia, and who were Muslims. The local Nepalese hill tribes, who were of Mongolian origin, assimilated the aristocratic Rajput immigrants

relatively peacefully, and many of the Rajput men took local brides. The offspring of these marriages created a powerful mix of Mongolian and north Indian blood, and a new Rajput nobility. In 1559, Drabva Shah, the younger son of Yasobam, king of Lamjung, seized the town of Gorkha and proclaimed himself king.[6] Drabva's immediate descendants were not very memorable, apart from the fourth of the line, Sri Rama Shah, who achieved some note as a legislator, introducing some weights and measures that are still in use today.[7]

In 1742, however, the tenth king of Gorkha, Sri Panch Maharaj Dhiraj Prithwi Narayan Shah (generally known as Prithwi Narayan), (1723–75), came to the throne.[8] His father had invaded the valley of Nepal (Kathmandu valley), but had been forced to retreat. Prithwi Narayan the Great inherited his father's ambition to conquer the populous and fertile valley (see Plates 5 and 6). He completed its conquest in 1768 and on 25 September established the Nepali capital at Kathmandu, where it has been ever since. By 1769, he had taken over the area of modern Nepal.

Hinduism, which holds cows to be sacred, was made the state religion, but with strong influences from Gorakhnāth's teachings, as well as from the Rajput nobles who ruled many of the forty-six small states – twenty-four in central Nepal (the Chaubisai Raj) and twenty-two in western Nepal (the Baisi Raj), now conquered by Prithwi Narayan. The Gurkhas took a fairly free-and-easy approach to Hinduism, which they confined to respect for the highly capable and aristocratic Brahman immigrants from the Indian priestly caste, who had fled northwards into Nepal to evade the Muslim invasion of India, and reverence for the cow.[9] This was one of the characteristics that the British thought made them good potential soldiers. One of their most distinguished chroniclers, Sir George MacMunn, writing in 1933, noted approvingly 'their lack of interest in Brahminical holiness'.[10]

Before learning how the Gurkhas came into collision, conflict and then collusion with the British, in Chapter 2, we need to understand the geography and ethnography of their homeland, Nepal. The country, which Prithwi Narayan created some 240 years ago

(see Figure 1), pre-dates most of the nation states of modern Europe.[11] It extends about 520 miles (830 kilometres) along the southern slopes of the Himalayas. Lying between the 85th and 88th parallels, it is nowhere more than 140 miles (225 kilometres) wide and, on average, is about 95 miles (150 kilometres) wide from south to north. It is divided into four broadly distinct strips in that direction, a veritable layer-cake. These strips are known as: the Terai (sometimes spelled Tarai); the 'Hills'; the Snows; and the very small area of the trans-Himalayan zone.

The Terai runs along the southern border and is only about 30 miles (50 kilometres) wide. It is low-lying, nowhere more than 1,000 metres above sea level, and is oppressively humid from April to June. The Siwalik 'Mountains', running parallel with the Himalayas, divide the outer from the inner Terai.[12] When the British and the Gurkhas first met, 200 years ago, the Terai with its forests and slow-flowing, grey-brown rivers (see Plate 2) swarmed with mosquitoes, and malaria was an ever-present danger. Some of the marshes have been drained but even today there is a risk of catching malaria in the Terai. Officially, there is 'no malaria in Nepal'.[13] However, foreign travel advice differs. Dharan, one of the key recruiting bases for the Gurkhas, is in a high-risk area, though the malaria that might be encountered there is far less lethal than the West African variety.[14]

North of the flat fields and forests of the Terai lie the 'Hills' (see Plate 3). Do not be deceived. The term is a misnomer. To a Western European, they are not 'hills' at all, but steep mountains. But compared with the icy glacis of the great Himalayan mountain range, of which they are the foothills, they are clearly of a subordinate order. The 'Hills' are the principal home of the Gurkhas recruited into the Indian and British armies, who refer to them as *pahar* – 'hills', in their own language.

The 'Hills' are inhabited up to 8,250 feet (2,500 metres) altitude, and grazed in the summer up to 13,200 feet (4,000 metres). Luxuriant green in colour at a distance, thickly sown with birch, bamboo and pine, the 'Hills' rise steeply, with roads snaking up and down. Those roads are shielded from the torrents of water that cascade down from higher ground in the monsoon by deep, stone-

lined drainage ditches and gabions – wire baskets full of stones – to hold back landslides. The 'Hills' recall the similarly cultivated and optimistically tamed features of Rwanda.

The main rivers, which rise in the high valleys of the Himalayas, cut through the Hills in a north–south direction. They typically flow at about 3,300 feet (1,000 metres) above sea level, cutting through hills twice that height. There are three main river basins: the Karnali in the west, the Gandaki (Kali Gandaki or Krishna Gandaki) in the middle, and the Kosi in the east. In the far west, the Maha Kali forms the country's western border and becomes the Sarda when it enters India. The climate in the Hills varies with the altitude, and in spring and autumn is very pleasant. The summer can be hot and oppressive, but the winter is not particularly cold and the temperature does not drop below freezing. The idea that the Gurkhas are from a harsh mountain environment is fallacious: their native climate is temperate, and varies rather less than that of the UK. The temperature in Kathmandu typically varies from just above freezing (3°C) as the December minimum to 29°C as the June maximum.[15] The monsoon usually begins in mid-June and lasts until the end of September with the heaviest rain in July and August. In 2010 it was raining heavily every day by late June.

The Pokhara plateau, with Pokhara itself as the country's second city, is important to our story. Pokhara, more pleasant and congenial a place to work than Kathmandu, is a tourist centre and one of the three Gurkha recruiting bases, along with Dharan and Kathmandu. It is usually classed as part of the Terai, and the climate in summer can be oppressive. It has, however, been developed as a tourist centre and most modern amenities can be found in Pokhara city, the 'hill capital of central Nepal'.[16] Once you get up into the hills, and in the Kathmandu valley and Pokhara plateau, the risk of malaria subsides, although there is a small seasonal risk between May and October in some low-lying valleys and hills in the Kavre District east of the Kathmandu valley itself.[17]

On a good day, looking north from Pokhara, the clouds part to reveal a spectacular view of the Himalayan 'Snows', beyond the 'Hills', including the several Annapurna peaks, centring on Mount Annapurna (26,566 feet; 8,091 metres) and Macchapucchre, the

'fishtail' mountain. Mount Everest (Sagarmatha), the world's highest mountain (29,030 feet; 8,848 metres), lies east–north–east of Kathmandu. But Nepal's northern border does not follow the crest line of the Himalayas everywhere, and there are strips of Nepalese territory to the north – the trans-Himalayan zone. North of the Himalayan crest, but still within Nepal, the inhabitants are Tibetans. Just south of the Himalayas, the Sherpas, closely related to the Tibetans, live on the southern slopes of the range.

The Kathmandu valley, or 'Valley of Nepal', is the country's cultural, administrative and historic heart. It is a flat and intensively farmed saucer, 300 square miles (570 square kilometres) in extent. Many hill Gurkhas still restrict the use of the name 'Nepal' (possibly from 'Ne' – another saint and *pal* from *palnu* – 'to cherish') to the valley itself. This geographical exactitude reminds us of how hard-pressed nineteenth-century pioneers in the American West sometimes referred, wistfully, to the distant eastern states as 'America'. In Nepali mythology, the Valley of Nepal was a lake that was drained by the god Krishna who, with a mighty sword, cut through the hills to the south. To this day the gorge where the river Bagmati leaves the Valley of Nepal (see Figure 1) is called 'The Sword Cut'. Geological evidence, as it often does, suggests that there is a grain of truth in the legend and that the valley, like many in the Himalayas, was indeed a lake once, before the river broke out to the south.[18]

Because of the influx of Hindus from India fleeing the Muslim invasion, and the influence of the Rajputs and Brahman priestly caste in the development of Nepal, Hinduism became the dominant religion. Prithwi Narayan, of Rajput descent and a Hindu himself, made Hinduism the state religion, but it is that no longer. However many of those conquered by the Gurkhas were Buddhists and traces of Buddhism persist among the religious practices of the various martial tribes. Nepal was, after all, the birthplace of Prince Siddhartha Gautama Buddha, at Lumbini, just inside the southern border and south-west of Butwal, in about 563 BC. Many of the Gurkha tribes are more likely to consult a Lama than a Brahman, and strong links persist with the Buddhism of neighbouring Tibet. The big festivals are celebrated by both Hindus and Buddhists.

Broadly speaking, the most orthodox Hindus live in the plains of the Terai and the Middle Hills. Elsewhere in the Hills, Hinduism becomes mixed up with Shamanism and Animism, while on the ridge tops and in the high Himalayas Tibetan-style Buddhism prevails. The Newar people of the Kathmandu valley practise an extraordinary mixture of Hinduism and Buddhism.[19]

The Gurkhas who serve with the British and Indian armies are therefore officially Hindus, although quite a few Nepalese Christians are now enlisted. Gurkhas serving in the British Army outside Nepal are excused by a Charter, originally issued by the guru of the British Raj, from all caste restrictions on food. These will vary from caste to caste and from tribe to tribe. The only exception was that, as Hinduism was the official religion of Nepal, they should not eat beef in any form, nor beef extract. On their return to India or Nepal, and before heading home, all Gurkhas used to have to perform a purification ceremony, which was conducted at the depot from which they were originally deployed. However, the last time this took place was in 1967.[20] The Gurkhas used to get different operational ration packs (formerly 'compo') from the rest of the British Army but that stopped after 1997 with the British withdrawal from Hong Kong and a further reduction in the size of the brigade. 'If you don't like it, don't eat it – or swap' was the pragmatic advice of a serving Gurkha officer, who added that the Nepalese Christians were now the most particular about food.[21]

Hinduism also traditionally imposed restrictions on travelling across the sea. Again, a special religious ceremony used to absolve those who needed to do so – like the Gurkhas who fought in both world wars, including the amphibious assault at Gallipoli in 1915. This restriction proved a convenient excuse for large numbers of Gurkhas not to deploy to Malaya.

However, again, this ritual was abolished in about 1965.[22] Any religious restrictions of this kind would have appeared absurd to the 1st Battalion, 7th Gurkha Rifles, which was transported from the UK to South Georgia aboard the liner *Queen Elizabeth 2* in May 1982, then transferred to the much smaller P & O ferry, *Norland*. They spent four days and four nights in rough winter seas before hitting the

beach adjacent to San Carlos Water in the Falkland Islands at 0300 hours on 1 June. With 70-foot (21-metre) waves, any military unit would most likely have suffered similar levels of seasickness.[23]

In order to understand the Gurkhas, we have to understand the recruiting policies applied, variously, by the East India Company from 1815, by the British-Indian government from 1857, and by the UK and an independent India from 1947 (the Republic of India from 1950). The Gurkha (or Gorkha) forces of the British and Indian armies have been, and still are, recruited from certain areas and racial groups within Nepal.

The racial groups (*jats*) identified by the British as suitable for service, albeit initially as irregulars and subsequently, were the Gurungs, Magars, Limbus, Rais, Tamangs, Sunwars, Thakurs and Chhetris. These, known as the 'martial tribes', had been prevalent in Prithwi Narayan's army, which captured the Valley of Nepal and Kathmandu in 1768. They were known collectively as Gorkhas, or Gurkhas, because they had assembled at Prithwi Narayan's fort at Gorkha, which stands today as a national monument (see Plate 4). After that, the definition of 'Gurkhas' was expanded to include the martial tribes of eastern Nepal. The Gurungs, Magars, Sunwars, Rais and Limbus remained the principal tribes recruited, however. Other tribes, not normally enlisted, have included Nepchars, Newars and others. The areas from which these groups have been recruited are shown on the map at Figure 1.[24]

The idea of 'martial tribes' may seem absurd to us today but it has long been prevalent in Asia and it became more prevalent in Western ideas soon after the Gurkhas were formed. As George MacMunn, (1869–1952) explained in 1911:

> It is one of the essential differences between the East and the West, that in the East, with certain exceptions, only certain clans and classes can bear arms; others have not the physical courage necessary for the warrior. In Europe as we know, every able bodied man, given food and arms, is a fighting man of sort . . . In the East, or certainly in India, this is not so . . . Nor are appearances of any use as a criteria. Some of the most manly looking people in India are in this respect the most despicable.[25]

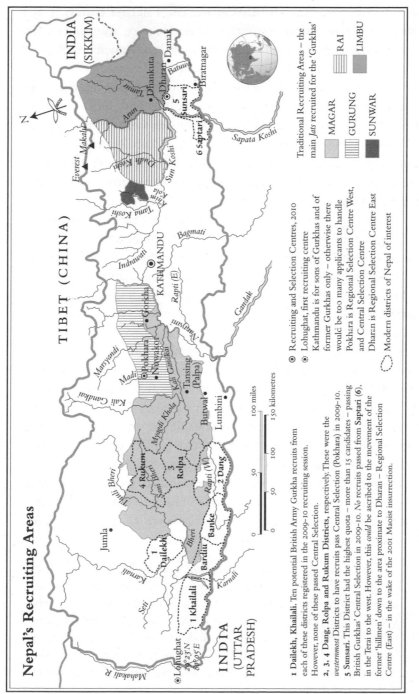

Nepal's Recruiting Areas

Traditional Recruiting Areas – the main *jats* recruited for the 'Gurkhas'

- MAGAR
- GURUNG
- SUNWAR
- RAI
- LIMBU

⊚ Recruiting and Selection Centres, 2010

⊛ Lohughat, first recruiting centre
Kathmandu is for sons of Gurkhas and of former Gurkhas only – otherwise there would be too many applicants to handle
Pokhara is Regional Selection Centre West, and Central Selection Centre
Dharan is Regional Selection Centre East

‿ Modern districts of Nepal of interest

1 Dailekh, Khailali. Ten potential British Army Gurkha recruits from each of these districts registered in the 2009–10 recruiting session. However, none of these passed Central Selection.

2, 3, 4 Dang, Rolpa and Rukum Districts, respectively. These were the *westernmost* Districts to have recruits pass Central Selection (Pokhara) in 2009–10.

5 Sunsari. This District had the highest quota – more than 15 candidates – passing British Gurkhas' Central Selection in 2009–10. No recruits passed from Saptari (**6**), in the Terai to the west. However, this *could* be ascribed to the movement of the former 'hillmen' down to the area proximate to Dharan – Regional Selection Centre (East) – in the wake of the 2001 Maoist insurrection.

FIGURE 1

From the 1890s the British-Indian Army started codifying the 'martial tribes' in a series of recruiting handbooks, although, as we have seen, these tended to be the people who had been recruited in the past and who generally made good soldiers. Lionel Caplan argues that 'the theory of martial race did not emerge sui generis to meet specific military needs, rather it was a deeper manifestation of the wider European doctrine of biological determinism or scientific racism'.[26] However flawed the motivation behind searching for the best 'fighting material', the recruiters often seemed to find it nonetheless.

As we saw earlier, selection for the Gurkhas today has to be free, fair and transparent and must withstand external scrutiny. One reason why recruiting in the past focussed on certain tribes and areas was simply that communications in Nepal were poor. Word of mouth and family tradition played a major role in determining who applied. Whereas recruits traditionally came from the 'Hills', the heaviest recruitment in 2010 was from Sunsari province, in the eastern Terai. Since the constitutional crisis of 2001, and the Maoist insurrection, which was concentrated in the 'Hills', large numbers of able-bodied young men left that area and flocked south, into teeming Terai towns like Damak, to avoid being forced to work for the Maoists.

The traditional differences between the Nepalese tribes are now breaking down as an inevitable result of globalisation, but a few interesting differences remain. One of the most important and relevant to this book is the view on the use of the kukri – the traditional Gurkha curved knife, which in skilled hands (or even in not-so-skilled hands) is a fearsome weapon (see Figure 2). Some tribes and clans – and it would be nugatory to list them – consider it bad form to draw the kukri unless you intend to use it, though not necessarily for any sanguinary purpose.[27]

The Gurungs, as the map at Figure 1 shows, occupy the most central position in Nepal. They are of Mongolian origin but their early history, like that of most of the ethnic groups, is unknown. Their ancient kings had strongholds in Kaski and Lamjung, north of the Pokhara plateau. Their language, Gurungkura, which they call Tamakiu, is Tibeto-Burmese and is closer to Tibetan than any other

Nepalese dialect. The Gurung tribe is divided into two. One is the Char *jat,* with four clans: Ghale, Ghotane, Lamchhane and Lama. The other is the Sora *jat,* the name of which implies sixteen clans, but all trace of these has disappeared. The Ghales were once considered to be the top clan, and are said to be descended from an old royal family of Lamjung. At the time of writing the Ghales are the only members of the Gurung *jat* who use their clan name – Ghale – instead of Gurung as a surname. The Gurungs follow the same twelve-year calendar cycle as the Chinese, with the names of the same animals and birds. Their closer link with Tibet is reflected in the fact that, although officially Hindu, the Gurung will call on a Lama for priestly services in preference to a Brahman.[28]

The Magars come from the area south and west of the Gurungs, but look very similar and are therefore probably from the same Mongolian stock, and their language, Magarkura, is of the same Tibeto-Burman group. Again, their early history is unknown but they probably occupied the area around Palpa, now Tansen, from early times. Because of their position towards the southern border they were the first to assimilate the incoming Indian immigrants who were fleeing the Mughals, and their religious beliefs conform more closely to those of orthodox Hindus than those of any of the other tribes. Their dietary habits are different from the Gurungs. Unlike the latter, they will not touch buffalo meat – probably because they are stricter Hindus and buffalo resemble cows – but they are happy to eat domestic pigs. There are seven clans, all officially of equal social standing: the Ale, Bura or Burathoki, Gharti, Pun, Rana, Roka and Thapa.

The Gurungs and Magars are the two western tribes. The eastern tribes have become much more intermixed, and the Limbus and Rais, also known as Khambus or Yakkas, are known collectively as Kiranti. When the Gurkhas conquered the Limbus and Khambus, as they were then known, the Gurkha king granted commissions to the more influential men among them to rule certain districts. The Limbus and Rais are sometimes more Mongolian looking than the Gurungs and Magars, suggesting a similar origin. Their dialects are also Tibeto-Burman, but more complex and closer to the dialects of Assam and Burma than Gurungkura and Magarkura.

Before 1887 most Gurkha regiments enlisted some Rais and Limbus but after the formation of the 7th and 10th Gurkha Rifles, those joining the Gurkhas usually headed for those two regiments. Gurkhas were also recruited into the Burma Military Police and the Assam Rifles.

Limbus have very few dietary restrictions and will eat meat of any kind. The Rais wear their Hinduism more lightly than some others, as Sir Herbert Risley observed in his *Tribes and Castes of Bengal* in 1891:

> By religion the Khambus [Rais] are Hindu; but they have no Brahmans and men of their own tribe, called Home, corresponding closely to the Bijuwas employed by the Tibetans, serve as priests. Their special god is the ancestral deity Parabhang, who is worshipped in the months of March and November with the sacrifice of pig and offerings of incense and Murwa beer . . . Another of their minor gods, Sidha, is honoured with offerings of dubo grass and milk. His origin is uncertain, but it seems to me possible that his name may be a survival of the stage of Buddhism through which the Khambus, like many other Nepalese castes, have probably passed.[29]

Although happy to eat pigs and drink beer, the Rais will not eat goat. There is a legend that once a goat on a hillside bleated and attracted a man's attention. He looked up, saw a landslide beginning and started running. The goat was killed but the man got away. He therefore swore that he and his descendants would never eat goat again.

Again, the Buddhist and Tibetan connexion is strong, suggesting that the imposition of Hinduism as the state religion by the Gurkha king was a convenient political device. There are parallels with British history.[30]

The last tribe shown on the map are the Sunwar. They are an agricultural tribe and claim to have come originally from western Nepal. They did intermarry with the western tribes when Risley was writing before 1891, but no longer do so, and their religious customs closely resemble those of the Magars, so there may be some truth in the claim. They were first recruited into the Gurkhas in 1909, but enlisted in very small numbers. Between 1940 and 1945,

during the Second World War, only 1,450 from this very small area enlisted, compared with 130,000 for the Gurkha units from Nepal as a whole and 30,000 for other units.[31]

The last 'martial' tribes are the Tamangs, Thakurs and Chhetris. The Tamangs live in the area north and west of Kathmandu, overlapping with the Gurungs. In the past they have also been known as the Lamas. Although they are not allowed to kill cows in Nepal, the Tamangs will eat beef killed by accident. For this reason, more orthodox Gurkha officers were, in the past, against the enlistment of Tamangs. However, they are of Tibetan-Nepalese stock and make excellent soldiers.

Apart from the priestly Brahman caste, the Thakur tribe has the highest social standing among Gurkhas. The king of Nepal is a member of the Shah, one of the Thakur clans. They do not come from a particular region of Nepal but are scattered across it.

The Chhetris were once known as Khas. They originated with the high-caste Indians fleeing the Muslim invasions of India from the twelfth century, which would make them the earliest of the Indian immigrants to Nepal. They gave the title Chhetri to those of the hill people whom they converted, and the name was also given to the offspring of Brahmans and local women. It is a corruption of the Sanskrit word *ksatriya*, meaning a member of the warrior caste – below Brahman, but still very prestigious. Because of their part-Indian origin, they tend to be found more in the southern part of the country, although they can be found across it. The 9th Gorkhas, which remained in the Indian Army after 1947 and who enlist Chhetris, like to recruit them in Gulmi, west-south-west of Pokhara, although there are also many in eastern Nepal, who tend to join the Nepalese Army.

A Chhetri may therefore come from three possible ancestral origins. He may be descended from the union of a Brahman and a woman of one of the hill tribes; he may be descended from a high-ranking convert to Hinduism; or he may be an Ektharia – a relatively pure-bred descendant of a Rajput or other warrior-caste north Indian (*ksatriya*), who served in Nepal as a military adventurer or mercenary. Whereas the Brahmans seem to have delighted in unions with the local women, the Rajputs and *ksatriyas* kept

themselves more to themselves, as the Chhetris still did up to the 1960s, marrying solely among their own kind.

Because of their ancestry, the Chhetris differ in appearance from the stocky Mongoloid tribes of Nepal. They are generally slighter, darker complexioned and more hirsute. They are fine soldiers, and many of the most distinguished Gurkha officers have been Chhetris. One was Bahadur Gambirsing Chhetri, who served with the British as a private (they became riflemen later) during the Indian Mutiny, capturing three guns and killing seven mutineers, armed with only – a kukri. He returned to Nepal and rose to be a full colonel in the Nepalese Army. He was presented with an engraved claymore by the then Prince of Wales, later Edward VII, in 1875, in recognition of his bravery in the British service.[32]

Among the tribes not normally enlisted, two deserve mention, as they were sometimes employed as clerks. These are the Lepchas and the Newars. The Lepchas are not Gurkhas but come from Sikkim, although some have lived in Ilam, in the extreme east of Nepal, for some time. They are primarily animists and highly superstitious. The Newars were the main inhabitants of the Kathmandu valley in the fourteenth century, and the source of its rulers until Prithwi Narayan conquered it in 1768 and reduced them to a subject people, which, to some extent, they remained. They are excellent craftsmen and the distinctive style of architecture and ornamentation in the Nepal valley, including the characteristic pagoda, may owe its origin to them. Although some people have speculated that the style emanated from Tibet or China, Sylvain Levi, an authority on early Nepalese history and archaeology, believes it may have originated in Nepal and spread north and east, not the other way round.[33] Newars are also still sometimes employed in the Gurkhas. In 2010, 1.7 per cent of those passing central selection were Newars.[34]

The Sherpas, who are of Tibetan stock and Buddhist by religion, have been enlisted into the Gurkhas in very small numbers, but mainly as mess servants. Given their mountaineering reputation, they would make first-class soldiers, but they do not fit the somewhat perverse religious template of the Gurkhas.

A knowledge of the so-called 'martial tribes' is important to understand the past history of the Gurkhas, but is less relevant today.

BREAKDOWN OF RECRUITS TO BRITISH GURKHAS, BY *JAT*,
2009–10

Jat	Registered (summer 2009), per cent	Passed regional selection (East, Dharan, West, Pokhara), per cent	Passed central selection (Pokhara), per cent
Brahman	1.63	0	0
Chhetri	7.19	4.8	3.41
Gurung	17.96	22.0	22.16
Limbu	14.44	14.8	18.75
Magar	21.29	20.8	23.3
Rai	19.2	18.2	15.91
Tamang	5.91	9.2	6.82
Thakuri	1.74	2.0	2.27
Others	10.64	8.2	7.38
Total	100	100	100

If we look at the recruit intake of 2010, there were applications from all but six of Nepal's seventy-five districts. As selection progressed, however, the traditional *jats* became increasingly prominent, and the successful candidates were concentrated in traditional areas, apart from the large concentration in Sunsari as a result of migration from the hills. This is best illustrated by a table (Table 1). Young men from some twenty *jats* applied, of which seven predominated. The Brahmans, interestingly, did not make it past the first major hurdle.[35]

Overlapping all the different tribes, and the clans within them, we also have to take note of the caste system. As we have seen, the Brahmans, the priestly caste, is the highest. The highest clan of the Brahman caste is the Upaddhe or Upaddhya, and you may encounter one of these as a regimental priest or religious teacher – the Gurkhas' equivalent of the British Army padre. The next is the *ksatriya*, or warrior caste. Members of both these castes wear the *janai*, or sacred thread. Third come the *vaishya*, the merchant or artisan caste, who do not wear the sacred thread, and, fourth, the *sudra* or menial caste.

Although logic might suggest that Gurkha soldiers, or the 'martial tribes' from which many of them come, should be *ksatriya*, it does

not work that way. The Brahmans never entitled the martial tribes to wear the *janai*. Therefore, in the main, they cannot be *ksatriya*, although some individuals are. The Thakurs and Chhetris are *ksatriya*, however, and wear the *janai*, but the other martial tribes occupy an indeterminate status between the *ksatriya* and *vaishya*.[36]

The caste system overlaps with the tribal system to provide tradesmen for the army to perform tasks forbidden to higher-caste Gurkhas. Four groups of tradesmen (which equate to tribes to some extent) – the Sarki, Kami, Damāi and Sumar – are recruited to do these jobs. Sarkis are leather workers and cobblers and are enlisted as shoemakers and saddlers, and to repair equipment. Kamis are blacksmiths who, in the recent and modern military context, equate to armourers. Damais may be musicians or tailors, and in the Gurkhas are employed as the latter. Sumars are goldsmiths and silversmiths. Finally, there are the Manjhis, or boatmen and ferrymen. Unsurprisingly, during the Burma campaign in the Second World War, many Gurkha units asked for Manjhi recruits.[37]

We have already come across the distinctive curved knife so characteristic of the Gurkha, the kukuri, better known as the kukri, in Devanāgarī खुकुरी. Some say it is based on the shape of a cow's hoof, and can be used as a tool as well as a close-combat weapon. As we have seen, the idea that it must always draw no blood when drawn is a myth. The cutting edge is inwardly curved in shape. Kukri blades usually have a notch, or often a double notch called the *kauda* or *cho*, at the base of the blade. The most practical reason for it is to stop the flow of blood or sap down onto the handle and the owner's hand,[38] but it also helps mark the base of the blade when it is being sharpened. The scabbard holds two further, smaller tools, the *karda* and the *chakmak*. The *karda* is sharp and can be used as a skinning knife. The *chakmak* is blunt and is used to hone the kukri blade or to start a fire with flint struck against it – the same principle as a flintlock musket. A modern service kukri is shown in Figure 2.

The first British intelligence report on the kukri appears to date from just before the outbreak of the 1814 war with the Gurkhas, although the British were not yet aware of its significance. On 20 October, twelve days before war was formally declared, Colonel

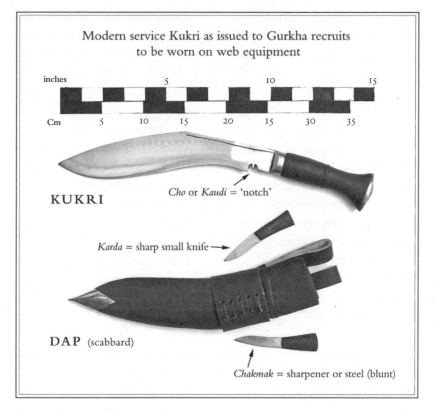

Modern service Kukri as issued to Gurkha recruits
to be worn on web equipment

KUKRI

Cho or *Kaudi* = 'notch'

Karda = sharp small knife

DAP (scabbard)

Chakmak = sharpener or steel (blunt)

FIGURE 2

G. H. Fagan, the adjutant general in the Bengal Army headquarters at Cawnpore, forwarded a paper by Captain Raper, *Memoir of Gurwall* [Gurhwal] *and Kamaon* [Kumaon]. Interestingly, he is not describing here the Gurkhas themselves, but the Kumaon irregulars commanded by Gurkha sirdars, or officers. 'Some of them carry also swords and bows and arrows, and all of them wear in their girdles a large curved knife called a *kookeree* or *boojalee*, which serves as a culinary implement as well as a formidable weapon of offence.'[39] 'The information in this paper,' Fagan added crisply, with a foresight commendable in someone about to direct a bloody war, 'may possibly be of use at this moment.'[40]

One of the best and most eloquent descriptions of the kukri and how it can be used was penned by the Reverend Wood in *Travels*

in India and Nepal, published in 1891, in the beautiful, if politically incorrect, style of the time:

> The blade is very thick at the back, measuring a little more than a quarter of an inch [6.5 mm] in thickness . . . The handle is made after a very remarkable fashion, and the portion which forms the hilt is so small that it shows the size of the hand for which it was intended. This smallness of the hilt is common to all Indian swords, which cannot be grasped by an ordinary English [sic] soldier. Indeed, the Gurkhas are so small that their hands, like those of all Indian races, are very delicate, about the same size as those of an English [sic] boy of seven. The point of the kukri is sharp as a needle and the weapon answers equally for cutting or stabbing. In consequence of the great thickness of the metal the blade is exceedingly heavy. It may be imagined that the blow from such a weapon as this must be a very terrible one. The very weight of the blade would drive it half through a man's arm if it were only allowed to fall from a little height. But the Gurkhas have a mode of striking which resembles the 'drawing' cut of the broad sword, and which urges the sharp edge through flesh and bone alike . . .
>
> In the hands of an experienced wielder this knife is about as formidable a weapon as can be conceived. Like all really good weapons, its efficiency depends much more upon the skill than the strength of the wielder and thus it happens that the little Gurkha, a mere boy in point of stature, will cut to pieces a gigantic adversary who does not understand his mode of onset. The Gurkha generally strikes upwards with the Kukri, possibly in order to avoid wounding himself should his blow fail, and possibly because an upward cut is just the one that can be least guarded against.
>
> When we were engaged in the many wars in India, the Gurkha proved themselves our most formidable enemies, as since they have proved themselves most invaluable allies. Brave as lions, active as monkeys, and fierce as tigers, the lithe wiry little men came leaping over the ground to attack moving so quickly, and keeping so far apart from each other, the musketry was no use against them. When they came near the soldiers, they suddenly crouched to the ground, dived under the bayonets, struck upwards at the men with their Kukris, ripping them open with a single blow, and then, after having done all the mischief in their power, darting off as rapidly as they had come. Until our men learned this mode of attack they were greatly

discomfited by their little opponents, who got under their weapons, cutting or slashing with knives as sharp as razors, and often escaping unhurt from the midst of bayonets. They would also dash under the bellies of the officers' horses, rip them open with one blow of the Kukri, and aim another at the leg of the officer as he and his horse fell together.[41]

Although the kukri is an icon associated with Nepal and the Gurkha regiments of the British and Indian armies, it is also a very practical tool. There is no prohibition on drawing it, but it is not a good idea to show it off, wave it around, or make trivial gestures with it. It is more helpful to think of it like any other superbly designed weapon or tool, like a soldier's rifle, a photographer's cameras, a carpenter's chisels, or a painter's brushes. It is to be guarded, kept clean and sharp and at the peak of efficiency, and simply to be treated with *respect*.

2

Collision, Conflict and Cooperation with the British

PRITHWI NARAYAN, 'THE GREAT', the tenth in the Gurkha line and a Rajput, ruled the Gurkha statelet and then Nepal from 1742 to 1775.[1] He was not a great field commander, but he made up for it with political guile, the tactics of state terror and psychological warfare – what we now call 'influence operations' – and by exploiting the incompetence of his adversaries. He smartly recognised the 'Valley of Nepal' – the Kathmandu valley – as the key to the kingdom, and his conquest of it highlights many characteristics manifested by the Gurkhas ever since. In 1749, Prithwi Narayan began by trying to seize Wallo Nawakot, now Nuwakot, 20 miles (30 kilometres) north-north-west of Kathmandu, but failed. He then tried to work his way round to the east, establishing a network of alliances. He besieged Kirtipur, 6 miles (10 kilometres) west-south-west of Kathmandu but, while he was busy doing so, the king of Kathmandu attacked him. Prithwi Narayan's forces were routed.[2]

However, the king of Kathmandu then upset some of the Kirtipur nobles who, out of spite, surrendered some strong points in the hills around the valley to the Gurkha king. Prithwi Narayan realised he was not yet strong enough to attack Kirtipur or Kathmandu directly, but blockaded the passes controlling access to the valley and hanged anyone attempting to supply food to it. Meanwhile, 2,000 Brahmans – the highest caste, who, unlike most people, were literate – were employed as public relations officers to try to bring round the neighbouring tribes to support Prithwi Narayan. It worked. The Kirtipur nobles, fed up with the way they had been treated by the king of Kathmandu, handed over the lower part of the town. However, the inhabitants were not entirely happy

and retreated into the strongly fortified upper part. Prithwi Narayan offered them an amnesty, so they surrendered. It was a ruse: the Gurkha king had the lips and noses of all males over the age of twelve cut off. Only boys under twelve and, in a bizarre gesture of cultural sensitivity, the lips of players of wind instruments, were spared. He had the town's name changed to Naskatipur – 'The City of Cut Noses' – an unfortunate pun on Kirtipur's original name. Prithwi Narayan was showing all the ingenious cruelty to be expected from an oriental despot. He went on to besiege Patan, then south of Kathmandu and now part of the metropolis, threatening to cut off the inhabitants' right hands as well as their lips and noses if they did not surrender.[3] The old-red brick city of Patan is now a picturesque tourist attraction within the sprawling conurbation of Kathmandu.

It was at this point that the first possible encounter between the Gurkhas and the forces of the Honourable East India Company might have taken place, but circumstances conspired to prevent it. The East India Company was a 'Crown Monopoly', founded in 1600 which, as we shall see below, by the mid eighteenth century effectively ruled large parts of India on behalf of the British.[4] The kings of Kathmandu and Patan requested help from the Company and a force was despatched under a Captain Kinloch. However, its advance was stopped by swollen rivers and the deadly malaria of the Terai. As a result the Company detachment never actually met the Gurkhas.[5]

With the threat of attack from the south removed, Prithwi Narayan returned to besiege Kathmandu. While the population was celebrating the eight-day late-summer festival of Indra Jatra, the Gurkhas infiltrated the city, unnoticed.[6] This again illustrates the incompetence of the defenders, as the Magar king of Palpa (now Tansing or Tansen), 40 miles (60 kilometres) south-west of Pokhara, had attacked the city in a similar way during a spring festival, Machendra Jatra.[7] Both these festivals are celebrated by Hindus and Buddhists. If Prithwi Narayan's capture of the city was not a stroke of particular brilliance, the king of Kathmandu's loss of it, given the earlier precedent, was careless in the extreme. Prithwi Narayan moved rapidly on to consolidate his control of the valley and

established Kathmandu as his capital, instead of Gorkha. He became the first ruler of unified Nepal on 25 September 1768. Resistance continued, however, and the Rajah of Tanhung (Tanjung), in the mountains north of the Kathmandu valley, inflicted a severe defeat on him, and did not submit to the Kathmandu government until after the 1814–15 war with the British.[8]

By the time of his early death in 1775, Prithwi Narayan had nevertheless consolidated his control over most of what is now Nepal. Although his forces never fought the British, he had travelled extensively in India and imported ideas from there, including flintlock muskets, the latest technology. His methods and legacy are therefore highly relevant in understanding the Gurkhas. The Newars, who had populated the Kathmandu valley, were reduced to the status of a subject race. Their kings disappeared and their nobles lost power – much like the fate of the Anglo-Saxon and Danish nobility in England after the Norman conquest of 1066.[9] Only the priestly Brahman caste, whom Prithwi Narayan had used for propaganda, retained their status. The hill peoples of the Chaubisai Raj and Baisi Raj were Mongolian in origin but had benefited from the leadership of the Rajput nobles and the intellect of the Brahmans, both of whom had fled the Mughal invasion of India. Prithwi Narayan was not a good military tactician, but he was clever and his victories owed more to guile, shrewd political manoeuvring and exploiting his enemies' incompetence. The Gurkha soldier has a measure of all three, to this day.

The British presence in India at the end of the eighteenth century presents some extraordinary parallels with the privatisation of warfare and the proliferation of private military companies and private security organisations today. The English East India Company, the oldest of several European companies formed to trade, initially, with the East Indies, was granted its Charter by Elizabeth I on 31 December 1600, and was therefore in business from 1601. It established its first 'factory' on the Indian mainland in 1611. In 1615, Sir Thomas Roe led an extraordinarily successful mission to the Mughal Emperor Nuruddin Salim Jahangir (reigned 1605–27), who granted the English exclusive rights to trade in his kingdoms, which was

conveyed to King James I of England and VI of Scotland in an exquisitely written letter.[10]

A rival English company then challenged the original Company's monopoly. As a result, the two companies were merged in 1708 to form the United Company of Merchants of England Trading to the East Indies, usually known as the Honourable East India Company (HEIC). It was often referred to, sometimes affectionately, sometimes cynically, as 'John Company'. Its rule in India, with its own regular army, effectively began in 1757 and lasted a century until 1858 when, after the 1857 Indian Mutiny had shown the Company to be incapable of running a subcontinent, the British Crown took charge with the so-called British Raj, which lasted another ninety years, until 1947.

The first East India Company fortified post had been Fort St George, near Madras, established in 1640. In 1665, English troops arrived in Bombay (Mumbai), following its transfer from Portuguese control in 1662. However, to protect its investments and secure the flow of goods, especially indigo, through Bengal, the East India Company began to recruit its own army, initially from the Muslim kingdom of Oudh, with its capital at Lucknow. The first authentic record of the existence of a regular native battalion on Indian soil is from 1741, when a unit was formed to garrison Bombay Castle. Seven years later Major Stringer Lawrence, 'the father of the Indian Army', was appointed commander-in-chief of the East India Company's field forces in India. His headquarters was at Fort St David, 100 miles (160 kilometres) south of Madras and only 12 miles (20 kilometres) from the then French town of Pondicherry. The war with France, which had temporarily ended in 1748, had driven both sides to recruit local Indian troops, since neither France nor Britain could spare their own regular troops for India. In 1757, the re-formation of the Indian troops into regular, organised battalions was entrusted by Major Lawrence to Robert Clive, later Lord Clive. That year was also famous for his victory at the Battle of Plassey, which gradually reduced French influence and led to an expansion of the Company's territories in India. The number of troops at its disposal increased correspondingly.[11]

Robert Clive created the first regular Indian infantry battalions.

Each of these had one British captain, two lieutenants, several British sergeants, forty-two Indian non-commissioned officers and 820 Indian rank and file – roughly 900 strong, in all. Clive was the first British officer in India to have Indian troops fully equipped, at the expense of the East India Company, which was popularly known as 'Sarkar'.[12]

In the 1770s the Company's officials began to compete with Indian rulers in recruiting peasant soldiers in Bihar, the Benares Raj and the Awadh Nawabi on the lower Ganges, in northern India. Bihar lies due south of Kathmandu. The company's success in recruiting soldiers inevitably drew these Indian states into its military and financial orbit. It also settled retired and wounded soldiers back in those same states, thus encroaching on the society and economy of the areas where the soldiers had come from. Something similar would later happen with the Nepali Gurkhas. By the end of the eighteenth century the East India Company had established its authority in most parts of northern India.[13]

At this point, the reader who is unfamiliar with military organisation might like to refer to the glossary, which includes military and British and Indian Army terms. In 1796 the Madras Army consisted of two European infantry regiments, four native cavalry regiments, two artillery regiments (battalions), each of five artillery batteries (companies), fifteen 'lascar' (voluntary tribal) companies and eleven native infantry regiments, each of two battalions. Between 1796 and 1824, the native infantry was raised to twenty-five regiments of two battalions each. Bearing in mind that battalions were each about 900 strong, assuming they were fully staffed, which they may not have been, eleven two-battalion regiments of infantry alone would mean a force of up to 20,000 strong, and, in the twenty-five regiments extant by 1824, a force of 45,000. And that was just the native infantry battalions, never mind the voluntary companies, each about 100 strong, or the native cavalry.

At this time the artillery was restricted to European troops, because it was felt to be too lethal and destructive to be given to native soldiers. This was, nevertheless, a very formidable private army indeed, about half the size of the British Army in total in 2010.

In 1803, Colonel James Skinner, another significant personality in the development of the East India Company's army, formed a regiment of irregular (light) horse from previous adversaries and put them at the disposal of John Company as well.[14] The cavalry's insatiable need for good horses and remounts further reinforced the Company's economic role in northern India.[15] With the British-led private army's need for soldiers, and the resulting economic interaction with the societies from which the recruits came, the precedents for the creation of the Gurkhas were already in place.

The first Briton to visit Kathmandu was Captain William Kirkpatrick, in 1793. His opinion of the Gurkhas was initially mixed. In his *Account of the Kingdom of Nepaul*, he wrote that they

> neither march nor carry their arms in a style anything superior to that of the rabble ordinarily identified with the title of sepoys in the service of the Hindustan powers nor would their discipline appear to be much stricter . . . [However] with all their defects I am disposed to think that they are on the whole no bad soldiers. They are brave, sufficiently tractable and capable of sustaining great hardships.[16]

He added that he did not see how 'artillery could be advantageously employed in such a rugged country', which was, again, of mixed accuracy. Kirkpatrick's evaluation may have been read by David Ochterlony, who was instrumental in creating the first East India Company Gurkha forces.[17]

Between 1796 and 1803, British influence in India was consolidated at the expense of the new French Republic. Two Irish aristocrats played a key role: Richard Wellesley, later the 2nd Earl of Mornington, who was Governor-General from 1798 to 1805, and his younger brother, Arthur, his military adviser. Arthur was an extremely talented young major general who made his military reputation in India and later became the Duke of Wellington. In 1796, as a colonel, Arthur went to India with his division. The next year, Richard was appointed Governor-General of the subcontinent, and when war broke out in 1799 against the sultan of Mysore, Tippu Sultan, Arthur was given his own division. Having won that campaign, Arthur was appointed to the supreme military and political command in the Deccan. He then defeated the bandit chieftain

Dhundia Wagh and, in 1803, the Marathas in the Second Anglo-Maratha War. When his elder brother retired as Governor-General in 1805, Arthur Wellesley returned with him to England, and was knighted.[18]

Meanwhile, in Nepal, Prithwi Narayan's son had survived him by only three years and he was in turn succeeded, in 1778, by Prithwi Narayan's infant grandson, Rana Bahadur Shah. The boy's uncle acted as regent and continued Prithwi Narayan's policy of conquest, moving into Sikkim to the east and then Tibet, which belonged, as it still does, to China. The Chinese retaliated and defeated the Nepalese, chasing them almost all the way back to the Kathmandu valley. However, the Chinese general was impressed by the courage and competence of the Nepalese – which effectively meant Gurkhas – and, having reached the culminating point of his attack, withdrew, having agreed that the Nepalese would send a trade mission to Beijing every five years. The regent, worried that the always formidable Chinese might beat him, requested help from the East India Company, but before a mission could reach Nepal, the Chinese had pulled back. From 1790 the regent moved west, into what is now India – Kumaon, Sirmoor, Gahrwal and the Simla Hill States. By 1794 the Nepalese Gurkha kingdom extended from Sikkim to the borders of Kashmir.

Gurkha rule in Kumaon, which lasted for twenty-four years until the British seized it back in 1815, was harsh. According to a report of 1846, the Gurkhas had 'oppressed Kumaon so cruelly that no sooner had British forces entered the hills . . . than the inhabitants began to join our camp and bring in supplies of provisions for the troops'.[19] The Gurkha invaders had divided each district into a number of small military commands, charging each Gurkha commander for the privilege of running it, and leaving him to 'wring out' as much as he could from the people.[20]

Prithwi Narayan's grandson, Rana Bahadur Shah, was now old enough to play power games himself. In 1795 he took over the government and imprisoned his uncle, whom he then executed in 1797. He returned to Kathmandu and made Bhim Sen Thapa – a Gurkha noble and the son of Amar Singh Thapa, one of the best Gurkha generals – his prime minister. He summoned his erstwhile

ally, the Rajah of Palpa (Tansen), to Kathmandu and killed him. The new king's murderous and sexually promiscuous behaviour was outrageous and he showed signs of insanity, but the prime minister, Bhim Sen, who was the only effective ruler from 1804, consolidated and extended the Gurkha conquests to the west.

In 1801 a treaty provided for the appointment of a British representative at the court of Kathmandu, and Captain Knox was appointed to the post. He was treated with haughty disdain, and withdrew in 1803. Richard Wellesley, the Governor-General of India, dissolved the short-lived alliance. Over the next eight years, incursions into British–protected territory became increasingly common. More intelligence about Nepal came in from an expedition by Alexander Knox and Francis Hamilton in 1802–3.[21] Hamilton reported that the military force among the petty chiefs was 'always large', but consisted of an undisciplined and ill-armed rabble. However, 'much order has since been induced by the chiefs of Gorkha, although both in arms and discipline the soldiers are still far behind the Europeans'.[22]

Then, pushing west, the Gurkhas ran into another formidable power with a military reputation, the Sikhs, who halted the Nepalese advance. In order to carry on the war Bhim Sen needed money and to get it, in 1807, he ordered the confiscation of Temple property and the Brahmans' personal wealth. This attack on the privileged and exalted priestly caste of the Hindu religion that had been imposed on the country by Prithwi Narayan was too much. In the tumult that followed, Rana Bahadur Shah was killed by a half-brother, who was killed in turn. The shrewd Bhim Sen was now in an unassailable position. He put on the throne the dead king's infant son by a Brahman wife, forced the dead king's beloved slave queen to burn herself on her husband's funeral pyre, and took his childless senior queen as co-regent. In order to head off any possible discontent he adopted a solution used by many dictators before and since: to divert internal dissent by engaging in foreign conquest. But where? With the Sikhs to the west, the Himalayas to the north and the Chinese to the north-east, the most tempting line of least resistance was the rich plains to the south. Memories were short, as they always are. Talk of young General Wellesley's victories died away,

and the East India Company was well known to be cutting back its forces and territorial ambitions, in part because of the costs of the great war against Napoleon.[23]

The senior Nepalese military commander, leading the Nepalese western army, was General Kaji Amar Singh Thapa (Amar Singh), aged about sixty. In April 1810 an East India Company officer, Colonel David Ochterlony, half American and half Scot, tried to agree the 'Principle of Limitation' with Amar Singh Thapa, which meant that the Company would not interfere with the Nepalese in the hills they had occupied if they did not intrude into the lowlands. But some of the hill states that the Gurkhas had occupied had claims to lowland territory, and, in any case, the whole idea of frontiers and boundaries was alien to Nepalese thinking and experience. In 1813, Amar Singh Thapa occupied some lowland villages that had formerly belonged to the Rajah of Hindur, whom the Nepalese had deposed. The Nepalese seemed anxious not to offend the British and the villages were restored by the end of October, but Ochterlony realised that the immediate threat to British East India Company interests was from Amar Singh Thapa's army. Ochterlony reported meeting Amar Singh Thapa at Kalka, just north of Chandigarh, south of Simla (Shimla) and west of Dehra Dun, on the edge of the hills, on 10 December 1813.[24] For the moment, peace remained, but it would not last long.

Nepal was an aggressive state under an aggressive prime minister who wanted to distract attention from any domestic concerns. Because military service was accepted in lieu of taxes, large armies were relatively easy to maintain. Nepal had already attacked and occupied large areas – Kumaon, Sirmoor and Garhwal – which were supposedly under the British East India Company's protection. It refused to accept another British Resident – effectively, an ambassador – or to negotiate with the Company boundary commissioners who were sent in response to repeated Gurkha raids. Gurkha inroads into British India grew more provocative, culminating with an attack on a British police post and its destruction. Some sort of war was inevitable.[25]

On 1 November 1814, Francis Rawdon-Hastings, 2nd Earl of Moira and the Governor-General of India from 1813 to 1823,

formally declared war. Operations had already commenced in October, as they always do when the attacker mobilises. He and the Company's army knew it would be a tough fight. The East India Company was taking on a proud and martial nation that had been conducting incursions into its territory on a front of several hundred miles. It should be stressed that in 1814 the 'Gurkhas', insofar as they could be defined, formed the core of the Nepalese Army that took the field against the British, and most of the officers, but not the major part, numerically.[26] As it turned out, the war would take the form of two separate campaigns, with the British driving the Nepalese out of Kumaon and Garhwal in the first (1814–15), but finding that they had to threaten Kathmandu in order to achieve the political objectives they wanted in the second (1815–16).

The East India Company force that assembled was very strong for the time. There were 30,000 regular troops, 12,000 Indian auxiliaries, 60 guns, 1,113 elephants and 3,682 camels. The regular troops comprised East India Company native soldiers with British officers and also purely British Crown regiments. Lord Moira's plan was good one. The force was split into four columns or divisions. In the centre Major Generals John Sullivan Wood and Bennet Marley were to attack towards Butwal, south of Pokhara, and south of Kathmandu, respectively, to engage Bhim Sen's centre of gravity in the Kathmandu valley. To the west, David Ochterlony, still a colonel at this stage, and Major General Rollo Gillespie attacked towards Simla, in Sirmoor, in the far west, and Dehra Dun, respectively. The fact that the talented Ochterlony, commanding a division, was only a colonel was a function of the East India Company Army's stultifying career pattern, which promoted only on the basis of seniority. In addition, two smaller columns of irregulars under Colonels William Gardner and Jasper Nicolls moved into Kumaon. Their job was to cut off the Gurkha forces further west and stop them withdrawing into Nepal. The three western areas of Garhwal, Sirmoor and Kumaon had all been captured and occupied by Gurkhas, but were outside Nepal itself.[27]

Like all good plans, Lord Moira's combined the psychological and political with the straightforward military and kinetic. The forces attacking in the west would destroy, or force the withdrawal

of, the Nepalese forces. The strike at the centre would appear to threaten the centre of gravity – Bhim Sen's government in Kathmandu. A big victory over the Gurkha regime would impress the native polities within India and convey the message of British supremacy, while perhaps making it possible to open up trade with Nepal and, indeed, a trade corridor through it to China.[28]

The forces started moving and entered the territories occupied by the Gurkhas in October, even before the formal declaration of war. This they were entitled to do, as the territory was under British protection. The two central columns that attacked Nepal were confronted by much smaller Gurkha forces but nevertheless failed to push on, and General Marley appears to have suffered a nervous breakdown.[29] Although the season – winter – is the best time of year to visit the Terai, where the temperatures are relatively mild and it is not oppressively humid, the difficulties of handling a force in the swampy forests of southern Nepal in 1814 must not be underestimated.

To the north-west (see Figure 3) the commanders did better. Gillespie probably had a force of 2,775 sepoys – native Indian troops – plus 100 Irish Dragoons and the 53rd Foot – maybe 3,500 to 4,000 altogether.[30] He captured the important town of Dehra Dun or Dehra Doon, north of Delhi and on the very edge of the hills (see Figure 3). It is now the site of India's military academy – the equivalent of Sandhurst or West Point. He was then halted before the hill fort at what British accounts call Kalunga. 'Kalunga' means 'fort', and the place is popularly called 'Nalapani ko Ladain' in Nepal. Built on a 495-foot (150-metre) high hill and surrounded by dense undergrowth, it was encircled by Gillespie's division. The Irishman reckoned the Gurkhas would surrender easily since the British, although by this time down to 2,700 men, still heavily outnumbered its garrison of 650. This figure may include a number of women who were there.[31] The first attack was beaten off, and Gillespie attacked again on 31 October.[32] This time, he, with his detachment of Irish Dragoons, got to within 30 metres of the Gurkha stockade when he was killed by a bullet through the heart, right next to his aide-de-camp, Lieutenant Frederick Young. The ferocity of the Gurkhas' defence of the fort, with 650 men against Gillespie's 2,700,

and the fate of his general were not lost on the twenty-eight-year-old lieutenant. Young (1786–1864) later founded and commanded the Sirmoor Battalion, later the 2nd Gurkha Rifles.

The battle and siege lasted for another month, until 30 November. At one point, the story goes, a Gurkha defender whose jaw had been shattered came out waving a handkerchief. The East India Company troops duly gave him treatment at the dressing station, and after he had recovered sufficiently, he returned to continue manning the defence. It is an extraordinary story and violates one of the basic laws of war. Although you should treat wounded prisoners, you do not then let them go to carry on fighting against you. Other accounts of the battle indicate that when Gurkha prisoners from the Nepali garrison first witnessed the British-Indian surgeons performing amputations, they were horrified, thinking it was a form of punishment that was going to be inflicted on them.[33] It had to be explained that it was to save the patient's life, in the long run. Unlikely though these details may seem, there can be no doubt that during the month-long battle both sides showed a measure of chivalry that was as unusual then as it would be now.

The British were hugely impressed by the resilience and courage of their opponents. The transformation of the British view of their 'Gurkha' enemies can be gauged from the memoirs of Lieutenant John Shipp. Tony Gould assesses Shipp's memoir, published in 1829,[34] as 'swashbuckling and riveting, if not entirely reliable', a view with which I concur. Shipp accompanied Ochterlony on the second, 1816 invasion of Nepal and noted how remarkably energetic he was for a seventy-year-old. Ochterlony would no doubt have been gratified, as he was only fifty-eight at the time. Shipp highlighted the contradiction that others, too, noticed about the Gurkhas and their environment:

> In this paradise of beauty dwelt a cruel and barbarous people, proverbial for their bloody deeds, whose hearts were more callous than the flinty rocks that reared their majestic heads above the woody mountains [a reference to the 'flinty' peaks of the Himalayan snows beyond the 'woody mountains' of the Hills]. They are more savage in their nature than the hungry tiger that prowls through their dreary glens; cruel as the vulture . . . cunning as the field of night, powerful

as the rocks on which they live; and active as the goat upon the mountain's brow.[35]

Of course the 'Gurkhas' – whoever, exactly, they were – could be as cruel as any other people engaged in life-or-death struggle, illustrated Shipp's description of the horrific torture inflicted on a spy whom they captured.[36]

The British-Indian force won, in the end, according to one report, because they got a local person to reveal the source of the water supply, which they then cut off. On 30 November, out of food, water and ammunition, Balbahadur Singh Thapa (Kanwar), the Gurkha commander, led about seventy able-bodied Gurkhas (some sources say eighty-five) away in the night, leaving the walls of the embattled fort piled high with the dead and dying, including women, but knowing that the British would look after the wounded as best they could. The British-Indian casualties over the month included 31 officers and 732 soldiers, while the Gurkha defenders lost 520. Two years later, two obelisks were raised at the site of the fort in honour of the British and their 'gallant adversary', including a memorial to General Gillespie.

The battle for Nalapani ('Kalunga') was the turning point in the creation of the British and Indian Army Gurkhas in several ways. The Gurkhas' facility for creating formidable fortifications that seemed to spring from the hillsides as the Company's forces advanced had not gone unnoticed. Alexander Fraser, an officer with the Company's army, in a series of letters to his no-doubt worried parents marvelled at the 'rude but efficient fortifications'[37] that sprang up 'at the shortest warning . . . the jungle which covers the sides of the hills furnishing the materials'.[38] The forts were built from the copious supplies of timber or bamboo, which were formed into two palisades about 4 or 5 feet (1.5 metres) apart, and the space between them filled with stones. Just inside these, the Gurkhas dug trenches which they covered with branches and loose earth. Incoming shells that came over the walls would land in the trenches and explode relatively harmlessly. Ochterlony was impressed with the Gurkhas' ingenuity and ability to create earthworks, in addition to their other fighting qualities.[39] Charles Callwell, author of the

classic work on *Small Wars* eighty years later, by which time the Gurkhas had proved themselves in British service, remarked how 'the Gurkhas, now so famed for their offensive tactics on the hill sides, showed remarkable aptitude in the rapid construction of stockades in the days of the Nepaul Wars.'[40]

After the Battle of Nalapani, Major General Gabriel Martindell, who had replaced Gillespie, advanced towards the fortress of Jaithak. After Christmas 1814 the British-Indian forces laid siege to the fortress, which could be approached only up a steep slope, and were driven back. But Ochterlony succeeded in outflanking Jaithak, to the east, pressing towards Malaun. Although Amar Singh, the Gurkha general, conducted a skilful withdrawal through a series of defended mountain positions, he was still withdrawing, and the local chieftains noticed. They had never liked being invaded by the Nepalese and sided with the British-Indian forces. Amar Singh also neglected to secure the mountain peaks that overlooked the fortress of Malaun. The occupation of commanding heights, whether in strength or with small groups, was a basic procedure in mountain warfare, which Ochterlony well understood. If only small groups were posted, the procedure became known as 'picketing', which is still a key tactic in Afghanistan at the time of writing.

On the night of 14 April 1815, two months before the Battle of Waterloo was to take place in distant Belgium, Ochterlony sent the first troops onto a hilltop, called Ryla (or Raila), overlooking Malaun and on the following day it was reinforced by a battalion-plus, with two guns. On the same day another force of about 2,000 moved onto another feature, known as Second Deonthal. The aim was to cut Malaun off from Surajgarh ('Soorajgurh') Fort, and it succeeded (see Figure 3, which is taken from a report of 20 April 1815).[41] Raila is A and Deonthal B. To prevent interference from the Malaun garrison, feint attacks were made as diversions on Nepalese camps below Malaun Fort. One was headed by a Captain Charles Showers of the 19th Regiment, Bengal Infantry, who on the next day (the 16th) killed the opposing commander in single combat, but was then killed in turn.[42] His family recall how he 'led one of the principal columns in a separate attack in the most gallant style and gloriously fell at its head, just when in personal conflict he had with

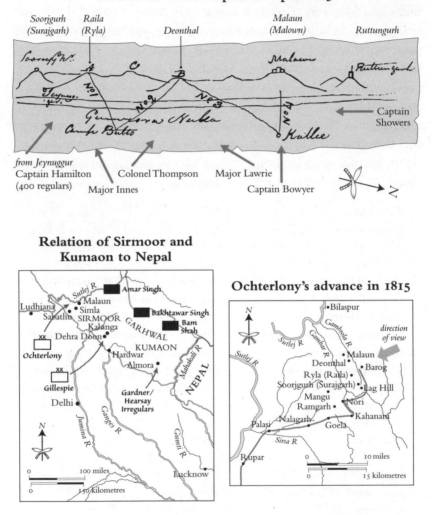

Lieutenant Ross's report 20 April 1815

Soorjgurh
(Surajgarh)

Raila
(Ryla)

Deonthal

Malaun
(Malown)

Ruttungurh

Captain
Showers

from Jeynuggur
Captain Hamilton
(400 regulars)

Major Innes

Colonel Thompson

Major Lawrie

Captain Bowyer

Relation of Sirmoor and Kumaon to Nepal

Sutlej R

Amar Singh

Ludhiana
Sabathu

Malaun
Simla

Bakhtawar Singh

SIRMOOR
Kalunga

GARHWAL

Bam
Shah

xx
Dehra Doon

KUMAON

Ochterlony
Hardwar
Almora

Gillespie
Gardner/
Hearsay
Irregulars

Mahakali R

NEPAL

Delhi

Ganges R

Gumti R

Jumna R

100 miles

150 kilometres

Lucknow

Ochterlony's advance in 1815

•Bilaspur

N

Gambola R

direction
of view

Sutlej R

Gambur R

Sutlej R

•Malaun

Deonthal
•Barog

Ryla (Raila)

Soorjgurh (Surajgarh)
Lag Hill

Mangu
•Nori

Ramgarh
Kahanam

Palasi
Nalagarh

Goela

Sirsa R

Rupar

10 miles

15 kilometres

FIGURE 3   The Approaches to Malaun, 1815

his own hand slain the chief of the enemy'. The family clearly believed this enemy 'chief' was called Bhim Sen, which may have led to confusion. A descendant, Colonel L. Showers DSO, wrote in 1965 that he had seen 'weapons used by Bhim Sen' in Kathmandu, including 'the very Kukri which might have chopped down my grandfather'.[43] Sadly, the latter were the weapons of Bhim Sen the prime minister and commander-in-chief, who was in Kathmandu at the time and was certainly not killed at Malaun that day.

The Nepalese commander who led the attempts to recapture Second Deonthal was Bakhti ('Bhugtee') Thapa. The accounts of timing are confusing, and the Nepalese may have tried to dislodge the British–Indian force more than once. On the morning of 20 April, according to Lieutenant Ross's letter of that date, he led the Nepalese counter-attack up the bare slope.

> This morning at the very first break of day the Gorkhas from Malown headed by Bhugtee Thappa made a grand attack on B [see Figure 3] which lasted nearly two Hours, and during which they sustained the hardest fire of grape and musquetry I ever heard. They returned there several times to the charge with most unparalleled intrepidity and endeavoured sword in hand to cut in upon our guns, during which as fast as one set of men were knocked down others springing up from behind rocks rushed forward to supply their places. They were finally driven back from all quarters with a loss which though not ascertained must have been very great. Bhugtee Thappa the most renowned Chief of their army fell just before their final retreat covered with wounds and glory, bayoneted, sabred and shot. Besides him they have lost Juskurrum Kajee and Jehr Singh, officers of note, whose bodies, originally brought into the camp, the General [Ochterlony] has sent to Ummar Singh [Amar Singh Thapa, the commander of the Malaun force], wrapped in shawls and with every mark of honour (Bhugtee's particularly) which their rank and valour merited.[44]

The 'approach of the dark hour' prevented Ross writing more, a reminder that these armies operated without the vision aids we have available today. Bakhti Thapa had attacked with 2,000 men but a quarter of them, including himself and two other key officers, were killed. Amar Singh Thapa withdrew into the fortress but had

too few troops to hold it. Ochterlony, shrewd as ever, offered him generous terms, and Martindell did the same at Jaithak, which was now cut off from Nepal proper. Some 1,500 Nepalese troops, plus 1,000 women and children, marched out of Jaithak, heading back to Nepal. The troops from both strongholds were allowed to withdraw with full military honours including 'arms and accoutrements, the colours of their respective corps', plus two artillery pieces from Malaun and one from Jaithak, back to the river Mahakali (Maha Kali), which would form a new, identifiable border with Nepal (see Figure 3).[45] The agreement signed on 15 May 1815 between Ochterlony and Amar Singh Thapa acknowledged 'the high rank and character of Kajee Ummer Singh Thappa and . . . the skill, bravery, and fidelity with which he defended the country committed to his charge'.[46]

Further to the east, and closer to Nepal proper, Colonels Gardner and Hearsey had advanced towards Almora. By April they had been joined by Lieutenant Colonel Jasper Nicolls, bringing the total British-Indian force to 5,000, and laid siege to Almora. By the end of April, the Nepalese were withdrawing from Kumaon, back into Nepal. The policy of letting them go with their arms was highly successful: the British-Indian object was never to invade Nepal per se, but to get the Nepalese out of Kumaon, a part of what was coalescing as British India. On all these occasions – engagements at Jaithak, Malaun and Amora – some of the Nepalese came over to the British.[47]

However, the war was not over because there was no guarantee, as yet, that the Nepalese would stay out of the East India Company's real estate. But the British-Indian authorities, in particular Ochterlony, had seen enough to start recruiting what became 'the Gurkhas'. It is estimated that about 5,000 former Nepalese troops remained in the area west of Nepal and joined British-Indian service.[48]

Bhim Sen, the prime minister and ruler of Nepal, was not prepared to accept the British terms. Lord Moira, now Marquess Hastings, thought the war was virtually over and appointed Ochterlony as his superintendent of political affairs and agent for the area west of Nepal. The Nepalese knew that the British still had to

deal with Napoleon, and therefore held out. Even after Waterloo, European politics was complicated and the British also had to worry about the powerful Sikh kingdom to the west. And then, lurking in the background, were the Russians who, as members of the victorious coalition, soon found themselves as far west as Paris. The expansionist Russian 'threat' to India, which had begun to smoulder into life in 1801, would soon be a major factor in Afghanistan, in British-Indian strategy and a key driver in the story of the Gurkhas.[49]

Although a treaty was signed between the British and the Nepalis at Segauli on 2 December 1815, it was not ratified by the stipulated deadline and the Nepalese refused to accept a British Resident – or ambassador – in Kathmandu. Hastings assessed that the regular, trained and experienced part of the Nepalese Army, which had been 12,000 strong at the outbreak of war in October–November 1814, was probably down to 7,000. Ochterlony was tasked to bring matters to a swift conclusion. He was appointed on 12 January 1816 although formally took command only on the 25th, by which time the first pioneer companies were already across the Ganges. His objectives were similar to those that the unfortunate Marley had failed to achieve a year before. Always hoping that the Nepalese government would bow to pressure and ratify the treaty, he was to occupy the Makwanpur valley and capture the forts there. If the Nepalese still did not give in, then he was to attack and capture the centre of gravity. The capital. Kathmandu.

Ochterlony commanded a main force comprising 19,400 men – a division – in four brigades. In addition there was another force of 6,600, under Colonel Nicolls, which would attack from the far west into western Nepal, and one of 4,900 under Major General Wood to mount a diversionary attack north from Gorakhpur, also west of the main thrust. Time was of the essence, and the cautious approach that had served Ochterlony so well in the first campaign in the west, cutting new roads and bombarding successive positions with artillery, would have to be discarded. On 9 February his force reached Bichakori, just beneath the Churia Ghati Pass.

Here he was confronted by the most depressing spectacle. The pass, the obvious route to Kathmandu, was defended by three stockades. In Lieutenant Shipp's words,

Hills rising like stairs, summit above summit, in beautiful succession, all of them wooded with the most gloriously variegated trees and shrubs. Among them majestic rocks lifted their heads, as if in proud defiance of the attacker. At the foot of the hills two strong piquets of the enemy were posted; one of them on a hill to the right . . . On our approach they withdrew to the nearby hills without a shot . . . This silence on the part of a brave, and subtle, foe let us know in plain terms that something was brewing for us. They seemed to be inviting us to advance, and take a look at their beautiful country. In the direction we had thought of taking [the Churia Ghati] there was nothing but stockade and fort upon fort. To risk failure at the beginning of a war, against such an enemy, would be to lay the basis of ultimate defeat and destruction. To go along on this route would be like knocking our heads on the rocks, or giving our bodies to fill up the trenches before their stockades . . . But we had at our head a Commander with just the right gifts for such a campaign, and he began to seek a more practicable route.[50]

Ochterlony's name was a problem for the Irishmen of Shipp's Irish 87th Regiment of Foot, so they called their general David Malony.[51] Ochterlony dug in at a fortified depot 5 miles (8 kilometres) directly south of the Churia Ghati Pass, while Lieutenant Pickersgill, his reconnaissance and intelligence officer, looked for a better route. On 14 February he told Ochterlony of an alternative pass, to the west, which was 'unguarded and practicable, though difficult'.[52] Leaving the 4th Brigade facing the Churia Ghati Pass as a deception, Ochterlony led the 3rd Brigade in a twenty-five-hour march that brought them 5 miles behind the forward Nepali defences. With their flank turned by this *desant* operation, which had much the same effect as an airborne assault, the shocked Nepalese withdrew to Makwanpur. The analogy comes from Shipp's account:

They thought us to be devils rather than men, who had dropped down upon them from the skies. Some of them even believed that we had been seen passing through the air in flying carriages, drawn by celestial elephants; until a few, who were braver than the rest, had a look at us and exploded the superstition. They were astounded that we had climbed that terrific mountain, indeed, looking at it

afterwards, we wondered ourselves how we had managed to get an army up it.'[53]

Ochterlony's action was seen as exemplary eighty years later. Charles Callwell, author of the 1896 classic treatise on *Small Wars* – which meant all wars other than those against major European adversaries, even if they were not 'small' – wrote:

When General Oughterlony was advancing on Katmandu in 1816, all the passes generally used over the first range of hills above the Terai were held by the Gurkhas, and reconnaissance showed the defences to be most formidable. A route was, however, discovered which the enemy had neglected by which the hostile positions could be turned. This route passed through a deep, narrow ravine for some miles, and it offered extraordinary difficulties to a march in the darkness. But one brigade starting after dark one night advanced by it, and reached the crest of the hill unopposed about dawn after an arduous march through most difficult country. The Gurkhas [the Nepalese – the enemy] were taken completely aback by this remarkable exploit, and they abandoned all their first positions.[54]

The actions that followed bore a striking resemblance to those at Malaun nearly a year before. Ochterlony discovered that an important hilltop position at Sikhar Khatri had been abandoned and occupied it with the 87th of Foot – Shipp's regiment. And, just as at Malaun, the Nepalese launched furious attacks up the killing ground of the slopes to try to dislodge them. Shipp's description of this enemy under fire has probably shaped the popular view of 'Gurkhas': 'Those we were now dealing with were no flinchers; but, on the contrary, I never saw more steadiness or bravery exhibited by any set of men in my life. Run they would not; of death they seemed to have no fear, though their comrades were falling thick around them, for we were so near that every shot told.'[55]

On 5 March 1816, Ochterlony was able to move heavy artillery to within 1,650 feet (500 metres) of Makwanpur fort. On 2 March his 1st Brigade took Hariharpur, 15 miles (23 kilometres) to the east. The East India Company was now within 20 miles (30 kilometres) of Kathmandu and threatening the Kathmandu valley. Bhim Sen gave in. 'At half-past two o'clock' on 4 March 1816 the

Treaty of Segauli, drawn up on 2 December 1815, was ratified by Chundur Seekhur Opadeea, 'agent on the part of the Raja of Nipal'.[56]

Articles 3 and 5 of the treaty confirmed the border, which is now the border between India and Nepal, and, in Article 8, that 'accredited ministers from each [state] shall reside at the court of each other'. The 'Resident', whom Bhim Sen and his top general Kaji Amar Singh had so opposed, would take his place in Kathmandu. Kaji Amar Singh had warned that the British would use the presence of a Resident to infiltrate troops, but this did not happen. The British were acutely aware of Nepalese sensitivities. This included not having any 'Gurkhas' – those who had obviously gone over to the British after the first campaign – in the Resident's escort. The escort must exclude 'any men who came over to us under such circumstances as would make their appearance at Catmandoo essentially an insult to their former masters'.[57] Ochterlony would have liked to have included a clause in the treaty allowing the recruitment of Gurkhas, but was anxious not to upset the Governor-General or to add any delay to the already protracted negotiations by introducing a subject of such sensitivity. On the recruitment of 'Gurkhas', the Treaty of Segauli is completely silent.

The two-stage war between the East India Company (acting as a 'state') and Nepal had been a very tough fight indeed: the toughest the British had yet encountered in the subcontinent. Lieutenant General George MacMunn, writing in *The Martial Races of India*, later said that

> It was to prove a long and arduous campaign because of the nature of the foe, long because of the inefficiency of the elderly commanders selected and the inferiority of some of the company's troops deployed. [The war with Nepal was] as serious as with Tipu Sultan and had it not been the years of the close of the Peninsular campaign [1808–14], or the war with America [1812–14], or the thrills of Hundred Days and the victory of Waterloo it would have attracted far more attention in Europe. The first thing to realize is that the Gurkha invasion of India was on a front of several hundred miles, and the Gurkha forces were established with strong points from the

44

Simla hills (to use an entirely modern term), far down to Dehra Dun, Almora and the road to Kathmandu.[58]

The idea of employing detachments of enemy prisoners against their former masters grew out of the age-old stratagem of breaking up enemy forces into their various components and disrupting alliances. At the start of the 1814–15 campaign, the idea was to try to recruit elements of the Nepalese Army who were *not* Gurkhas. Ochterlony may have had the idea in mind at the start of the war. As early as 21 November 1814, Fagan, the adjutant-general, wrote back to Ochterlony, still a colonel commanding the 3rd Division of the Field Army:

> The Commander-in-Chief [Lord Moira] would think it politic to adopt any measure which had a tendency, particularly at the onset of the contest, to disorganize or break up the enemy's force, as that of occasionally entertaining detached bodies of it evidently has; but the characteristic treachery of the natives of Goorka proper would render such a measure, if pursued to any extent and without using the utmost precaution, extremely hazardous. Could the Goorkas be discriminated from the other various tribes of which the armies of Nepal are composed and many of whom, it is said, serve in them with reluctance, the measure in question might be resorted to, whenever recommended, by policy or the circumstances of the moment, without incurring the dangers which seem to attach to the unrestricted grants of service to the troops of Nepaul, and still more their employment with ours. The Commander-in-Chief understands the Goorka troops; those properly so-called are markedly distinguished by dialect, appearance and other peculiarities, from the natives of other countries of which the Nepaul army is of great degree formed; and those distinguishing features may possibly, in most cases, serve as a discriminating criterion . . . The Commander-in-Chief is sensible how safely it may be left to your judgment and prudence to adopt the measure in question or not.[59]

The letter is tantalisingly ambiguous. The most obvious interpretation is that it would be necessary to distinguish Gurkhas from non-Gurkhas, to prevent Gurkhas infiltrating East India Company units and then turning on the other nationalities and British officers. But

Ochterlony may already have been thinking of recruiting Gurkhas, as opposed to the non-Gurkhas who might be prepared to fight them. It is impossible to tell from the letter. The idea of trying to recruit non-Gurkha subjects of the Nepalese ruling class and the inhabitants of occupied territory would have been fairly obvious to many at the time. To take that idea and turn it on its head, as Ochterlony did shortly afterwards, and recruit the Gurkhas themselves because they were good soldiers, was a stroke of utter genius. Ochterlony would do just that within a few months.

David Ochterlony's lateral thinking may have owed something to his upbringing. He was born in Boston, Massachusetts, then a British colony, in February 1758, and went to India as a cadet in 1777, after having attended the Dummer Charity School, now known as the Governor's Academy, in Boston. He therefore left America at the start of the War of Independence, to join the British. By the time he led his East India Company division against the Nepalese, the British had fought not just one but two wars against the Americans, the latter in 1812–14. For Ochterlony, the country of one's birth was no doubt a supreme irrelevance, when determining one's military or company loyalty. And so, naturally, he might have assumed was the case with the Gurkhas.

The British could clearly distinguish between the Kumaonese, who resented the Nepalese invasion and the imposition of 'Gurkha' rule, and the 'true Gurkhas'. 'Nature has drawn a very striking difference,' wrote Captain Raper, 'for the slender form of the Kamaonese cannot be put in competition with the stout Herculean limbs of the Goorkali soldier.'[60] William Fraser, a civilian on Gillespie's staff, wrote that Gillespie had agreed 'to raise some bodies of light irregular troops to push forward into the mountains, for the purpose of giving confidence to the inhabitants, destroying the few detached parties scattered about, and to collect the revenue and awe the people, and seizing difficult passes and strengthening them if necessary with stockades or barriers'.[61] On 30 November 1814 the Political Secretary, John Adam, passed on the Governor-General's approval for the creation of an 'irregular corps' on this basis, which was to be commanded by Lieutenant Young. It must be stressed that very few, if any, of these 'irregulars' were 'true

Gurkhas'. On the contrary, they were 'natives of the country who supported the British' against the Gurkha regime of Nepal.

This body of irregulars soon ran into trouble. On 21 February 1815 they were sent to intercept a party from Amar Singh's army that included non-combatants and treasure. Young's irregulars, about 3,000 strong, were repulsed by about 800 Nepalese Gurkhas, and about 200 of them then counter-attacked. According to Fraser, Young's irregulars fled 'like a flock of sheep. Many were not killed for they ran too fast but a number broke their legs and necks by tumbling down precipices.'[62]

There is a story that Young did not flee with his men and was captured by the 'Gurkhas' (the enemy). The story continues that, when interrogated and asked why he had not fled, he said he had come too far to run away. It has been repeated religiously, but seldom challenged. The Gurkhas supposedly responded by saying, 'We could serve under a man like you.' His daughter, one Mrs Jenkins, said more than a hundred years after the event that she did not know how long her father had been a prisoner, but that he had used the time to become conversant with his captors' customs and religion and to learn their language. He must have been a very quick learner, because, after allegedly being captured on 21 February, just five days later, on 26 February, he and Fraser signed a letter describing the event. It detailed the total strength of Young's force (3,305), the number of men engaged (2,312), those who fled and subsequently deserted (1,451), those killed (180) and wounded (83). Neither Young nor Fraser made any reference to Young being taken prisoner, and it seems highly unlikely that he was.[63]

However, the 'Affair of the 21st' must have convinced Young – if he needed convincing, after General Gillespie had collapsed dead in his arms at Nalapani on 31 October 1814 – that the British-Indian Army did not really need the people who made up the force that had disintegrated around him. It needed 'Gurkhas'.

Meanwhile, the East India Company forces were taking small numbers of 'true Gurkhas' as prisoners. They were not initially armed, because they were seen as too dangerous, nor were they committed to fight their former bosses. They were used instead to instruct the 'irregulars' in how to build the stockades that Alexander

Fraser had so admired. 'The irregulars make a stockade in the Goorkha fashion – a Jemmadar [Lieutenant – see Table 2] and a party of the regular Goorkha company show them the way'. Their appearance, at this stage, did not endear them to conventional military or refined European taste. James Fraser recalled on 28 March 1815:

> Last night my brother's Goorkha company came in. Such ragamuffins I have seldom seen. They have Chinese faces, sallow complexion, dark shaggy hair cut short by the ears and very bushy. Upon their heads they wear a peculiar turban somewhat like the broad Scottish bonnet. Their garments are filthy. They carry besides a short crooked knife in their cummerbunds.[64]

The recruitment of 'Gurkha' volunteers, as opposed to the employment of Gurkha prisoners, had begun even earlier. On 24 January 1815, Ochterlony signed and sealed a note offering businesslike terms for the transfer of Nepalese soldiers and officers to British service. The initial pay was a reward of 10 rupees, followed by pay at the same rates as applied in the Nepalese Army. For the mighty East India Company, as hard-headed a business operator as you could find, this was a good deal. Senior officers who brought over companies or battalions would be granted especially high rates of pay.[65]

The number of Nepalese Gurkhas, mostly prisoners, joining the British began to increase. They appeared eager to make themselves useful, rather than languish as prisoners of war, and their expertise at constructing engineering works was especially valued. By early April 1815, just before the critical battle at Malaun, Ochterlony had 324 Nepalese prisoners in his camp. He told Hastings (formerly Moira), the commander-in-chief, that he proposed to form them into a 'Nusseeree Pulteen', or battalion. In the correspondence of the time, the word 'Nusseeree', which nowadays would be transliterated as 'Nasiri', goes without explanation. But it is pregnant with meaning. It comes from the Hindustani word *nasir*, meaning 'defender' or 'friend'. This in turn is linked with the Arabic word *nasr*, meaning 'help' or 'victory'. At the most basic level, therefore, the Nusseerees or Nasiris were 'friendlies' – as the US cavalry would have referred

to certain Native American tribes in the West – as opposed to 'hostiles'. But in 1804, Ochterlony had defended Delhi and the Mughal court from the Marathas and was given the title Nasir-ud-Daula ('helper' or 'victory-giver of the state') by Shah Alam. He wrote in April 1815 that he considered himself the Nusseerees' 'Commandant and Patron. These trifles have great weight and I must confess myself sanguine in my hopes of their not discrediting my favour.'[66] There was something deeper here, as Coleman observes,[67] something that perhaps evokes the romanticism of the time: Scottish loyalty to kith and kin and friends, extraordinary vanity, who knows. These men were FOOs – Friends of Ochterlony.

The first British officer to lead Nepalese Gurkhas into action was also a friend of Ochterlony. Lieutenant Peter Lawtie was Ochterlony's chief field engineer, a post that, given the prevalence of siege warfare and the Gurkhas' ability make stockades spring from the hillsides, gave him importance far above his rank or years. As we have seen, rank in the East India Company's army depended on length of service and thus, in large measure, on age, but the jobs to which one could be assigned did not. Lawtie's meticulous reconnaissance contributed to Ochterlony's unlocking of the Malaun defences. On 14 April, Ochterlony put Lawtie in charge of his Nusseeree (Nasiri) battalion, 'a corps', he wrote on 18 April, 'in which I feel a great and peculiar interest'.[68]

Lawtie's account of the night move up onto the heights commanding Malaun on 14 April 1815 sets the tone for 200 years of Gurkha service in the Indian and British armies: 'the closeness of their files and the perfect silence with which they moved on the night of the 14th instant over the most rugged roads proved them to be peculiarly adapted for operations which require celerity and concealment.'[69] The Nasiris were in action for the next three days. Lawtie noted that everything 'was done with cheerfulness, good humour and an acknowledgement of gratitude for the kindness of their present employers', in a report written to help Ochterlony 'to judge the value of a new and so peculiarly formed a Corps'.[70] A special force, indeed.

Meanwhile others resisted arming the Gurkhas, notably Martindell, who prevaricated. William Fraser, a man of some

ambition, took matters into his own hands and went over his head to the Governor-General. Hastings concurred and on 8 May replied that 'a Corps of the description formed by Major-General Ochterlony has been found to be of the utmost utility, and that Officer's experience has shewn that the utmost reliance may be placed in their fidelity, while regularly paid and well treated. Of their value in all the essential qualities of soldiers there can be no doubt.'[71]

Lawtie, meanwhile, had fallen ill with typhus and on 5 May he died. Ochterlony was devastated and ordered his division's officers to wear mourning for a month. In Lawtie's place, Ochterlony appointed Lieutenant Robert Ross to command the Nasiris. On 3 May, Ross led the Nasiris in an operation to open up and secure a road that Nepali troops could use to evacuate a redoubt that had been under British-Indian bombardment. Many of them did so, along with their womenfolk, and came over to the British-Indian side.

The 15 May agreement ended the first campaign of the war and the three main Nepalese field commanders crossed the Kali river, back into Nepal. They left behind about 5,000 Nepalese troops who had joined the British-Indian force, mostly in the far west. Under the terms of Clause 5 of the 15 May convention, all those Nepalese troops, with the exception of the personal guards of the Nepalese commanders, were 'at liberty to enter into the service of the British Government [that is, the East India Company], if it is agreeable to themselves and the British government choose to accept their services'.[72] Those who were not so employed would be paid an allowance until peace was concluded between the 'two states'. That happened with the signature of the Treaty of Segauli on 4 March 1816.

Therefore, the formal agreement between the East India Company and Nepal related just to the employment of 'Gurkhas' who had been captured or gone over to the British while fighting outside Nepal during the first campaign a year earlier. The Treaty of Segauli contained no further provision relating to Gurkha service with the British.

We do not know for sure how many of the 4,700 to 5,000 Nepali soldiers of the western army who went over to the British-Indian Army could properly be defined as 'Gurkhas'. Most of the accounts of the Nepalese Army, analysed in depth by Coleman, suggest that

about a third of it were 'true Gurkhas'. This means that perhaps 1,500 or so of the Nepalese Army units that came over to the British would have been from those same *jats*. They would have been Gurkhas or Gorkhas from the Chhetris, Magars and Gurungs of western Nepal, whom Prithvi Narayan Shah would have recognised as 'Gorkhalis'. As we have seen, the 'true Gurkhas' tended to hold more senior ranks in the Nepalese Army. Thus, of eight sirdars working for Ochterlony in May 1815, six were 'Gurkhas'.[73]

By 1 July 1815, after the Nepalese withdrawal from Kumaon and Garhwal, and while a final peace deal was in the balance, there were therefore two groups of 'Goorkhas' in British-Indian service: Young's 'corps', 1,553 strong, and four battalions under Ochterlony, known as 'Nusseerees' , totalling 2,102. Ochterlony was slightly contemptuous of Young's 'corps', pointing out that Young's people 'came over uninstigated from the highest to the lowest' – implying they were deserters, while his Nasiris, who were prisoners of war, were not. On 27 July, the commander-in-chief ordered that these 3,655 soldiers – officers and other ranks – plus a small number of associated non-combatants should be reorganised into three battalions: two Nasiri battalions and one, based on Young's, the Sirmoor battalion.[74]

The precise date of the foundation of the Gurkhas in British-Indian service, if such a thing could ever be pinned down, is disputed. The very word *lahuré*, the Nepalese word for a Nepali in foreign military service, actually pre-dates the British East India Company's direct involvement altogether. It was first used to describe the Nepalis who headed for Lahore to serve the rajah of that Indian state, Ranjit Singh, as early as 1806–9.[75] The British East India Company Governor-General's order of 27 July 1815 was the de facto formalisation of an arrangement that had come into place over the preceding eight months, since Ochterlony's ambiguous exchange with the adjutant general in November 1814.

> Major-General Ochterlony will be pleased to form the whole of the Goorkhas who came over during the late Campaign to the westward, both Nusserees and those under Lieutenant F. Young into three battalions . . . the Nusseree and Sirmoor Battalions are to be

armed with musquets [the standard, long, smooth-bore weapon of the infantry] until a sufficient number of fusils [shorter carbines carried by light troops and cavalry – see glossary] can be obtained. Each man to maintain and wear his kookrey [kukri] in a leather waistbelt.[76]

There can be little doubt that these were what we would now recognise as 'Gurkhas'.

However, to make this formal the order of the Vice-President in Council of the East India Company was required, which came on 26 August. The formation of the First and Second Nasiri (Gorkha) Battalions, and the Sirmoor and Kumaon ('Kemaon') Battalion, is given as 24 April 1815 in a later document dated 2 May 1823.[77] An Indian history also cites the Governor-General's orders of 24 April 1815 as the official date. Hastings, the Governor-General, was then on tour and Coleman, whose meticulous history is unsurpassed, doubts whether the order ever existed.[78] Nevertheless, there is no dispute that there were four battalions – each of about 1,000 troops – in existence, by summer 1815. These were: the 1st Nasiri Battalion, who were Ochterlony's protégés, under Lieutenant Ross, who had succeeded the tragically missed Lawtie; the Malaun Battalion, which became the 1st Gorkha Regiment; and the Sirmoor Battalion, which became the Sirmoor Rifles (later the 2nd King Edward's Own Gurkha Rifles), under Lieutenant Frederick Young. A 2nd Nasiri Battalion was also established, initially commanded by Lieutenant McHarg, but was disbanded in 1829 and its members all redistributed to the 1st Nasiris or the Sirmoor Rifles. Finally, there was the Kumaon Provincial Battalion, which was formed from remnants of Nepalese forces captured at or near Deonthal and Almora under Sir Robert Colquhoun. This later became the 3rd Queen Alexandra's Own Gurkha Rifles.[79]

These four battalions gained progressive levels of official approval, possibly through an untraceable Governor-General's order of 24 April 1815,[80] but certainly through the commander-in-chief's (Hastings') order of July, and the Vice-President in Council's order of late August. Each European commanding officer was allocated a European adjutant, although almost all the officers were native

'Gurkhas' – who had been the officer-class in their own country. Each battalion had a nominal establishment of 1,330 officers and men, including 1,088 with muskets or fusils.[81] However, none of these units was used – and therefore deployed directly against their former masters – in the second East India Company campaign against Nepal. There was no particular reason why they should have been. They had been raised to secure and defend the western hills of Kumaon and Garhwal, recovered from Nepalese incursions. Their purpose was to release British and other native infantry units, who were not so suited to hill combat, to fight on the plains against the Marathas, or anyone else proving difficult. Given where the 'Goorkha' battalions were raised, there was no pressing reason to commit them to an assault on central Nepal, and they were in the wrong place. Nevertheless, between autumn 1815 and the start of 1816, Young's battalion was moved to Sitapur to link up with Nicolls' detachment, which was on standby to move into western Nepal. But the second campaign, which lasted but a few weeks, was over before the Sirmoor Battalion could be committed. Nicolls, interestingly, was impressed by the way this special battalion was equipped for 'hill' (mountain) fighting, but felt he could not trust the men to fight against their own Nepalese kith and kin so soon after defecting. Young, as might be expected, had no such doubts, but the war ended before their commitment could be fully tested.[82]

The moment hostilities ceased, the East India Company – a 'state' with a particularly commercial ethos – was keen to cut costs and disband units raised temporarily during the conflict. However, as Hastings stressed in his 1815 report on the first phase of the war, he was convinced of the 'Gurkhas'' loyalty because of 'the active, zealous and meritorious services performed by those who were embodied by Major-General Ochterlony in the progress of the campaign. [His] despatches . . . will show your Honourable Committee the sense of their value entertained by these officers.' He also stressed that it would be neither 'prudent nor consistent with good faith to discharge from the service of the British Government any portion of the troops who came over from the enemy'.[83] Having been separated from their own country, the 'Gurkha' soldiers were not immediately liable to be seduced back

into Nepalese service by their former commanders. However, if kept idle, they might be tempted to lend their martial services elsewhere, to parties that might include Ranjit Singh, the rajah of Lahore, or 'predatory associations' – bandit chiefs. Hastings therefore reassured the Secret Committee of the Court of Directors of the East India Company that it made sense to maintain the four battalions raised, but that their recruitment had been a temporary measure and that their numbers would inevitably diminish as a result of natural wastage.[84] As it turned out, other pressures – notably competition for the Gurkhas' services – meant that their strength in the service of the British-Indian Army would not be allowed to diminish, but would be maintained and even, later, increase.

In 1815, the year the British-Indian Gurkhas were officially formed, the four battalions, on paper, had a strength of about 5,000 men. There were probably fewer, in practice. That equated, and equates, to a brigade. In 2010 the UK Brigade of Gurkhas has two battalions of infantry, plus a regiment of Gurkha Engineers, a regiment of Gurkha Signals, and a Gurkha Logistics regiment, totalling about 3,000 men and, in the latter three – known as the 'corps regiments' (Engineers, Signals, Logistics), women. If Hastings, Ochterlony, Lawtie, Fraser, Ross and Young were brought back to life two centuries on, the modern organisation would be the same size as the one they created. It, and its people, would be instantly recognisable to them. So, too, would be public-private partnerships, the employment of private military companies and contractors. But they might be surprised that there were more British and fewer Gurkha officers than in their day, and that the computerised dead hand of Whitehall bureaucracy was as tortuously frustrating as the lengthy manuscript letters penned by East India Company clerks.

3

Proving Competence and Loyalty

D AVID OCHTERLONY'S VICTORY over Nepal in a second campaign lasting less than two months was a stupendous achievement. He received thanks from both Houses of Parliament in the UK, and, now a major general, was the first East India Company officer to be made a Knight Grand Cross of the Order of the Bath (GCB). Sir David took up residence at Delhi as the East India Company's number two in the subcontinent. However, after Governor-General Hastings left in 1823 and was succeeded by Lord Amherst, Ochterlony fell out of favour.

He was a product of the 'nabob' era, when British officers submerged themselves in the native culture, which in many cases included taking as many native wives as they could afford. Ochterlony was, therefore, in part, a victim of the growing tide of political correctness – in public, anyway – that we associate with the ensuing Victorian age. Stories about his extravagance spread, among them that he had thirteen wives who took the Delhi air every evening, each on her own elephant.[1] Fortunately for Ochterlony, perhaps, there were no credit cards in 1816. One of his wives, who became the most powerful, was Mubarak Begum, a former Brahman dancing girl, who converted to Islam. She was the mother of Ochterlony's youngest children, and attracted grave disapproval because of her background, her pretensions and her extravagance. She called herself 'Lady Ochterlony', which upset the British, and was widely known as 'Generallee Begum'.

Early in 1825, Ochterlony, still evidently with some energy to spare, prepared to march on Bharatpur, where the heir to the throne, whom he had undertaken to support, had been pushed aside by a cousin, but Amherst countermanded the order. As Amherst

expected, it was clearly a blow, and Ochterlony resigned. His health rapidly deteriorated. On 14 July 1825, aged sixty-seven, the canny and flamboyant Scottish-American general died. Mubarak Begum inherited a Mughal-style tomb that he had built in the north of the city, which respectable society shunned, calling it 'the Prostitute's Mosque'. Ochterlony's own monument in Calcutta stands a full 165 feet (50 metres) high. But his most lasting memorial and service to Britain and India is what his much lamented friend Lawtie had described as 'a new and so peculiarly formed a Corps'.[2] The Gurkhas.

Ochterlony's friend, William Fraser, who had also played a key role in creating the Gurkhas, not least by going over Martindell's head to Hastings when Martinell demurred on this issue, was a candidate for the new post of Resident in Kathmandu. Edward Gardner got the job instead, and that may again have been due to Fraser's risqué lifestyle. He reportedly had six or seven wives who lived with their numerous children 150 miles from Delhi.

Gardner, and his successor, Brian Houghton Hodgson, who arrived in Kathmandu as his assistant in 1821, found themselves virtually imprisoned by the shrewd and defensive Bhim Sen.[3] With the borders of Nepal firmly defined by the Treaty of Segauli, the strong army that Bhim Sen had built up for expansion and conquest was too big for British comfort. But it was his main power base. Although not an immediate threat to British India, the Nepalese army might again become one, especially if there was internal trouble in Nepal and Bhim Sen wanted to divert attention. Hodgson thought that diverting the 'Gorkhas' – at that point the western *jats* of Khas, Magars and Gurungs – into British-Indian service as mercenaries would help solve the problem by strengthening the Bengal Army and creaming off Nepalese martial manpower.

Bhim Sen was determined that this should not happen. Hodgson reported typical remarks made by Nepalese:

they say the English is good service but our Government won't hear of our entering it – nor can we leave the country without permission, obtainable only once in several years under the pretence of pilgrimage . . . Were we to run away our families would answer for

the offence, and such being the hazard how can we think of attempting it – especially under such an uncertainty of success?[4]

Word of the smartness and discipline of the newly raised 'Gurkha'
battalions quickly spread to Ranjit Singh, the ambitious Sikh rajah
of Lahore. In March and April 1816, Ross and MacHarg's 1st and
2nd Nasiri Battalions both reported attempts by emissaries from
Ranjit Singh to recruit their officers and soldiers at slightly higher
rates of pay than those paid by the East India Company. Ross's
Gurkha officers immediately passed on the information, but were
clearly unimpressed by the offer. MacHarg put Ranjit Singh's envoy
under arrest. However, Ranjit Singh had other successes, notably
recruiting Balbahadur Thapa who had commanded the defence of
Nalapani (Kalunga) against the ill-fated Gillespie and then Martindell.
Balbahadur Thapa commanded Ranjit Singh's Gurkha battalion,
and was killed fighting against the Afghans in 1823. The Afghans
were reputedly fearsome opponents, then as now, and Ranjit Singh
wrote that 'of all my trained soldiers, only the Gurkhas stood their
own against the Muslim attack'.[5]

Ranjit Singh's military build-up was another problem for the
British. His army grew in strength from just over 4,000 in 1811 to
15,000 by 1823, by which time it had become a well-trained, well-
equipped, balanced fighting force. Ranjit Singh recruited deserters
from the Bengal Army to train his troops, including Europeans, as
only they had expertise with artillery. The first European artilleryman joined him in 1809 and two French mercenaries, Ventura and
Allard, joined the Sikh force in 1822. Ranjit Singh continued to
recruit Gurkhas, and by 1842 the Sikh army had two Gurkha battalions.[6] Although at first he paid better than the East India
Company, pay for Gurkhas in the Sikh army later fell behind that
offered by the British.[7]

The East India Company's army continued to recruit a small
number of Nepalese, in spite of the Nepalese government's ban on
British-Indian recruiting, but most would have come from the hill
areas west of Nepal secured by the 1815 campaign. In a report of
December 1829, Frederick Young, now a major, described how in
1815 a school had been set up at Dehra Dun for the sons of 'Native

officers and men', who were brought up to provide new recruits for the Sirmoor Battalion. He noted that the stocky original Nepalese Gurkhas were physically stronger, but that the mixture of old Gurkha blood with taller, slimmer native Indian women produced recruits who looked better on parade because of their 'upright and soldier-like carriage'.[8] Comments of that kind would not be permitted today.

The main role of the two Nasiri Gurkha Battalions and the Sirmoor Gurkha Battalion was to defend the Cis-Sutlej hills (that is, the hills on 'our' side of the Sutlej) and Garhwal from possible invasion from the west by the ambitious Ranjit Singh. The Kumaon battalion was to prevent any incursion from Nepal out to the west. The fixing of the Nepalese frontiers brought about a period of political stability in northern India, and the Gurkha battalions – which we can now call them, using the modern spelling used by the British from 1891 – played a role in stabilising the region. They saw little active service for the first few years. In 1817–18 men from the Sirmoor Battalion served under Ochterlony during the war against the Marathas and Pindaris, but did not get any 'trigger time'.[9]

In 1824, however, a detachment of 350 men from the Sirmoor Battalion, commanded by Young, was sent against 'a gang of rebels and outlaws who had plundered the Treasury Party, and possessed themselves of the mud fort of Koorka (Kunja); the fort was stormed by means of a battering ram applied to the gate'.[10] This brief account summarises a dramatic story. The Gurkhas spent much of their time pursuing bandits, known as 'dacoits'. Led by someone called Kulwa and his brother Bhoora, a dacoit band 800 strong had seized a consignment of treasure guarded by 200 police. They seized the fort at Kunja and were committing 'every species of atrocity'. Just 200 men of the Sirmoor Battalion, plus some local police and volunteers, went to take them on. After breaking into the fort, near Saharanpur, the Gurkhas killed 153 of the 'rebels and outlaws', many of them with their kukris. Kulwa was killed and his severed head hung in a cage over the entrance to Dehra Dun jail for several years afterwards.[11]

This was the first time that any of the Gurkha battalions formed in 1815 had seen any real action, and Young and his men received

due thanks from succeeding levels of the East India Company hierarchy. This small action is important because Kunja is not in the
hills, where the Gurkhas were expected to serve, but down in
the plains. The Sirmoor Battalion also attacked it after covering 36
miles (54 kilometres) in twelve hours – quite a forced march.
Finally, the Gurkha force showed a certain amount of ingenuity.
Finding their way barred by a massive gate, which, covered by fire,
was a serious obstacle, they felled a tree and then trimmed it with
their kukris to make the battering ram. In memory of their first
action, the Sirmoor Battalion, later the 2nd Gurkha Rifles and
the now 1st Battalion the Royal Gurkha Rifles, adopted a ram's
head – the classical Greek or Roman battering-ram furniture – as a
prominent emblem on their cross-belts. There were also dacoit
women in the fort, and Young thought it worth noting that none
of them was molested by his troops.[12]

The first Burma War of 1824–6 created a crisis for the new
Governor-General, Amherst. Regular East India Company troops,
normally based near the main population centres in northern India,
were sent to Burma, given the cost and time it would have taken to
bring the King's Regiments from the UK. The British Bengal
Native Infantry, who were modelled on regular line infantry, wearing red coats, were recruited from the plains of northern India and
often of high caste. High caste brought certain problems, which did
not apply to Gurkhas. There were numerous jobs – including carrying food and water – which the high-caste sepoy did not do. Meals
were attended by religious prohibitions and rituals, as a result of
which feeding a force of sepoys took an inordinate amount of time.
Finally, the Hindus, as we saw in Chapter 1, had rigid rules about
seaborne travel. Rumours started spreading among the strict Hindu
troops that they might be used for a seaborne assault on Rangoon,
which led to a mutiny by the 47th Native Infantry stationed at
Barrackpur (Barrackpore).

Although, as we have seen, Gurkhas were nominally Hindus,
they had little time for high-caste rituals and dietary restrictions.
Writing to the adjutant general in India on 29 December 1829,
Major Young pointed out how the Gurkhas 'look down on the
regular Native sepoys, to whom they consider themselves superior,

but they have the highest opinion of the Europeans as soldiers, and respect their courage and discipline'.[13] He added that as long as the Gurkhas knew that their families in the base at Dehra would be looked after, 'they are ready to undertake any service, however distant'.[14] In a report the following year, Captain Kennedy, commanding the Nasiri Battalion, also noted 'the absence of all fastidiousness in regard to nature or preparation of their food adds greatly to the efficiency of the individuals composing the bulk of this corps and enhances their value as soldiers'.[15]

Another emerging problem at this time was an increasing alienation between the British and their Indian soldiers. This was not just noticeable among officers of the King's (UK) Regiments, but also among East India Company officers and their own soldiers. The Company officers tended to emulate their King's officer counterparts' 'disdain for all things Indian, including the language'. The same trend worked against nabobs like Ochterlony and Fraser who had, to a very large extent, 'gone native'. In the Gurkha battalions, however, the bond between the senior British officers – just three per battalion, at this stage – and their Gurkha officers, NCOs and men grew ever stronger. In part, this was due to Young's recommendation that British officers should be properly selected with reference to 'the duties they are intended to discharge and to their knowledge of the Asiatick [sic] character', and to Ochterlony's stress on the need for 'intelligent European officers'.[16]

Under these circumstances it would make sense to make more use of the Gurkhas, and to have more of them. The new commander-in-chief, Lieutenant General Sir Edward Paget, who had taken over from Hastings (who had been both Governor-General and commander-in-chief) on 13 January 1823, was not unsympathetic. In January 1825 his adjutant-general told the Political Secretary, George Swinton, that the commander-in-chief would support the establishment of a recruiting base at Lohughat in eastern Kumaon, just across the border from Nepal (see Figure 1). It was difficult to get new recruits for the two Nasiri and one Sirmoor battalions, in the face of Nepalese opposition and Ranjit Singh's poaching of recruits. The Governor-General had ordered that 'an augmentation of the two Nusseera [sic] and Sirmoor battalions is

directed and that Goorkahs are specified as the class to be entertained'.[17]

Lohughat was just a day's trek from the Nepalese border. The Nepalese enlisted their soldiers for a year and then discharged them, so there was a ready flow of potential recruits. As the proposed depot was right up against the border with Nepal, it would be far closer to the source of recruits than Ranjit Singh's rival Sikh headquarters at Lahore. On 14 January 1825, Swinton wrote to Edward Gardner, the Resident at Kathmandu, asking his opinion and stressing that the Nepalese authorities should know nothing about the plan. However, although the possibility of sending Gurkhas 'on expeditions beyond seas' was clearly being considered, Gardner then blocked it. He thought it 'improbable that men accustomed to the pure air and temperate climate of the hilly countries in which these people are accustomed to serve, would be able to preserve their health and continue efficient for a length of time in low and marshy situations'.[18] Given the Gurkhas' performance in Burma in the Second World War, and in Malaysia and Borneo subsequently, and their deployment to Hong Kong and Belize, Gardner could hardly have got it more wrong. But the Gurkhas were not sent to Burma, this time. Instead, another operation beckoned.

As we saw, in early 1825, Ochterlony had prepared to march on Bharatpur ('Bhurtpore') to rescue the legitimate heir, Bulwant Singh, whose accession had been usurped by his cousin, Durjan Singh. Amherst, nervous about a repetition of a failed assault on Bharatpur in 1805, told him in a most peremptory fashion to stop. But Charles Metcalfe, a friend of Ochterlony's and now Resident at Delhi, advised Amherst that he was obliged to uphold Bulwant Singh's claim to be rajah of Bharatpur. Ochterlony died at Meerut on 14 July. Lord Combermere (General Sir Stapleton Cotton), who had replaced Paget as commander-in-chief, then moved with a force of 21,000 troops and 100 guns against Bharatpur, by which time Durjan Singh had strengthened his defences. As if to honour their founder, the Sirmoor and 1st Nasiri battalions played a leading role in the assault. Two companies of the 1st Nasiris were attached to His Majesty's (King's – UK-based) 14th Foot.

The Major-General [Reynell, commanding the Division] impowers him from his own observation to assert that the conduct of the two Companies forming the detachment was calculated . . . to reflect the highest credit on the Regiment to which it belongs, and the Major-General has much satisfaction in assuring the two Commanding Officers, Major Young [Sirmoor Battalion] and Captain Kennedy [1st Nasiri Battalion], that the spirited behaviour of the men of both detachments whenever called upon for any particular enterprize or service not only attracted the notice of the Right Hon'ble the Commander-in-Chief but left in his Excellency's mind a most favourable impression of the Goorkha Sepoys.[19]

Although the Gurkhas disliked being referred to as sepoys, a term more usually associated with Indian native troops or, even worse, as 'NI' ('Native Indian'), which was definitely wrong, there could be no doubt that their star was in the ascendant. The Gurkhas were different, and for decades they fought to have that difference recognised. Thirty years later, in 1855, Ensign (Second Lieutenant) Gepp, a British officer who would be killed in the Indian Mutiny two years later, wrote sarcastically to his parents that 'you have been for the last three or four months most desperately insulting my dignity by two very simple letters, viz., NI affixed to the Regimental designation'. He went on to explain 'the excellencies of "The Goorkhas" in general and their undoubted superiority to the rest of the Indian Army . . . In religion they are Hindus but *far less bigoted than the ordinary Hindu, as they will eat and drink anything; they get on capitally with Europeans and associate with, but do not condescend to mix with, NIs* [emphasis added].'[20] But, going back to 1825, Bhurtpore was awarded as a battle honour to the two Gurkha battalions, later the 1st and 2nd Gurkha Rifles.

At this time, it will be remembered, there were two British-led armies in India with separate chains of command, each deriving from very different ethos. One was the East India Company's army, known as the Indian Army, essentially a private army, reporting to the Governor-General in council. That, in turn, was divided into the three armies of the three presidencies of Calcutta, Madras and Bombay. Of these, the Bengal Army, based at Calcutta, was by far the largest, and from 1813 it formed more than half the

Indian Army. In 1825 the Bengal Army accounted for 158,612 officers and men out of 276,548 for the Indian Army as a whole. The soldiers, NCOs and junior officers were natives – or Gurkhas – and the senior commanders British. The Company's armies were also divided into line regiments and 'irregulars', the Gurkhas being the latter.

But the other army comprised the King's Regiments, which were all British, and these were the armed forces of a post-Westphalian nation state.[21] By the 1820s there were 20,000 King's troops in India, making up almost a quarter of the entire British Army. The Indian government paid for this force and therefore regarded it as reinforcement to its own armies. The government in London, on the other hand, saw the King's Regiments based in India as an imperial strike force, to be deployed anywhere it was needed to defend British interests in southern Asia or elsewhere. As the Russian threat appeared to coalesce, this became more of an issue.

Another issue was that the two armies had different conditions of service. Promotion in the East India Company's forces was much slower – twenty-five years from commissioning to the rank of major in the Company's service as against twelve to seventeen years in the King's Regiments. In 1826 there were eighteen generals in India for three of the Company's armies 291,000 strong, although most of the generals had risen in the King's and not the Company's service. In October 1827 a note from Calcutta argued that

> The present period when the recent employment of two armies in the field has procured for officers of His Majesty's service who distinguished themselves the high honour of being promoted in the Army by Brevet appears . . . to be a favourable occasion for arguing upon the notice of the Honourable Court of Directors a subject which has already been laid before them by my predecessors . . . allowing officers of the service to be eligible for the same honourable distinction of Promotion by Brevet as the officers of H.M. Service. His Majesty has declared officers of both services alike eligible to receive the honour of the Bath, but they never can be considered as of an equity until they are declared alike eligible for promotion by Brevet.[22]

East India Company regiments were commanded by full colonels, while King's Regiments had lieutenant colonels. Therefore the COs of King's Regiments in India were made brevet colonels to prevent the East India Company officers claiming seniority over them. Giving East India Company officers the right to promotion by brevet restored their unfair advantage. The debate ground on until 1837, by which time the constant jockeying for position between senior officers of the King's and Company services had been under discussion for forty years. In 1837 'local rank was introduced', and 'the Commander-in-Chief in the East Indies conferred the Local Rank of Major-General upon ten Brevet Colonels of Her Majesty's Forces in June 1837 for the purpose of preventing them being superseded by their juniors in the Company's service who had obtained the rank of Major General by the Brevet of the 10th January preceding'.[23]

Within the Indian Army combat units, the British officers were extraordinarily few in number, and among the Gurkhas they were the fewest of all. When they were originally raised, in 1815, the Gurkha units included large numbers of Nepalese Gurkha officers, who had come over from the Nepalese Army, and the British officers like Frederick Young were the very top management. As originally raised, each Gurkha 'corps' (battalion) had just three British officers: a commanding officer (captain), an adjutant (lieutenant) and an assistant surgeon. With a nominal strength of 1,327 per battalion, that was one British officer to 440 Gurkhas. In the King's (later Queen's) Regiments of the British Army, the ratio was 1:30; in the Native Infantry of the line 1:90; and in other irregular infantry (of which the Gurkhas were part, at this stage) 1:180. This added to the Gurkhas' obvious economy and efficiency. The small number of British officers in the Gurkhas is more remarkable because of their irregular role, scattered over the landscape, which would normally require more officers than the tightly packed masses of line infantry.

The commanding officers of the 1st Nasiri and Sirmoor battalions were also political agents of the Governor-General in their respective territories. Although the arrangement had clearly grown from the particular circumstances of the Gurkhas' inception, there was

perhaps precedent as well as pragmatism. The rank structure and organisation would have been very familiar to members of the British ruling classes, who were soaked in classical history and military literature from an early age. The Indian Army was officered much like the Roman. In the Roman Army, centuries – 80 or 160 men, equivalent to companies – were commanded by centurions, who were usually senior non-commissioned officers (NCOs), risen through the ranks. The centurions took it in turns to command the cohort – the equivalent of a battalion. The Roman aristocracy got involved only at the tribune level, with five junior tribunes and one senior tribune forming the equivalent of a brigade staff. A Roman legion at the time of Caesar was 5,120 strong – equivalent to a brigade. The tribunes, effectively staff officers, were responsible for higher tactics and administration. The similarity with the role of the tiny number of British officers in Indian Army battalions and higher staffs, responsible for politics and operational planning, is clear. Day-to-day administration and command of the soldiers was left to centurions, in the case of the Roman Army, and to native officers in the case of the Indian Army.[24]

Meanwhile, Brian Houghton Hodgson, the Resident in Kathmandu, kept up gentle pressure for the British to recruit Nepalese Gurkhas. The Nepalese military system was in some ways remarkably efficient. In 1825, Hodgson reported that there was a standing army of 10,000, and a reserve of 10,000, who rotated annually. The 10,000 in reserve were unpaid and unemployed, and had little to do but 'hunt game and amuse themselves at home', but if war came, then the trained strength of the Nepalese Army would double very quickly. By 1832, when Hodgson wrote his *On the Origin and Classification of the Military Tribes of Nepal*, the strength of the reserve was estimated at 30,000, with a full-time regular force of 15,000. Hodgson said he did not see 'any insuperable obstacle to our obtaining, in one form or other, the services of a large body of these men'. He continued: 'they are by far the best soldiers in India . . . their gallant spirit and unadulterated military habits might be relied upon for fidelity . . . our good and regular pay and noble pension establishment would serve to counterpoise the influence of nationality.'[25]

The government in India thanked Hodgson for his advice, but nothing came of it immediately. Lord William Cavendish Bentinck, who succeeded Amherst as Governor-General of Bengal in 1828, and then became Governor-General of all India from 1833 to 1835, seems to have had no particular interest in the Gurkhas. He noted the glowing reports about their value in the hills, but that was all, and he did not share Hodgson's anxiety about a possible Nepalese attack on British India. As part of a general retrenchment the number of Gurkhas actually declined, in spite of calls for more to be recruited as confidence diminished in the Indian sepoys of the Bengal Army.

As part of these cutbacks, the 2nd Nasiri Battalion was disbanded on 1 February 1830, although some sources say it was 1826.[26] Men with fewer than six years' service were discharged, while those with more who were 'residents of the Nypal territory' – that is, true Nepalese Gurkhas – were transferred to the 1st Nasiri Battalion or the Sirmoor Battalion. The rest were offered transfer to the Kumaon Battalion or to line regiments of the Indian infantry. During Bentinck's term of office the Gurkha component of the Bengal Army was reduced by more than a third.[27]

Between February and May 1832, a Select Committee of the House of Commons examined the affairs of the East India Company, but the case for more Gurkhas was not well made. Holt Mackenzie, the Secretary to the Territorial Department in Bengal, gave evidence on 19 April. When asked about the Gurkhas, the exchange on a spring day in London went as follows:

> [Mackenzie] [They are] very superior in the point of physical strength and moral courage to any troops with whom we have had to do. They have a strong feeling of patriotism, with a great deal of personal pride and are described, indeed, as equalling any troops in the world in the moral qualities of a soldier.
>
> [Questioner] What difficulty is there in having a greater number of Goorkhas in our service?
>
> [Mackenzie] The chief difficulty that immediately occurs to me is this, that they are hardly fit for general service in the plains . . .
>
> [Questioner] Would they [Gurkhas] not form a cheap substitution for European forces?

[Mackenzie] I should not consider it safe to rest upon them as a substitute for Europeans.

It was also put to Mackenzie that 'the Hindoos especially appear to
suffer from their prejudices as to food'. He was then asked: 'Are the
Gurkhas Hindoos?' to which he replied, missing a crucial opportunity to stress the Gurkhas' relaxed approach to Hinduism, 'Yes, they
are all Hindoos.'[28] General Sir Edward Paget, and Major Generals
Jasper Nicolls and Sir Thomas Reynell, appeared before the
Committee. They all had a high regard for Gurkhas, but none of
them made any special mention of them and Reynell made no
mention of their outstanding role at Bharatpur, which he had
praised at the time.

However, factors within and beyond the subcontinent would
soon supervene to ensure the continuance of the Gurkhas. The
most distant was the rise of Russia and its thrust into Central Asia,
setting off alarm bells in India. Russia's campaign in the Caucasus
brought her into collision with Persia and in 1826 war broke out
between the two empires. The Russians defeated the Persians easily
and the war ended with the Treaty of Turkmenchay on 2 February
1828. According to the terms of the treaty, the Trans-Caucasian
Khanates of Yerevan and Nakhichevan passed to Russia. The shah
granted the Russians the exclusive right to maintain a navy in the
Caspian Sea and agreed that Russian merchants were free to trade
anywhere they wanted in Persia.

In the short term, the treaty undermined the dominant position of
the British in Persia and marked an intensification of the 'Great
Game' played between the empires in Central Asia, Afghanistan and
the North-West Frontier for the rest of the century. Henceforward,
the Caucasus and large areas of Trans-Caucasia would be tied, like it
or not, to Russia. It also opened the way to Russian expansion into
the khanates of Central Asia, and thus towards Afghanistan and India.
Lord Ellenborough, the President of the Board of Control of the East
India Company, wrote in his diary in September 1829:'I feel confident we shall have to fight the Russians on the Indus, and I have long
had a presentiment that I should meet them there, and gain a great
battle.'[29] A Russian attack on India was constantly predicted for the

rest of the century, but never came. One of the reasons for that was the slightly difficult country that came to lie between the Russian and British empires: Afghanistan.

The second factor, closer to the areas of India controlled by the Company, was the rising power of the Sikh state under Ranjit Singh. The third was the continued discontent among Indian sepoys, which would eventually lead to the Indian Mutiny of 1857. All three would provide the Gurkhas with opportunities to shine.

On 4 September 1835 a new commander-in-chief, Sir Henry Fane, arrived in Calcutta. Fane would prove a friend of the Gurkhas. Almost immediately he asked the Governor-General to approve more favourable pension arrangements for 'men of the three Goorkah or Hill Corps [Nasiri, Sirmoor and Kumaon] who came over to the British [sic] Army from the Nepaul Government in 1815'.[30] In March 1836 he made a far-sighted argument for the maintenance of regimental schools for the Nasiri Battalion and other Gurkha units in the North-West, giving as his reason that 'A number of children of the original soldiers of these Corps are at this time entering the service and replacing their fathers, and no doubt such will be the continuing practice so that, should the Government see fit to extend the proposed advantage to them, the benefit will be reaped hereafter.'[31]

Fane's portrait reveals a smooth operator, with a slightly lascivi-ous mouth, who would no doubt make a cutting after-dinner speech. He was very shrewd. In February 1837 he began a tour of the north-west territories, which lasted more than a year, by which time the young Queen Victoria had ascended the British throne. He said the North-West was the weakest frontier, that the Indus was easily crossed and that the Sutlej was the river line to defend (see Figure 5). The only exception to this was that Ferozepur, just north of the Sutlej, should be occupied. In all this, he concurred with Ochterlony's opinions from thirty-three years before. The Cis-Sutlej hills were vital and the 1st Nasiri and Sirmoor battalions had the responsibility of guarding them.

In March 1837, just after starting his tour, he was invited to attend the wedding of Ranjit Singh's grandson at Lahore. He clearly

rated Ranjit Singh's power and his French-trained army. To conquer the Punjab, he noted – perhaps, who knows, on the wedding invitation – would take two years and 67,000 troops. The Sikhs were likely opponents in the future and so, too, were

one mountain tribe, the Nepaulese, whose position is dangerous to the neighbouring province of Bengal because it has been the policy of former Governments (a most unwise policy in my opinion) to permit the state to organize, equip and arm a large body of their Goorkah subjects (45,000). These people have no cavalry and little efficient field artillery and therefore would not be formidable [sic] to contend with on the plains.[32]

However, a lot of resources had to be tied up in case of any 'eruption from their mountainous country'. Fane included a meticulously detailed intelligence report of Nepalese strength in his diary, which must have emanated from the Resident in Kathmandu. The figure of 45,000 must have come from Hodgson's report of 1832.[33] Although intelligence had been conducted with extreme professionalism throughout the Napoleonic War period, there was a notable advance in the scientific rigour with which intelligence was gathered during the 1830s, which coincided with the creation of new military-scientific research institutes.[34] Fane appears to have been a first-rate operator.

Towards the end of his tour, in 1838, he ordered the administration of the Kumaon Battalion to be transferred from the civil to the military department, where, from February 1839, it sat more logically alongside the Nasiri and Sirmoor battalions. He also moved its base to Lohughat, a day's march from the Nepalese border. It will be recalled that a recruiting station here had been mooted in 1825. This was a clear message that the Kumaon Battalion had a real role in defending Kumaon against a Nepalese attack and it also established a border recruiting base, which would make it easier to recruit Gurkhas.[35]

In Nepal, Bhim Sen Thapa died on 29 July 1839 after a failed suicide attempt nine days before. Bhim Sen's mistress, the queen-regent Tripura Sundari, had died in 1832 and after her death Bhim Sen's grip on power began to loosen as the maharajah, Rajendra

Bikram Shah, exploited factional disputes. He was twice imprisoned on dubious charges and tormented, including a threat to parade his wife naked through the Kathmandu streets. Eventually, a kukri was placed conveniently near by, and Bhim Sen used it, although he botched the attempt and took a long time to die.[36]

Following Bhim Sen's death a radical party wrested power in Nepal and, with British attention now diverted towards Afghanistan, a party of Nepalese soldiers crossed the border and seized some British territory. Hodgson was extremely vulnerable, but he survived, his diplomacy prevailed, and a less militant party came to power in Nepal.

While their Resident in Kathmandu was clinging on by the skin of his teeth, in 1838 the British sent an envoy to Kabul to form an alliance with the emir of Afghanistan, Dost Muhammad, against Russia. The emir was not unsympathetic, but asked for British help in recapturing Peshawar, which Ranjit Singh's Sikhs had captured in 1834. The British were wary of upsetting Ranjit Singh, and said no. Dost Muhammad then began courting the Russians who had also sent an envoy to Kabul. The Governor-General of India from March 1836, Lord Auckland, concluded, perhaps wrongly, that Dost Muhammad was anti-British. To make things worse, the Russians and their new-found Persian allies laid siege to Herat in the far west of Afghanistan, fanning the prevailing fears of a Russian advance on India.

Auckland issued the Simla Manifesto in October 1838. It said that, in order to ensure the welfare of India, the British needed an ally on India's western frontier. They chose Shah Shuja Durrani, who had been deposed as ruler of Afghanistan in 1809 and taken refuge with various Indian potentates, including Ranjit Singh. The British line was that they were supporting Shah Shuja's army to retake the throne that was legitimately his. In fact, there can be little doubt that Auckland was trying to install a pro-British leader in Afghanistan to guard against the Russian threat. The result was the first Anglo-Afghan War of 1839–42, which proved an unmitigated disaster for the British.[37]

An army of 21,000 British and Indian troops under the command of Sir John Keane set out from the Punjab in December 1838, but

there were no Gurkhas in it. By late March 1839, the British forces had crossed the Bolan Pass and begun their march to Kabul.

As often happens in wars in Afghanistan, the invaders seeking regime change made good progress initially, but were unwelcome. After taking Kandahar on 25 April 1839, the British-Indian force reached Kabul. Shah Shuja was restored to the throne by the British on 7 August 1839. But as, again, often happens, the Afghans were unhappy with the new ruler and, even more, with what they saw as British occupation. The majority of the British and Indian troops returned to India, but it soon became obvious that more British and Indian forces would be needed to keep Shah Shuja in power.[38] The British Resident, MacNaghton, allowed the soldiers to bring their families, to improve morale, which further reinforced Afghan suspicions that they were an army of occupation.[39]

Then, on 28 April 1840, a General Order of the commander-in-chief called for volunteers from the Nasiri and Sirmoor battalions to serve in a 4th (Gorkha) Regiment of infantry, specially raised as part of Shah Shuja's force. This short-lived battalion is not mentioned in most of the official histories, but it existed. Each of those two established battalions (not the Kumaon Battalion) provided three volunteer havildars (sergeants), four naiks (corporals) and six sepoys, who were all promoted to the next-highest rank and who would, furthermore, be paid still more – the same as those higher ranks in the Bengal infantry of the line. It was clearly a special posting. The havildars therefore became jemadars – the lowest officer rank, equivalent to a lieutenant. The rank structure of the Indian Army, including the Gurkhas, is set out in Table 2.

Where the rest of the '4th (Gorkha) Regiment' came from is unclear. Sir John Chapple, in his *The Lineages and Composition of Gorkha Regiments*, says that the 4th Regiment of Light Infantry of Shah Shuja's contingent, which was 'entirely Gorkha', and Broadfoot's Sappers (Engineers), of whom about one third – 200 – were Gurkhas, were raised in 1838, in which case they must have been raised separately from existing established Gurkha units. It seems more likely that most of the men in the 4th were Afghan supporters of Shah Shuja officered by Gurkhas. There is also mention of a 'Corps of Jezailchees' – a jezail being a large-calibre musket –

which included a number of Gurkhas in this campaign.[40] The 4th Gurkha Light Infantry unit after 1840 was commanded by a British officer, Captain Codrington.

Early in November 1841 supporters of the now deposed Dost Muhammad's son, Muhammad Akbar Khan, deposed Shah Shuja and destroyed the British garrison. The 4th (Gorkha) Regiment was stationed in Charikar 40 miles (64 kilometres) north of Kabul (see Figure 5), and on 14 November was overwhelmed. Codrington was killed, but about 150 men escaped into the hills. Some of these were rescued ten months later, in September 1842, when Kabul was recaptured by British forces withdrawing on a circuitous route. They were subsequently enlisted into the Bengal Army's three established battalions.[41] Shah Shuja, captured by Muhammad Akbar Khan's faction, had, meanwhile, been killed in April 1842. It was not the last Afghan campaign in which the Indian and British armies were involved, nor was it the last in which Gurkhas would see action.

The 4th (Gorkha) Afghan Battalion, raised for a very specific task, was a short-lived predecessor to the 4th Prince of Wales's Own Gurkha Rifles, who were officially raised in 1857 and served in the Second Afghan War of 1878–79. The fact that Gurkhas were selected to lead, and presumably instruct, a force personally linked to the Afghan ruler, possibly from 1838 and certainly from 1840, is fascinating. Given the perspective of the twenty-first century, when Gurkhas have been used to train new armed forces in post-conflict states, to have deployed them in that way would make complete sense. And it would be one of the first examples anywhere of a military mission of this type.

In July 2010 a chilling parallel struck home in Britain's Fourth Afghan War, when as described in the Prologue, three British Army Gurkhas were killed by a rogue Afghan sergeant with whom they were working.[42] There had been Gurkhas in the First Afghan War 170 years before, although none of the established Gurkha units served in it, and none has it as a battle honour. But the Gurkhas were there, in some cases because of their special talents. This almost unknown commitment of an, admittedly, very small Gurkha (or Gurkha-led) force deserves further research, if any evidence can be found.

At this point, it may be worth consulting the 'family tree' of the Gurkhas (Figure 4). It shows the evolution and expansion of the Gurkhas in the Indian Army from 1815, the split that led to the transfer of four regiments to the British Army after 1947, and the continuation of the Indian and British lines to the present day.

Having been humiliated by the Afghans, the British found themselves at war with, first, the emirs of Sind and then the Sikhs. Sir Charles James Napier (1782–1853) was sent out to India, initially to command Sind and Baluchistan. A hardened and much shot-at veteran of the Peninsular War (1808–14), in 1842 he was appointed, at the age of sixty, as major-general to the command of the Indian Army within the Bombay presidency. In a campaign in 1842–3 he defeated the emirs of Sind (a province in the lower delta of the Indus, in present-day Pakistan), which gave rise to a famous story. General Napier supposedly sent a dispatch (not a telegram, bearing in mind that telegrams, a wonderfully economical form of communication, had been around for only ten years), bearing an appropriately succinct message: 'Peccavi' – Latin for 'I have sinned' (Sind). Besides the similarity of sound, it was later claimed that he was under orders not to actually capture the province, which added to the double meaning. The alleged pun later appeared in a spoof article entitled 'Foreign Affairs' in *Punch* magazine in 1844, but the original message almost certainly never existed.[43]

The Gurkhas were not involved in the Sind campaign but would be in the next. Ranjit Singh, the Sikh ruler of Punjab, whom the British had so carefully watched, died in 1839, while British India was preoccupied in Afghanistan. The Sikhs now started stirring up revolt among neighbouring Indian Army regiments. The new commander-in-chief, General Sir Henry Hardinge, another Peninsular War veteran and a former (1828) UK Secretary of War, who arrived in Calcutta on 23 July 1844, prepared for a fight. The British needed to control the Punjab. In late November 1845 the Sikhs began moving forces to the Sutlej river, and crossed it on 11 December. Meanwhile, Henry Lawrence, who had taken over from Hodgson as Resident in Nepal on 1 December 1843, wrote on 25 May 1845 that although he was not worried about Nepal as a threat

The Gurkha Family Tree

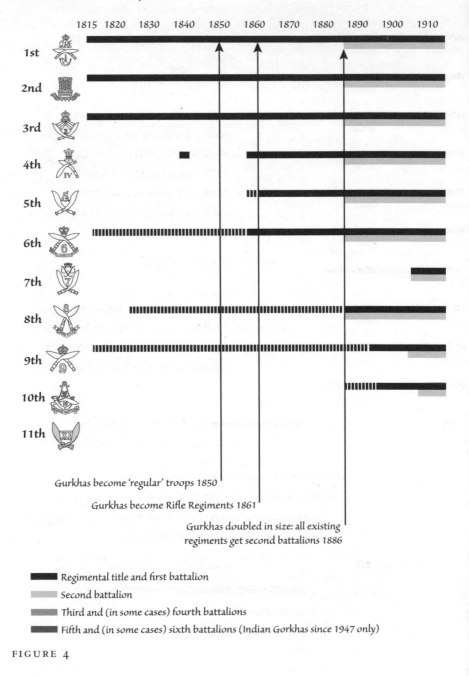

1815 1820 1830 1840 1850 1860 1870 1880 1890 1900 1910

1st
2nd
3rd
4th
5th
6th
7th
8th
9th
10th
11th

Gurkhas become 'regular' troops 1850

Gurkhas become Rifle Regiments 1861

Gurkhas doubled in size: all existing
regiments get second battalions 1886

Regimental title and first battalion
Second battalion
Third and (in some cases) fourth battalions
Fifth and (in some cases) sixth battalions (Indian Gorkhas since 1947 only)

FIGURE 4

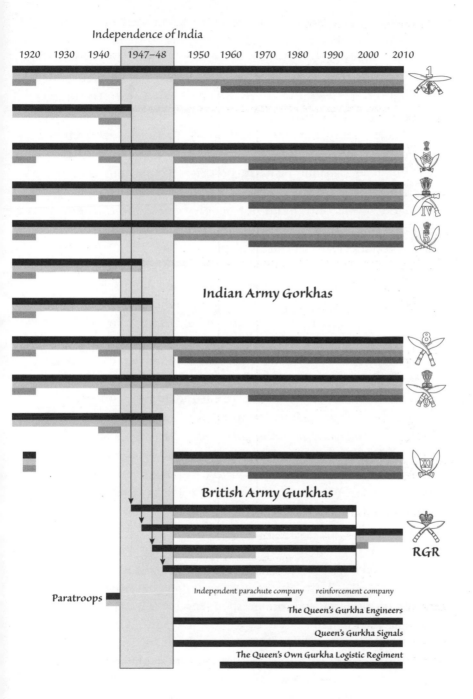

Independence of India

1920 1930 1940 1947–48 1950 1960 1970 1980 1990 2000 2010

Indian Army Gorkhas

British Army Gurkhas

RGR

Paratroops

Independent parachute company   reinforcement company

The Queen's Gurkha Engineers

Queen's Gurkha Signals

The Queen's Own Gurkha Logistic Regiment

to India, 6,000 or 8,000 Gurkhas should be recruited into regular Indian regiments, but not with the view of using them to occupy their own homeland.[44]

On Christmas Eve 1845, Sir Henry Lawrence was recalled from Kathmandu to replace the agent to the Governor-General of India, who had been killed in action at Ferozeshah, not far from the Sutlej river. While Henry Lawrence was away there was a coup in Kathmandu – the so-called Kot massacre in September 1846 – which put Jang Bahadur Rana in power as prime minister. The Rana family would control Nepal for a century. Jang Bahadur, who was friendly to the British, did not openly oppose the recruitment of Gurkhas to the British-Indian Army, but tried to make sure that no really good recruits became available.

The Nasiri and Sirmoor battalions were brought in to reinforce the East Indian Army fighting the war with the Sikhs. They moved immediately to the key depot at Ludhiana, where the Sikhs were starting to demolish the installations. The Gurkhas attacked and drove them away. However, they then took part in the ferocious battles of Aliwal on 17 January 1846 and Sobraon on 10 February 1846 (see Figure 5).

At Aliwal the Sikhs awaited the British-Indian force at a bend on the Sutlej river. This was a ferocious hand-to-hand battle in which, once their single-shot muskets had been discharged and close-quarter battle joined, the Gurkhas' short kukris were pitched against Sikh swords. The Sirmoor Battalion lost its colour, but one of the Gurkha havildars (sergeants), Badal Singh Thapa, leaped forward and recovered it. He was awarded the Indian Order of Merit (IOM), one of its first recipients.[45]

The medal had been introduced in 1837 and was the first British award ever to be given purely in recognition of gallantry. It was the only gallantry medal available to native soldiers between 1837 and 1907, when the Indian Distinguished Service Medal was introduced, and 1911, when the Victoria Cross (introduced only in 1856) was made available to them. Until then, the IOM was sometimes awarded for acts of gallantry that could equate to those that would have merited a Victoria Cross. At Aliwal the Gurkhas suffered heavy casualties that would be seen as intolerable today: forty-nine dead

and wounded from the Sirmoor Battalion and twenty-two in the Nasiri Battalion – close to 10 per cent.

The Sikhs pulled back but at Sobraon the armies clashed again. After a heavy British-Indian bombardment, the Sirmoor Battalion was sent forward. Its commanding officer, Captain John Fisher, was killed and another 144 of his battalion were killed or wounded. The Nasiris lost 7 killed and 77 wounded.[46] Four Gurkhas won the Indian Order of Merit.[47] One of them was Havildar (Sergeant), later Subedar Major (Major), Jase Rajput, one of the first Gurkhas ever to be photographed, shown in Plate 10. The divisional commander commended the Gurkhas' 'bravery and obedience' but the commander-in-chief went further in a despatch of 30 January:

> I must . . . especially . . . notice the determined hardihood and brav-ery with which our two battalions of Goorkahs, the Sirmoor and Nusseree [sic], met the Sikhs whenever they were opposed to them. Soldiers of small stature but indomitable spirit, they vied in ardent charge with the Grenadiers of our own nation, and armed with the short weapon of their mountains [the kukri] were a terror to the Sikhs throughout the great combat.[48]

Although 'irregulars' – which meant they werc paid less and were therefore cheaper – the Gurkhas were clearly being equated in value with the more highly paid regular or 'line' troops of the Bengal Army and even with the 'British Grenadiers'. Given the large scale of the war under way, the constant praise lavished on these two bat-talions is remarkable. Hardinge's son noted that his father, a very experienced soldier, often repeated that he was more than surprised to see the support that the native regiments – all of them – gave to their European comrades but that, in particular, 'the Gurkha [sic] battalions behaved admirably'.[49]

The fact that the 'irregular' and less well-paid Gurkha battalions were now being equated with the better-paid if (in many people's view) overly devout, prissy and 'pampered'[50] Bengal line infantry was significant.

The Sikhs, as we know, also had Gurkhas in their army. Ranjit Singh had employed them before 1815, before the British did. In 1845, as the Sikh War started, the Sikhs had two battalions – about

1,500 men in total – of Gurkhas, out of a total strength of 54,000, most of whom were Sikhs. However, none of the Gurkhas of the Sikh Army seems to have been employed against the British.[51] If that was a deliberate decision, it was probably shrewd, as the good relations between the Company's Gurkha troops and their British allies was by now well known.

Whereas the British had been able to negotiate with a strong leader like Ranjit Singh, they could not tolerate 'uncontrolled space', which the Sikh state of Punjab had become on his death. The parallels with our own time are very clear. In March 1846, after the British-Indian victory, Hardinge told Lawrence to reorganise the Sikh Army and establish a permanent government, based in the Sikh capital of the Punjab, Lahore. Effectively, this meant an extension of British rule, again. The fate of the 1,500 Gurkha soldiers of the former Sikh Army is unknown. The Treaty of Lahore of 9 March 1846 meant that the Sikhs renounced claims to the key Cis–Sutlej territory, transferred a 50-mile wide strip of land north of the Sutlej river (see Figure 5), as far as the Beas, to the British, and paid an indemnity of £500,000. Hardinge did not want to annex the Punjab – like his counterparts in Russia, who were desperate not to take on more Central Asian territory that they could not control.[52] He therefore agreed for a British-Indian 'stabilisation' force – there is no other word for it, really – to remain in Lahore for a year, at the Sikh government's expense.[53]

The Sikh War removed any remaining doubts about the Gurkhas' ability to operate in the plains and marshes. At Sobraon they had assaulted a fortified position on the banks of the flooded river Sutlej. Hardinge, Lawrence and Sir Hugh Gough, the commander-in-chief, added their praise to that of Henry Fane and the Gurkhas' founders: Ochterlony, Fraser and Young, and the former Resident in Kathmandu, Hodgson. It made sense to recruit more Gurkhas at a time when the Bengal Native Infantry was becoming increasingly restive. The problem remained the Nepalese government's refusal to permit British-Indian recruitment of 'Gurkhas' from Nepal, however ill defined they might have been as a group.

In spite of the two treaties of Lahore of 9 and 16 March 1846, the Sikhs were not pacified. In April 1848, after a Sikh tax collector

responsible for Multan had been found guilty of embezzlement and corruption, two British political agents were murdered and their heads handed to the tax collector in exchange for a reward. The British political agents had been protected by an escort of a regiment of infantry, 'Goorkhas, too, famous for their fidelity', plus some cavalry and artillery with guns.[54] The escort troops went over to the tax collectors' force and the two officers were butchered, without any resistance on the part of the escort. It is important to note that these 'Goorkhas' were members of the quasi-independent Lahore state force, and had nothing to do with the Gurkha battalions of the Bengal Army, although some of them may have been Gurkhas formerly employed by Ranjit Singh. It was not the best publicity for Gurkhas in British-Indian service, although no long-term damage seems to have been done by the story.

The Second Sikh War was the result. Gough, the commander-in-chief, launched a costly assault on the Sikh fortified camp at Chillianwallah on 13 January 1849. It was so costly that on 5 March the eighty-year-old prime minister, the Duke of Wellington, asked the distinguished Sir Charles Napier, of the alleged 'I have Sind' fame, who was then in UK, to go back to India to take over from Gough. He added that if Napier, now a lieutenant general, would not go, 'then I must'. As that was not a realistic prospect, Napier headed for India to a series of public plaudits on the way. The Lord Mayor of Portsmouth's eulogy typifies the enthusiasm with which the British public regarded Napier's appointment:

> The consummate strategy displayed in the conquest of Sinde [sic] gives reason to hope that you may not meanly achieve fresh victories in the field but that you will stamp the impress of your genius on Indian warfare for all time to come, by the abuses you will labour to eradicate and the improved methods you will introduce – your interesting exploits on the Indus proved that intrepidity and wisdom combined could bring British interests out of difficulties and dangers to which, in modern times, there has been no parallel.[55]

It would prove uncannily prophetic, not least because it implied that Napier's genius extended beyond the 'meanly' military. As a result Napier clashed with the imperious and autocratic new Governor-General, thirty-five-year-old James Ramsay, 1st Marquess

of Dalhousie, who had taken over from Hardinge in January 1848. Before Napier got to India, however, the British-Indian forces had won a decisive victory at Gujerat on 21 February 1849.[56] Again, the Gurkhas were not involved in this victory but Napier's arrival as commander-in-chief in Calcutta on 6 May 1849 was of profound significance for them.

Napier liked the Gurkhas. While his relations with Dalhousie were peppery in the extreme – Dalhousie was prepared to allow him absolute authority in military matters but he must never intrude into his own responsibilities for empire – they agreed they were both sitting on a 'volcano'.[57]

In July 1849 the first eruption occurred. A special allowance paid to sepoys – native Indian troops – in the Second Sikh War was withdrawn in April, but the reasons were not properly explained. Four Native Infantry regiments (the 22nd, 13th, 41st and 32nd) refused to accept the reduced pay. Napier handled the situation well and a rebellion by the other twenty-four battalions in the Bengal Army was averted. Napier later noted that, meanwhile, the Gurkhas were starving on much lower pay. To Napier, the solution was obvious. He told Dalhousie, who has half his age, that the time had come to 'win the Goorkha's heart' with money and the (then) red uniform of regular Indian infantry. He was fully cognisant of the European officers' view that Gurkhas were as reliable and efficient as European troops, that they were cheaper, and that 'the great advantage of enlisting these hillmen will be that, with 30,000 or 40,000 Goorkhas added to 30,000 Europeans, the possession of India [would depend on] . . . an Army able with ease to overthrow any combination among Hindoos, or Mohamedans, or both together.'[58]

There were two themes here that would recur throughout the history of the Brigade of Gurkhas up to 1947 and, as to their relative cheapness, almost to the present day.[59] The first was that the Gurkhas were a cheaper substitute for Europeans, but just as reliable, and, second, that they formed a 'third force' in India. They were clearly not European, but neither did they empathise with the other native troops, whom they openly despised.

Dalhousie agreed. While he was waiting to get clearance from the East India Company Court of Directors to increase the Gurkhas'

pay to regular levels, however, another mutiny broke out. On 25 February 1850 the 66th Native Infantry at Govindargh revolted and threatened to seize the fortress with armaments, ammunition and treasure recently seized from the Sikhs. Dalhousie was away so, in a General Order of 27 February 1850, Napier ordered the 66th to be disbanded and their colours – and regimental identity – to be transferred to the Nasiri Gurkha Battalion. A more flagrant example of identity transfer would be hard to imagine. The disbanded and disgraced 66th henceforward became the 66th Goorkha Regiment. Napier said he was fulfilling a 'promise' to one of the three Gurkha regiments – a recommendation he had made in October 1849 that he would bring the irregular Gurkhas into the Bengal line infantry.

Dalhousie was presented with a fait accompli. He agreed with the decision, but was slightly put out by the way Napier had done it. On 22 March 1850, Napier's General Order no. 173 stipulated that 'In recognition of their entire willingness to perform all the duties required of Corps of Native Infantry of the line . . . the Sirmoor and Kemaoon Battalions, as well as the new Nusseree Battalion' should be given the same pay, allowances and privileges as all the other Native Infantry regiments.[60]

The British officers of the mutinous 66th were transferred to the Nasiri Battalion, a slightly irregular move, since officers for the Gurkha battalions were usually selected specially. In his 27 February 1850 order, Napier, fully aware of the Gurkhas' strong points, stressed that young European officers should associate with the native officers as much as possible and, through them, acquire a thorough knowledge of what was going on in the regiment. It is clear that the Gurkhas were already a role model. Furthermore, 'the nationality of these corps [the Malaun and Kumaon battalions], and of the 66th or Goorka regiment, shall be kept up *by the careful exclusion of men as recruits, who are not Goorka* [emphasis added].'[61] Given the Nepalese government's continued opposition, recruiting was actually very difficult.

Since the Nasiri (Nusseeree) Battalion had taken over much of the identity of the disbanded 66th, a new Nasiri Battalion was raised, commanded by Major O'Brien, who had commanded the old Nasiri Battalion until 27 February 1850. In part, this was done by

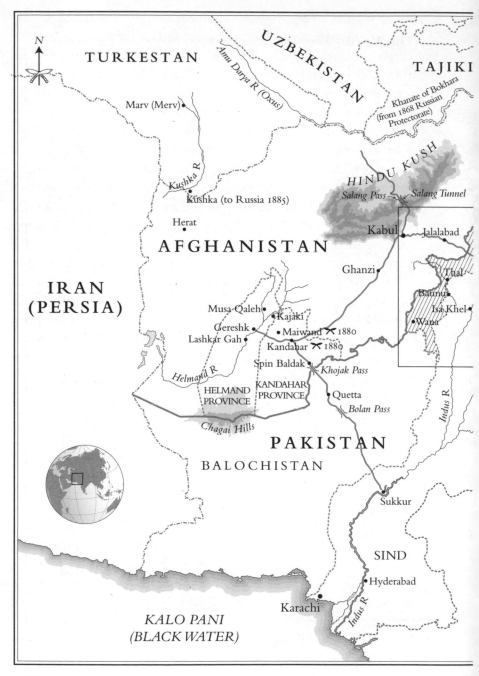

FIGURE 5

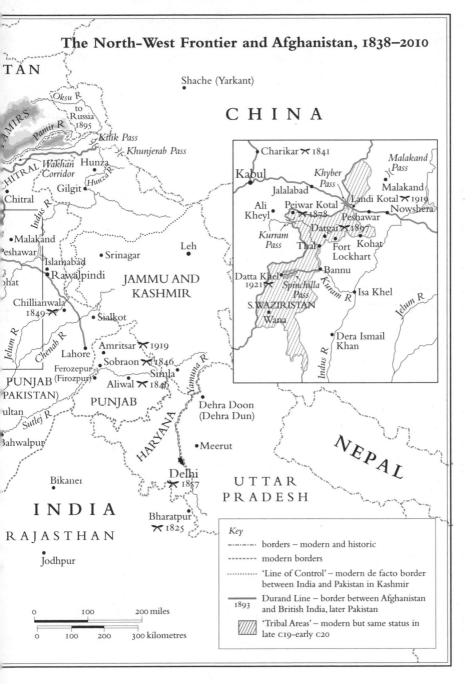

The North-West Frontier and Afghanistan, 1838–2010

TAN

Shache (Yarkant)

CHINA

Oksu R

to
Russia
1895

Pamir R

MIRS

HAIRS

Kilik Pass

Khunjerab Pass

CHITRAL Wakhan Hunza
Corridor

Charikar ✕ 1841

Malakand
Pass

Kabul

Khyber
Pass

Malakand

Jalalabad

Landi Kotal ✕ 1919

Gilgit

Hunza R

Chitral

Indus R

Ali
Kheyl

Peiwar Kotal
1878

Nowshera

Peshawar

Malakand

Leh

Kurram
Pass

Datgai ✕ 1897

Peshawar

Islamabad

Srinagar

Thal

Fort
Lockhart

Kohat

Rawalpindi

JAMMU AND
KASHMIR

Datta Khel
1921

Bannu

Chillianwala
1849 ✕

Sialkot

Spinchilla
Pass

Isa Khel

Jelum R

S. WAZIRISTAN

Kuram R

Jelum R

Chenab R

Wana

Dera Ismail
Khan

Indus R

Lahore

Amritsar ✕ 1919

Ferozepur
(Firozpur)

Sobraon ✕ 1846

Simla

PUNJAB
(PAKISTAN)

Aliwal ✕ 1846

ultan

PUNJAB

Sutlej R

Yamuna R

Dehra Doon
(Dehra Dun)

HARYANA

Bahwalpur

Meerut

NEPAL

Delhi
✕ 1857

UTTAR
PRADESH

Bikaner

INDIA

Bharatpur
✕ 1825

RAJASTHAN

Jodhpur

0	100	200 miles
0	100	200	300 kilometres

Key

-----·----- borders – modern and historic

-------- modern borders

·········· 'Line of Control' – modern de facto border
between India and Pakistan in Kashmir

———— Durand Line – border between Afghanistan
1893 and British India, later Pakistan

▨ 'Tribal Areas' – modern but same status in
late C19–early C20

transferring some individuals from the Sirmoor and Kumaon battalions and in part by new recruiting. Correspondence from O'Brien
refers to the difficulties involved, and indicates that illicit recruiting
was still going on in Nepal. In 1851 he shrewdly advised that, while
the Khas (Chhetris), Magars and Gurungs from Nepal were the best
soldiers, a good mix of talents makes any team stronger. He recommended that a small proportion of Gurkha units – a third or a
quarter – should be the children of older Gurkhas, and men from the
British-controlled hill areas across the Sutlej river. The old Nasiri
Battalion became the 66th Goorka Regiment of the line, while the
new Nasiri Battalion, and the Kumaon and Sirmoor battalions, were
all given the same terms of service as regular Native Infantry.

The establishment of the Gurkhas as regular soldiers of the Bengal
Army was finalised by a Governor-General's Resolution of 15 July
1850. It had taken thirty-five years to turn the Gurkhas from lower-
paid irregulars to regular soldiers on full East India Company pay, in
spite of the fact that they had proved far more cost-effective and far
lower-maintenance than other 'sepoys', while their military prowess
was recognised, not only by their own officers, but by generals and
civilian bosses across the empire. Meanwhile, Napier's abrasive relationship with Dalhousie had got worse. In November 1850, Napier
sailed from India. He warned darkly of problems 'rising on the
horizon' – the forthcoming Indian Mutiny.[62]

In 1852, Napier appeared before the Select Committee of the
House of Lords. He once again referred to one of the Gurkhas' most
enduring and appealing qualities – low maintenance:

> they are excellent soldiers . . . everybody says that their courage is
> equal to that of our own men; they have no caste, so there is no dif-
> ficulty as to their food; they mess and do everything without causing
> any difficulty, and they are excessively attached to the European
> troops; they feel the greatest possible pride in the British uniform.
> When I turned a Goorkah [sic] regiment into the 66th, their delight
> at wearing a red coat was great.[63]

The comment about red coats is important. The Sirmoor
Battalion had always worn the dark rifle green that we associate
with the Gurkhas, and before 1850 the Nasiri battalions did so as

well, although with many variations. Until the late nineteenth century dyes were not fast and colours varied enormously. Although the Nasiri and Sirmoor battalions each had a rifle company from 1842, the green uniform was because they were irregular hill regiments, not because they were at that stage associated with the British rifle regiments. That would come later.[64] The Gurkhas' uniforms are often described as 'black', and very nearly were, at least until the colour ran after service in the field. British officers serving with the Gurkhas also wore a dark-green uniform very similar to the King's or, now, Queen's Rifle Regiments celebrated in Bernard Cornwell's *Sharpe* novels, and the TV series of the same name. After 1850, the 66th Gurkha Regiment wore the red they had inherited from the disbanded 66th, and retained it from 1861, when they were redesignated as the 1st Gurkha Regiment, until the 1880s. They alone rejoiced in the title 'Lal Kurti Paltan' – 'Red Coat Regiment'. The other Gurkha regiments wore rifle green throughout, although by the 1870s they were wearing khaki in the field, which had first been introduced in the Indian Army for the Corps of Guides (see below), in 1848.[65]

In 1857, Napier's dark prediction came true as the seeds of dissent and revolt among native Indian troops, exacerbated by the increasingly arrogant attitude of some British officers, sprouted into all-out rebellion. Fear of forcible conversion to Christianity was one factor. The immediate cause, as is well known, arose from the introduction, in January 1857, of new Enfield rifles, which required greased cartridges. Rumours, spread by those who opposed British rule, variously reported that the shiny cartridges, made with a different kind of paper, were greased with beef fat, which was offensive to Hindus, or pork fat, which was offensive to Muslims. In fact, it was some form of tallow, which can be made from beef, mutton or pig fat. The contractors were not given any instructions as to the type of fat to be used, so the sepoys' suspicions were not unreasonable.[66] All the British had to do was to convince the native soldiers that it was mutton fat, or some sort of mineral oil, and the problem might have been solved, but the growing alienation between British officers and their sepoy soldiers contributed to the problem.

On 29 March there was an incident in the 34th Regiment at Barrackpore, followed by a serious mutiny at Meerut with the murder of British officers, which broke out on Sunday evening, 10 May. The mutiny spread rapidly across northern India, but the Gurkhas, who had few religious or dietary scruples, were not interested. Shortly before the mutiny, Lieutenant Duncan Macintyre, who was with elements of all three Gurkha battalions on a small-arms course at Ambala, reported that

> they did not like being mixed up with the *kala log* ('black folk') as they called the native Sepoys, whom they reported as showing very bad feelings in their conversations regarding the use of the greased cartridges. At the same time, they requested that these might be served out to them, in order to show the *Poorbiahs* [*Purbiya* – men, usually Brahmans and Rajputs from Oudh, Benares and Behar, where most British sepoys were recruited] that they had no fellow-feeling with them on the cartridge question.[67]

Not all European officers were convinced of the Gurkhas' loyalty, however. Some who had sworn that their own native Indian troops would never revolt were hacked to death, so the suspicion was understandable. However, the nearest the Gurkhas came to rebellion was an incident involving the new Nasiri Battalion, formed in 1851 after the original Nasiri Battalion took over the identity of the 66th. Theirs was a much more Gurkha grievance – they had not been paid, so they refused to escort artillery to Ambala, where the British were assembling a relief force for Delhi, and some of them helped themselves to pay from the Treasury at Kasauli. Reports spread to the nearby hill station at Simla where large numbers of Europeans had gone to escape the lowland summer heat. News came of the mutinies at Meerut and, now, Delhi, which the mutineers had reached on 11 May. The Europeans knew how lethal the Gurkhas could be, and they panicked and fled the town. The situation was quickly brought under control, however, and the Gurkhas handed back the money. An amnesty was granted to the entire regiment, apart from the detachment who had helped themselves. Frederick Roberts, later a field marshal and commander-in-chief of India, who had completed his training at Addiscombe in

1853 and won the VC as a lieutenant in the Indian Mutiny in January 1858, later recorded that 'before the year was out the battalion did us good service'.[68]

On 14 May, less than four days after the mutiny at Meerut had begun, the Gurkha Sirmoor Battalion, 490 strong, based at Dehra Dun, was ordered to Meerut, 100 miles away, to subdue the uprising (see Figure 5). Major Charles Reid, the battalion commander, ordered his men to move immediately. Each man carried sixty rounds of ammunition and two elephants carried the ammunition reserve.[69] Reid was an outstandingly competent and shrewd officer – he later became a major general: one of the 'intelligent' types that Young and Ochterlony had insisted should officer their 'peculiar' corps of Gurkhas.

When they reached the town of Roorkee, on the Ganges canal, Reid ordered a halt for rest. Mutinous sepoy sappers appeared and tried to persuade the Gurkhas that – horror of horrors – they were being given ground bullock bones to put in their chapatis. The Gurkhas just laughed. They then headed down the river by boat and near a village called Bhola came under fire from mutineers. The Gurkhas counter-attacked, found the rebels had seized government property and captured eighteen of them. After a minimalist court martial, thirteen were shot. The Gurkhas moved on to another village and found more misappropriated government property. Three men were hanged and when two of the ropes snapped Reid ordered the struggling men to be shot. All three, and five of the thirteen shot earlier, were Brahmans. The significance of this act by the Gurkhas cannot be underestimated. Brahmans were the highest caste, inviolate. There could be no better test of the Gurkhas' loyalty to their East India Company employers, of their contempt for the *kala log*, and their relative indifference to the orthodoxies of the Hindu religion.[70]

At Delhi, starting on 11 May, the mutineers had killed many of the resident British Army personnel and civilians. A small group of British soldiers had stopped the city's arsenal falling into the mutineers' hands, but only by blowing it up. Several hundred mutineers were killed but so were some of the defenders. The telegraph office just managed to tap out the message, 'THE SEPOYS HAVE COME IN FROM MEERUT . . . WE MUST SHUT UP'.[71] The industrial revolution in

warfare helped the British response, whereas the mutineers' actions were uncoordinated, yet did nothing to diminish the horror that accompanied the release of their pent-up frustration.

Reid's Sirmoor Battalion moved on to Delhi to join General Sir Henry Barnard's small relief force. It had comprised two British and several native regiments, but one of the latter mutinied, leaving perhaps 4,000 men. The first commander, General Anson, fell ill with cholera and died, and the same fate met Barnard a few weeks later. But Reid still found the British distrustful. The Gurkhas were sent up to the commanding position of Hindoo Rao's house on the Badle-ki-Serai ridge, just north of the city, on 8 June. Here, Barnard's force had met a huge attack by about 30,000 mutineers, but they were badly coordinated and defeated. The Sirmoor Battalion found their tents had already been pitched for them. The reason, Reid later discovered, was so that they were under the eyes of the artillery, who were 'ready to *pound* us if we misbehaved [emphasis in original]'.[72] It must be remembered, however, that they had moved in such haste and had travelled so light that they had brought no tents of their own.

The so-called 'siege' of Delhi was not really a siege at all. The British, with a few loyal non-British troops – the Gurkhas – never surrounded it. The city's circumference was 7 miles (11 kilometres), and the British could not prevent entrance to or egress from it. They merely occupied the ridge just over half a mile (about a kilometre) away and fought off all attempts to dislodge them, while awaiting reinforcements and launching occasional attacks on the city gates. At the start, Reid faced continued questioning about his men's loyalty. 'Time will show,' he replied. But, he added, 'shooting Brahmins was a pretty good test'.[73]

Hindoo Rao's house (see Plate 13) was about 3,630 feet (1,100 metres) from the Mori Bastion of the city. As soon as the Gurkhas were in position, alongside two companies of the British 60th Rifles, who also came under Reid's command, the mutineers in the city came out to attack. It was the first of twenty-six attacks that the Gurkhas repulsed between 8 June and 14 September.

Reid knew that he and his 490-strong Gurkha battalion were in the spotlight:

we were under arms for sixteen hours. How fearful: my little fellows behaved splendidly, and were cheered by every European Regiment. It was the only Native Regiment with the force [a strange comment, as if, whilst the Gurkhas were 'natives', they were not native to India], and I may say every eye was upon it. The General was anxious to see what the *Goorkhas* could do, and if we were to be *trusted*. They had (because it was a *Native* Regiment), *doubts* about us, but I think they are satisfied [emphasis in original].[74]

The photograph in Plate 14 shows an officer and men of the Sirmoor Battalion during the Indian Mutiny. You can tell a lot about soldiers by looking at them, and there can be no doubting the toughness and professionalism of this group, captured on camera more than 150 years ago with remarkable clarity. Conditions on the Badle-ki-Serai ridge were dreadful. It faced due south, and so was exposed to the sun all day, and there was no clean source of water. The number of decaying bodies helped make the area an ideal breeding ground for dysentery and cholera. The chaplain noted when visiting the men: scoundrels

> nearly every man . . . [was] languishing from that terrible disease cholera. It required strong nerves to withstand the sickening sights of these infirmaries. The patients [were] constantly retching . . . The flies, almost as innumerable as the sand on the seashore, alighted on your face and head, and crawled down your back, through the openings of the shirt collar and occasionally flew even into your throat.[75]

At just over half a mile (just over a kilometre) from the northern bastion of the Delhi city walls, the ridge was 'under the fire of the enemy's heavy bastions morning, noon and night from first to last'.[76] If the conditions, disease and enemy fire were not enough of a test of loyalty, the mutineers' taunts added to the stress. 'Come on, Goorkhas,' they taunted, 'we won't fire upon *you* – we expect you to join us [emphasis in original]'.[77] . . . 'Oh, yes,' was the reply, 'we are coming'. Then, according to Reid, 'They closed upon their centre, and when within twenty paces they gave the mutineers a well-directed volley, killing some thirty or forty of the scoundrels.'[78]

The Gurkhas were showing the same cunning as their forebears who had fought the British in 1814–16. After this incident, the mutineers raised the reward for a Gurkha's head to 10 rupees – the same as for a British soldier.[79] It was the ultimate compliment. During the three months that they held on to the ridge, the Gurkhas formed a close relationship with the two companies of the British 60th Rifles that were also under Reid's command. The 60th later became the 2nd Battalion the Royal Green Jackets and is now part of the British regiment that has returned to its historic title, the Rifles. Reid recorded: 'The 60th Rifles is truly a fine Regiment, so totally different to every other. My men are very fond of them, and they get on famously.'[80]

The 60th also appreciated the Gurkhas' knack for showmanship. On 24 June, James Hare of the 60th wrote that, the day before, 'a sepoy had gone into a hut and was shooting out at the door when two little Ghoorkas [sic] set out to catch him. They sneaked up, one on either side of the door, and presently the sepoy put out his head to see if the coast was clear, when one grabbed him by the hair and the other whacked off his head with his cookery [sic].'[81] The story spread and may have inspired similar accounts, including that portrayed in the contemporary picture at Plate 11, where two vulnerable British soldiers are saved by an alert Gurkha grabbing a sepoy by the hair and drawing his kukri at the same time. The latter incident occurred after the capture of Delhi, in Subzincandi vegetable market, where two Lancashire Fusiliers decided to chill out and were saved by an alert Gurkha.[82]

By mid-July Reid had lost 206 killed and wounded out of his battalion – nearly half of the 490 he started with.[83] On 19 July he recorded the twenty-first attack by mutineers, in this case 'Pandies', a sobriquet given to mutineers who were high on *bhang* (hashish), thanks to Mangal Pande who had started the first revolt at Barrackpore while in a similar state. While the drugs banished fear among the attackers, it did not help their shooting, while the Gurkhas and the 60th were very good shots indeed. Discipline and cohesion were crucial to the defenders' ability to fight off vastly superior numbers, again and again.

On 9 August, John Nicholson, 'The Lion of the Punjab', having

been made a brigadier general to give him more political influence, arrived ahead of a relief force of 4,000 highly trained troops organised in a 'movable column'. The column arrived five days later, on 14 August. Nicholson had used this force decisively in the north-west region to disarm mutineer regiments and to prevent the mutiny spreading further. He had become a legend, and the Punjab Sikhs gave him the reverential nickname of Nikalseyn. His force was joined by Pathans, Afghans and Multanis who were loyal to him and keen to exploit the opportunity to take on lowland Indians. Nicholson was immensely tall and appeared arrogant, and at first Reid took a dislike to him. However, during August they became friends, often talking during the night on the roof of Hindoo Rao's house. On one occasion a shell burst over them, the shrapnel hitting Reid's telescope (which can be seen in the Gurkha Museum) and two Gurkhas below, but missing the two British officers.[84]

Nicholson's distinctive figure was instantly recognisable and everyone on the ridge knew him, but the Gurkhas had orders to ask everyone for the password, without exception, and they always did. Nicholson was slightly annoyed, but realised it was a measure of their discipline.

More Gurkhas were also on the way. The Kumaon Battalion arrived in time to play an important part in the next stage – Nicholson's assault on the city. On 12 September heavy guns began bombarding the northern walls and bastions of Delhi. After three days of bombardment, on 14 September, the British, Gurkhas, Sikhs and other loyal 'native' troops attacked in four columns. Nicholson led the column that entered through a breach in the Kashmir Gate bastion. The Royal Engineers blew up the Kashmir Gate itself, although most were shot dead as they tried to place the charge. Colonel Campbell of the 52nd Foot then led a column through the gate. The attackers became separated and isolated from one another. Nicholson himself was shot in the back as he advanced down a narrow street – a classic casualty of street fighting. He was carried to safety but died soon afterwards. Major Reid's luck held, even though he was hit in the head as he led forward what was left of the Sirmoor Battalion, and at first was presumed dead. A Gurkha picked

him up, put him on his back and carried him away. As he was doing so, Reid came round and eventually recovered. Out of the 490 (or possibly 540) men of the Sirmoor Battalion, 327 (some sources say 319) were killed or wounded. Of nine British officers, only one was unscathed.[85]

Major Reid's unceasing energy and determination received due recognition. On 17 July he was mentioned in the Governor-General's orders – equivalent to a mention in despatches – because he had withstood the 'most frequent and constant attacks of the enemy . . . admirably recorded by the troops under his command comprising parties of Her Majesty's 60th Royal Rifles and other corps and the gallant Sirmoor battalion and Corps of Guides'.[86]

The Guides provided 'reliefs' to the Sirmoor Battalion and the 60th, and could be the mysterious extra ninety troops mentioned by Roberts. That would equate with one of the companies of Guides.[87] The Guides were a specialist reconnaissance unit, created in 1846, who often worked with the Gurkhas, reinforcing the view that units of this kind were the first British 'special forces' and are therefore part of the Gurkha story.[88] They were the idea of Sir Henry Lawrence (1806–57), and were raised by Lieutenant Harry Lumsden. Lawrence was agent to the Governor-General in charge of political relations of the British government with the Sikh Durbar, and then the Resident at Lahore, as well as agent to the Governor-General for the North-West Frontier. He was one of the first casualties of the Indian Mutiny, being mortally wounded by an exploding shell at Lucknow on 2 July 1857.

Raised in Peshawar in 1846, the Corps of Guides initially comprised a troop of cavalry and two companies of infantry. The Corps of Guides was part of the elite Frontier Force Brigade. They were almost certainly the first unit in the Indian or British armies to dress in 'khaki' – the 'dust-colour' uniform that became common later. They were often used in small detachments, usually supported by other reliable troops who were similarly mobile and independent of heavy supply chains such as the Gurkhas and Sikhs.[89]

On 16 September 1857, the commander of the British–Indian field force, Major General Wilson, reported that Reid had been wounded in the assault two days before:

Major C. Reid, commanding the Sirmoor Battalion, whose distinguished conduct I have already had reason to bring prominently to
the notice of superior authority . . .however, [was] severely wounded
on this occasion . . . His column consisted of his own Battalion, 'the
Guides', and the men on duty at Hindoo Raos (the main piquet),
numbering in all about 1,000 supported by auxiliary troops of his
Highness the Maharajah Rambeir Singh under Capt R. Lawrence.[90]

Major General Wilson, commanding the Delhi field force, commended Colonel G. Campbell, who had led the 52nd through the
Kashmir Gate, and 'that intrepid and excellent officer Major C.
Reid of the Sirmoor Battalion, both wounded whilst gallantly leading columns of attack'.[91] The General Order of 4 December 1857
said that 'the example . . . set throughout the operations by courageous and indefatigable exertions of Major Reid commanding the
Sirmoor Battalion is warmly acknowledged by the Governor
General in Council'.[92]

Although the despatches constantly highlight Reid's extraordinary energy, drive and luck, he just missed out on a new medal: the
Victoria Cross. The VC was introduced in 1856 and could be
awarded retrospectively back to the start of British involvement in
the Crimean War in 1854. Today the criterion and the procedures
for recommending somebody for it are well defined and understood. Most awards are posthumous – there is a 90 per cent chance
that any recipient will die. Today, the criterion is 'most conspicuous
bravery, or some daring or pre-eminent act of valour or self-
sacrifice, or extreme devotion to duty in the presence of the
enemy'.[93] When it was introduced, however, the criterion and the
procedures were far less clear. The public records are full of recrimi-
nations. In March 1858 a letter complained that one Colonel
Campbell had conferred the VC on Bugler Robert Hawthorn and
Lance Corporal Henry Smith via the major general commanding
the field force rather than going through Sir Colin Campbell, the
Commander-in-Chief India. In future, it was decided, all recommendations for the VC should be sent through the commander-in-
chief.[94] Every senior officer wanted to recommend people for the
new medal, so there were too many recommendations.[95]

On 16 April 1858 the Chairman and Deputy Chairman of the East

India Company wrote to the Earl of Ellenborough, the former Governor-General of India and now President of the Board of Control, which was responsible for overseeing the Company and running Indian affairs. They recommended eight people for the VC but not Lieutenant Colonel Charles Reid or Sergeant Major Sheats of the 52nd Regiment. 'The grounds for omitting these two,' a minute of 12 April stated, 'are that no *specific* acts of gallantry are alleged [emphasis added].'[96] It was probably a fair point. But their enormous achievements in protracted conflict were recognised in other ways. Reid had already been promoted and awarded the Companion of the Bath, a military order normally given to major generals, while Sergeant Major Sheats was commissioned as an officer.

Although the Sirmoor Battalion's role at Delhi has attracted most attention, as we have seen, the Kumaon Battalion also took part in the assault. Meanwhile the new 1st Nasiri Battalion and the 66th Regiment (the former Nasiri Battalion) also fought well. The 66th confronted a force of mutineers vastly superior in numbers, who were aiming to drive the British from Kumaon and Garhwal, which Ochterlony had prised from the Nepalese forty-two years before. Ironically, while Reid missed the VC, the first Gurkha VC was awarded to Lieutenant John Tytler (1825–80), the adjutant of the 66th Regiment. He led an attack on horseback and, although wounded three times, survived. The citation for the first Gurkha VC reads:

> On the attacking parties approaching the enemy's position under a heavy fire of round shot, grape, and musketry, on the occasion of the Action at Choorpoorah, on the 10th February last [1858], Lieutenant Tytler dashed on horseback ahead of all, and alone, up to the enemy's guns, where he remained engaged hand to hand, until they were carried by us; and where he was shot through the left arm, had a spear wound in his chest, and a ball through the right sleeve of his coat.[97]

Tytler later rose to the rank of brigadier general and commanded the 4th Gurkha Rifles. For the non-British Gurkha soldiers and officers, the VC would not be a possibility until 1911, but many won the Indian Order of Merit. The IOM can be seen in Plate 10.

The Indian Mutiny was largely confined to Bengal, although there was trouble elsewhere, notably in Bombay. The British under Sir Colin Campbell (later to become Lord Clyde) recaptured Lucknow on 21 March 1858, marked by one of Campbell's better-educated aides-de-camp with a message mimicking Napier's alleged 'Peccavi': 'Nunc fortunatus sum' ('I am in luck . . . now').[98] A century and a half later, one can hear the groans. But it was not the end of the mutiny. The British response to the rebellion was often vindictive and excessive, and that, in turn, encouraged resistance. At Lucknow, and also at Jhansi, 133 miles (200 kilometres) to the south-west, British troops followed victory with drunkenness and looting. The British had defeated the rebel sepoys, who were poorly coordinated, but now faced increased resistance from local rulers who sensed, probably correctly, that British rule would become more intrusive. These included Khan Bahadur Khan, who was proclaimed the rebels' Viceroy at Bareilly, in Rohilkand, 133 miles (200 kilometres) north-west of Lucknow, and the mysterious Maulvi of Faizabad, east of Lucknow. Jhansi was captured on 3 April 1858, the British soldiers being ordered to 'spare nobody over sixteen years – except women, of course'.[99] Campbell defeated Khan Bahadur Khan in a pitched battle on 5 May, but the rebels kept the British on their toes with guerrilla warfare. The Maulvi was killed after clashing with the pro-British rajah of Pawayan on 5 June, but it was several more months before the rebellion finally died down.

The four Gurkha battalions in existence at the start of the Indian Mutiny had all been involved on the British side and their performance had ranged from exemplary to legendary. A new battalion, known initially as the 'Extra Regiment', was formed by Lieutenant MacIntyre at Pithoragrh and Lahughat, the old recruiting station on the western border of Nepal, on 6 August 1857. It served at Almora before the mutiny ended, and then became the 4th Gurkha Rifles. The 5th Gurkha Rifles, which traced their origins to the Gurkha force formed by Ranjit Singh, was formed as the 25th Regiment of Punjab Infantry, or the Hazara Goorkha Battalion, in May 1858. In October 1858 the first recruiting expedition set off, not to Nepal, but to Kumaon. The men enlisted were Gurkhas, Garhwalis and Kumaonis, in roughly equal numbers. 'Gurkhas', so-called, were

serving too in the Assam Light Infantry battalions in north-east India. These battalions also had hill peoples – Garhwalis and Kumaonese – in about the same proportion as 'true' Gurkhas. Although the mutiny did not take hold in this area, they fought against the rebels. Among them was the Sylhet Light Infantry, which included some Gurkhas from eastern Nepal. They were formally designated Gurkhas in 1886, and eventually became the 8th Gurkha Rifles, with the first battalion so named forming in 1903 and the second in 1907.[100]

The Indian Mutiny, and its brutal suppression, strengthened British rule in India in the short to medium term. Although it has been called the 'First War of Indian Independence', a term sometimes wrongly attributed to Karl Marx,[101] independence did not come for another ninety years. Bahadur Shah II, king of Delhi – the aged heir of the Mughal emperors, who had been present, aged eighty-two, during the 'siege' – was put on trial and exiled in 1859. Neither the last of the Mughals, nor the East India Company, survived the mutiny. On 1 November 1858, with military pomp and circumstance, and followed by church services and firework displays, the East India Company was abolished. The British Crown took direct control of India. Earl Canning, who had been Governor General of India from February 1856 and who had overseen the horrors of the Indian Mutiny, became the first Viceroy of India. The East India Company's treaties with native princes would be honoured, however. Rebels who had not taken part in killing Europeans – those who were still alive, that is – were pardoned; there would be religious toleration and ancient customs would be respected.[102]

From the same moment, the Indian Army came under the British Crown, although it remained a separate army with a separate chain of command and its own, different, rank structure. The Indian Mutiny had been a catharsis for the Gurkhas. Their loyalty and efficiency were now no longer in any doubt and more battalions had already been recruited. Above all, their 'special force' status was confirmed. They were now seen, as Tony Gould puts it, 'not simply as courageous and indomitable soldiers, but as a kind of honorary British, a race apart, *in* but not *of* the Indian Army [emphasis in

original].' Confirmation of this came in 1858 when the soldiers of the Sirmoor Battalion were designated as "riflemen" – after their equally valiant bothers in the 60th Rifles – rather than mere "sepoys".'[103] The demands of their next theatre of operations would make some of them "special forces" in other ways, too.

4

Riflemen, and Afghanistan's Plains . . .

When you're wounded and left on Afghanistan's plains,
And the women come out to cut up what remains,
Jest roll on your rifle and blow out your brains,
An' go to your Gawd like a soldier.

Rudyard Kipling, 'The Young British Soldier',
Barrack Room Ballads, 1892.[1]

After its achievement at Delhi in 1857, and in recognition of its close association with the 60th Rifles, the Sirmoor Battalion was designated as a 'rifle regiment' in 1858. The evolution of all the Gurkha Regiments can be traced through the 'family tree' in Figure 4.

Originally, rifles – long-barrelled firearms with spiralling grooves down the bore to make the bullet spin – had been rare and expensive, and were also slow to load because the tight-fitting bullet had to be pushed down the barrel, engaging the rifling as it went. They were therefore used by huntsmen, by frontiersmen in America and, from the later eighteenth century on European battlefields, by specialist troops, called *jägers* ('hunters') in German, or *tirailleurs* in French, or 'light infantry' by the British. Their job was to skirmish in open order and soften up the enemy before the massed volleys of the line infantry, firing smooth-bore muskets, were unleashed at closer range. Although shorter-ranged and less accurate, muskets were much quicker to load. The latter were also fired in volleys, rather than concentrating on aimed shots at individual targets, as was the practice of the riflemen. Rifles were not always the ideal weapon. In the British-American War of 1812–14, British rifle

units, armed with the superb Baker rifle used in the Peninsular War by the likes of Richard Sharpe,[2] were sometimes at a disadvantage faced with faster-firing smooth-bore muskets. But being armed with rifles also meant a different way of operating. The Gurkhas were naturally suited to the skirmishing, light infantry role and, as we have seen, had been fulfilling it since their formation in 1815. The 'rifles' title therefore accurately reflected their former role and proven expertise, but was also an honour, conferred on elite troops. The Russians, whom the British in India were preparing to fight, similarly used the adjective *strelkovy* to denote 'rifle' units, as opposed to ordinary infantry – *pekhota*. Later, the Red Army, sensitive to such issues, called most of its infantry units *strelkovy* – 'rifle'.[3] By the end of the 1850s, however, as a result of the industrial revolution, which was transforming warfare, just about everyone who could get hold of them was firing rifles.[4]

Because of its achievements at Delhi, the Sirmoor Battalion was also privileged with the grant of a third 'colour', a colour being the highly visible flag, carried by the most junior officer (hence 'ensign'), about which regiments rallied in time of trouble. Ordinary regiments of the line normally carried only two. Then, inconveniently, in 1863, the authorities decreed that rifle regiments, as fast-moving specialist troops, should not carry colours. Charles Reid, now recovered from his Delhi-induced headache, as well as a colonel and a GCB, came up with an answer, approved by Queen Victoria. Instead of the third colour, the regiment was presented with a truncheon 6 feet (1.83 metres) high, which could be dismantled into five pieces, each easily able to be carried by a Gurkha in his pack. Thus was born the 'Queen's Truncheon', presented to the Sirmoors, at that point called the 2nd Goorkha Regiment, in 1863. Being a big bronze standard, liberally ornamented with bronze Gurkha riflemen, silver rings and kukris, the Queen's Truncheon has tended to outlast traditional colours.[5] As Plate 12 shows, it looks more delicate than might be imagined. Today, the British Royal Gurkha Rifles, the successors to the 2nd, 6th, 7th and 10th Gurkha Rifles, which transferred to the British Army in 1947, still have the Queen's Truncheon as an alternative 'colour'. That makes the Royal Gurkha Rifles unique – the only

British regiment to carry the same standard as one of its several predecessors 150 years ago.[6]

The other 'Gurkha' regiments effectively became rifle regiments, although, apart from the 2nd, they were not designated as such immediately. The 1st Regiment (the Malaun Regiment) became the 1st Goorkha Regiment (Light Infantry) in 1861. The 3rd Regiment became the 3rd Goorkha Regiment in 1861, although it was not formally designated 'Rifles' until 1891. The same happened with the 4th Regiment, the 'Extra Goorkha Regiment', which was redesignated the 4th Goorkha Regiment in 1861 and, again, a Gurkha rifle regiment in 1891. And the same happened with the 5th, which had been raised as the Hazara Gurkha Battalion in 1858 and became the 5th Goorkha Regiment in 1861 and the 5th Gurkha (Rifle) Regiment in 1891.[7] However, it remained an 'irregular' regiment, part of the Punjab Irregular Force (PIF) as the Trans-Frontier Brigade, raised on 18 May 1849, had been renamed in 1852. Initially the PIF comprised individual companies of Punjabi Muslims, Pathans, Dogras, Sikhs and Gurkhas. In 1858 the Gurkha troops of the Punjab Irregular (Frontier) Force were formed into the Hazara Gurkha Battalion. Because of their origins in the PIF, what became the 5th Gurkhas were known henceforward as 'Piffers'.[8] So it was not until 1891 that all the Gurkha regiments became 'rifle' regiments. The distinguished title 'rifleman' further aligned the Gurkhas with the British and distanced them from the sepoys. The idea of the Gurkhas as a 'third force' – and the trappings thereof – was getting stronger.[9]

In 1858 and 1859 a Royal Commission – the 'Peel Commission', named after its chairman, Major General Jonathan Peel, the Secretary of State for War, and not Sir Robert, the former prime minister, who had died in 1850 – examined the reform of the Indian Army.[10] Generals are often criticised for planning to fight the last war rather than the next and the Commission was no exception. It focussed on the causes of the Indian Mutiny, on how to prevent the recurrence of such a disaster, and hence on internal security. Therefore, the extraordinarily inefficient arrangement, by which there were three separate armies for the three presidencies – Bengal, Madras, and Bombay – was retained. The Madras and Bombay

armies had been virtually untouched by mutinous intent and had therefore been available to intervene against the Bengal mutineers. For the moment, therefore, 'divide and rule' made sense. For the same reason, Indian troops were not assigned to artillery, apart from light mountain guns, leaving the most lethal and long-ranged weapons in British hands alone.

While some argued that the Indian Mutiny had made firmer British rule essential, many realised that British rule in India, just like a modern peace support operation, depended on a certain amount of consent. India was too vast and its population too numerous to hold down by force. Sir Bartle Frere, later Governor of Bombay, grasped that that meant that Indian troops had to be trusted, as Reid had so acutely observed while fighting off attacks north of Delhi. 'They could not be *half* trusted,' said Frere.[11] However, many British continued to do just that, resulting in a step back from the progressive thinking of men like Henry Lawrence, now dead, who had advocated giving native talent maximum scope for development. 'We firmly believe,' he wrote in 1844, 'that is absolutely required some new grade where, without risking the supremacy of European authority, he may obtain and exert on our behalf those energies and talents which under the present system are too liable to be brought into the scale against us.'[12]

The nearest to what he was describing could be found in the Gurkha regiments. The system of Viceroy's Commissioned Officers – an extra layer of non-British officers between the warrant officers who play such a key role in the British Army and British officers holding the King's or Queen's Commission – existed throughout the Indian Army. Its evolution can be seen in Table 2. However, Gurkha officers controlled the day-to-day running of the unit and the subedar majors – including one holding the office of 'Gurkha major', advising the British commanding officer – exercised power and autonomy probably unmatched in most Indian Army units.

The main way of utilising native manpower while keeping it under control was to have mixed units. After the Indian Mutiny, Gurkhas and Sikhs were particularly welcome in the Bengal Army, to displace the Brahmans and Rajputs who had proved unreliable,

	British Army	Indian Army Infantry Viceroy's Commissioned Officers (VCOs)	Indian Army Cavalry Viceroy's Commissioned Officers (VCOs)	Indian Army Commissioned Officers, Junior Commissioned Officers (JCOs), warrant officers and NCOs post 1947	British Army King's (Queen's) Gurkha Officers (K/QGOs) post 1947 (1953), until 2007	Gurkha Commissioned Officers (GCOs) post 1957
King's/Queen's Commissioned Officers	general			general		
	lieutenant general			lieutenant general		
	major general			major general		
	brigadier (brigadier general until 1922)			brigadier		
	colonel			colonel		
	lieutenant colonel			lieutenant colonel		
	major			major		major
	captain			captain		captain
	lieutenant			lieutenant		lieutenant
	second lieutenant					

Intermediate layer	(major)	subedar major	risaldar major	subedar major/ risaldar major	gurkha major
	(captain)	subedar	risaldar	subedar/risaldar	gurkha captain
	(lieutenant)	jemadar	jemadar	jemadar (from 1965, naib subedar/risaldar)	gurkha lieutenant
Warrant Officers	Warrant Officer Class 1 (regimental sergeant major) Class 2 (company sergeant major)	havildar major	daffadar major	battalion havildar major/daffadar major company havildar major/daffadar major company quartermaster havildar/squadron quartermaster daffadar	As British Army

COMPARATIVE BRITISH AND INDIAN (INCLUDING GURKHA) RANKS, AND THEIR EVOLUTION, 1815–2010 (CONTINUED)

British Army	Indian Army Infantry Viceroy's Commissioned Officers (VCOs)	Indian Army Cavalry Viceroy's Commissioned Officers (VCOs)	Indian Army Commissioned Officers, Junior Commissioned Officers (JCOs), warrant officers and NCOs post 1947	British Army King's (Queen's) Gurkha Officers (K/QGOs) post 1947 (1953), until 2007	Gurkha Commissioned Officers (GCOs) post 1957
Non-Commissioned Officers					
staff or colour sergeant	No equivalent	No equivalent	No equivalent		
sergeant	havildar	daffadar	havildar/daffadar		
corporal	naik	naik	naik		
lance corporal	lance naik	lance naik	lance naik		
private/rifleman/ trooper	sepoy	sowar	sepoy/sowar		

Viceroy's Commissioned Officers (VCOs) and King's or Queen's Gurkha Officers (K/QGOs) after 1947 were commissioned from the ranks. The first Gurkha commissioned officers who trained at Sandhurst graduated in 1957. In the Indian Army before 1947 jemadars and subedars normally served as platoon commanders and company second-in-commands (2i/cs), but were junior to all British officers, while the subedar major was the commanding officer's trusted adviser on the men and their welfare. For a long time it was impossible for Gurkhas to progress further, except that honorary lieutenancies or captaincies were occasionally awarded to Gurkhas on retirement. Honorary major titles have also been awarded occasionally since. The QGO commission, the Short Service (Gurkha) Commission and the system of awarding honorary rank ended on 8 March 2007. On that day the Gurkha Terms and Conditions of Service (GTACOS) Review was announced. Among its recommendations were that all Queen's Gurkha Officers were transferred to the Short Service Commission (Late Entry) (SSC(LE)) group, subject to meeting the standard. All future candidates except Direct Entry (Sandhurst) officer candidates would be commissioned into the SSC(LE) within the Brigade of Gurkhas. Gurkha Other Ranks could also seek commissions in other arms and corps.[13] The Indian Army has kept the same ranks as the British Indian Army. The historic titles of jemadar (now naib subedar) (infantry) or naib risaldar (armour), subedar (risaldar), and subedar (risaldar) major have been kept for junior commissioned officers (JCOs). These still form a separate layer of officers commissioned from the ranks. In the modern Indian Army, full commissioned officers do not command platoons; junior commissioned officers do.[14] Indian JCOs are distinguished by a transverse red and yellow stripe on the epaulette, reminiscent of the distinctive stripe that VCOs in the Indian Army and QGOs in the British Army also wore.

but neither they nor their British officers wanted them to mix too closely. A compromise solution was to have mixed regiments like the 42nd Assam Light Infantry, with companies each composed of a single ethnic group. Thus, in 1865, the 42nd had two companies of Sikhs, four companies of 'Gurkhas' (each of which had 25 per cent Jarhwals, a local hill people, and not true Gurkhas), and two companies of 'Hindustanis' – one Hindu, one Muslim.[15]

By the time the Indian Army Gurkhas had achieved their regular status in 1850, there was a new ruler in control of Nepal, who would play an important role in the Indian Mutiny and the story of the Gurkhas. He was Jang Bahadur Kunwar (1816–1877).

Although he was not of royal blood himself, but a descendant of Bhim Sen, one of his daughters married royalty, creating the Rana dynasty of Nepal. His real name was Bir Narsingh Kunwar but he became famous by the name Jang Bahadur. After various adventures, he arrived at the Nepalese court in 1842 and rose to be prime minister. Queen-Regent Rajya Laxmi Devi (Lakshmidevi) and her son King Rajendra were condemned by the Nepalese aristocracy and exiled after a hatching plot to kill Jang Bahadur, but the king still coveted the throne and began plotting to return from India. In 1847, Jang Bahadur denounced the exiled king's treasonable activities, announced that he was dethroned and put Rajendra's son on the throne as Surendra Bikram Shah (1847–81). By 1850, Jang Bahadur had eliminated all of his major rivals, installed his own candidate on the throne, appointed his brothers and friends to all the important posts, and made sure that, as prime minister, he made the major administrative decisions by himself. He then made an extraordinary move by travelling to Britain and France, in spite of all the prohibitions on high-caste Hindus crossing the 'black water' – the sea. He left Calcutta in April 1850 and returned to Kathmandu in February 1851. The British government fended off his attempts to deal directly with its top people while he was there, but the exotic Nepalese leader was a hit with London society. The British took care, however, that he saw the wealth and industrial might of the country for himself. It made an indelible impression on Jang Bahadur, who was also extremely shrewd and admired British pragmatism and adaptability. He became convinced that keeping in with

the British was the best guarantee of Nepal's independence and of his own power.[16]

When the Indian Mutiny broke out some of the British thought that Nepal would side with the mutineers, which could well mean disaster for the British, who were hard-pressed as it was. However, Jang Bahadur proved to be a reliable ally. With hostilities in Tibet, and Chinese intervention between 1854 and 1856, the Nepalese Army had been increased to around 25,000 troops. When news of the mutiny reached Kathmandu, many Nepalese saw it as an opportunity for revenge for their defeat in 1816. But, Jang Bahadur argued, 'We may enrich ourselves for the time being. We may prosper for two or three years, but our time will infallibly come, and we shall then lose our country.'[17] He had a big army itching for action, so the solution was clear. Rather than fight the British, the Nepalese should help them.

Although there was some opposition in Nepal, Jang Bahadur wisely directed his forces against the predominantly Muslim rebel movement in Oudh, rather than against fellow Hindus. Three Nepali regiments – about 3,000 men – crossed the border and, joined by British officers (what we would now call 'military advisers)', did well to clear the Gorakhpur area of mutineers. The main force, another 9,000 troops, which followed at the end of 1857, led by Jang Bahadur himself, did less well. It headed for Lucknow but fought no major engagements and moved agonisingly slowly. William Howard Russell of *The Times*, the first independent war correspondent in an era when the popular press was expanding in power and influence – a revolution in media affairs to parallel the revolution in military affairs that was well under way – was accompanying General Sir Colin Campbell's force on its way to relieve the city.[18] In his diary he relates how the general was infuriated by 'that terrible impedimentum, Jung Bahadoor'. Lord Canning, the Governor-General and later first Viceroy, urged Campbell 'not to move without the Goorkhas' – the Nepalese Army Gurkhas, this time. If the British took Lucknow by themselves, 'we might give him offence and drive him back to his mountains in a huff'.[19]

Jang Bahadur eventually arrived on 11 March, ten days before the coded message, 'Nunc fortunatus sum', announced that the

British were in Lucknow. Russell was acutely contemptuous of Jang Bahadur but modified his comments as time went on. The Nepalese troops, having done little to support the British victory at Lucknow, still took part in the appalling looting. They then headed back to Nepal laden with treasure. Prime Minister Jang Bahadur returned to Nepal triumphantly in March 1858, but continued to help the British in hunting down mutineers who had crossed the Nepalese border and sought refuge in the Terai. Among them was Nana Sahib, also known as Dhandu Pant, who was blamed for the massacre of British people – especially the women and children – at Cawnpore on 27 June 1857. Nana Sahib was a Brahman, the highest Hindu caste, and therefore entitled to the greatest protection, but Jang Bahadur knew the British wanted him – dead or alive. In true Nepalese fashion the story came out that Nana Sahib and his brother were dead, and although most people were sceptical, nothing was heard of them thereafter.[20]

Gurkha recruitment remained a problem for the British-Indian Army. Jang Bahadur had offered help to the British during the Sikh Wars, knowing that the British would refuse it, and again during the Indian Mutiny, when the British were desperate, and accepted it. But he continued to oppose and obstruct the recruitment of Gurkhas from Nepal to the British-Indian Army, for good reasons. Why should his best military material join a neighbouring power that was, potentially, an overwhelming threat? The difficulties of recruiting true 'Gurkhas' – from Nepal – continued. In 1859, Jang Bahadur forced the British to abandon their illegal cross-border recruitment attempts. The recruiters were already liable, technically, to be sentenced to death. In 1859 he reiterated that recruiters were liable to be arrested and that 'no subject of the four classes and thirty-six castes of our country shall go to India for recruitment without prior approval'.[21] Anyone who disobeyed this order might forfeit his house and land, and forgo certain rights under Nepalese law, including that most natural of rights: to kill his wife's lover.[22]

Because recruiting in the 'hills' on the Nepali side of the border was so difficult, and so resisted by the Nepalese authorities, the British-Indian service inevitably attracted some outlaws, deserters and renegades. In 1864 the British abandoned sending undercover

recruiting teams into Nepal, because it was so dangerous, and relied on word of mouth to bring volunteers across the porous border.[23] Jang Bahadur played a brilliant game. He got on the right side of the British and in so doing maintained Nepal's independence. But he strongly resisted the recruitment of his best military people by the British. His successors eventually succumbed to that convenient arrangement, but he never did. Many of the men in the photographs of Indian Army 'Gurkhas' in the later nineteenth century look like 'true' or 'wild' Tibeto-Burman Gurkhas, rather than Kumaonese or the so-called 'line boys' from mixed marriages. But, given the difficulties of recruiting inside Nepal, and the huge constraints on British-Indian recruiters, it is, frankly, hard to explain how they got there. Meanwhile, the wider strategic situation was changing.

> The most important political question on which modern times have to decide, is the policy that must now be pursued, in order to maintain the security of western Europe against the overgrown power of Russia: a power that hangs in threatening darkness over the west, as the thunder cloud of the tropics hangs over the lands destined to feel the fury of the desolating tornado.[24]

If Major General Sir John Mitchell, writing before 1838, was worried about Europe, the British in India were even more worried and would become still more so as the century went on. Russia was not only the principal competitor to the British empire, at least in Eurasia. It was also, notwithstanding the similarity of the British and the Russian approaches to subject peoples, the antithesis of British free-market capitalism and aspirations towards democracy. By the 1830s, British attitudes to Russia had crystallised into 'a distinct Russophobia',[25] and in spite of – or, rather, because of – Russia's defeat in the Crimean War, the bear embarked on a programme of quite radical military reform. And it set its sights on Central Asia.

The reform was led by a 'liberal' war minister, Dmitry Milyutin, and the abolition of serfdom in 1861 – two years before slavery was officially abolished in the United States – was motivated as much by modern military as by humanitarian and philanthropic concerns.[26] On 25 August 1859, the Russians captured the Imam Shamil, one of

the top guerrilla commanders of all time, who had been diverting them in a protracted and bloody war in the Caucasus for twenty years. In 1864 the Russians declared the Caucasus War over. Their attention now swung south and east, towards Afghanistan, where they had been heavily involved in 1838–41, and to India (see Figure 5).

It is unlikely that the Russians had a really serious grand strategic plan to capture India. In the last quarter of the nineteenth century they compiled voluminous reports in more than forty volumes of the *Collection of Geographical, Topographical and Statistical Materials on Asia*, including 'The Military Communications along the Indo-Afghanistan Frontier' and a translation of a British article on the defence of India.[27] In 1878, when the British invaded Afghanistan and fear of the Russian threat reached its height, General Skobelev, the flamboyant, white-uniformed hero of the Central Asian campaigns, authored a plan that, among other things, would 'organize hordes of Asiatic horsemen, who to a cry of blood and plunder, might be launched against India as a vanguard, thus reviving the days of Timur'.[28]

In June 1886, General Kuropatkin, later Minister for War and later, land commander in the 1904–5 Russo-Japanese War, formulated a plan for an advance into Afghanistan and on to India. Kuropatkin considered that the possibility of war existed 'beyond any doubt' and that it would be best to launch the attack in November as 'the weather is healthier for the men and all the Russian ports would be frozen', negating the British advantage at sea. The British obtained a copy from 'a most secret source' and Lord Roberts, the Commander-in-Chief India, no less, had a look at it.[29] Although they appeared threatening, the Russians also felt threatened. They were more concerned that the British, strengthened by their effective suppression of the Indian Mutiny, would trespass on what the Russians regarded as their real estate in Central Asia.

Writing in 1874, in his account of the Russian expedition to Khiva in 1839–40 that had coincided with the first disastrous British intervention in Afghanistan, Russian General Mikhail Ivanin explained:

In Asia you rule the richest of lands [India]; 150 million are bound to you [roughly the same population as Russia at the time]; in India you have an army of 100,000 men; your huge factories are flourishing, you can supply arms and war *matériel* to our enemies in central Asia, and therefore we do not wish you to extend your dominion and influence beyond the Indus. We consider every step of yours beyond the right bank [the west, given the direction of flow] of the Indus hostile to our trade and political stance. As a naval power you can extend your trade and political enterprises across the whole Asian littoral; only leave the interior countries of Asia for our trade. Otherwise we must regard every step you make beyond the Indus or the Himalayan chain with suspicion.[30]

Ivanin's account of the 1839–40 expedition is, however, interestingly illustrated with up-to-date 1870s maps including the railways, which were not there when the expedition had taken place. The British were, not unreasonably, concerned, and the more distant Russian 'threat' compounded that from the uncontrolled space, as they saw it, in Afghanistan. The prevailing view from the 1860s was encapsulated by General Sir Colin MacGregor, the quartermaster general in India. Writing in 1884, he said: 'The aims of Russia as regards England [sic] are altogether so aggressive and unprovoked that I hold we are justified in using every means in our power, in the event of war, towards breaking up the Russian Empire into fractions that cannot for a long time become dangerous to us.'[31]

MacGregor calculated that the Russians could deploy 185,000 infantry and 40,000 cavalry against India. They could get to Herat in western Afghanistan, to Kabul, the capital, and to Chitral, in what is now north-west Pakistan, close to the Afghan border, before the British could deploy troops to prevent them. Once in Kabul, they could count on another 20,000 Afghan troops, who would side with perceived might. MacGregor's assessment, like all military assessments, was a 'worst case', but it underlines that at the height of its power the British empire was modestly realistic about its capabilities. And his comment does not overly flatter the Indian Army: 'It is not the power of Afghanistan we shall have to meet, but that of Russia, not the efforts of a few thousand undisciplined men, but those of a *scientific, well-disciplined army*, backed by an incalculable

number of irregular troops drawn from the whole of Asia [emphasis added].'[32]

British assessments of the 'Russian threat' and comparisons with the Indian Army's native troops remained pessimistic. Major J. M. Home, of the Gurkhas, one of the British observers of the 1904–5 Russo-Japanese War, noted Russian claims (and they were Russian claims; not necessarily his own view) that 'their Central Asian troops were . . . vastly superior to our native troops and fully the equal of the British soldier'.[33] Whether Home thought the Russians were referring to Gurkhas as well is unclear, but he would probably have assumed not. The idea that the Gurkhas, too, were fully equal to the British soldier had been around since the 1840s, reinforced by the experience of the Indian Mutiny, and would have been further reinforced by operations in the later nineteenth century. The Russian threat to India, real or imagined, was another trump card the Gurkhas could play.

The Indian writer Nirad Chaudhuri, writing in 1930, divided British-Indian Army recruiting into three phases. In the eighteenth century anyone who volunteered, including many ne'er-do-wells, might enlist. From the end of the eighteenth century and into the nineteenth the Bengal Army was dominated by Brahmans and Rajputs from the Ganges basin, which had its effect in 1857. After the mutiny, therefore, the British concentrated on 'the broken-up elements of the once hostile military powers'.[34] This meant playing Gurkhas off against Sikhs and Sikhs against Gurkhas, while isolating the favoured 'martial races' from the rest of the population. However, political circumstances now also favoured the Gurkhas. Chaudhuri believed 'the whole attitude of the British authorities in India in favour of the men of the North was due to historical circumstance . . . that by 1880, due to the growth of the Russian menace, the North-West Frontier had become the principal theatre of operations for the Indian Army'.[35]

The North-East Frontier, with Burma, was also a key theatre of operations, sometimes very bloody. The 42nd (Assam) Regiment of Bengal Native Infantry, based on the Cuttack Legion originally founded in 1817, acquired that name in 1861, becoming the Bengal Native (Light) Infantry in 1864 and eventually acquiring the title

Goorkha in 1886. It later became the 6th Gurkha Rifles. The 8th and the 10th Gurkha Rifles also originated on the North-East Frontier, the latter raised to police the border with Upper Burma.[36]

The massive expansion in the Gurkha units of the Indian Army in the later nineteenth and early twentieth centuries was therefore a function of the increasingly 'scientific' (or pseudo-scientific) 'martial race' theory, combined with the *realpolitik* of opposing the north-western tribes, including Afghans, and possibly the Russians, in sometimes mountainous terrain, with troops of the required quality. The Gurkhas met all these requirements.

The Gurkhas' next campaign would be on the North-East Frontier, not the North-West – the Lushai campaign of 1871–2 (see Figure 6). Events on the North-East Frontier were less comprehensively and accurately covered in the press than those on the North-West, for understandable if not forgivable reasons. There was no vigorous native power comparable with Afghanistan and the area was not a gateway for Russia into India. Neverthless, in the words of a political officer writing in 1836, 'In a commercial, a statistical or a political point of view no country is more important. There our territory of Assam is situated in almost immediate contact with the empires of China and Ava [Burma-Myanmar], being separated from each by a narrow belt of mountainous country.'[37]

As in the north-west, the idea of 'frontiers' was hard for the local peoples to grasp and repeated raids against the British-controlled territories, including the precious tea plantations, were met with reprisals. In 1871 there was a spate of significant raids by the Lushai tribes, in which a six-year-old British girl, Mary Winchester, was seized and a fortified tea plantation attacked.[38] In July 1871, the Viceroy and Governor-General in Council – as the replacement for the East India Company's Governor-General was now known: the head of the British administration in India who oversaw the provinces of Punjab, Bengal, Bombay, Madras and others – decided to launch an expedition against the Lushais on the southern part of the border with Burma. The force was to consist of two columns, one starting from Chittagong, the other from Cachar (see Figure 6). Five Gurkha battalions were involved – the 2nd, 4th, what would later become the 6th (the 42nd (Assam) Regiment of Bengal (Native)

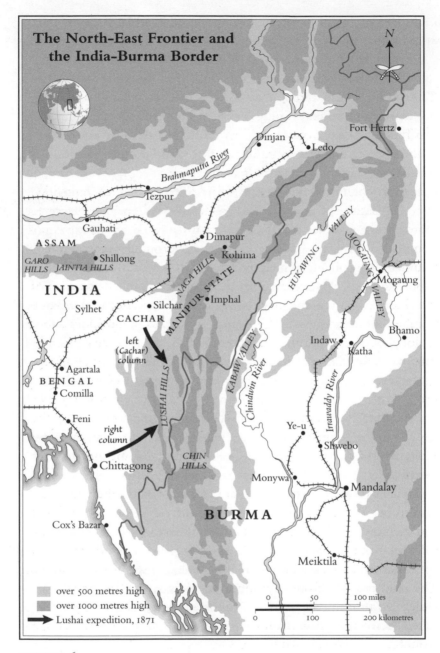

The North–East Frontier and the India–Burma Border

N

Fort Hertz

Dinjan

Ledo

Brahmaputra River

Tezpur

Gauhati

ASSAM

GARO HILLS

JAINTIA HILLS

Shillong

INDIA

Sylhet

Silchar

CACHAR

Dimapur

Kohima

NAGA HILLS

MANIPUR STATE

Imphal

HUKAWING VALLEY

MOGAUNG VALLEY

Mogaung

Bhamo

Indaw

Katha

left (Cachar) column

Agartala

BENGAL

Comilla

Feni

right column

LUSHAI HILLS

KABAW VALLEY

Chindwin River

Irrawaddy River

Ye-u

Shwebo

Chittagong

CHIN HILLS

Monywa

Mandalay

Cox's Bazar

BURMA

Meiktila

over 500 metres high
over 1000 metres high
Lushai expedition, 1871

0   50   100 miles

0   100   200 kilometres

FIGURE 6

Light Infantry), and two battalions of what would later become the 8th Gurkhas (the 43rd and 44th).[39]

Former expeditions in 1849, 1861 and 1869 had been unsuccessful. Colonel Raban, who commanded an expedition from the Chittagong side in 1861, made various recommendations, including that 1,000 porters would be the smallest number required, and that hillmen alone would be of any use. Some of these, in addition to the fighting troops, would be 'Gurkhas'. In 1871, all the recommendations made by Colonel Raban ten years earlier were carried out. Each column would consist of three regiments, accompanied by a half-battery of artillery and a company of sappers and miners, representing a force of nearly 2,000 men, with about an equal number of 'coolies' – porters and other non-combatants – and a number of elephants. The Cachar or left column of the Lushai expedition included a company of sappers and miners; 500 men of the Punjab Native Infantry under Colonel Stafford; the same number of the 42nd Assam Light Infantry (later 6th Gurkhas) under Colonel Rattray; and the same number of the 44th Assam Light Infantry (later the 1st Battalion 8th Gurkhas) under Colonel Hicks. Brigadier General Bourchier, commanding the North-Eastern Frontier District, was selected to command the left column. His staff included Lieutenant Colonel F. Roberts RA VC CB, the deputy assistant quartermaster general, later Field Marshal Lord Roberts of Kandahar. The right column included the 2nd and 4th Gurkhas.[40]

The left column's general and staff arrived at Mynadhur, about 29 November 1871, with one wing of the 44th (later the 8th Gurkhas) and the sappers. The jungle in the Mynadhur area consisted principally of bamboo, and so the force experienced no difficulty in constructing barracks, hospitals, magazines and officers' quarters. The road onwards from Mynadhur was similar in character to that which led to it, 'precipitous and Jungly'.[41] Four camps were established between Mynadhur and Tipai Mukh. It was an operation that would have been very familiar to Ochterlony and his colleagues far to the west in 1815. Lieutenant Thorpe, of the engineers, of the Topographical Survey Department of India, attached to the left column, noted that after they

Arrived at the halting place, all the troops went to work cutting down branches of trees and bamboos, collecting leaves, grass, &c. In this work the active little Goorkhas of the 44th N. I. [Native Infantry], were much more at home than their up-country brethren in arms, who at first used to look helplessly on, while the former, springing into trees like monkeys, lopped off branches, collected bamboos, &c., and had quickly constructed comfortable ranges of cantos [bivouacs], with a low raised bamboo floor as a sleeping place, before the others had made up their minds what to do.

All the Sepoys had been supplied with kookries, a peculiar kind of native knife, most effective in cutting jungle when successfully used. The Goorkhas, as a rule, were possessed of their own, but those supplied by Government were soon useless, often breaking after the first few blows, efficiency having been sacrificed to economy.'[42]

The Gurkhas were clearly well equipped and fully conversant with that famous British Army maxim: '*Any fool* can be uncomfortable.'

Thorpe also noted how the Gurkhas' tactics and fieldcraft helped shield the column as it was conducting a withdrawal. On 26 December 1871, the column pulled back, knowing full well that, on previous experience, the Lushais would probably let the leading combat troops pass and lie in wait for the long string of 'coolies' – and fire into it.

The 22nd formed the advance. The baggage and sick were sent on in front, under the protection of some of the 44th [later the 8th Gurkhas], distributing a couple of files between the coolies at short intervals. The remainder of the 44th formed the rear-guard, and were accompanied by the General himself, and Colonel Roberts.
. . . The Lushais then discovered the manoeuvre, but too late, for the coolies were well ahead, and the rear-guard was between them. They tried, however, wherever the nature of the ground gave them a chance, to get by the rear-guard and attack the coolies; but *they were baffled by the Goorkhas*, 'who', in the words of one of the staff-officers present, 'extending rapidly where the ground allowed, retired through their supports as if on parade'. The troops were admirably led by Colonel Nuthall and Captain Robertson [emphasis added].[43]

The right column, meanwhile, advanced from Chittagong and on 4 January 1872 reached the stockaded village of Lalgnoora. That

was believed to be the Lushais' 'capital', insofar as such things existed, 'their chief stockaded village', and therefore a formidable obstacle.[44] It was surrounded, as the Gurkhas would have known only too well, by high palisades, made from sharpened logs or bamboo, the approaches to which, in turn, were surrounded by *panji* spikes – sharpened stakes. That is a British-Indian Army term, still in use today, taken from the Hindi *panja*, meaning a hand or a foot. Often they are concealed in holes in the ground, to impale unsuspecting or hasty attackers, and were so used in the Vietnam War. Major Donald MacIntyre, a forty-year-old staff officer in the Bengal Staff Corps attached to the 2nd Gurkha Rifles and temporarily serving as second-in-command, was an unlikely candidate to lead an attack. But, for reasons that are unclear, he led the assault on the stockaded village of Lalgnoora.

> Colonel MacPherson C.B., V.C. Commanding the 2nd Goorkha Regiment, in which Lieutenant-Colonel Macintyre was serving at the time as second in command, reports that this Officer, who led the assault, was the first to reach the stockade (on this side from 8 to 9 feet [just over 2.5 metres] high); and that to climb over and disappear among the flames and smoke of the burning village, was the work of a very short time. The stockade, he adds, was successfully stormed by this Officer under fire, the heaviest the Looshais delivered that day.[45]

Donald MacIntyre (1831–1903) was a distinguished scholar and artist who became a Fellow of the Royal Geographic Society and later retired as a major general. He had joined the East India Company army in 1850 and served with the 66th Gurkhas – the former 1st Nasiri Battalion, now wearing red coats – as a subaltern under Sir Colin Campbell in 1852, in expeditions against the hill tribes on the Peshawar frontier. He had also served under Sir Neville Chamberlain in the expedition of 1856, again with the 66th Gurkhas in Afghanistan at the Kurram valley. Later, in the Afghan campaign of 1878–9, he commanded the 2nd Gurkhas with the Khaibar column in both expeditions to the Bazar valley.[46]

On that day, 4 January 1872, Major MacIntyre won the Gurkhas' second Victoria Cross. For ease of reference, the Victoria Crosses awarded to the Gurkhas up to the time of writing are shown in Table 3.

GURKHA WINNERS OF THE VICTORIA CROSS, OR THOSE ATTACHED TO THE GURKHAS AT THE TIME, UP TO THE TIME OF WRITING

	Name	Rank on date of action	Date of action	Regiment and/or affiliation	Place/campaign	Date of London Gazette citation
1.	J. A. Tytler	Lieutenant	10 Feb 1858	Bengal Staff Corps, serving in the 66th Bengal Native Infantry, later 1 GR. Later commanded 4 GR.	Indian Mutiny	23 Aug 1858
2	D. Macintyre	Major	4 Jan 1872	Bengal Staff Corps, serving in 2 GR (2 i/c)	Lushai Campaign Burmese border	27 Sep 1872
3	G. N. Channer	Captain, Brevet Major	20 Dec 1875	Bengal Staff Corps, serving in 1 GR	Malaya	12 Apr 1876
4	J. Cook	Captain	2 Dec 1878	Bengal Staff Corps, serving in 5 GR	Afghanistan, Peiwar, Kotal	18 Mar 1879
5	C. J. W. Grant	Lieutenant	27 Mar 1891	Indian Staff Corps, serving in 12 Burma Regiment and commanding detachment of 43 GR which became 2nd Battalion, 8 GR	Manipur	26 May 1891

6	R. K. Ridgeway	Captain	22 Nov 1879	Bengal Staff Corps, serving in 44 GR, which later became 1st Battalion 8 GR	Naga campaign	N/K
7	G. M. Boisragon	Lieutenant	2 Dec 1891	5 GR	Hunza campaign	12 Jul 1892
8	J. Manners-Smith	Lieutenant	20 Dec 1891	Indian Staff Corps, serving with 5 GR	Hunza campaign	12 Jul 1892
9	W. G. Walker	Captain	22 Apr 1903	1st Battalion 4 GR, attached to Bikanir Camel Corps	Somaliland	7 Aug 1903
10	J. D. Grant	Lieutenant	6 Jul 1904	1st Battalion 8 GR	Tibet	24 Jan 1905
11	Kulbir Thapa	Rifleman	25 Sep 1915	2nd Battalion 3 GR	France, Western Front	18 Nov 1915
12	G. C. Wheeler	Major	23 Feb 1917	2nd Battalion 9 GR	Mesopotamia	8 Jun 1917
13	Karanbahadur Rana	Rifleman	10 Apr 1918	2nd Battalion 3 GR	Egypt	21 Jun 1918
14	Lalbahadur Thapa	Subedar	5/6 Apr 1943	1st Battalion 2 GR	Tunisia	15 Jun 1943
15	Gaje Ghale	Havildar	24/27 May 1943	2nd Battalion 5 RGR	Burma	30 Sep 1943
16	M. Allmand	Acting Captain	11/23 Jun 1944	Indian Armoured Corps (Duke of Connaught's Lancers) attached to 6 GR	Burma	26 Oct 1944

GURKHA WINNERS OF THE VICTORIA CROSS, OR THOSE ATTACHED TO THE GURKHAS AT THE TIME, UP TO THE TIME OF WRITING (CONTINUED)

	Name	Rank on date of action	Date of action	Regiment and/or affiliation	Place/campaign	Date of London Gazette citation
17	Ganju Lama	Rifleman	12 Jun 1944	1st Battalion 7 GR	Burma	7 Sep 1944
18	Tulbahadur Pun	Rifleman	23 Jun 1944	3rd Battalion 6 GR	Burma	9 Nov 1944
19	Agansing Rai	Rifleman	24/25 Jun 1944	5 RGR	Burma	5 Oct 1944
20	Netrabahadur Thapa	Acting Subedar	25/26 Jun 1944	2nd Battalion 5 RGR	Burma	12 Oct 1944
21	F. G. Blaker	Temporary Major	9 Jul 1944	Highland Light Infantry, attached to 3rd Battalion 9 GR	Burma	26 Sep 1944
22	Sherbahadur Thapa	Rifleman	18 Sep 1944	1st Battalion 9 GR	Italy	28 Dec 1944
23	Thaman Gurung	Rifleman	19 Nov 1944	1st Battalion 5 RGR	Italy	22 Feb 1945
24	Bhanbagta Gurung	Rifleman	5 Mar 1945	3rd Battalion 2 GR	Burma	5 Jun 1945
25	Lachhiman Gurung	Rifleman	12 May 1945	4th Battalion 8 GR	Burma	27 Jul 1945
26	Rambahadur Limbu	Lance Corporal	21 Nov 1965	2nd Battalion 10 GR	Borneo	22 Apr 1966

Non-British Gurkhas became eligible to win the VC from 1911. Before that, many won the Indian Order of Merit, which in many cases equated. Table complete up to August 2010.

Source: *For Valour.* Poster, Gurkha Memorial Museum, Pokhara, Nepal; http://www.army.mod.uk/gurkhas/14281.aspx, Honours and Awards, Victoria Cross. Retrieved 25 July 2010

In the Lushai campaign twenty Lushai villages were destroyed and Mary Winchester was rescued. There were no more significant Lushai raids for the next decade.[47]

The eastern frontier would soon see the Gurkhas' third VC, and the second to be won by a British officer of the 1st Gurkha Rifles. In 1874 the British government sent its first Resident to Perak, an independent state in what is now north-west Malaysia. The Resident, perhaps appropriately called Birch, started taking charge of government administration, but in doing so upset the sultan of Upper Perak and other Malay chiefs, who resented his interference in matters such as revenue collection and slavery, and in 1875 allegedly had him murdered. In response, the British government sent troops from Hong Kong and Calcutta, including the 1st Gurkha Rifles, at that point called the 1st Goorkha Regiment (Light Infantry). The sultan was deposed, other chiefs were punished and British influence in Malaya (as it was then known) increased although, unsurprisingly, later Residents were more inclined to consult the local chiefs.[48]

It was the 1st Gurkhas' first trip overseas. The circumstances in which Captain George Nicholas Channer (1843–1905) won his VC were not unlike MacIntyre's. Channer had been sent by the commander of the Malacca column to procure intelligence as to the strength and position of a stockade inconveniently sited where British artillery could not hit it. According to the citation in the *London Gazette* of 14 April 1876, Channer, by this time a major, got the supreme award

> For having, with the greatest gallantry, been the first to jump into the Enemy's Stockade, to which he had been dispatched with a small party of the 1st Goorkha Light Infantry, on the afternoon of the 20th December, 1875, by the Officer commanding the Malacca Column. Major Channer got completely in rear of the Enemy's position, and finding himself so close that he could hear the voices of the men inside, who were cooking at the time, and keeping no look out, he beckoned to his men, and the whole party stole quietly forward to within a few paces of the Stockade. On jumping in, he shot the first man dead with his revolver, and his party then came up, and entered the Stockade, which was of a most formidable nature, surrounded by

a bamboo palisade; about seven yards within was a log-house, loop-holed, with two narrow entrances, and trees laid latitudinally, to the thickness of two feet [0.6 metres].

The Officer commanding reports that if Major Channer by his foresight, coolness and intrepidity, had not taken this Stockade, a great loss of life must have occurred, as from the fact of his being unable to bring guns to bear on it, from the steepness of the hill, and the density of the jungle, it must have been taken at the point of the bayonet.[49]

Although events on the North-West Frontier have attracted more attention, the fifth Gurkha VC was also won on the North-Eastern, underlining the difficult character of the operations there and the continuous nature of the Indian Army's engagement. On 22 November 1879, Captain Richard Kirby Ridgeway, of what became the 8th Gurkha Rifles, won his.

On 14 October 1879, Deputy Commissioner G. H. Damant was shot dead, with thirty-five of his men, on a visit to the Angami 'village' of Konoma – a formidable hilltop fort, and effectively a tribal capital. Two days later 6,000 Angamis attacked the British headquarters at Kohima, the garrison of which included the 43rd (Assam) Regiment of Bengal (Light) Infantry, but were repulsed. The British counter-attacked and captured Konoma.[50] Ridgeway won his VC

> For conspicuous gallantry throughout the attack on Konoma (Eastern Frontier of India), on the 22nd November, 1879, more especially in the final assault, when, under a heavy fire from the enemy, he rushed up to a barricade and attempted to tear down the planking surrounding it, to enable him to effect an entrance, in which act he received a very severe rifle shot wound in the left shoulder.[51]

Meanwhile, the Russian threat loomed on the North-West Frontier (see Figure 5). Sher Ali succeeded his popular and strong father Dost Muhammad as ruler of Afghanistan in 1863. The Russians persuaded him to accept an envoy, which alarmed the British. They wanted to send their own, Major Pierre Louis Cavagnari (1841–79),[52] but the Afghan government would not let him into the country. Therefore, in November 1878 the British invaded Afghanistan

for the second time. This time the British were not initially intent on regime change, although that happened later, but on detaching some of the frontier provinces from Afghanistan and bringing them under British control.

The 'frontier', which was not yet defined and would not be until Sir Henry Mortimer Durand established the imperfect 'Durand Line' in 1893,[53] centred on a stretch of tribal territory varying from 10 to 100 miles [16 to 160 kilometres] in width from Chitral in the north down to Baluchistan in the south (see Figure 5). Fighting there, between the Indian Army and the warlike and cruel Pathan tribes who lived in the wild, forbidding terrain – Wazirs, Mahsuds, Yusafzais and Orakzais – was pretty constant. However, invading Afghanistan, which had some of the trappings of an independent country, was a different proposition, although, then as now, the ruler's writ did not run much outside Kabul.[54]

The regular Afghan Army took prisoners sometimes. But the tribesmen were renowned for cutting up the wounded, and starting before they were dead, which often meant cutting off the victim's genitals and stuffing them in his mouth.[55] The phrase 'Save the last bullet for yourself' is sometimes wrongly attributed to Kipling, but he never published those words, which were reportedly coined by the US Army in not dissimilar circumstances in the Plains Indian Wars, at about the same time.[56] The last verse of Kipling's poem, 'The Young British Soldier' (1892), however, meant the same thing.[57] Additional delicacies included staking out prisoners or wounded, then peeling a piece of skin from the stomach and letting heat, dehydration, blood loss, ants and carrion birds do the rest. A small piece peeled away for a slow death, a more extensive one for a less slow death.[58] Therefore, rescuing the wounded became an overriding preoccupation in Indian Army operations, and extraordinary measures were taken to do so, even under heavy fire.[59]

All five Gurkha Regiments now in existence were involved in the Second Afghan War. The Gurkha soldiers were still less well equipped than their British colleagues, armed with Snider rifles – a breech-loading conversion of the former Enfield from twenty years before – as opposed to the new Martini-Henry box-chamber rifle carried by British regiments.[60] Both rifles were single-shot, with

black powder cartridges, since smokeless cordite did not come in until the 1890s. The Snider fired a massive 0.577-inch (14.66-mm) calibre round; the Martini-Henry, sighted up to 800 yards (728 metres), a 0.45-inch (11.4-mm). Both therefore had formidable 'stopping power', greatly valued when fighting fanatical tribesmen.

The British-Indian force of about 40,000 fighting men was distributed into three columns, which penetrated Afghanistan at three different points – a common Victorian technique to dislocate and confuse the enemy. Splitting one's force is often considered a sin at the tactical level but, as Callwell pointed out, at the strategic level, and in 'small wars', it may be opportune. He highlighted Afghanistan as a case in point:

> As long as the separated portions of an army are strong enough to hold their own against any hostile bodies likely to be brought against them, they run no risk . . . Thus in the Afghan wars the cities of Kabul and Kandahar have always been in the first instance aimed at, necessitating at least two entirely different lines of advance . . . In roadless inhospitable districts . . . quick movements of large armies are impossible, and in such theatres of operations the mobility of a body of troops is in inverse proportion to its size. Supply is a great difficulty, and only a certain body of supplies can be moved along a particular route within a given time . . . All this tends often to make it preferable, even if not absolutely necessary, to move in several columns instead of moving concentrated . . . Moreover, moral effect has to be taken into consideration . . . There can be no doubt that the spectacle of several well appointed columns of regular troops pouring into their territory alarms the semi-civilized races and savages more than does a single army, and for this reason division of force is often expedient [emphasis added].[61]

The northernmost column was led by Lieutenant General Sir Sam Browne, famous for designing the eponymous belt,[62] and this force advanced from Peshawar towards Kabul. In the centre, Lieutenant General Sir Frederick Roberts VC led a column through the Kurram valley towards Ali Kheyl, also eventually heading for Kabul. In the south, Lieutenant General Sir Donald Stewart led a column towards Kandahar (see Figure 5). Browne's force included

the 4th Gurkhas; Roberts' force included the 5th Gurkha Rifles, known as the 'Frontier Force'.

Sam Browne's column fired the first shots of the war in the attack on the fortress of Ali Masjid. It lay very close to the border with India and was reached within hours of the declaration of hostilities. Browne, who crossed the border on 20 November 1878, planned to split his forces into three columns. One column (the 3rd and 4th Brigades) would advance along the shortest route to the fort, up the Khyber valley, to act as a holding force to fix the enemy until the other columns (the 1st and 2nd Brigades) were in position. The two flanking columns were sent up a parallel valley, called the Lashora valley, to the north but running in the same direction. One of these flanking columns would occupy the heights over the fortress, whilst the other would move to the rear of the position so as to be able to launch an attack from behind the fortress. Success would depend on the speed and coordination of attacks from each of these three columns.

The 4th Gurkhas were in the 1st Brigade, which followed behind the 2nd up the Lashora valley. The 2nd Brigade was commanded by none other than Brigadier General Tytler VC, the first Gurkha VC winner, although he now had no Gurkhas under his command. Although Ali Masjid is one of the 4th Gurkhas' battle honours, they did not have to do very much to win it. The 3rd and 4th, who had carried on straight up the Khyber, shot it out with the Afghans on 21 November, and ceased firing in the evening to await completion of the encirclement. But on the 22nd it became obvious that during the night the Afghans had quietly withdrawn from the fort and escaped along the river Khyber to the north. The flanking brigades, meant to trap the garrison, had not yet got that far. Not all battle honours were to be so easily won.

Soon after crossing the frontier from Thal on 21 November, Roberts's column found its way blocked by Afghan forces under Karim Khan holding the Peiwar Kotal – the Peiwar Pass – leading to Ali Kheyl and beyond into Afghanistan. He had three British regiments including the 72nd (Seaforth) Highlanders. The Indian regiments were mostly Punjabis (Sikhs), but included the 5th Gurkhas and two mountain batteries, also components of the Frontier Force.

With winter approaching, it was imperative that the British forces move quickly. Roberts had decided that he would capture Peiwar Kotal before settling down for the winter. He had no idea exactly what Afghan troops opposed him in the Kurram valley, nor how good they were. He knew that there were forts at nearby Khapianga and at Kurram itself, but nothing about their garrisons.

The British forces reached the fort at Kurram on 25 November. Local people told the British-Indian force that the Afghans had withdrawn towards Peiwar Kotal (see Figure 5). On 28 November, Roberts went in pursuit to try to catch and trap the Afghans while they were attempting to evade the British. Two Indian battalions reached the Peiwar Kotal but found that the Afghans had dug in, supported by artillery and able to fire down into the pass from three sides, making attack a suicidal prospect. Roberts, a gunner himself, was wary. On the 29th he sent the 5th Gurkhas to cover the withdrawal of the Indian battalions.

Like Sam Browne at Ali Masjid, to the north, or Ochterlony in 1816, Roberts decided to send a turning column up around a parallel valley – the Spingawi valley, to the north-east – and then over the Spingawi Kotal, to the right of the Afghan position at Peiwar Kotal. But unlike Browne at Ali Masjid, he decided to send most of his troops as the turning column itself. To disguise the flank movement, the British and Indians established a gun line in the valley beneath the Kotal and made sure they appeared to be reconnoitring the Afghan positions. The holding force was in fact as small as possible, assisted by deception. Maximum noise was made to simulate the presence of the full force, and most of the supplies were left behind, while a strong fighting column moved round to the Afghans' left, led by Roberts himself. The 900-strong flanking force included the 5th Gurkhas and the 72nd Seaforth Highlanders, plus the 23rd and the 29th Bengal Native Infantry, the 2nd Punjab Infantry, and mountain artillery. At 2200 hours on 1 December, the flanking force began the 12-mile (18-kilometre) trek over treacherous terrain through darkness. They marched all night until they had come level with the right flank of the Afghans.[63]

At 0500 hours on 2 December, the artillery from the holding force began to bombard the Afghan positions, a further distraction

1. 'Free, fair and transparent.' Gurkha recruiting sign at Pokhara, 2010

2. The Terai: British Army Land Rover crosses the Batuwa River, just outside Damak, eastern Nepal

3. The 'Hills', eastern Nepal

4. The Gorkha Durbar – the fortress–palace–temple complex at Gorkha,
where Prithwi Narayan Shah was born and where he gathered his
Gorkha army for the conquest of the Kathmandu Valley

5. Prithwi Narayan Shah, 'the Great', unifier of Nepal (portrait in the National Museum of Nepal)

6. Prithwi Narayan Shah shows his nobles the Kathmandu valley (impression in the Gorkha Museum, Gorkha)

7. Major General Sir David Ochterlony GCB (1758–1825), father of the Gurkhas

8. Gurkha soldier, c.1830

9. General Frederick Young (1786–1864), one of the founders of the Gurkhas, as a 'colonel'. From his appearance, it is likely that this was drawn around 1833, when he was agent at Dehra Dun while a lieutenant colonel

10. Subedar Major (Major) Jase Rajput who won the Indian Order of Merit at Sobraon in 1846. He was one of the first Gurkhas to be photographed, in the 1850s. The IOM is the eight-pointed star worn on his left breast

11. An incident during the Siege of Delhi

12. The Queen's Truncheon, presented to 2nd Gurkha Rifles in 1863, in place of a colour

13. Survivors of Reid's Sirmoor Battalion after repelling twenty-six assaults by mutineers, 1857. They are standing in front of Hindoo Rao's House on the Badle-ki-Serai Ridge, north of Delhi, looking to the south

14. A British officer – seemingly called Alex – and Gurkhas at the time of the Mutiny, or just after; one of very few contemporary photographs. An Indian Army List for 1858 lists a Major A. Bagot as commandant of the New Nasiri (Rifle) Battalion, but it is not certain that 'Alex' is him

15. British officers of the 4th Gurkhas, Second Afghan War. Captain C. A. Mercer standing left, Lieutenant Colonel Rowcroft, CO, third from right

16. British officers of the 5th Gurkhas, Second Afghan War.
Lieutenant W. Yielding standing behind Lieutenant Colonel Fitzherbert, CO

17. Bayonet team of the 5th Gurkhas, Second Afghan War

18. Mercer and Mainwaring's tent, 4th Gurkhas, Jellalabad, March 1879, painted by a press correspondent

from the Gurkhas' and Highlanders' advance. At 0600 hours, the Gurkhas had managed to move to within 165 feet (50 metres) of the Afghans before being spotted. They and the Highlanders immediately launched a ferocious attack on the Afghans, who were surprised, and within an hour had captured two guns and won a Victoria Cross.

The VC went to Captain John Cook, serving with the 5th Gurkha Rifles, the Gurkhas' fourth. Again, Cook was not a regimental officer but a member of the Bengal Staff Corps, attached to the 5th. The citation from the *London Gazette* of 18 March 1879 says he gained the award

> For a single act of valour at the action of the Peiwar Kotal on the 2nd December, 1878, in having, during a very heavy fire, charged out of the entrenchments with such impetuosity that the enemy broke and fled, when, perceiving at the close of the melee, the danger of Major Galbraith, Assistant Adjutant-General, Kurum Column Field Force, who was in personal conflict with an Afghan soldier, Captain Cook distracted his attention to himself, and aiming a sword cut which the Douranee avoided, sprang upon him, and, grasping his throat, grappled with him. They both fell to the ground. The Douranee, a most powerful man, still endeavouring to use his rifle, seized Captain Cook's arm in his teeth, until the struggle was ended by the man being shot through the head.[64]

As the turning column came crashing in round the Afghan left, the frontal fixing force also joined in. The infantry started moving along the ridge just north of the pass, again towards the Kotal. The pine trees that the Gurkhas and Highlanders had used to get within 165 feet (50 metres) of the Afghan defenders also helped the defenders. Roberts's turning force also ran into difficulties for the same reasons. The British-Indian forces crawled along from tree stump to tree stump. At about midday, however, the two forces did manage to join up.

Roberts then decided to withdraw his turning column forces and conduct a second turning movement. The Afghans realised what was going on and tried to get clear of the British forces before the turning column cut them off. By 1430 hours it was clear that the British-Indian forces had won a major victory.[65]

The British-Indian forces moved on into Afghanistan, and Sher Ali died. Muhammad Yaqub Khan (1849–1923), his son, took over as emir of Afghanistan from February to October 1879. On 26 May 1879 the Treaty of Gandamak, negotiated by Cavagnari, and signed by Yaqub Khan as Sher Ali's successor, ended what turned out to be the first phase of the war. The Afghans accepted Cavagnari as British Resident in Kabul where he arrived on 24 July. However, the British presence did not last long. On 3 September the Afghans rebelled, killing a number of British in Kabul including Cavagnari. Early in the morning they stormed the Residency, killing the Resident early in the attack. His small bodyguard of twenty-five Guides cavalry troopers and fifty-two Guides infantrymen, who were in other flat-roofed buildings within the complex, faced a desperate choice. It was uncertain how the Afghans who had occupied Kabul would treat them, so the Guides chose to stand their ground and fight. By evening only a dozen Guides, commanded by Jemadar Jewand Singh – a Viceroy's Commissioned Officer – were still standing. After a hurried consultation, the group decided to attack. The action was over in a few minutes. After a defence lasting twelve hours, some 600 Afghans reportedly lay dead around them. But all the seventy-seven defenders were themselves certainly dead too.[66]

The British had largely withdrawn their forces, but the death of Cavagnari, plus the gallant stand of the Guides, aroused fury combined with determination, and they resolved to return. The command of the northern attack on Kabul was given to Roberts, the commander of the Kurram Valley Field Force in the first phase, and generally considered to have performed best of the three force commanders. Now he commanded the Kabul Field Force.

Roberts again reached Ali Kheyl near the head of the Kurram Pass on 6 September 1879. Yaqub Khan realised that the death of Cavagnari made his position as emir untenable, left Kabul and headed to see Roberts, enabling the British to claim, completely disingenuously and for a very short time, that the invasion was to support the emir's rule.

On 3 October 1879 the Kabul Field Force began the final 33-mile (50-kilometre) march to Kabul. On the evening of 5 October, Roberts reached Charasiab (Charasiah) village near the river Logar

and camped there with his two leading brigades. These were the 1st Infantry Brigade, commanded by Brigadier General Macpherson VC, and the 2nd Infantry Brigade, commanded by Brigadier General Baker, which included the old combination of the 72nd Highlanders and the 5th Gurkhas.[67] To the north of the camp the route to Kabul lay through the Sang i Nawishta defile along the river Logar. Roberts planned to remain in Charasiab while his draught animals returned to the logistic base at Safed Sang and brought up the supplies he had left there, along with the remaining troops.

Then, on 6 October, the Afghans appeared: not just tribesmen, but also elements of the regular Afghan Army, complete with artillery, 8,000 strong in all, stretching across a front of 3 miles (5 kilometres). Afghan tribesmen were also threatening Roberts's supply lines, so there was only one way of escape. Forward. The 5th Gurkhas were in the 1st Brigade, and advanced head-on against the numerically superior Afghan force. They drove them off one ridge, and the 2nd Brigade, which had been reconnoitring the river, attacked the Afghan left flank. Three days later Roberts was outside Kabul.[68]

It is a measure of Sir Frederick Roberts's regard for the 72nd Highlanders and the 5th Gurkhas that when he was ennobled, becoming Baron Roberts of Kandahar in 1892, he chose a representative of each of those two regiments to put on his coat of arms.[69] Roberts's personal regard for the Gurkhas, as well as their aptitude for the particular type of warfare on the North-West Frontier, was a major factor in the massive expansion of the Gurkhas before the First World War. Roberts (1832–1914) was one of the most successful commanders of the Victorian era and after he died of pneumonia while visiting Indian troops in France, he was one of only two non-members of the royal family to get a state funeral. The other was Winston Churchill. With a friend like that, the Gurkhas were on to a winner.[70]

Roberts marched into Kabul on 13 October and restored order, but Yaqub, suspected of collusion in the murder of Cavagnari, abdicated and was exiled. The British looked at two replacement candidates: Yaqub Khan's younger brother, Ayub Khan, the

Governor of Herat, and his nephew, Abdur Rahman Khan. Emir Abdur Rahman Khan, a British protégé, was recognised as emir in July 1880, but Ayub Khan offended by the British choice, started stirring up anti-British feeling and disrupted British plans for evacuating the country by moving out of his power base in Herat in early June with 10,000 followers. The British sent a force to intercept him, comprising one infantry and one cavalry brigade – 1,500 British and 1,200 Indian Army troops, together with Afghan levies, commanded by Brigadier General George Burrows.

From now on, the British held Kabul, although the rest of the country was unstable in the extreme. The 4th and 5th Gurkhas were stationed in Kabul for some of the time, but were constantly in action around Afghanistan. When they were not on operations, their commanders made every effort to keep them occupied and train their fighting skills at the same time. Thus, Plate 17 shows the bayonet team of the 5th Gurkhas. Military skills could easily be turned into competitive sports, and were.[71]

The British-Indian force met Ayub Khan at Maiwand, on 27 July 1880. Many of the Indian troops in British service, who were new and inadequately trained recruits, gave way under pressure of exhaustion, heat and enemy fire. The Afghan levies had already switched sides, unwilling to fight against their countrymen. Despite gallant resistance by the British 66th Regiment (not to be confused with the 66th Goorkah Light Infantry, which had been renamed as the 1st Goorkha Regiment in 1861) and inflicting 2,500 casualties on the enemy, the British lost. Some of the survivors made it to the nearby British-held fortress at Kandahar, where they were besieged.

No Gurkhas were in the force defeated at Maiwand, but they formed part of Roberts's Kandahar relief force. 'I wished,' Roberts explained later, 'that the force should be composed, as far as possible, of those who had served with me throughout the campaign.'[72] Roberts supported the 'martial races' idea and rated the services of the Gurkhas and Sikhs far higher than the other Indian troops. The Kandahar relief force was specially picked, from units whose individual strengths, weaknesses and stamina were known to Roberts and to each other. The force now had a great deal of experience and it travelled light. As usual in colonial campaigning, Roberts

deliberately mixed the units he had available, to ensure that the most committed soldiers were not concentrated all together. To further boost morale in what he hoped would be a quick campaign, Roberts promised the soldiers that they would be allowed back to India as soon as the fighting was over.

On the Kandahar relief march there were 9,700 troops, excluding officers, of whom 2,562 were British. Each of the three infantry brigades had four battalions of between 500 and 700 soldiers, and each brigade contained one British and one Gurkha battalion. The other battalions in the force were virtually all Sikh or Punjabi. Thus both British and Gurkha forces were distributed in order to stiffen each brigade with elements of the so-called 'martial races'.[73]

The 1st Brigade therefore included the 2nd Gurkha Rifles, under Lieutenant Colonel Battye. The 2nd Gurkhas had arrived at Ali Masjid in December 1878, about two weeks after its capture, before taking part in two expeditions into the Bazar valley. In March 1879 the regiment had moved on to Basawal and was in action at Deh Sarak. After the Treaty of Gandamak, the 2nd Gurkhas returned to India, but when hostilities were renewed in the autumn, the regiment moved back through the Khyber Pass to Daka, Jalalabad and Gandamak. After some fighting with Ghilzais, the regiment arrived at Sherpur at the end of December 1879. They saw action on the Chardeh plain in April 1880, before joining the Kandahar force and playing the most prominent role of the three Gurkha regiments at the Battle of Kandahar.

The 2nd Brigade included the 5th Gurkhas whom Roberts regarded so highly, commanded by Lieutenant Colonel A. Fitz-Hugh. The colonel can be seen, along with his British officers, in Plate 16. Having won a VC at Peiwar Kotal and wintered in the Kurram valley, the Gurkhas had formed part of the ill-fated Sir Pierre Louis Cavagnari's escort as far as the Shutagardan in July 1879. After his murder triggered the second campaign, the Gurkhas had been in the lead of Roberts's march on Kabul, fighting at Charasiab on the way. The 5th Gurkhas were then stationed at the fortress of Bala Hissar, outside Kabul, where they relieved any risk of boredom by engaging in bayonet competitions (Plate 17) and other relevant training.

But the internal security situation remained dangerous. Roberts initiated reprisals for the murder of Cavagnari and hanged the ringleaders. This upset the Afghans and they resorted to terrorist acts, one of which may have been the mysterious explosion at the emir's armoury at Bala Hissar on 16 October 1879. The fire spread, threatening further explosions, and the guards withdrew, apart from the 5th Gurkhas who waited until they received clear orders. In the explosion the 5th Gurkhas lost all their greatcoats, which were in store waiting for the Afghan winter. Their friends the 72nd Highlanders lent them theirs, so that they did not get too cold until replacements arrived.[74] During December they were involved in winter preparations at Sherpur, and fighting actions at Karez Mir, the Chardeh valley, Takht-i-Shah and the defence of the cantonment in Kabul. In May and June 1880 they operated in the Logar and Wardak valleys, before joining the march to Kandahar in early August.

The 3rd Brigade included the 4th Gurkhas, commanded by Lieutenant Colonel F. F. Rowcroft who can be seen, again with his fellow British officers, in Plate 15. Among them is Captain Mercer, who compiled a fine collection of photographs and sketches, which is now in the National Army Museum.[75] He was clearly media-aware, and before moving into Afghanistan he shared a tent with Major Mainwaring, also in the photograph, which a press reporter sketched (Plate 18). After missing serious action at Ali Masjid, the regiment advanced through the Khyber Pass and successively occupied Daka, Jalalabad and Gandamak. Part of the regiment was further involved in engagements at the Bokhar Pass in January 1879, and another company were part of the pursuit of Azmatallah Khan into the Lughman valley in March. The end of the first campaign saw them in Bukloh.

The start of the second campaign forced them to return to Gandamak in November. The 4th Gurkhas then marched to Jagdalak in December and were involved in fighting there before moving on to help relieve Sherpur. The regiment arrived on 24 December 1878 and camped at the Bala Hissar. In April they went with General Ross to cooperate with Stewart's force moving on from Ghazni, and were then involved in operations around the

Maidan district, including actions at Shekabad and Zaidabad. June saw the Gurkhas around Koh Daman and engaging with the enemy at Sofian. They marched from Kabul to Kandahar in August, were in action at Absabad on the day of the reconnaissance of Ayub Khan's forces, and were further engaged in the Battle of Kandahar the following day.[76]

On 23 August 1880 the force, which had been covering about 20 miles (30 kilometres) a day, reached Kalat-i-Ghilzai. The pace of the march in the August heat was starting to tell, with soldiers falling sick at the daily rate of 500. Messages from Kandahar suggested there was now no very immediate urgency as the garrison was still able to hold out for some time yet. With 90 miles (130 kilometres) to go, Roberts therefore allowed his force to rest at Kalat-i-Ghilzai. When he moved on, Roberts took the British garrison with him, since he no longer needed to hold the town. Then, on 27 August, word reached Roberts that Ayub Khan had abandoned his siege of Kandahar and withdrawn westwards, back towards Herat.

The Kabul Field Force reached Kandahar on 31 August 1880 and entered the city. Roberts's 10,000 troops had marched 300 miles (480 kilometres) in three weeks. Rather than let Ayub Khan escape back to Herat, Roberts resolved to attack him the same day. Ayub's camp lay to the west of Kandahar. The main assault would be made by the three brigades of the Kabul Field Force with Bombay troops providing a diversion. On the morning of 1 September the 3rd Brigade took station on the left, the 2nd in the centre and the 1st on the right, attacking north-west. Of the Gurkha battalions, one in each brigade, the 2nd Gurkhas saw most action. Following an artillery bombardment, the 92nd Highlanders and the 2nd Gurkhas, supported by the 23rd and 24th Bengal Native Infantry (BNI), who were Punjabis, attacked the village of Gundimullah Sahibdad. After two hours of close-quarter fighting the village was carried and the troops moved on to the next fortified village, Pir Paimal.

During the attack on Gundimullah, Lieutenant Menzies of the 92nd found himself attacked by numbers of Ayub Khan's troops. Knocked to the ground, Menzies was rescued first by Drummer Roddick from his own regiment and then by a Gurkha.[77] Major George White of the 92nd, who had already won the VC at

Charasiab, led the final attack on the Afghan fortified camp. He was followed by Sepoy Inderbir Lama of the 2nd Gurkhas, who marked an Afghan gun as taken for his regiment by hanging his green cap, with a black-and-red chequerboard pattern, over the muzzle. White later commanded the British force besieged in Ladysmith in the Boer War and became a field marshal.[78]

Following their return to India, the 2nd Gurkhas were eventually deployed to Dehra Dun. The 4th left Kandahar on 8 September, operating for a while in Panizai and later Marri country, eventually arriving at Bukloh on 9 December 1880. After the Battle of Kandahar, the 5th Gurkhas were involved in MacGregor's operations against the Marri in October before returning to Abbottabad on 7 December. Roberts's promise to get everyone home from Afghanistan as soon as possible had been fulfilled.

British and Indian regiments finally withdrew from Afghanistan in April 1881. By the Treaty of Gandamak a substantial swathe of Afghan territory became nominally part of the British domain in India, including much mountainous tribal territory. The unintended result was to intensify sixty-five years of almost incessant warfare between those tribes and the British and Indian armies.

After the Second Afghan War, with Roberts a celebrity and the Russian bear still threatening the North-West Frontier, the Indian High Command determined to *double the number of Gurkha troops* by raising second battalions for each of the five Gurkha regiments. The problem was where to find the Gurkhas. This required the cooperation of the Kathmandu Durbar – the Nepalese government – and they were still not cooperating. The more pressure the British Resident applied, the more the Nepalese, mindful of what had happened in Afghanistan, were wary. They empathised with Afghanistan, which shared their position as a mountainous country with tenuous independence from Britain on one side and another country on the other. For Afghanistan it was Russia; for Nepal, China. And both countries were, in themselves, unstable. 'It is not so much that the Durbar credits the British Government with a fixed determination to encroach,' wrote Brevet Major Elles of the Royal Artillery in his *Report on Nepal*, published in 1884, 'as that it believes in the

irresistible course of events, perhaps by some inadvertence of its own, an occasion for interference will arise.'[79] The Nepalese were, indeed, so suspicious of the British that when the newest, cutting-edge lamp-posts were installed in Gorakhpur, the Durbar sent agents to check that they were not some new form of (presumably long-range) gun.[80] The British, on the other hand, were aware that a number of ex-Indian Army Gurkhas were returning to Nepal, providing the Nepalese with a pool of very well-trained soldiers.

In 1884–5 the British managed to recruit just 657 Nepalese Gurkhas, far short – only 10 per cent – of what they would need to create five new battalions.[81] But then circumstances changed. Jang Bahadur had died in February 1877 and his successor, Ranodip Singh, was more inclined to accept British arms and ammunition in exchange for providing Gurkha recruits. He was then assassinated in November 1885, but Bir Shamsher, who took over, needed British support to stay in power. He therefore stopped opposing British recruitment of Gurkhas, although he would not allow recruiting teams into the hills.[82] Roberts became Commander-in-Chief India in 1885, a post he held until 1893, and quietly supported the recruitment of more Gurkhas. Many of the potential recruits who approached the British were of poor quality and trying to escape conscription into the Nepalese Army. With the growing popularity of the 'martial race' theory, recruiters were also becoming too particular about who they accepted. They wanted Magars and Gurungs only, and excluded Rais and Limbus (see Chapter 1). But, as Captain C. A. Mercer, the feisty 4th Gurkha (see Plate 15), realised, 'we may yet find that we have as good fighting material among the tribes of eastern Nepal, and should this prove to be the case, we shall have a large additional area upon which to draw for recruits.'[83]

In September 1886 second battalions had been successfully raised for the 1st, 2nd and 4th Gurkhas but not for the 3rd and the 5th. The adjutant general, still foreseeing problems with the Nepal Durbar, saw no prospect of raising two additional battalions and therefore ordered concentration on one battalion for the 5th Regiment. There had been a minor case of mutiny in the 3rd Gurkhas because of reductions in pay resulting from tightening up on the payment of food allowances.[84] The investigation,

unsurprisingly, found that the battalion was badly run and poorly disciplined. Four 'ringleaders' of the minor revolt were imprisoned and the commanding officer removed. The 3rd (the Kumaon) Goorkha Regiment used the opportunity to get rid of the 'Kumaon' element in its title and in May 1887 Roberts approved the change of name to the 3rd (Goorkha) Regiment. The 3rd Gurkhas also got their second battalion, although they were pretty much entirely Garhwalis, rather than Gurkhas. Roberts was a fan of the Garhwalis and, in an off-duty moment, told young Nigel Woodyatt, one of the 3rd's officers, that 'nearly every so-called Gurkha who had won the Indian Order of Merit had been a Garhwali or Kumaoni'. Woodyatt checked it out and found that, indeed, 90 per cent of them were.[85] The definition of what a 'Gurkha' was, exactly, remained blurred.

From 1890 the British also started encouraging their Indian Army Gurkhas to marry – or, at least, they removed the traditional military obstacles in the way. There were two reasons. The first was the massive incidence of venereal disease, which steady monogamous relationships under favourable circumstances tended to reduce. The second was the continued difficulty of recruiting 'true' Gurkhas from Nepal. Although the British were wary of the 'line boys' and 'line girls' produced by Gurkha soldiers' marriages in India, fearing that the 'wild' Gurkha stock would become too domesticated, they had little choice. By 1892, cases of venereal disease were well down.

In 1888 the new Viceroy, Lord Dufferin (1826–1902), a former Governor-General of Canada, made a further attempt to improve relations with Nepal.[86] Bir Shamsher responded positively, with a proclamation that, for the first time, officially permitted Gurkha recruitment into the Indian Army. In 1888, after seventy-three years, the recruitment of Gurkhas into the Indian Army was finally sanctioned by the Nepalese government.[87] It was a final and decisive breakthrough accomplished through quiet diplomacy and 'soft power' – backed by increasingly apparent latent force. It opened the way to massive recruitment to expand the Gurkha regiments for service with the Indian Army on the North-East and North-West Frontiers of the Raj, and in both world wars.

Its consequences resonated far beyond. The relations that had

taken so long to build bore fruit in the Nepalese reinforcements sent to help the British in India in the First World War, in the Third Afghan War in 1919 and in the Second World War. The tolerance of foreign recruiting now established was also crucial to the un-opposed recruitment of post-1947 Indian Army Gurkhas, and of British Army Gurkhas right up to 2001, when, after the Maoist in-surrection, British-Nepalese relations took a backward step again.

5

Gurkhas in the 'Great Game'

B Y 1890 THE 'Great Game' between Britain and Russia in the highlands of Asia had reached its peak. Colonel George Arnold Durand (1854–1923) was one of its most flamboyant exponents, along with Francis Younghusband (1863–1942), who later led the invasion of Tibet in 1904. The latter famously bumped into Bronislav Grombchevskiy (Bronisław Grąbczewski),[1] a Polish officer in the Imperial Russian Army, when they were both scouting around in the Hunza, valley in 1889. Grombchevskiy had entered Hunza, in 1888 with six Cossack escorts who were received cordially by the ruler of Hunza, Mir Safdar Ali Khan. Before his return to Russia, he also promised Mir Safdar Ali that he would come back with important proposals from St Petersburg, the capital of the Russian empire. This act of temerity by Captain Grombchevskiy and his host Mir Safdar Ali was considered by the political agent of Gilgit – Durand, appointed in 1889 – as an open threat to the British empire.

The British response was for Durand to send young Lieutenant Younghusband to track down Grombchevskiy and negotiate with the Mir of Hunza, while also locating a secret pass through the mountains that Hunza raiders had been using to attack the caravan route due north from Leh in Kashmir to Yarkand (Yarkant, now Shache) in the Xinjiang province of China (see Figure 5). Besides its part in the wider picture of the British-Russian 'Great Game', which proved so important for the evolution of the Gurkhas, Younghusband's exotic mission casts an important light on their role.

His escort, as revealed in Patrick French's outstanding biography, was to be seventeen Kashmiri sepoys, six Gurkha riflemen, along with two Balti guides and a Pathan surveyor from the 11th

Bengal Lancers.[2] Younghusband, now promoted to captain, set off from Leh on 8 August 1889. At the end of the month he met the Kirghiz chief, Turdi Kol, who had narrowly escaped being killed by the Hunza raiders, and was inclined to seek protection from the British. Younghusband arranged an impressive show with the Kashmir sepoys presenting arms and the Gurkhas firing three volleys. He left some sepoys to guard the Kirghiz chief but, significantly, took all the Gurkhas with him. On being told that the Hunza (called Kanjutis by the Kirghiz) would kill the first man to enter their territory, Younghusband said to the 'corporal' (naik) in charge of the Gurkhas that he should go first. 'The little man was quite delighted,' Younghusband recalled, in the slightly condescending way that many British used of their Gurkha colleagues, 'and beamed with satisfaction at the prospect. Little touches like this show up in a flash the various characteristics of different races.'[3] Younghusband was clearly another devotee of the 'martial races' theory.

He pressed on, taking Turdi Kol with him in disguise. The Mir of Hunza, it later emerged, was determined to have Turdi Kol's head, as he had killed one of his men in a slave raid the previous year. The party reached Darwaza, a stone fort on top of a precipitous cliff at the gateway to Hunza territory. Younghusband, claiming to have been sent directly by Queen Victoria, negotiated his way in. During the negotiations he pretended that Turdi Kol was a lowly herdsman called Sattiwali. He said he was going on to meet the Mir but would send his Kirghiz colleagues home. As he was leaving he later said that one of the Gurkhas carelessly called Turdi Kol by his real name, which could have been a fatal gaffe. 'Gurkhas are brave, cheery little men,' Younghusband commented later, 'but they have not the wits of a hog.'[4]

As we have seen, derogatory comments about Gurkhas are very rare. Furthermore, in this case we know Younghusband was not telling the truth. Patrick French has pinpointed a contradiction between this account, published in 1896, and Younghusband's earlier 1890 *Report on a Mission to the Northern Frontier of Kashmir in 1889*. In the latter he says it was he, not a Gurkha, who made the gaffe. He admits he said, 'Salaam, Turdi Kol,' instead of 'Salaam,

Sattiwali'. His interpreter covered the mistake by shouting at another Kirghiz called Sari Kol, which sounded similar.[5] So it was Younghusband who had 'not the wits of a hog' on this occasion. The way Younghusband picked on a Gurkha to excuse his own carelessness, and his comment about the Gurkhas being 'brave' and 'cheery', if sometimes lacking intellect, highlights the reputation they were acquiring at the time. If you want to blame someone for saying something indiscreet, choose someone known for not being too bright. Fortunately, Younghusband's duplicity is clear to see.

Younghusband, now escorted only by six Gurkhas, set out to meet the ruler of the raiders and challenge the mighty Russian empire far from the British realm of the sea. As he was approaching the Taghdumbash Pamir, the plain on the edge of the Kun Lun range, a horseman galloped up to him with a letter. It was an invitation to meet from Colonel Grombchevskiy of the Imperial Russian Army. Younghusband accepted, of course. The two men were obviously rather similar, oddballs in their own society and more at home in the wilds where they could play at being bigger men than they were at home. He found Grombchevskiy escorted by Cossacks, as he was by Gurkhas. The similarities are easy to see. They sat down to 'a very substantial repast of soup and stews, washed down with a plentiful supply of vodka'.[6]

They conversed in French, the common language of educated people of the time. Before long, it became obvious that Younghusband and Grombchevskiy had, indeed, been hitting the vodka. Grombchevskiy then explained that the Russians had 400,000 men to invade India, and the people there would also rise against the British. This assertion, when reported to New Delhi, probably added to 'Algy' Durand's concern. Younghusband was still sober enough to ask how the Russians planned to supply this vast army, to which Grombchevskiy responded that the Russians had never worried too much about that sort of thing. They would direct their forces, who would live off the land.[7]

The next morning the British captain and the Russian colonel paraded their small but select forces. Younghusband reported that the Russian was 'much taken with the appearance of the Gurkhas,

and with the precision and smartness of the few drill exercises they went through'.[8] The Gurkhas, however, did not think much of the Cossacks, saying they were slack and ill equipped. Grombchevskiy set his box camera – the latest technology – on delay to take a photograph of the extraordinary encounter, reproduced in French'soutstanding book.[9] The day after, the British force left. The Gurkhas – riflemen – presented arms and the Russian Cossacks saluted back with swords. Grombchevskiy was obviously impressed, and said that 'he hoped we might meet again, either in peace at St Petersburg or at war on the Indian frontier; in either case I [Grombchevskiy] might be sure of a warm welcome'.[10]

Younghusband headed on into Chinese territory, in search of the Mir of Hunza, having recommended that the Russian take an impossible route to his proposed destination, Ladakh. That journey very nearly resulted in Grombchevskiy's death. Meanwhile the devious Captain Younghusband and his six Gurkhas persuaded the Chinese that their mission was legitimate and eventually reached the Mir at the village of Gulmit in November. Dressed in his scarlet British uniform, with the Gurkhas in their smart rifle green, Younghusband endeavoured to make the right impression. The Mir of Hunza was known to be a dangerous operator, having poisoned his father and thrown two brothers over cliffs. Younghusband decided that a show of force might shake 'such a man as this', and had his Gurkhas go through small-arms drill very smartly before firing volleys at rocks on the other side of the valley. The Mir was impressed, and asked if they would fire at a man walking on the opposite side. Younghusband said the Gurkhas were such accurate shots that they would certainly hit the target. 'What does it matter if they do?' replied the Mir. 'He belongs to me.'[11] Younghusband nevertheless declined to have the man shot.

After returning to Calcutta, Younghusband was back in the Pamirs in 1891, playing the Great Game with the Russians. Gurkhas were again assigned to escort the British officers playing this cloak-and-dagger game, a role for which they were obviously well suited.[12]

While Captain Younghusband played cat and mouse with the Russians and set up a spy network, his superior, Colonel Algernon

Durand, the British agent at Gilgit, was equally anxious to ensure that the British and not the Russians dominated the area, known as the Dard states. The Hunza and Nagar chiefs who ruled the area had a long tradition of independence and resented the presence of the British. Durand began building up a force, which by 1891 totalled 1,000 troops, including the 5th Gurkhas – the 'Frontier Force'. But as the British began consolidating their hold on these proudly independent tribal areas, the tribes began to acquire modern rifles and ammunition. The British suspected Russian involvement, probably rightly.[13]

In late November 1891, Durand moved up a force of 1,000 men and two guns to Chalt to prevent any invasion force from Nagar and Hunza from coming down the gorge to reach the British stronghold at Gilgit. He built a new bridge across the Hunza gorge to replace the terrifying rope bridge illustrated in his book, and entered Nagar territory, overlooking the fortress of Nilt. Here the 'Dards' – shorthand for tribesmen from Hunza, Nagar and anyone else who joined them – were waiting for him, armed with perhaps 100 modern weapons. The British mountain guns could make no impression on the fortress's strong walls, however. Eventually, on 2 December 1891, the British blew up the main gate. Edward Knight, a war correspondent for *The Times* who also temporarily found himself in command of some native troops, modestly explained that 'I occupied the fort, one of the most gallant things recorded in Indian warfare.'[14] Durand, standing in full view of the enemy, was wounded by a home-made bullet of a garnet encased in lead, and was out of action for the remainder of the campaign. He later sent the bullet to his sister as a souvenir.

Although Knight thought he had captured the fort, the Indian Army and the *London Gazette* did not totally agree. According to the latter of 12 July 1892, Lieutenant Guy Hudleston Boisragon of the 5th Gurkha Rifles won the Victoria Cross

> For his conspicuous bravery in the assault and capture of the Nilt Fort (Hunza) on 2nd December, 1891.
>
> This Officer led the assault with dash and determination, and forced his way through difficult obstacles to the inner gate, when he returned for reinforcements, moving intrepidly to and fro under a

heavy cross fire, until he had collected sufficient men to relieve the hardly pressed storming party and drive the enemy from the fort.[15]

He was lucky to get it, and probably would not have done so, had it not been for a letter of 12 December from Durand to Lord Roberts:

> Colonel Mackenzie will have written to you I know to tell you of one fight on the second [of December]. So far as it went it was a brilliant little success, due entirely to the splendid pluck of Aylmer RE [Royal Engineers – for blowing up the gate], Boisragon and Babcock 1/5th Gurkhas. Bradshaw who is now in command has sent in a recommendation for the VC for all three in, I am afraid, a surprisingly feeble letter. I have added one and done my best. I do not suppose they will give three VCs for it but they might give two and in that case I think Aylmer and Boisragon are the most deserving and young Badcock might perhaps get a DSO [Distinguished Service Order].[16]

Durand got his way. Captain Fenton Aylmer, Royal Engineers, also got the VC.[17]

Unfortunately, as the attackers had rushed into the fort, the defenders rushed out and, by the next day, had re-formed behind a network of prepared defences on the far side of the precipitous ravine, which was in fact a much stronger position than the one they had occupied at Nilt. There was no way round the stone breastworks, on which the mountain guns made no impression. The advance halted for three long weeks, the invading force suffered from the cold and morale plummeted. It could have been a disaster but on 20 December a force of 100 British and Gurkhas, who had moved down into the Nilt ravine under cover of darkness, scaled the sheer precipice under the Dard fortifications and stormed the breastworks. The defenders fled, now at last providing an easy target for the British guns. Lieutenant John Manners-Smith, 5th Gurkha Rifles, won the VC, for 'conspicuous bravery' but also, as the citation makes clear, skilful fieldcraft and climbing skills:

> The position was, owing to the nature of the country, an extremely strong one, and had barred the advance of the force for seventeen days. It was eventually forced by a small party of 50 rifles, with

another of equal strength in support. The first of these parties was under the command of Lieutenant Smith, and it was entirely due to his splendid leading, and the coolness, combined with dash, he displayed while doing so, that a success was obtained. *For nearly four hours, on the face of a cliff which was almost precipitous, he steadily moved his handful of men from point to point, as the difficulties of the ground and showers of stones from above gave him an opportunity, and during the whole of this time he was in such a position as to be unable to defend himself from any attack the enemy might choose to make.*

He was the first man to reach the summit, within a few yards of one of the enemy's sungars [sangars], which was immediately rushed, Lieutenant Smith pistolling the first man [emphasis added].[18]

An advance party then crossed the Hunza river and occupied the Mir's palace in Baltit, bringing all resistance at an end. The Hunza and Nagar, who only a few weeks before had fought the British so bitterly, now welcomed them, and the Mir of Hunza fled to Sinkiang, China. The whole campaign was probably unnecessary as, in 1892 and again in 1895, the Hunza people voluntarily provided a force of irregulars to serve under British orders in Chitral. Hunza had been an independent principality for centuries. Mir Safdar Ali Khan, who ruled from 1886 to the British conquest in December 1891, was its last. The Tham (Chief/Mir) of Hunza escaped to China. His younger brother, Mir Muhammad Zazim Khan, was installed by the British and became maharajah (rajah) of Kashmir in September 1892. The British retained Hunza's status as a 'princely state' until 1947.

By the time the Pamir Boundary Commission had completed its work in 1893, and drawn the Durand Line in the sand (or rock), it had also become clear that an invasion force from the north or north-west could never even have reached Hunza, let alone Kashmir. Durand had been so obsessed with the Russian threat that on one occasion he arrested three Europeans found in the area, assuming they were Russians. They turned out to be well-known French explorers. In 1893 the 'Durand Line' established what is now the still-porous frontier between Pakistan (the former British Raj), and Afghanistan. The 'Wakhan Corridor', a narrow strip of Afghanistan that reaches as far as China, was inserted as a kind of

'peace wall', to keep the British and Russian empires apart. The Durand Line left some Pushtun (Pashtun) people on the British-Indian side, while the majority were in Afghanistan. The emir of Afghanistan saw the line as threatening the Pashtun ascendancy in his country, but ordinary Pashtuns ignored the Durand Line altogether. Consequently when fighting broke out in the 1890s, Pashtuns from the 'Afghan' side took part in the resistance and offered safe havens for those driven off by British troops.[19]

The Afghans' acquisition of modern rifles, thousands of which found their way into the hands of tribesmen in the areas nominally controlled by the British, created a serious problem for the Indian Army. The ability of the Pashtun marksmen to pick off the British officers rapidly became apparent. This suggests the Pashtun fighters knew that British assaults and the coordination of their fire were to a large extent dependent on the officers. Killing them would seriously disrupt the British ability to bring down effective fire and to manoeuvre. One officer noted that 'Hundreds of these [Pashtuns] . . . have been in our service, and they not only easily recognise our officers by their conspicuous head-dress and gallant leading, but they well know their value, and undoubtedly they select them for their attentions and pick them off.'[20] By the 1890s, a number of fighters had indeed served in the Indian Army and, their service over, they had returned to the hills. Here, the expertise in fire control and minor tactics, which they had learned – and, perhaps even more important, the weaknesses in command and control, including the key position of the British officers – were eagerly absorbed and assimilated by the hillmen.

From 1891 the 5th Gurkhas started employing carefully picked soldiers known as 'scouts'. These became the 'Gurkha Scouts' who established a fearsome reputation on the frontier. Two British officers, F. G. Lucas and the Hon. Charles Granville Bruce, seem to have got the idea after the Black Mountain campaign in 1891, and from conferring with Colonel Hammond of the Corps of Guides – the original Indian Army special forces.

The Scouts fulfilled three interrelated roles. The first was reconnaissance, 'feeling for the enemy with the greatest circumspection and the utmost celerity, the scouts themselves being invisible and

unheard'.[21] The second was sending patrols out at night to intercept enemy forces who had the irritating habit of firing on British camps out of the darkness. The British were reluctant to deploy large forces at these times, where without vision command and control would be next to impossible, but small groups of Gurkhas could do it. The third was the anti-sniper role. Enemy snipers, now sometimes armed with 'weapons of precision', a phrase first encountered in the 1890s, were a lethal threat to British officers, in particular, and thus to the very command and control that they ensured. As riflemen, with a special emphasis on long-range, accurate shooting, the Gurkhas were perfect to provide this special capability. General Sir William Lockhart, the commander of the Tirah Field Force, singled out the Scouts of the 3rd and 5th Gurkhas for praise because they were able to climb steep slopes, carry out ambushes at night and 'surpass the tribesmen in their own tactics'.[22]

Lucas and Bruce, both of whom subsequently became brigadier generals, then developed the idea. In the Waziristan expedition of 1894, '"Gurkha Scouts" were used freely as a separate body to act as "eyes" in front of British or other troops advancing, retiring or attacking.'[23] By 1897 there was a platoon or more of Scouts with each battalion. Neither battalion of the 5th Gurkhas was detailed for the 1897 Tirah expedition, but their expertise was clearly so valuable that Bruce went to see Sir William Lockhart, commanding the Tirah Field Force, to request the employment of the Scouts of both battalions of the 5th under Lieutenant Lucas as 'Gurkha Scouts' – for 'leading at night, covering advances and retirements, acting as flanking parties far out [sic], for reconnaissance duties, and to work against snipers'.[24] The general said that if Bruce wanted to command he had better take them himself, as Lucas was senior, but Bruce explained that he and Lucas were old mates and could work together. He also requested the 3rd Gurkhas' Scouts as well. Lockhart agreed, and he was given ninety Scouts of the two battalions of the 5th Gurkhas, plus thirty of the 3rd Gurkhas under Lieutenant A. B. Tillard.[25]

The Scouts were not subordinate to any brigade or division but were *army* troops – deployed at the discretion of the field force commander. They were 'specially trained to work on the steepest

hill-sides, and selected for their wiry physique, fleetness of foot and skill as marksmen'.[26] A group of what may be Gurkha Scouts photographed at the time is shown in Plate 19. The platoon – forty strong – appears to be from the 5th Gurkhas, as they are wearing shorts that were first introduced in that regiment in the Dargai campaign in 1897. The officer is unidentified, but his shoulder titles, when seen through a magnifying glass, also show him to be a 5th Gurkha. Bruce was a very big man, and later led the second and third British expeditions to Everest in 1922 and 1924. He was so imposing, and rather clumsy, that his men called him Bhalu – 'the bear'.[27] The more slightly built officer in the photograph is obviously not Bruce, and may be Lucas, who was made a brevet major for his outstanding role in the campaign. Tillard was mentioned in despatches twice for his work in the Tirah campaign, 'for his conspicuously able leading with the scouts', and also gained the DSO.[28] Subedar Major Chamu Sing, Subedar Harkbir Gurung and six other ranks were awarded the coveted Indian Order of Merit.

The tribesmen showed no mercy to prisoners or wounded, and the Gurkhas were not inclined to be too soft, either. Plate 20 shows a Pashtun tribesman, or Afghan, captured by the Gurkha Scouts. As a warning to other tribesmen or Afghans tempted to snipe at the Gurkha Scouts, his head was subsequently displayed as a form of deterrent on top of a cairn marking his former firing position, with a placard saying 'Gurkha Scouts trophy'. The evidence is another photograph not used here.[29] Unlike British or Gurkha prisoners and wounded who fell into the tribesmen's hands, however, the Gurkhas would have killed him first, quickly.

The role of the Gurkha Scouts in stalking snipers was highlighted by Callwell in his definitive book on *Small Wars*:

> The best method of dealing with the nuisance is to dispatch small parties out to stalk the snipers, or else to arrange ambushes for them . . . These stalking parties do not shoot, they trust to the cold steel. The Gurkha scouts in Tirah revelled in enterprises of this nature and were most successful in surprising the Afridi sportsmen. The European soldier is not at his best at this sort of work, but Gurkhas and Pathans are great adepts at hoisting nocturnal prowlers

with their own petard. Lord Roberts relates how in the Ambela campaign the tribesmen used to call out to the Gurkhas and Pathans when on outpost duty, 'We do not want you! Where are the Sikhs and Europeans; they are better sport.' When the adversary falls back on this essentially guerilla mode of fighting, he is very careful of himself; if he thinks he is being stalked he will probably sneak off, hoping for a better and safer opportunity.[30]

The 1897 Tirah campaign was in response to the largest and most serious outbreak of fighting on the North-West Frontier during the colonial era, the Pathan Uprising of 1897–8. The revolt was actually a series of local insurrections involving over 200,000 fighters, including Afghan volunteers, and it required over 59,000 regular troops to suppress it.[31] It was the largest deployment in India since the Indian Mutiny of 1857–8. Two powerful tribes, the Afridi and Orakzai, massed thousands of fighters and attacked the forward British outposts on the Samana ridge, in the Khyber Pass 33 miles (50 kilometres) to the north, and in Malakand (see Figure 5). On 23 August 1897, the Afridis attacked and captured the three British strongholds in the Khyber Pass of Landi Kotal, Ali Masjid and Fort Maude. The surviving British and Indian forces withdrew to Jamrud, leaving the Afridis with large quantities of valuable weapons and ammunition. The British assembled a large force – two divisions, each of two brigades. At this stage the force totalled 34,882 officers and men, and about 20,000 supporting personnel, commanded by Lockhart. The aim was to invade Tirah, along the route south of the Khyber Pass. Although the British tried to keep their plan secret, the Afridis got wind of it and on 18 October the British found their way potentially blocked at the Dargai heights, overlooking the route that the force would have to take.

The Gurkha Scouts from the 3rd and the 5th Gurkhas led Brigadier General Kempster's 3rd Brigade, part of 1st Division. General Westmacott, commanding the 4th Brigade, led a frontal advance as a diversion, while the 3rd Brigade would conduct a lengthy turning movement and come in on the right and rear of the enemy position. With 4th Brigade advancing on their front and with the risk of their withdrawal being cut off by 3rd Brigade's flanking movement, the Pashtun (Orakzai) tribesmen quit their

position in the afternoon. The two brigades met and occupied the Dargai heights on 18 October, having faced relatively little opposition. The heights and the path of the British advance are shown in the contemporary photographs at Plates 21 and 22.

The Pashtun tribesmen put down some fire but gave way as soon as the British began to close on them, and they were prompted to retreat as soon as they came under fire from the flanking force under General Kempster. On the approach march and in the frontal assault across a killing ground barely 660 feet (200 metres) wide, the British had lost nineteen killed and wounded. However, after this relatively easy gain, the divisional commander then made the fatal decision to withdraw: first, because there was no water supply there; second, because the forces in that advanced position might be vulnerable to a night attack; and third, because the high ground to the right in the photograph would also need to be occupied. The Gurkha Scouts pulled back, and the 5th Gurkha Scouts were redeployed. The sound of gunfire, meanwhile, had attracted large numbers of Pashtun reinforcements. During the nights of 18 and 19 October, they returned, occupied the ridge in strength and also constructed sangars. Again, former members of the Indian Army who had returned to the tribal areas probably advised on building – and siting – these formidable small fortifications, the equivalent of 'pillboxes'.

When the field force advanced again, at 0430 hours on 20 October, they faced a very different proposition. The Pashtuns had known that the British were coming and what route they would take. The ground had been carefully selected and it channelled the attackers into a specific killing area. The 3rd Gurkha Scouts, commanded by Tillard, who knew the ground from two days before, led the 2nd Gurkhas into the attack, backed up by the Dorsets and the Derbys, and then by the Gordon Highlanders.

The Gurkhas were the first to be sent up, but were pinned down. Then the Derbys and the Dorsets tried to rush the entrenchments, but their attack also faltered. Finally, the (1st) Gordon Highlanders and the 3rd Sikhs were ordered to advance. The Gordons came up the hill to the dead ground where remnants of the previous assault waves were crouching. By this time all the British and Indian regiments, and the 2nd Gurkhas, were mixed up. The regiments that

had been pinned down joined with the Gordons and the 3rd Sikhs, and, headed by the Gordons' pipers, they then charged across the strip of exposed ground. From here it was 'one eager spurt up the precipitous goat track to the summit and, if report speaks truly, Tillard got there first'.[32] As he was the leader of the Gurkha Scouts who formed the point of the attack, and as he knew where to go, it may be that he was. As noted already, Tillard was mentioned in despatches. Rifleman Hastbir Thapa, who was with him as he reached the top of the ridge, was immediately promoted to naik.[33]

In forty minutes the combined force of three British battalions, one Sikh battalion and one Gurkha battalion (the 2nd), with the 3rd Gurkha Scouts as the pathfinders, had captured the Dargai heights (see Plate 22), at a cost of three officers and thirty men killed and wounded on the way. The conduct of the pipers, in particular, has appealed to the popular imagination. Piper Findlater was shot through both feet and was therefore unable to stand. Instead, he sat up under a heavy fire and continued playing 'The Cock o' the North' to encourage his comrades – the Gordon Highlanders and the 2nd Gurkhas – while his kilt became red with blood.[34] The incident is the subject of a famous painting by Vereker Hamilton, now in the Gordon Highlanders Museum, Aberdeen. It shows the Gordons equipped with the newer Lee-Metford magazine rifles and the Gurkhas still using the old single-shot Martini-Henry.[35]

When the British and the Gurkhas took the heights, they found that many of the sangars had already been vacated. Almost all the British casualties occurred in one small area that could be swept by small-arms fire. Robert Johnson suggests that, after keeping the Gurkhas, Dorsets and Derbys under sustained fire for three and a half hours between 1130 and 1500 hours on 20 October, the Pashtuns were running out of ammunition. The Gordons' and Sikhs' final assault went in just after 1500 hours. It is quite conceivable that the weight of fire was beginning to slacken at this point. The British had suffered 200 casualties. While the tribesmen were forced to abandon the Dargai position, they had inflicted an awful lot of damage. In the three days of the Dargai operations, the 2nd Gurkhas had lost seventeen killed and forty-eight wounded, and the 3rd Gurkha Scouts seventeen killed and forty-six wounded. The

British-Indian force had been held up, while the Pashtuns had managed to escape with their own forces largely intact, and they had carried away most of their own dead and wounded. Pashtun losses were never calculated, but were probably 'trifling'.[36]

The attack on Dargai received a good deal of attention. The decision to withdraw on 18 October and to allow the enemy to install themselves in strength has been widely criticised. Piper Findlater's story naturally appealed to the public, and the attack merited a poem by none other than William McGonagall, probably the world's worst poet. McGonagall concentrates on the Gordons, and does not mention the Derbys, Dorsets, Gurkhas or Sikhs at all.[37] The Tirah campaign as a whole contained numerous lessons for the interaction of regular troops and special forces, exemplified by the Gurkha Scouts, that have resonance today.

After the capture of the heights, the 5th Gurkha Scouts found themselves constantly occupied in anti-sniper and pathfinding activity. Captain Badcock of the 5th Gurkhas was a victim of a sniper shot, losing his left arm to a large-calibre bullet, but this did not stop him excelling at tennis and squash.[38] On 29 October the 5th Gurkha Scouts, again acting as brigade reconnaissance, led British troops in the capture of the Sampagha Pass. The Pashtuns were trying to interpose themselves between the Yorkshire Regiment and the 3rd Sikhs, but the Scouts sneaked up on them. Havildar Kaman Sing Burathoki surprised a body of the tribesmen and killed a number of them, while the rest fled.[39] Bruce, made a brevet major for his role in the campaign and later a brigadier general, said that

> we [the 5th Scouts] were employed with every brigade in succession, that we covered the advance of most troops, seizing the heights in the dark, and were usually left to find our own way home . . . Work at night, other than seizing points before dawn, consisted in stalking small sniping parties, and was very exciting if not always very successful. Karbir, however, brought off a very brilliant coup in stalking a party of Afridis and accounting for some six of them.[40]

This was Subedar Karbir Budhathoki, an accomplished mountaineer, who later accompanied Bruce on other mountaineering expeditions.

Bruce also noted how the Gurkha Scouts, as snipers, could work with regular troops who still used volley fire, not always effectively. Firing a volley necessitated orders beforehand: 'In those days when volley firing was in vogue, the enemy frequently dodged the word of command most successfully. Many of our little local successes were gained by utilizing these words of command; men were specially posted to take advantage of the carelessness of the enemy *after* a volley had been fired [emphasis added].'[41]

In order to try to win over the locals, the British sometimes promoted the 'hearts and minds' strategy that has formed a basis for counter-insurgency ever since. With that in mind, General Lockhart ordered that there was to be no further looting. Bruce, like all British Gurkha officers, was utterly devoted his men, and, knowing what they had been doing, must have been worried to find himself in Lockhart's presence one day: 'One of the most nervous incidents during the retirement down the Bara valley was after an order had been issued that there was to be no further looting of villages. The scouts marched past Sir William Lockhart with every haversack stuffed with chickens. Luckily the Gurkha face can look more innocent than anything on earth!'[42]

Peace negotiations were under way when, on 29 January 1898, empire troops experienced a serious reverse at Spin Kamar, and there was a possibility that the tribesmen might take encouragement from this. Lockhart therefore started preparing for a spring campaign. According to the official history, he 'arranged to increase the efficiency of his forces by increasing the number of Gurkha Scouts'.[43] Their strength was brought up to a total of eight British officers, seven Gurkha officers, and 660 NCOs and men. They were also issued with the new Lee-Metford magazine rifle, which had first been issued to British troops from 1888, making them the first Gurkhas to get it.[44] The Lee-Metford was an interim design, with the new small 0.303-inch (7.69-mm) calibre and an eight-round magazine, but still designed for a black powder cartridge, instead of the new 'smokeless powder' – cordite, which was used in the newer Lee-Enfield, introduced in 1895.[45] To become familiar with the new weapon, the Gurkha Scouts were sent on a course at Peshawar. While there they won a great victory in a hill race against local

Pathans, which further reinforces their similarity with modern special forces, with their stress on physical fitness as well as skill at arms.

The Spin Kamar affair did not have the effect the British feared and the tribes began to comply with the terms imposed. The field force was dispersed and, with it, its 'army'-level pathfinders, the Gurkha Scouts. They came to an end as an organised body in April 1898 and rejoined their peacetime units.[46] It was an understandable but short-sighted decision. The Gurkha Scouts were, however, re-formed for the Third Afghan War in 1919 (see Chapter 7). John Morris, who was detached from the 3rd Gurkhas to join the re-formed Scouts in the latter, and who verifies that their role then was very similar, said: 'The Gurkha Scouts had proved so useful in this earlier campaign [1897] that it is difficult to understand why they were not retained as a permanent corps. Their success was due almost entirely to freedom from orthodox military methods and depended largely upon individual enterprise, neither of which appealed to the higher command.'[47]

The fact that Gurkhas, rather than any British soldiers (apart from their officers), were suited to this role calls many of the stereotypes about them into question. The Gurkhas had, according to sources at the time, been the basis for a force deployed at the discretion of the high command as a 'force-multiplier', specialising in long-range reconnaissance, anti-sniper work, night operations, equipped (at the end) with the latest weaponry, and with special stress on physical fitness, skill at arms, 'freedom from orthodox military methods' and 'individual enterprise'. By any criteria, these were special forces.

The frontier remained an extremely dangerous place until the present day. At the time of writing the very same border is still 'transparent', with Al-Qaeda having taken refuge on the Pakistani side, American drones – pilotless aircraft – attacking targets in Pakistan, and aid, arms, ammunition and fighters reaching the Afghan Taliban from their brothers-in-arms in Pakistan. The nature and demands of fighting such adversaries in such terrain would have been utterly familiar to British soldiers 100 years ago. Technology has helped a little, in making soldiers' lives a bit more comfortable and in making movement less physically arduous. It has also helped

reduce casualties. It would be inconceivable for British forces in Afghanistan today to sustain the same level of casualties as the Indian Army in its operations there and on the North-West Frontier.

Two more VCs were won by British Gurkha officers. Captain William George Walker of the 4th Gurkha Rifles, serving in Somaliland, was awarded his for an action on 22 April 1903. He was part of a rearguard that came under fire, and held off large numbers of attackers to save a wounded fellow officer.[48] Then, in December 1903, following an unsuccessful diplomatic mission, Younghusband, promoted to colonel to enhance his status as a negotiator, led a British expedition into Tibet. Younghusband's Expeditionary Force included elements of two of the newer Gurkha regiments: six companies of the 8th Gurkhas, and transport and Maxim gun detachments from the 1st Battalion 9th Gurkhas. The Tibetans were hopelessly outgunned by the Indian Army, but nevertheless put up stiff resistance, again often relying on forts on top of high crags.

One was Gyantse Jong, which looked impregnable and was considered the key to Tibet. There was an old Tibetan tradition that if it fell to an enemy, further resistance was useless.[49] The assault began on 5 July 1904. The British artillery, now equipped with high-explosive shells, blew a hole in the stone and also, following a tip-off from a local woman, managed to detonate the powder magazine. On 6 July, the storming company, heading for the resulting hole in the wall, was led by Lieutenant John Grant of the 8th Gurkha Rifles.[50] The circumstances were similar to those in which many other Gurkha VCs had been won. The attacking team had to advance up 'a bare, almost precipitous rock-face, with little or no cover available, and under a heavy fire from the curtain, flanking towers on both sides of the curtain, and other buildings higher up the Jong. Showers of rocks and stones were at the time being hurled down the hillside by the enemy from above. One man could only go up at a time, crawling on hands and knees, to the breach in the curtain.'[51] Grant, followed by Havildar Karbir Pun, also of the 8th Gurkha Rifles, at once attempted to scale it, but on reaching the top he was wounded and hurled back, as was Havildar Karbir Pun. The citation continued:

Regardless of their injuries they again attempted to scale the breach, and, covered by the fire of the men below, were successful in their object, the Havildar shooting one of the enemy on gaining the top. The successful issue of the assault was very greatly due to the splendid example shown by Lieutenant Grant and Havildar Karbir Pun. The latter has been recommended for the Indian Order of Merit.[52]

It seems manifestly unfair – and unnecessary – that the two men, doing exactly the same thing, got two different awards: the VC for Lieutenant Grant, the IOM (First Class) for Havildar Pun. Maybe this incident contributed to the change in policy that would follow soon after.

The doubling of the Gurkha strength in the 1880s, which owed much to the Gurkhas' performance in Afghanistan and Roberts's influence, was followed by the creation of new Gurkha regiments. This partly reflected the extension of Gurkha recruiting to the eastern parts of Nepal. The name changes can all be followed in the 'family tree' in Figure 4. After the 1st to the 5th Gurkhas all got a second battalion, other Indian Army regiments acquired the 'Gurkha' designation. In 1886, the 42nd (Assam) Regiment of (Light) Infantry, originally the Cuttack Legion from the east coast of India, became the 42nd Regiment Goorkha Light Infantry. In 1903, after further name changes, it became the 6th Gurkha Rifles. Similarly, also in 1886, the 43rd (Assam) Regiment of Bengal (Light) Infantry became the 43rd Regiment Goorkha Light Infantry. After more name changes, and the adoption of the spelling Gurkha in 1891, it became the 7th Gurkha Rifles in 1903 and then, confusingly, the 2nd Battalion 8th Gurkha Rifles in 1907. The 7th Gurkha Rifles were raised in 1902 as, rather confusingly, the 8th Gurkha Rifles, and, after a flirtation as 2nd Battalion 10th Gurkha Rifles from 1903, became the 7th Gurkha Rifles in 1907. The 9th Regiment of Bengal Infantry became the 9th (Gurkha Rifles) Regiment of Bengal Infantry in 1894 and the 9th Gurkha Rifles in 1901. The 10th Regiment (1st Burma Rifles) Madras Infantry acquired the Gurkha name in 1895, and became the 10th Gurkha Rifles in 1901. The 8th and 10th were both raised as North-East Frontier protection forces and the 6th had strong links

with that frontier as well, having fought there virtually continuously from 1824 to the Burma War of 1885–9.[53]

As the twentieth century dawned, the British Raj in India looked unbeatable, although the seeds of Indian and Pakistani independence were already sprouting. Queen Victoria had been proclaimed Queen-Empress of India in 1877. In 1911, the new King- and Queen-Empress of India, Victoria's heirs-but-one, King George V and Queen Mary, decided to hold what was effectively an Indian coronation at Delhi. A Durbar had been held in 1903, to celebrate the coronation of Edward VII, but the king himself had not attended, although 100 Indian princes did.[54] The Delhi Durbar and Coronation was an even more extravagant affair, to which all the Indian rulers were invited. It was recorded on colour film, the edited version of which lasted more than two hours, using the revolutionary Kinemacolor process invented by Charles Urban. The Durbar, held in December 1911, was filmed in black and white by several film companies but when Urban's colour film opened at the Scala theatre on 2 February 1912, complete with a set looking like the Taj Mahal and an orchestra, it was a massive success.[55]

The Delhi Durbar was an appropriate occasion to announce that certain British awards would now be available to Indians and other non-British people. Among them was the Victoria Cross. How many of the winners of the Indian Order of Merit from 1837 to 1911 would have got the Victoria Cross if it had been available instead is impossible to determine, but there would have been many. Havildar Pun would undoubtedly have been one. Now the supreme award for valour was available to the Indian Army, including Gurkhas. Many VCs had been awarded on the frontiers. But soon the Indian Army and the Gurkhas would face new enemies, more scientifically organised and armed, in circumstances few had imagined.

6

The Great War for Civilisation, 1914–19[1]

IN 1903, FIELD Marshal Lord Kitchener of Khartoum became commander-in-chief of the 'Army *of* India', which comprised the Indian Army, made up of locally recruited troops with British officers, and the British Army *in* India, which consisted of British units stationed there. He had been due to take over in 1900 after his victory over the Mahdist regime in the Sudan but was sent to South Africa instead, to take over from Roberts, also a former Commander-in-Chief India. Like Roberts, Kitchener was a great believer in 'martial races', to the exclusion of other native troops, so his lengthy tenure from 1903 to 1909 did the Gurkhas no harm.

Soon after arriving, Kitchener clashed with the new Viceroy, Lord Curzon, who ruled India from 1899 to 1905. Both men had supreme egos, and the clash was inevitable. The commander-in-chief had been responsible for fighting the numerous wars in the subcontinent, while a Military Member of Council advised the Viceroy on matters affecting supply and administration. The system worked when communications were poor, but now, in an age of telephones and wireless, Kitchener railed against the system of 'dual control', regarding the Member of Council – a mere major general, in the pocket of the Viceroy – as a nuisance. Curzon saw that if Kitchener had his way, he would become military dictator of the British Raj. Eventually, in August 1905, Curzon resigned although he stayed on until November to host a visit by the Prince and Princess of Wales, later George V and Queen Mary.[2]

The presidency armies had been abolished with effect from 1 April 1895 by an order of 1894[3] unifying the three of them into a single Indian Army. Kitchener pursued the aim of cementing the separate armies into a single force, and abolished the designations of

Madras, Bombay and Bengal, which persisted in regimental titles even after the presidencies had gone. He also established four main principles. The main role of the Army of India was to defend the North-West Frontier, guarding against a Russian invasion through Afghanistan; the army's organisation, training and deployment should be the same in peace as in war; internal security was a secondary role for the army (albeit an important one); and all troops should get experience of fighting on the North-West Frontier.[4]

The Russian 'threat' diminished after the British-Russian Agreement of 1907, which followed the Entente with France in 1904 and thus created the alliance (though not formally designated as such) that fought the First World War. Kitchener complained that the army was scattered 'all higgledy-piggledy over the country without any system or reason whatever'.[5] The new structure of the Army of India was established at nine divisions. These, together with three independent infantry brigades, would serve in India. The Indian Army also supplied a division in Burma and a brigade in Aden. Divisions were based in fixed geographical areas but units – battalions – within those divisions were rotated every several years so that everyone got experience of the North-West Frontier.

Kitchener pressed for the introduction of the latest weapons including the excellent 0.303-inch (7.69-mm) magazine rifle and a new mountain gun. Training was improved, including the establishment of a Staff College at Deolali in 1905 to train staff officers, most of whom would have been British, with special reference to local Indian conditions. In 1907 it moved to Quetta, and the college there still continues to train Pakistani Army officers for the higher ranks.[6] The fact that Kitchener was preparing the fight the Russians, if necessary, meant that in 1914 the Indian Army was to some extent prepared for a European war, though not as well as the British divisions it would have to reinforce. With long hindsight, however, Kitchener's reforms made the Indian Army much better able to cope with an unexpected role than it would otherwise have been.

In 1914 the Indian Army was the world's largest volunteer army with a total strength of 240,000 men in two armies, the Northern and the Southern. These two armies contained 39 cavalry regiments, 138 infantry battalions (including 20 Gurkha battalions), the

Corps of Guides – which, as noted, was essentially a joint cavalry–infantry special forces reconnaissance unit – and three engineer regiments and twelve mountain artillery batteries.

By this time there were ten Gurkha regiments, each with two battalions, numbering in all about 20,000 men – *8 per cent of the entire Indian Army*. As can be seen from Figure 4, some of the more recent regiments with higher numbers in their names traced their origins way back, but became 'Gurkha' regiments only in 1886 (the 6th and the 8th), in 1894 (the 9th) and in 1895 (the 10th), while the 7th was founded only in 1902. This was a result of increased recruitment of so-called 'martial races', their concentration in particular units, and the more cooperative attitude of the Nepalese government.

In 1901, Maharajah Chandra Shamsher Jang Bahadur Rana (1863–1929), known as Chandra, took over from his brother in a bloodless coup. He was happy to support the British in their aim of expanding the Gurkhas, in exchange for British arms, ammunition and training, and also perhaps to make the troops so trained and equipped available to the British. He made a pointedly timely visit to Britain in 1908. The policy paid dividends for Britain and Nepal. Nepal retained a large army, for internal political reasons, but had no one to fight. In 1915, the British, desperately short of troops for the Middle East and Europe, reluctantly accepted Nepal's offer of 6,000 men in six battalions, followed by another four battalions nine months later, bringing the Nepalese contingent up to 10,000 men. They were trained in India at Dehra Dun and Abbotabad, and then deployed on the North-West Frontier.[7] In 1919, nearly 16,000 Nepalese soldiers fought with the British on the North-West Frontier and in the Third Afghan War.[8]

The forces sent to India between 1915 and 1919 included some of the elite senior Nepali Gurkha battalions from the mountain village of Gorkha itself. One was the Shree Kali Buksh Battalion, credited with 'defeating' the East India Company at Sindhuli in 1767, which was sent to Abbotabad. Another was the Shree Bada Bahadur Battalion, which also served at Sindhuli and was sent to Dehra Dun. The Shree Sabuj Battalion, another holder of the Sindhuli battle honour, was sent to the North-West Frontier 'to maintain peace', and also put in readiness to be deployed against

Afghanistan in 1919, although it was apparently not used. The Shree Purano Gorakh Battalion, first used at Sindhuli, also served on the North-West Frontier between 1915 and 1918.[9] These battalions would be made available to help the British in the Second World War.

Britain entered the First World War on 4 August 1914. Its politicians and senior commanders initially expected to fight an overwhelmingly maritime war, with a small but highly professional British Expeditionary Force of six divisions, reinforcing the left flank of the mighty French Army against the German attack that hooked in through Belgium in accordance with the Schlieffen Plan. By November the manoeuvre period of the land war was largely over in the west, although operations on the Eastern Front remained far more mobile. In the West, the two sides had become locked in an increasingly trench-bound stalemate that would last until 1918. In autumn 1914, two Indian Army divisions, the 3rd Lahore and the 7th Meerut, which included several Gurkha battalions, were sent to Egypt to replace British troops sent to France, but they, too, quickly followed those that they replaced.

Lieutenant Hamish Reid, a descendant of the formidable Charles Reid who had defended Hindoo Rao's house overlooking Delhi in 1857, negotiated a transfer from the 10th Gurkha Rifles, who were in Burma, in order to go to France. He transferred to the 2nd Battalion 2nd Gurkha Rifles (henceforward the 2/2nd), the Sirmoor Rifles, his illustrious ancestor's regiment. He noted that 'a very large proportion of the Indian Expeditionary Force is Gurkhas'.[10] There were four Gurkha battalions in the Meerut Division (the 1/9th, 2/2nd, 2/3rd and 2/8th), and two in the Lahore Division (the 1/1st and 1/4th). That made the Gurkhas the biggest identifiable component in the Indian Corps, as these two divisions were known, accounting for a full quarter of the corps' strength.[11] Reid recorded the way that his Gurkhas 'take an extraordinary interest in the various places and peoples they have seen on the way and in the Torpedo Boats and French Battleships we saw in Port Said, but more, I honestly think, in the flying fish and porpoises than all the rest put together!'[12]

The culture shock when the Gurkhas arrived in Marseilles (see Figure 7) was massive. The French welcomed the small, stocky soldiers from the Himalayas as conquering heroes, while the Gurkhas, newly issued with woollen vests and pants to counter the European December cold, put them on *over* their uniforms. It must be assumed that this was an error, rather than a deliberate attempt to promote a 'Superman' image for the Gurkhas.

On their arrival in northern France, the locals were not initially welcoming, but soon changed their minds. One French farmer was difficult about letting the Gurkhas help themselves to straw for their palliasses – the straw-filled mattresses that used to be issued to soldiers in the field. The Gurkhas found some eggs and, very correctly and politely, asked the farmer if they might have them. The farmer later a told a British officer, 'Your men must be good men; if they had been French *poilus* they would not only have kept my eggs, but would be cooking and eating my chickens now.'[13]

The Gurkhas' adaptability surprised even their own officers.

> 'Johnny Gurk'; clad in serge tunic and balaclava cap, sitting in a French peasant's kitchen with his feet on the stove, smoking a pipe and drinking beer or coffee, and discussing life and the war situation in halting and broken French! The Gurkha was deservedly popular with his temporary hostesses for his cheerful spirits, his good discipline and cleanly habits, and for his rather extravagant ideas which appealed very much to the French madame.[14]

Exactly what the regimental historian of the 9th Gurkhas meant by the last sentence is unclear. It may be that the Gurkhas rated their chances with the local women, but they were punctiliously behaved and, if so, their aspirations in that direction were usually unsuccessful.

At the end of October the 2nd Gurkhas reached Neuve Chapelle, shown in the main Figure 7 map, where, in Hamish Reid's words, 'the HELL (no apology, please) of a battle' was going on. It was one of the big battles of 1915. It was also Reid's last letter to his parents, ending with a refererence to Kismet – fate. A note scribbled on the envelope in the Oriental and India Office Collection (now the Asia-Pacific and African Collection), found by Tony Gould, says 'killed 2 November'.[15]

The Gurkhas, like other Indian Army units and formations, were more lightly equipped than their British equivalents, with two machine-guns per battalion instead of the usual four, thirty field guns per division as opposed to seventy-six, and no trench mortars or – most critically – hand grenades.[16] The 2nd Battalion, 2nd Gurkhas were, in the words of Sir James Willcocks who commanded the Indian Corps in France, 'dumped' on an exposed salient near Neuve Chapelle on the night of 29–30 October.[17] The Gurkhas were exposed to a storm of well-directed German fire and driven back, but the commanding officer, Lieutenant Colonel C. E. Norie, led an attack with the Royal Scots Fusiliers, which recaptured the trenches they had lost. Sir John French mentioned him in despatches, while Willcocks acknowledged the 'discipline and tenacity of the Gurkhas of Nepal'. Reid fell, 'after hard fighting . . . whilst coolly conducting a relieving party of the Connaught Rangers to the Gurkha trenches'.[18]

However, reading between the lines, it looks as if the 2/2nd Gurkhas gave way. Norie said that his battalion had been virtually annihilated, but officers from other regiments clearly believed they had fled. There was no disgrace in that: many British soldiers reacted to the infernal mechanics of 'machine-age' warfare in the same way. On 30 October the 2nd Battalion of 8th Gurkhas had also given way. But there were no 'martial races' now. Everyone had the same reaction. Captain Grimshaw, commanding D Squadron of the Poona Horse, who were fighting as infantry, recalled

> Little Gurkhas slopping through the freezing mud barefooted. Tommies [British soldiers] with no caps on and plastered with mud and blood from head to foot, Sikhs with their hair all down and looking more wild and weird than I have ever seen them [Sikhs do not cut their hair], . . . misery depicted in their faces. I stopped some Gurkhas and asked why they walked in bare feet. Those that replied said 'Sahib, our feet hurt terribly, but in boots they hurt worse.[19]

The Gurkhas had arrived unacclimatised and often without cold-weather clothing. Trench foot – prolonged immersion in freezing water – proved a terrible problem.

During the First World War, 306 British and Commonwealth

soldiers were shot for cowardice and desertion, and Gurkhas were not immune. Lieutenant Bagot-Chester of the 2nd Battalion 3rd Gurkhas recorded in his diary on 31 December 1914 that the previous day he had had 'the unpleasant duty of being present at the corporal punishment of a [Gurkha] Rifleman with thirty lashes for sleeping at his post when a sentry'.[20] And then, on 5 February 1915, came a story that everyone would have wanted to suppress, but the import of which is clear. 'Never do I want to command a firing party [firing squad] again. They died bravely and it will take a long time to forget this morning's work.' They must have been his own men. Gurkhas, court-martialled, probably for desertion.[21]

The circumstances of the trench warfare on the Western Front were unspeakable and the Indian Army troops, whether Gurkhas or not, acquitted themselves as bravely as anyone else. On 31 October 1914, the 57th Wilde's Rifles was attacked by nine German battalions, who got round to a flank. A platoon commanded by Indian Army jemadar Kapur Singh was wiped out. The jemadar killed himself with his last round, rather than be captured by the Germans. The lessons of the North-West Frontier were holding good. On the same day, at Hollebeke in Belgium, an infantryman — Sepoy (later Subedar) Khudadad Khan of the 1st Battalion, 129th Duke of Connaught's Own Baluchis, who were part of the same Lahore Division – became the first Indian soldier to win a Victoria Cross. One of the battalion's two machine-guns was knocked out by a shell, killing the machine-gun officer, and five of the six-man crew of the remaining gun were also killed. Khudadad Khan fired the machine-gun himself until knocked unconscious. He was left for dead but revived and crawled back to his own lines. The Cross was presented to him on the battlefield itself.[22]

In March 1915 the Indian Corps was tasked to retake Neuve Chapelle, from which it had been driven the previous autumn, and to move on further, to capture the Aubers ridge, which overlooked the British positions. It was the first major British offensive since the Battle of Mons in September 1914, so the involvement of the Meerut Division of the Indian Corps was something of an honour. After a bombardment by 420 British guns – the biggest of the war so far – the Garhwal Brigade, which included the 2nd Battalion 3rd

The Gurkhas in the First World War

Southern boundary of Ottoman Empire (approximate)

Grand Strategic rail route linking Central Powers

Major front lines 1915 (approximate)

FIGURE 7

Gallipoli

N

Suvla Bay

Salt Lake

1/6th 8 August

Aegean Sea

Ari Burnu

Z Beach

Chunuk Hill Q
(Chanak) Bair

Koja Chemen
Tepe (Hill 971)

Sari Bair Range

Boghali

Lone
Pine

Maidos

Nagara
Point

The Narrows

Chanak
Kale

Gully Spur or Ridge
(Gurkha Bluff)

Gully Ravine
(Bruce's Ravine)

Y Beach

1/6th 12–13
April

X Beach

W Beach

V Beach   S Beach

Cape Hellas

Kum
Kale

Krithia

Achi Baba

Sari Siglar
Bay

furthest line
reached by
British fleet
18 March 1915

Dardanelles

R. Menderes

0   5   10 kms

- - - - approximate front line end April 1915
⟶ initial British and ANZAC landings 25 April

RUSSIA

CAUCASUS FRONT

Akhaltsike

ARMENIA

BLACK SEA

Erzurum

OTTOMAN EMPIRE

PERSIA

Arbil

Mawsil (Mosul)

Ash Sharqat
(Sharqat)

Kirkuk

MESOPOTAMIA

Tigris

Baghdad

Euphrates

Ramadi

Kut

Al Amarah

As Samawah

An Nasiriyah

Basra

Abadan

PERSIAN GULF

POLI

CYPRUS

Haifa

Tel Aviv

PALESTINE

Jerusalem

Damascus

Amman

Dead Sea

Maan

Alexandria

Port Said

Cairo

Suez

Akaba
(Aqaba)

Tabuk

Hejaz Railway

Mada'in Salih

Medina

Yanbu

RED SEA

Jeddah

Mecca

0   100   200   300   400   500 miles

0   200   400   600   800 kilometres

Gurkhas, would attack, followed by the 2nd Battalion 2nd Gurkhas and the 1st Battalion 9th Gurkhas. The British and Indian forces captured the German trenches and the village of Neuve Chapelle. Rifleman Gane Gurung of the 2nd Battalion 3rd Gurkhas moved into one house alone and, after a tense pause, to everyone's surprise, emerged with eight German prisoners. The event was witnessed by the British 2nd Rifle Brigade, which was the spearhead of the 8th Division, to the Meerut Division's right, which had closed on the same objective. Seeing the diminutive Gurkha herding eight large Germans, the 2nd Rifles burst into spontaneous and prolonged applause for their fellow rifleman.[23] As often happened, the British advance ran out of steam before the Aubers ridge could be captured. But the attack by the Indian Corps, involving three Gurkha battalions, was a limited success, in a set-piece battle designed to counter French criticism of British inactivity.

Later in 1915, the British and Indian forces were involved in the Battle of Loos, one of the most important British offensives mounted on the Western Front in 1915. It was the first time the British used poison gas during the war, referred to as 'accessory' in all the preliminary orders, to preserve secrecy, and it was also the first large-scale use of new 'Kitchener Army' units comprising volunteers from civilian life. Kitchener had decided to raise a large-scale army on continental lines, although they were still all volunteers, and the use of Indian Army forces had, to some extent, been a stop-gap until the new army was ready. The British IX Corps consisted of two 'New Army' divisions, the 21st and the 24th. The battle was the British component of the Third Battle of Artois, a combined British and French offensive. Immediately prior to the troops attacking the German lines, at around 0550 hours on 25 September the British released 140 tons of chlorine gas, but in some places the gas was blown back onto British trenches, causing about 2,000 casualties, although only seven men died.[24] The use of gas was another innovation for which the Gurkhas were ill prepared, but probably not much more so than anyone else. The Meerut Division of the Indian Corps did not participate in the main attack, but was used on 25 September in a subsidiary attack.

The British broke through the forward German trenches and

captured the town of Loos. However, there were the usual supply and communications problems, and delays bringing up reserves, so the breakthrough could not be exploited. The British artillery failed to cut the German wire as had been hoped, and losses were heavy. The German defence recovered, and the Germans repelled further attempts to continue the advance.

South of Mauquissart, the 2nd Battalion 3rd Gurkha Rifles were involved in the supporting attack. Rifleman Kulbir Thapa was wounded on the first day, 25 September 1915. After crawling through gaps in the wire and rushing the Germans, he was suddenly alone, and wounded. However, according to the *London Gazette*,

> he found a badly wounded soldier of the 2nd Leicestershire Regiment behind the first line German trench, and, though urged by the British soldier to save himself, he remained with him all day and night. In the early morning of 26th September, in misty weather, he brought him out through the German wire, and, leaving him in a place of comparative safety, returned and brought in two wounded Gurkhas one after the other. He then went back in broad daylight for the British soldier and brought him in also, carrying him most of the way and being at most points under [the] enemy's fire.[25]

Rifleman, later Naik, Kulbir Thapa was the first non-British Gurkha soldier to win the VC. But individual acts of gallantry made little impact on the massed, mechanical destruction that characterised the war on the Western Front. The fighting around Loos subsided on 28 September with the British having retreated to their starting positions, and the Germans subsequently counter-attacked. Ironically, Bagot-Chester, who had had to witness his men being flogged and shot, was Kulbir Thapa's company commander. He was wounded the day before Thapa got his VC, and 86 of the 120 men in his company were either killed or wounded, Thapa among the latter.

By this time Kitchener's new armies were coming into the fray and the Indian Corps was severely depleted. A big problem for the Gurkhas, and for the Indian Army in general, was that British officers who were trained to make decisions and to liaise with British and French units were few and far between. Although there were more British officers than the three in the original Gurkha battalions

100 years before, there were still only twelve or thirteen in a Gurkha battalion: the CO, the second-in-command, sometimes an adjutant, the quartermaster, the machine-gun officer and then two officers – the company commander and a 'company officer', who was the second-in-command – for each of four companies. It was quite possible that all the British officers might be wiped out in a single attack, leaving command to the Gurkha Viceroy's Commissioned Officers who were not trained in staff work nor expected to show much initiative. The British officers had also spent years learning their men's language and gaining their trust and confidence, a relationship that was impossible to replicate.

Major Allanson, whom we will meet commanding the 1st Battalion 6th Gurkhas at Gallipoli, was explicit about the vulnerability of Indian units to losing their British officers:

> Everyone is unanimous that the Indian Brigade has done well, but that it depreciates 10 per cent [sic] for the loss of each British officer, and 20 per cent when the CO [British commanding officer] goes! After our experience in France, this brigade should have gone up with 30 officers, the same as a British regiment. It would have been interesting to see the result, and an example for all time as to the difference in value. The Indian Brigade started with two Punjab regiments, the 1/6th Gurkhas and the 14th Sikhs. After the first action the first two regiments were relieved by the 1/5th and the 2/10th Gurkhas . . . I know how extremely highly trained the 1/5th and 1/6th Gurkhas are, and they have had the advantage of six months in Egypt. No troops could be at a higher level of peace training, but nothing can compete with the disastrous effect of the loss of British officers.[26]

The fact that the Indian Army performed better in the Second World War may be due to a number of related factors. There were comparatively fewer British officer casualties (and casualties generally); steps had been taken to train VCOs better, while burgeoning nationalism and Indianisation had produced some Indians who were commissioned on a par with British officers. The latter were King's Commissioned Indian Officers – KCIOs. All this led to a general increase in the troops' self-esteem and ability to exercise initiative.[27]

Withdrawing the Indian troops from France had been on the cards since early 1915. They had been sent there in 1914 only because of a shortage of trained British troops. They filled a gap, because the new Kitchener armies were not ready, and would not be deployed until Loos in late September 1915. The Indian Corps mail censor, E. H. Howell, warned in January 1915 that the troops were close to breaking point and that the 'door of hope' should be opened. On the other hand, he had reservations about withdrawing the Indian Army soldiers from France as they were clearly anxious to prove that they were as good as the British – and the Germans.[28] Had they had better equipment, more appropriate training and more officers trained to the same standard as British officers, they would have done so. But other theatres now offered the Gurkhas scope to use their particular talents to the full.

Turkey entered the war at the end of October 1914 after failing to respond to a British ultimatum issued on the 30th. By 1 November the two countries were at war, with Russia joining in against Turkey on 2 November.[29] As part of a grand strategic encirclement of the Austro-German Alliance, which would also open up links with Russia – now transformed from an ominous threat to a glorious ally – Churchill devised the Dardanelles campaign.

Initially, the British hoped to break through the Dardanelles with naval forces alone but a British naval attack was repulsed on 18 March. In order to break through the Dardanelles, threaten Istanbul, and have a secure ice-free route to Russia, it was necessary to seize the Gallipoli (Gelibolu) peninsula with land forces. This is shown in Figure 7. The peninsula lies in Europe, to the west of the Dardanelles, which, at their narrowest point – conveniently known as 'The Narrows' – are only a mile (1500 metres) wide. However, the channel is extremely deep and the current very strong.

On 12 March 1915, General Sir Ian Hamilton was summoned to see Kitchener, an old comrade of his from the Boer War, and told he was to have command of the military force being sent to support the fleet now at the Dardanelles. It would consist of the Australian and New Zealand Army Corps (ANZAC), and the British 29th Division. Hamilton wrote to Kitchener on 25 March 1915, saying he was 'very anxious, if possible, to get a Brigade of Gurkhas, so as

to complete the New Zealand divisional organization with a type of man who will, I am sure, be most valuable on the Gallipoli Peninsula. The scrubby hillsides on the southwest face of the plateau are just the sort of terrain where these fellows are at their brilliant best.'[30]

It was a case of horses for courses. Each Gurkha 'might be worth his full weight in gold at Gallipoli', Hamilton continued. On 1 May 1915, the 1st Battalion 6th Gurkhas arrived from Egypt, part of the 29th Indian Infantry Brigade, and later reinforced by the 1st Battalion 5th Gurkha Rifles and the 2nd Battalion 10th Gurkhas. The commander of the 1/6th Gurkhas was none other than Lieutenant Colonel the Hon. Charles Granville Bruce who, as a member of the 5th Gurkhas, had played such a key role in developing the Gurkha Scouts in the 1890s. He spent seven weeks at Gallipoli before being evacuated, having been wounded in the legs. He said that 'from start to finish the whole thing was one long nightmare', which, to someone with his background, used to outwitting the enemy with guile and cunning, it undoubtedly must have been.[31]

Major Cecil Allanson (1877–1943), who recounted Bruce's comment and took over command of the 1/6th Gurkhas from him, revealed that while the operation was being contemplated, the students at 'the Staff College' – presumably the Indian one – had come up with a clever plan to get troops into the theatre without exciting suspicion on the part of the Turks or their German mentors. They had 'decided that the best plan was to create a riot in Egypt, bring out a mass of troops from England to quell it, and suddenly shoot them off at right angles to the Dardanelles. This scheme would have worked most perfectly, I imagine, instead of the disastrous loss of life that is now taking place.'[32]

Creative imagination was alive in the British and Indian armies, then as now. But often it failed to penetrate the layers of bureaucracy above. By the time the 1/6th Gurkhas arrived, the British empire troops had been ashore for six days, having first landed at Anzac Cove on 25 April.[33] Bruce reconnoitred the Turkish positions from a light cruiser on 9 May, while a Gurkha officer, Subedar Gambirsing Pun, reconnoitred by land. Bruce later confirmed that 'we were fighting a very brave enemy, well equipped and in a

magnificently defended position'.[34] He was probably aware that the German General Otto Liman von Sanders was commanding the defence, but possibly not of the significance of von Sanders' decision to appoint Mustafa Kemal to command the Turkish 19th Division. Mustafa Kemal later became Kemal Ataturk, the leader and creator of modern, secular Turkey.

The Gallipoli peninsula can be seen in the inset to Figure 7. On the morning of 25 April 1915 the British 29th Division landed on five beaches around Cape Helles on the southern tip of the peninsula. The main landings at 'V' and 'W' Beaches on the Aegean coast were opposed and the British suffered heavy casualties. A supporting landing made at 'Y' Beach to the north encountered no opposition but the troops had no orders and stopped. At that time, the first-day objectives of the village of Krithia and the nearby hill of Achi Baba, from which four ravines run down to the cape, were virtually undefended. Then Turkish reinforcements arrived and the British were forced to evacuate the 'Y' Beach landing – some sources say it was an unauthorised withdrawal – and so a major opportunity for quick success was lost.

On 28 April the British launched an attack on the village of Krithia and Achi Baba. As they advanced they encountered the four ravines, down which Turkish machine-guns could fire. On the extreme left the British ran into the deep, 3-mile (5-kilometre) long Gully Ravine with a stream called Zighin Dere running down it. Between the ravine and the abandoned 'Y' Beach on the coast, and running parallel with both, there was a steep ridge, at first known as Gully Spur. The spur was an excellent fire position for the defending Turks. Two battalions of the 87th Brigade (1st Border Regiment and 1st Royal Inniskilling Fusiliers) got into the ravine but were halted by a machine-gun post near 'Y' Beach. No further advance would be made up the ravine until the spur was captured. The only way of doing that was to scale a cliff 300 feet (91 metres) high. The Royal Marine Light Infantry and the Royal Dublin Fusiliers both tried and failed.

Then, on the rainy night of 12–13 May, Bruce's 1st Battalion of 6th Gurkhas, who were in their element – a rock face at night – swarmed up the cliff and found the ridge lightly defended, although

they lost twelve killed and forty-two wounded in the initial attack. In addition to the Turks who were shot, twelve were decapitated with kukris.[35] The Turks then counter-attacked but could not dislodge the Gurkhas. It was a brilliant feat, and Gully Ridge was henceforward known as 'Gurkha Bluff', under an order signed by Hamilton, while the ravine became 'Bruce's Ravine'. The latter offered protection from Turkish fire, and quickly became the main artery for communication as the force tried to press northwards. Near its entrance at Gully Beach were sited the divisional headquarters, hospitals, rest quarters, horse and donkey lines, and a pier for landing supplies.

Henceforward, the Gurkhas were used to lead British attacks, much as the Scouts had been in the Tirah campaign. On 28 June the 2nd Battalion 10th Gurkhas carried out another successful assault up a steep cliff that the Turks had assumed to be unassailable. They surprised the Turks at the top and drove them back 1,000 yards (1 kilometre), but then had to hold the ground for three days. As in France, losses among the officers were a particular problem. In its first thirty-five days at Gallipoli the 2nd Battalion 10th Gurkhas lost 40 per cent of its other ranks but three-quarters of its British officers.[36] At the end of June the Gurkha Brigade, which had been in the lead on numerous attacks, was withdrawn for a month to rest on the island of Imbros.

The Gurkha Brigade returned at the beginning of August as part of 20,000 reinforcements for the British empire forces pinned down on the peninsula. On 6 August, Hamilton launched another attack. The empire forces were still pinned down on the southern end of the peninsula, and a diversionary attack was made from there, but this time the main focus was on the Sari Bair ridge ('Yellow Ridge'), behind Anzac Cove, on the eastern shore of the peninsula, some 10 miles (15 kilometres) to the north, where there was also a beachhead (see the inset to Figure 7). Hamilton recorded:

> The first step in the real push – the step which above all others was meant to count – was the night attack on the summits of the Sari Bair ridge. The crest line of this lofty mountain range runs parallel to the sea dominating the Anzac position. From the main ridge a series

of spurs run down towards the level beach, and are separated from one another by deep, jagged gullies, choked up with dense jungle. It was our object to effect a lodgement along the crest of the high main ridge with two columns of troops.[37]

The description of a 'lofty mountain range' would have amused the Gurkhas, given that its highest point was less than 1,320 feet (400 metres) above sea level. The 29th Indian Brigade was the left column. The Sari Bair ridge rises gradually from south-east to north-west, with a series of peaks: Baby 700, Battleship Hill, culminating in Chunuk Bair, known as Hill 971 (see Figure 7, inset).[38]

With Bruce out of action, command of the 1st Battalion 6th Gurkhas was in the hands of Major Cecil Allanson. Allanson had spent much of his career as a staff officer and barely spoke Gurkhali. He also had a reputation for being self-serving, and one therefore has to question his account of what happened next.

On the morning of 7 August the empire forces had still not reached the ridgeline. The 29th Indian Brigade's advance on the left had gone well but the right column had encountered stiff resistance. The 1/5th and 1/6th Gurkhas were therefore ordered to swing right and help them. Two companies of the 1/5th who had got lost during the night reinforced the New Zealanders for an attack on the summit of Chunuk Bair, but were driven back. Slow progress continued on 8 August, with the Royal Navy pounding the Turkish positions with heavy shells. The danger of hitting one's own troops – 'blue-on-blue' –[39] was obvious, so the Gurkha battalions in the Sari Bair assault wore red circles about the size of dinner plates on their backs to help the naval observers identify them.[40] The 2nd Battalion 10th Gurkhas wore white armbands for the same reason. It was a simple and fairly effective recognition device. In the Battle of the Somme the next year the advancing British had reflective triangles on their backs, which should have been even more effective.

In the confusion, the various elements of the attacking force got mixed up but in the morning of 8 August the 1/6th Gurkhas – Allanson's battalion – found itself well forward of everyone else and in the middle of the line, quite possibly because the Gurkhas were

good at scrambling up this steep ground. Allanson thought he could take Hill Q, just to the north of Chunuk Bair, and gathered reinforcements. They climbed up the cliff and, completely cut off from the rest of the force, clung on near its summit all day. Like gargoyles they perched in nooks and crannies on the cliff face, sheltered precariously from the Turkish fire. As Alan Moorehead observed, 'it was not so much fighting as mountaineering'[41] – something the Gurkhas were very good at. They inched their way up a little further at dusk, and hung on during the night. Allanson, whose whereabouts had been unknown, managed to make contact with the main British force and was given some reinforcements – two companies of the Staffordshire regiment and one of the Warwickshires. The Warwickshire company included a Lieutenant William Slim, later Field Marshal Bill Slim, who was to have a close association with the Gurkhas, which began that day. He was seriously wounded in the assault, but survived. Allanson had direct orders from General Godley, the divisional commander, to keep his head down until the bombardment stopped and then to rush the Turkish trenches just above him on the top of the steep ridge.

At 0430 hours on 9 August the navy and the Royal Artillery opened fire again, ignoring Koja Chemen Tepe, the height to the north, and concentrating every single gun on Chunuk Bair and Hill Q, where the empire forces were tantalisingly close, and the 1/6th Gurkhas the closest of all. Hill Q was a key knoll on the Sari Bair between Chunuk Bair Point, where today's war memorials are located – one to the New Zealanders and also a more recent and slightly higher one of Mustafa Kemal – and the highest point, Hill 971 (see the inset to Figure 7). The bombardment was due to stop at 0516 hours. Allanson's diary records that

> The roar of the artillery preparation was enormous; the hill, which was almost perpendicular, seemed to leap underneath one. I recognized that if we flew up the hill the moment it stopped, we ought to get to the top. I put the three (Lancashire) companies into the trenches among my men, and said that the moment they saw me go forward carrying a red flag, everyone was to start. I had my watch out, 5.15. I never saw such artillery preparation; the trenches were being torn to pieces; the accuracy was marvellous as we were only

just below. At 5.18 it had not stopped, and I wondered if my watch was wrong. 5.20. Silence. I waited three minutes to be certain, great as the risk was. Then off we dashed, all hand in hand, a most perfect advance and a wonderful sight. I did not know at the time that the GOC Division [divisional commander] Godley was in a torpedo boat destroyer, and every telescope was on us. I left Cornish with 50 men to hold the line in case we were pushed back and to watch me if I signaled for reinforcements. At the top we met the Turks: Le Marchand was down, a bayonet through the heart, I got one through the leg, and then, for about ten minutes, we fought hand to hand, we bit and fisted, and used rifles and pistols as clubs; blood was flying like spray from a hair wash bottle. And then the Turks turned and fled, and I felt a very proud man; the key of the whole peninsula was ours, and our losses had not been so very great for such a result. Below I saw the Straits, motors and wheeled transport, on the roads leading to Achi Baba.

As I looked round I saw that we were not being supported, and thought I could help best by going after those who had retreated in front of us.[42]

The Gurkhas were now on the key objective, but the troops meant to be supporting them were nowhere to be seen. Allanson ordered his men to pursue the retreating Turks down the hill.

We dashed down towards Maidos, but had only got about 300 feet [95 metres] *when I saw a flash in the bay* and suddenly our own Navy put six 12-inch [305-mm] monitor shells into us and all was terrible confusion. It was a deplorable disaster: we were obviously mistaken for Turks and had to turn back. It was an appalling sight. The first hit a Gurkha in the face: the place was a mass of blood and limbs and screams and we all flew back to the summit and to our old position just below. I remained on the crest with about fifteen men; it was a wonderful view; below were the straits, reinforcements coming over from the Asia Minor side, motor-cars flying. We commanded Kilid Bahr, and the rear of Achi Baba and the communications to all their Army there [emphasis added].[43]

What caught the Gurkhas and British reinforcements in their moment of triumph has been hotly disputed. The Royal Navy always denied Allanson's assertion that the fire came from their

'monitors' – shallow-draught vessels designed for shore bombardment – and those closer to the action, watching from just below,
were not sure what had happened. They saw that Allanson's men
had caught the Turks in the open as they were running back to the
trenches after the bombardment and they saw the excited figures of
the Gurkhas and the British of the Lancashire Regiment waving on
the skyline. Philip Haythornthwaite, on the other hand, believed
that the salvo came 'almost incontrovertibly' from the British
ships.[44] The Gurkhas should have been visible to the observers on
the ships and the divisional commander was watching. A visit to the
site reveals that the sea can be seen from there, and therefore it can
be seen from the sea. ·

The same is not true of the view from the Australian artillery
position at Lone Pine, a set of Turkish trenches south of Johnston's
Jolly, taken, with the award of nine VCs, and held by the Australians
during the August fighting. Lone Pine is in dead ground. It is therefore possible that the Australian artillery, who could not see the
Gurkhas with red circles on their backs, rather than the Royal
Navy, fired the shells.[45] However, that in turn suggests the
Australians were firing blind, without direction by forward observers who could see the target. That would have been an irregular
procedure in 1915.[46] There are few if any places from which such
observation could be carried out.

Allanson's account contains a number of inconsistences, including the death of Lieutenant Le Marchand, who was attached from
56th Punjab Rifles, and it would have been hard to be sure that
the sudden unexpected bolt from the blue came from '12-inch
monitor shells' without some serious forensics. Allanson's assertion is supported by the fact that many of the Gurkha dead were
found covered in a yellow powder, which suggested the explosive
contents of shells used by RN monitors. However, the Royal
Navy had been pounding the same target just before the Gurkhas
moved up, and the powdery residue could have been left on the
ground where they subsequently fell. Ninety-five years after
the event, it is impossible to be sure whether the fire came
from the Royal Navy, the Australians, other artillery positions on
the plain below, or the Turks. And if, let us suppose, the Turkish

counter-attack had been the real reason the Gurkhas were stopped and pushed back, a 'friendly fire' incident would have been a convenient additional factor to excuse the Gurkhas' failure to hold the ridge.[47]

The most recent analysis of the battle cites a message Allanson sent to General Cox on 9 August, in which he just says that at 0525 hours 'artillery reopened fire (I think it must have been ours)'. He added that he did not think that the casualties should have been enough to cause the retirement but that 'all the troops concerned had had an extremely bad night and had only just clung on'.[48] Robin Prior, author of the most recent study of Gallipoli, has concluded that Allanson's battalion was not '"shelled off the ridge", because it never really occupied it in the first place'.[49]

Nevertheless, Allanson had led a remarkably successful attack and been wounded. He won the DSO, although he expected the VC.[50] His diary includes a despatch referring to a recommendation from Brigadier General Cox, commanding the 29th Indian Brigade, recommending Allanson for 'the highest possible decoration for gallantry, and Marchand had he lived'.[51] In a section in his 'Diary', which was obviously compiled long after the event Allanson emphatically said it was 'not a V.C. attack; I only obeyed orders throughout and could not have done otherwise: it was a theatrical feat, and I think it would have been fitting to have given the regiment a V.C., and let them choose who should wear it. The thanks is due to a splendidly trained regiment, for which I was in no way responsible.'[52] It was the right thing to say, but one senses that Allanson was protesting too much.

Captain Tomes of the 53rd Sikhs was Allanson's replacement, underlining the scarcity of British officers. But he was killed within twenty-four hours and command devolved on the senior Gurkha VCO, Subedar Major (Gurkha Major) Gambirsing Pun. On 10 August, realising that the position seized by the Gurkhas was utterly critical to the entire Turkish defence of the peninsula, the Turks launched a counter-attack that retook the heights at a cost of 5,000 casualties. The Gurkhas were the last to leave, six hours after all the other empire forces. Pun did not speak much English but organised a highly disciplined and successful withdrawal. The medical officer,

Captain Edward Phipson, the only British officer left, translated for him when he needed to communicate with neighbouring units or higher command.[53]

The Gurkhas' achievement was in vain. The campaign bogged down again, and the intense summer heat with the stench of rotting corpses and innumerable flies gave way to bitter rain and cold. Kitchener visited Gallipoli in November and decided, though he did not advertise it at the time, to pull the empire troops out. The Turks were too strongly dug in. The Gurkhas retained their traditional resilience and stoicism. It is – or was – an officer's duty to inspect his men's feet. Captain Watson-Smyth, a company commander in the 1st Battalion 6th Gurkhas, eventually decided he had to inspect those of his orderly, Hastabir Pun. He found them 'black with gangrene from neglected frost bite. He had never said a word to me and never would have.'[54]

The withdrawal from Gallipoli conducted by General Sir Charles Monro, Hamilton's replacement, was, in contrast, one of the slickest and most successful manoeuvres of the war. Between the nights of 18–19 November 1915 and 8–9 January 1916, the Royal and Merchant navies withdrew 83,000 men, 4,500 animals, 1,700 motor vehicles and 200 guns under the noses of the Turks. The total British, Anzac and Indian Army casualties totalled 250,000 out of 410,000 deployed, while the French lost 47,000 out of 79,000 and the Turks between 250,000 and 300,000 out of 500,000.[55] The Gurkhas had been among the first in and were among the very last to leave. On 12 December, battalion commanders were told in great secrecy that it was intended to evacuate the Anzac and Suvla areas of the peninsula. At 1600 hours on 21 December the 1/6th left Murdos on the SS *Knight Templar* and arrived in Alexandria on Christmas Eve. The withdrawal from Gallipoli, like that from Dunkirk, rates as one of the most extraordinary and paradoxical victories in British military history. But it was far more successful as an operation. No living soldier was left behind.[56]

The 1/6th, 1/5th and 2/10th Gurkhas all distinguished themselves at Gallipoli, and the 1/4th also served there, but arrived after the main fighting was over. Lieutenant General Sir Reginald Savory, who served at Gallipoli with the 14th Sikhs, later said that

the 1/6th Gurkha Rifles were 'the outstanding battalion of the Gallipoli Campaign'.[57] The 2/5th Gurkhas tied strips of blanket around their boots to muffle the sound of their footsteps as they trudged down the beach to the Royal Navy boats waiting to take them off. Sir Ian Hamilton's secretary wrote to the colonel of the 6th Gurkha Rifles: 'It is Sir Ian Hamilton's most cherished conviction that if he had been given more Gurkhas at the Dardanelles then he would never have been held up by the Turks.'[58]

With the failure of the Gallipoli campaign clear to see by the end of 1915, the only remaining axis of attack against the Ottoman Turkish empire was in the Middle East, through Mesopotamia (modern Iraq) or Palestine.

On the outbreak of war with Turkey at the beginning of November 1914, a British force was despatched to seize the Turkish port of Basra on the Shatt-al-Arab waterway (see Figure 7). The reason was very specific. Oil. Basra is a mere 50 miles (80 kilometres) upstream on the river Tigris from the Persian (now Iranian) port of Abadan, where the recently established Anglo-Persian Oil Company refined and then exported the increasingly precious war-winning commodity of oil. Britain needed to protect its supply of diesel oil for the navy and, as warfare was becoming increasingly dependent on all forms of motor transport, oil generally.

General Sir John Nixon was given authority to 'control lower Mesopotamia and such portions of neighbouring territory as may affect your operations'.[59] It was a blank cheque, which would bounce, resulting in a Parliamentary Commission.[60] Basra was captured on 22 November 1914 by a joint navy and army attack, and a defensive outpost was established 50 miles (80 kilometres) further north at Qurna, at the junction between the Tigris and the Euphrates (see Figure 7). Having captured Basra, the British set about developing it as a massive military and industrial base. Arriving there in 1920, Lieutenant General Sir Aylmer Haldane thought it had become 'a miniature Liverpool, the creators of which had not only provided for the necessities of the vast force which overcame the Turks, but had prepared for the development of the country such as might not be attained for half a century'.[61] Back in 1915, as the Gallipoli campaign failed, the political, strategic and

energy-security advantages of seizing what is now Iraq from the Ottoman empire became more apparent.

Major General Charles Townshend, commanding the 6th Indian Division, and Major General George Gorringe, commanding the 12th Division, from India, were ordered forward, Townshend up the Tigris, in boats, and Gorringe up the Euphrates where the navigable water soon gave way to swamps. Townshend, on the Tigris route, took Amara on 3 June 1915. The 2nd Battalion, 7th Gurkhas were part of Gorringe's force. In July they reached Nasiriya, in appalling heat and pestered by mosquitoes, which caused malaria. On 24 July, however, the 2/7th Gurkhas helped unlock the defence after Naik Harkarat Rai – one of the eastern *jats* recruited into the relatively new 7th and 10th Gurkhas – led an attack with the cry '*Ayo Gurkhali*' and brandishing a kukri. His company followed, clearing the Turkish trenches with bayonets and kukris and beheading several Turks. The 7th Gurkhas celebrate 24 July – Nasiriya Day – as their Regimental Day. On 30 July a message from Kitchener about the capture of Nasiriya, described as 'another great victory in Mesopotamia' and saying it opened the way to Baghdad, was read out to sceptical troops at Gallipoli, including the Gurkhas.[62]

What had started as a limited operation to protect the Abadan oil installations had been quickly expanded. Townshend was now put in charge of both divisions and ordered on, with the 6th Division heading west along the Tigris to Kut al-Amarah, 100 miles (160 kilometres) short of Baghdad. He outflanked the Turkish position east of Kut and captured the city after the Turks withdrew. Here, the two divisions joined up. Eventually, only 22 miles (33 kilometres) from Baghdad, at Ctesiphon, on 22 November, Townshend's force was stopped by a Turkish force under the expert command of the German Field Marshal Kolmar von der Goltz. The empire troops were driven back and the 2/7th Gurkhas, by now only 400 strong, made an epic defence, on one of a number of mounds that covered the remains of the ancient city, against the Turkish 35th Division.

Exactly a year after the successful capture of Basra, Townshend ordered the remnants of his force back to Kut. There they were

trapped. The Turks went round them and concentrated on countering the relief force, while Townshend waited. He had had
experience of a similar situation on the North-West Frontier, where
he had been besieged in a fort in Chitral for more than six weeks.
The 2/4th Gurkhas claimed a special interest in relieving Townshend,
since they had done exactly the same in 1895.[63]

But relief never came. The Turks tried an assault on Kut, but
were repelled. Thereafter they settled for sniping, and waiting.
Townshend's force remained under siege until, on 29 April 1916,
the British commander was finally forced to surrender. The remaining 10,000 British, Indian and Gurkha soldiers, out of an original
force of 13,000, were taken into Turkish captivity. Townshend was
allegedly wined and dined by the Turkish commander-in-chief,
while his troops were condemned to a 1,200-mile (1,900-kilometre)
forced march back to, and across, Turkey.[64]

The soldiers of the 2nd Battalion, the 7th Gurkhas, were separated from their officers and formed part of the captive column.
However, by all accounts, they maintained discipline and, in so
doing, gained the respect of the Arabs and the Turks. There was,
apparently, 'no straggling', as a result of which the Gurkhas avoided
the worst of the abuse meted out to those who fell by the wayside.
'Each man took strength from his comrades, cohesion and membership were never lost.'[65] The regimental history identifies as
worthy of special praise Colour Havildar Fatehbahadur Limbu – the
senior NCO who took command of the remnants of the battalion
after the officers, including any surviving VCOs, were taken away;
Colour Havildar Bhotri Khattri, who took on the duties of adjutant; and Havildar Hari Singh Khattri, the Sikh quartermaster
clerk.[66]

As at Gallipoli, the outstanding discipline, tactical skill and expertise displayed by the Gurkhas on numerous occasions was let down
by failings at the higher command level. It would be tendentious
and wrong, however, to say this was uniquely bad luck for the
Gurkhas. It happened to a great many individuals and units in
the First World War, and indeed, it happens in all wars.

On 16 February 1916, the British War Office had taken over
responsibility for running the Mesopotamian campaign after the

Indian government had proved less than competent. The arrival of the Meerut and Lahore divisions from France made it possible to assemble a relief force of three divisions for Kut. It was commanded by Lieutenant General Sir Fenton Aylmer, who, ironically, was the engineer who had won his VC alongside Boisragon in the Hunza campaign in 1891, and was also at the relief of Townshend's fort at Chitral in 1895. It was a small world, in some ways. The 1/1st and 1/9th Gurkhas were in the relief force. It got to just 7 miles (10 kilometres) from Kut and could have taken the Turks by surprise, but Aylmer delayed to organise an artillery bombardment. As a result, the Turks occupied positions that the relief force had found deserted, and inflicted heavy casualties on them when they did eventually attack. The 1/9th lost 31 killed and 107 wounded. 'This costly failure,' the 9th Gurkhas' regimental history recorded, 'sealed the fate of the beleaguered garrison at Kut.'[67]

Four months after the fall of Kut Major General Stanley Maude, who had brought the 13th Division with him from Gallipoli, took over command of, first, the Tigris Corps, and then the army in Mesopotamia. By the end of 1916 he therefore had I Indian Corps, III British Corps and a cavalry division under his command. This force included no fewer than six Gurkha regiments, and there were fifteen Gurkha battalions serving in the Middle East (Mesopotamia and Palestine) as a whole, making it the largest theatre for Gurkha deployments in the First World War.[68]

After reorganising his force, Maude, who had a reputation for being methodical, directed his greatly reinforced army towards Kut. The city on the Tigris was strongly defended so in February 1917 he resolved to get round behind it, which necessitated crossing the river west of Kut, at the Shumran bend. Three crossing points were selected, with a battalion to secure each. These were the 2/Norfolks, the 2/9th Gurkhas and the 1/2nd Gurkhas. The Norfolks were happy to row themselves but the Gurkhas were rowed by the 1/4th Hampshire Regiment, a Territorial Army battalion with many watermen from Southampton docks among them. Although it is not specifically stated in the accounts, it will be recalled from Chapter 1 that the Manjhi caste are boatmen and ferrymen, a menial

job forbidden to higher-caste Gurkhas, and there would have been no Manjhis with the 2nd or 9th Gurkhas in Mesopotamia in 1917. With the 9th Gurkhas comprising higher-caste Chhetris and Thakurs, rowing a boat would definitely be out, and the same was probably true for the artisan class Magars and Gurungs of the 2nd Gurkhas.[69]

At 0530 hours on 23 February 1917, just before dawn, thirteen boats carrying the 2/9th Gurkhas crossed the river, which was flowing fast. They immediately came under heavy Turkish fire. As soon as they hit the bank the commander, Major George Campbell Wheeler, led his men in hand-to-hand combat with the Turks using bayonets, kukris and hand grenades, and they secured a hold on the far side of the river. He was awarded the VC

> For the most conspicuous bravery and determination.
>
> This officer, together with one Gurkha officer and eight men, crossed a river and immediately rushed the enemy's trench under heavy bombing, rifle, machine gun, and artillery fire.
>
> Having obtained a footing on the river bank, he was almost immediately afterwards counter-attacked by a strong enemy party with bombers. Major Campbell Wheeler at once led a charge with another officer and three men, receiving a severe bayonet wound in the head, but managed, in spite of this, to disperse the enemy.
>
> This bold action on his part undoubtedly saved the situation. In spite of his wound, he continued to consolidate his position.[70]

Presumably the fact that the action took place on the river Tigris was withheld for operational security reasons.

The 1/2nd Gurkhas were even more exposed to enemy fire and so boatloads of dead and wounded went drifting downstream. However Lieutenant Toogood and fifty-six men made it across, in part thanks to Toogood's initiative in using a lantern to guide the boats. Those of the 1/2nd and 2/9th who had not yet crossed then moved to the Norfolks' crossing point, which was less exposed. In spite of Turkish counter-attacks the bridgehead on the far bank held and a pontoon bridge was built. The Turks, realising they were being cut off, started withdrawing from Kut towards Baghdad.

Under pressure of being outflanked, they abandoned Baghdad, in spite of German pressure to the contrary, and Maude's army entered it on 11 March 1917.[71] The first task was to restore order, which had collapsed when the Turks left. The lessons for the invasion of Iraq in 2003, when a 'security gap' opened up with the collapse of Saddam Hussein's forces, but before US and other coalition powers could install proper policing, are only too apparent. Law and order broke down in Baghdad, there was much looting, and 'spoilers' opposed to any peace process moved in. A study of the Mesopotamian campaign, as well as of the Allied occupation of Germany in 1945, should have paid dividends.

After occupying Baghdad and taking steps to ensure internal security, Maude's army pressed on up the Tigris and Euphrates. The two rivers come close again at Baghdad, and then diverge again to north and south. The 1/8th Gurkhas were involved in the indecisive battle at Istabulat railway station, north of the capital. Some 50 miles (80 kilometres) north of Baghdad, the Adhain (Uzaym) river flows into the Tigris from the north near a town of the same name. Here the Turks planned to concentrate their forces with the corps on the Tigris joining the corps withdrawing eastwards in the face of Russian troops moving through Persia. The 1/2nd, 2/4th and 2/9th Gurkhas were all involved in a big battle on 30 April. The Gurkhas captured the town, then a village, but under cover of a sandstorm the Turks counter-attacked and pushed them back, releasing 400 of their own prisoners and taking British empire captives. All three battalions were engaged, with the 1/2nd Gurkhas trying to cross the big river to envelop the Turks. However, when the next day dawned they found that the Turks had withdrawn. It was too hot to fight and both sides agreed to suspend hostilities. The temperature in Iraq often reaches 45° Celsius *in the shade*, which at the time would have been expressed as 113° Fahrenheit, and in high summer may reach 50°C, which would be 122°F. During the long, unspeakably hot summer, the Gurkhas were involved in protracted guard duties on the long and vulnerable lines of communication stretching all the way back to Basra. Again, the difficulties of protecting communications between Basra and Baghdad along the two rivers in the Iraq operations from 2003 to

2009 present obvious parallels. In 1917, the Gurkhas also became involved in railway construction.

In September the heat began to diminish and Maude renewed his advances up the Tigris and Euphrates. On the south bank of the Euphrates, the 15th Indian Division was engaged in a big battle at Ramadi about 60 miles (100 kilometres) west of Baghdad where there was an important Ottoman garrison. Its defeat would allow the British to advance further along the river. There had already been an abortive attack on the town on 11 July (in spite of the summer 'ceasefire') by the re-raised 2/7th Gurkhas. The original 2/7th had become prisoners at Kut, so a new battalion had been raised. However, they were repulsed with 566 casualties.

General Brooking ordered the building of a dummy bridge and road on the north bank, to fool the Turks that the assault they expected would come from that side. He then sent the 6th Cavalry Brigade in a classic enveloping manoeuvre to take up positions to the west of the town to cut off the Turkish line of retreat. The attack began on 28 September, on the south bank of the Euphrates, with two brigades of the 15th Division attacking the town directly. The 42nd Brigade, which was mainly Gurkha, would attack frontally and 12th Brigade attacked the right flank. The 42nd Brigade included 1/4th Dorsets and three Gurkha battalions – 1/5th, 2/5th and 2/6th. Although the Turks expected an enemy assault, the British made ample use of armoured cars, which surprised the defenders, and the Ottoman garrison was quickly outflanked and surrounded. The British cavalry intercepted an attempt to escape at night, and the Ottoman forces surrendered on the morning of 29 September.[72]

Then there was an unexpected tragedy. On 18 November 1917, General Maude died of cholera in Baghdad, in somewhat suspicious circumstances. It was rumoured that he had been given milk for his coffee containing the cholera bacillus while watching an Arabic production of a Shakespeare play.[73] Alas, poor General Maude . . . He had turned around the administrative and logistic support of the army in Mesopotamia and driven to Baghdad and beyond, accomplishing a series of victories. He was sorely missed.

After Maude's death, the 42nd Brigade, with the same components, including the same three Gurkha battalions, was then engaged

in the last big battle of the Mesopotamian campaign. In the spring of 1918, British empire forces continued to press up the Euphrates and met a Turkish force with German commanders and reinforcements at Khan Baghdadi, about 100 miles (160 kilometres) west of Baghdad. The Dorsets, the 2/5th and 2/6th Gurkhas, with the 1/5th Gurkhas as a reserve, attacked after a heavy artillery barrage, and the Turks gave in on 27 March. Two Turkish generals, two senior German advisers and a number of German soldiers were among the 5,200 strong force that surrendered.[74]

However, that was not the end of fighting in Mesopotamia. There was little action in the months that followed but on 23 October 1918, as an armistice with Turkey was expected, the new commander-in-chief, Sir William Marshall, determined to secure control of the Mosul oilfields north of Baghdad. A British-Indian force under Sir Alexander Cobbe moved north from Baghdad the same day. Its progress was remarkably swift: within two days it had covered 80 miles (120 kilometres), reaching Little Zab river, where Cobbe planned to meet and if necessary fight the Turkish 6th Army under Ismail Hakki Bey. The speed of Cobbe's dvance was assisted by the use of cavalry and also the presence of two Gurkha battalions, the 1/7th and 1/10th. The 1/7th covered 36 miles (58 kilometres) in thirty-six hours to keep up with the cavalry trying to outflank the Turks.[75] Hakki retreated to Sharqat a further 66 miles (100 kilometres) to the north. Cobbe nevertheless caught up with him and attacked on 29 October. The 1/10th were in the main attacking force but within a day Hakki surrendered to Cobbe, despite the fact that his lines had not yet been breached by the British empire forces. However, the political situation in the Ottoman empire was so precarious that fighting seemed pointless. During this last battle in Mesopotamia, 18,000 Turkish soldiers were taken prisoner by the British, who lost a little under 2,000 men. Mosul itself was peacefully occupied by an Indian cavalry on 14 November 1918.

The fighting in Mesopotamia, over land familiar to us as Iraq, was over. But the focus of attention in the Middle East had already shifted west, to places that are equally familiar today.

★

At the end of 1917, Russia effectively left the First World War following the second revolution on 25 October – in fact, on 7 November 1917 by the modern calendar. The Russians had been fighting, and beating, the Turks in the Caucasus since December 1914, and holding down large numbers of German and Austrian troops on the Eastern Front. Their withdrawal from the Great War and diversion into their own bloody civil war had major implications for the remaining members of the Entente, Britain and France. The Americans, although now formally part of the war, would not be deploying significant land forces until summer 1918. The Russian resignation released large numbers of Turkish troops to fight the British empire in the Middle East.

In early 1918 the Germans took advantage of the slackening of pressure on the Eastern Front to launch the innovative and potentially fatal Michael offensive against Britain and France on the Western Front. All this put extra stress on the British command in the Middle East.

In June 1917, General Sir Edmund Allenby took over command in Egypt and started to plan the invasion of Palestine, as the Ottoman empire began to disintegrate. It was a largely conventional strategy but Allenby used the Arab revolt, guided by the enigmatic T. E. Lawrence, to guard his flank and to gain additional support by promising the Arab leader Prince Faisal a share in the Ottoman empire. Allenby moved through Palestine and what is now Israel in late 1917 and captured Jerusalem by Christmas. Allenby was a cavalry general, and manoeuvre and speed were essential to his style. Armoured cars had been in use since the start of the war, but were expensive and needed good roads. Tanks were still little more than armoured bulldozers for breaking through barbed wire and trenches, and hardly used in the Middle East. Here, the arm of speed and manoeuvre remained the cavalry, but cavalry needed masses of forage and water. That was not available in Mesopotamia, but it was in the more fertile country of Palestine. Allenby therefore needed infantry who could, as near as possible, keep up with the cavalry. And the best choice for that were Gurkhas.

The end of the fighting in Mesopotamia meant that Allenby had

six Gurkha battalions: the 1/1st, 2/3rd, 3/3rd, 2/7th, 1/8th and 4/11th. The 11th Gurkhas, whose British service was short-lived, was formed on 18 May 1918 from other Gurkha detachments serving in Mesopotamia. Four battalions were raised and the 1st and 2nd were used in Iraq to put down the Arab rebellion there in June 1920. They also served in Afghanistan before being disbanded in 1921 and 1922 as part of the inevitable reduction of the Gurkha Brigade after the 'war to end war'. In accordance with the best modern management practice, last in, first out.[76] However, the 11th Gurkhas were revived by the newly independent Indian Army after 1947 (see Chapters 7 and 9).

The other five preformed Gurkha battalions were with Allenby before the 11th Gurkha Rifles was formed. The Turks kept up resistance as the British pushed north through Palestine, again with German advisers and detachments. After the capture of Jerusalem in time for Christmas 1917, resistance continued in the Plain of Sharon, north of Tel Aviv, near the coast.

In April 1918 one German machine-gun on the plain was proving particularly difficult. On 10 April, Rifleman Karanbahadur Rana, 3rd Gurkha Rifles, became the third member of the Gurkhas, and only the second non-British Gurkha, to win the VC in the Great War. He won it

> For most conspicuous bravery, resource in action under adverse conditions, and utter contempt for danger.
>
> During an attack he, with a few other men, succeeded under intense fire in creeping forward with a Lewis gun in order to engage an enemy machine gun which had caused severe casualties to officers and other ranks who had attempted to put it out of action.
>
> No. 1 of the Lewis gun [the gunner] opened fire, and was shot immediately. Without a moment's hesitation Rifleman Karanbahadur Rana pushed the dead man off the gun, and in spite of bombs thrown at him and heavy fire from both flanks, he opened fire and knocked out the machine-gun crew; then, switching his fire on to the enemy bombers and riflemen in front of him, he silenced their fire. He kept his gun in action and showed the greatest coolness in removing defects which on two occasions prevented the gun from firing. During the remainder of the day he did

magnificent work, and when a withdrawal was ordered he assisted with covering fire until the enemy were close on him. He displayed throughout a very high standard of valour and devotion to duty.[77]

While operations of a relatively conventional kind were going on up the coast, a different kind of war had been under way inland, and especially in the desert to the south. The Arab revolt was being synchronised with British military action through T. E. Lawrence 'of Arabia'. Much of the action focussed on the Hejaz railway (see Figure 7), which had been completed in 1908 and ran all the way from Damascus and Haifa down to Medina. It linked with main lines further north, and therefore extended Turkish rail communications from Istanbul right down into Saudi Arabia.[78] In January 1917, Lawrence intercepted a Turkish communication saying that the Turks were planning to withdraw from Medina, and he recommended that the railway should be cut to prevent them from doing so. The first train was derailed at Towaira in February 1917. Attacks on it would continue for more than a year, as the Turks withdrew northwards. Among Lawrence's helpers during the final phases was a team of about thirty Gurkhas.

Little has been published about the Gurkhas who worked with Lawrence, but an article appeared in 1942, including an interview with one Havildar Manbahadur Gurung.[79]

Gurung referred to his time in the desert as *Unt ka kam* – 'camel work'. He had served in France and arrived back in Egypt in April 1917. He was then at the Battle of Gaza and took part in the capture of Jerusalem in December 1917, where he was wounded. He spent about a month in hospital in Suez, and then returned to the front. In July or August 1918, volunteers were requested to go on a camel training course in Jerusalem. Because his arm hurt when he did drill, Gurung volunteered, even though he did not like camels. He said he was in the '3rd Battalion', which suggests the 3/3rd, the only 'third battalion' present in Allenby's forces. His testimony is a good indication of how a typical Gurkha might react to taking part in the 'swirling campaigns', to use Lawrence's words,[80] and to totally unfamiliar circumstances.

'From our battalion one Havildar and twelve sepoys volunteered. I was only a sepoy then. There were also volunteers from other Gurkha regiments. In all there were about twenty-four of us.

We were put in a train but instead of getting to Jerusalem we arrived at Suez. I thought it was a mistake but the captain Sahib who was in charge of us said it was all right. He told us that there was no course, that the story about the course was only a lie to deceive the enemy and that we were going on a secret and important mission. At Suez we went on board a steamship. We were several days and nights on board the ship and then we arrived at a place called . . .'

'Was it Akaba?'

'Yes, yes, Akaba. That was the name. At Akaba we did one week's training in camel riding. After the week none of us were very good camel riders and all of us were stiff. But we were then ordered to march and were sent off into the desert. We rode for more than twenty days into the desert in a north-easterly direction. I began to think that we would go on riding forever. We never had a rest, never stopped more than one night in the same place. It was hard work for we were still untrained camelmen but the worst difficulty was food.'[81]

Gurung explained that his regiment normally ate rice but they had been issued only with flour and that during the one-hour halt during the day there was not time to cook chapatis. Gurung did not remember where his small group of camel-riding Gurkhas had stopped, but they might possibly have done so at Azrak. They then met up with some Egyptian sappers and miners.

'The next day we went out with the Egyptians to break the railway line. We rode for a long way and then broke the rail for the first time near Maan.'

'Did you help break it or was that sapper work?'

'We Gurkhas did some of the breaking. We tore down the tele-graph lines and broke them by hammering the wires between two stones. When we finished the work we retired into the desert and rode north towards Amman. We travelled one or two days on the way. Near Amman we broke the line again. This time our party was employed on covering work only. After this we rode again to a place about six miles north of Deraa. We arrived at our objective about daybreak after riding all night and we started work on the railway

line about six o'clock in the morning. This time the Turks attacked us but we had Lewis guns as well as rifles and we drove them back; they never got nearer than six hundred yards from us.'

'Were there no other covering troops?'

'Oh yes, some "badus" [irregular troops], the small French cannon and an armoured car. They helped us. We worked right on at breaking the line and bridges until about twelve o'clock when a great number of Turkish aeroplanes came and attacked us.'[82]

Gurung described an attack by large numbers of Turkish aircraft with only one Allied aircraft to counter them. The Allied plane landed, while the Gurkhas and other members of the force fired at the Turkish aircraft. Gurung held a Lewis gun up to his shoulder and fired it. The Turkish aircraft were forced to fly higher as a result. Then they continued destroying the line.

'We worked all day and destroyed about four or five miles of line as well as the bridges; we helped the sappers. When it became dark the General sahib came and said that the Egyptians could not see at all in the dark, so we Gurkhas would have to hold night piquets over the area.'

'What was the general sahib's name?'

'I forget.'

'Was it Lawrence? No? Joyce, Peake?'

'No sahib, I forget, but *he was the burra sahib who was in charge of the Arab militia people.* We held the piquets until one o'clock in the morning when our captain sahib whose name I forget also came and ordered us to retire. He told us that our troops in Palestine had orders to attack the Turks on the next day and that we had broken the railway line behind the enemy's position in order to prevent reinforcements reaching them. Now, if all went well, it was too late for the Turks to repair the line; for we would win the war first [emphasis added].'[83]

The phrase 'burra sahib' adds to the mystery. It means something like 'old man', but referring to the man as he is, or might be, now, rather than as he was then.[84] And Rifleman Gurung would himself have been very young. The sahib was clearly a British officer. Could this 'general' in charge of the Arab militia have been the youthful Lawrence?

The Gurkhas marched for the rest of the night and all the next day, and then had several days' rest. 'Then one of our aeroplanes came and told us that we had attacked and defeated the Turks near Jaffa. The Turks were completely beaten and the war was over. We had helped a lot by destroying the railway.' Gurung said he and the other Gurkhas had nothing to do with the other soldiers. 'They were all Mussulmans or something like that, not a Hindu among the lot. We had our own captain sahib, who was from a Gurkha regiment, and we kept separate.'

Gurung's attitude typified that of many Gurkhas. The camel riding made him ache, but it was better than walking. As for the extraordinary special-forces-style operation, working with the Arab militia and striking at long range across the desert, 'It was all right; not worse than the rest of the war. Though the cooking was difficult, of course. We did get rum sometimes, but not always.'[85]

Lawrence's forces had started attacking the railway lines around Deraa on 17 September, as a prelude to the famous (and not the first) Battle of Megiddo from 19 September to 1 October. Allenby's victory at Megiddo precipitated the break-up of the Turkish forces, and on 30 October the Armistice of Mudros (Moudhros), ending the war in the Middle East, was signed on board HMS *Agamemnon* in the harbour of that name on the Greek island of Lemnos.

During the First World War the Gurkhas had fought in trenches and against chemical weapons in France. They had landed from ships from the sea, and crossed the desert on its 'ships' – camels – in special operations comparable to those of the SAS and the Long Range Desert Group in the Second World War. They had played a disproportionate role, given their numbers, in Hamilton's unsuccessful Gallipoli operation, and in Maude and Allenby's well-planned, well-supplied and well-executed victories. They had borne up better than anyone else in terrible conditions when taken prisoner at Kut. The total number of Gurkha casualties in the First World War is estimated at more than 20,000, of whom more than 6,342 – the number of known dead recorded by the Commonwealth War Graves Commission – were killed.[86]

Nobody expected to fight another war like this ever again, and the Gurkhas would return to the same challenges and problems in

India and Nepal that they had left behind. Lawrence of Arabia, who had a small number of Gurkhas in his force, bemoaned how 'We lived many lives in those swirling campaigns, never sparing ourselves: yet when we achieved and the new world dawned, the old men came out again and took our victory to remake in the likeness of the former world they knew . . .'[87] For the moment, the Gurkhas returned to the former world they knew until, twenty years hence, there would be another world war.

7

Empire Under Threat

I N 1932, NEARLY fourteen years after the First World War ended, the British published a report on its lessons. The *Kirke Report* noted the prevailing view that such a war, involving massive deployment of British empire troops against a first-division, first-world continental adversary, was unlikely to recur. However, it added a note of caution. Adversaries in future wars were difficult to predict. 'At present the enemy cannot be defined and the absence of a basis to the problem adds greatly to the difficulties of its solution.'[1]

The First World War – 'the war to end war' – had been so unprecedented and extraordinary that one must forgive many people for thinking that nothing like it would ever happen again, certainly not within a generation. One of the most extraordinary things about it was that the British had fielded a mass army, against all historical precedent, and had assumed the main burden of the increasingly high-technology war on the Western Front after the French mutinies and Russian revolutions of 1917, and before the arrival of the Americans at the very end of the war. They had then shot and bombed the Germans to pieces, using the latest technology and extraordinarily good staff work. This extraordinary achievement – what Gary Sheffield has called the 'Forgotten Victory' – was, if acknowledged at all, seen as a one-off, never to be repeated.[2]

The demands of a first-division war in Europe and the Middle East, and the use of the best of the Indian Army, including a disproportionate number of Gurkhas, had denuded the North-West Frontier. Besides the constant threat of the frontier tribes and the uncertain intentions of Afghanistan, there was the increasing danger

of insurrection in India as nationalism began to grow. As we have
seen, Nepalese troops were brought in, and the British also deployed
some Territorial Army units, who were only partially trained and
unsuited to facing the warlike tribesmen. There were regular British
units, too. The author's grandfather, Robert James Buckland,
commissioned into the Royal Norfolk Regiment after serving as a
sergeant at the Battle of the Somme, was sent with that regiment to
India in 1917.

During the First World War, Emir Habibulla of Afghanistan had
resisted German and Turkish attempts to persuade him to take their
side against Britain and its empire. In February 1919 he was
murdered, and his son Amanulla took over. Many of Amanulla's
advisers were strongly anti-British. Almost immediately, in March
and April 1919 there were outbreaks of disorder in India, which
directly contributed to the Third Afghan War.[3] As often happens
when internal security is threatened, the Indian government passed
legislation providing for internment without trial, and trial without
a jury – the Rowlatt Acts. The same thing happened in Northern
Ireland in 1971, with similar results. Indian nationalists exploited
the special measures to stir up opposition to British rule. Amritsar, the
main city of the Punjab and site of the Sikhs' holiest shrine, became
a particular hotbed of resentment. It was the time of the Baisakhi
festival, so the 160,000 population of the city was swollen by thousands of pilgrims. Brigadier General Reginald Dyer, commanding
the 16th Division, was told to restore order and use his judgement
about how to do so.

Dyer moved to the city and reinforced his available forces with
260 men from the 9th Gurkhas whose troop train had been halted
by the disorder. They were recruits who had just finished training,
and their instructors. They had no rifles so they were issued with
100 rifles from the Amritsar armouries. To be fired accurately, a
rifle has to be zeroed for the individual firing it, and this did not
happen. On 13 April, in defiance of a ban on public meetings, 5,000
to 6,000 people congregated in a large open space – nominally a
'garden', although there was no cultivation anywhere – enclosed by
walls and houses, called the Jallianwallah Bagh. Dyer appeared with
a force of twenty-five of the newly trained 9th Gurkhas and

twenty-five men from the 54th Sikhs and 59th Scinde Rifles, the latter being Pathans who, like the Gurkhas, had little affection for the Indians.

According to Second Lieutenant, later Brigadier, McCallum, who had just joined the 1/9th Gurkhas, and was not present at what happened next, he was told by Jemadar Jitbahadur – a Gurkha VCO of commensurate rank – that 'General Sahib [Dyer] had been informed that a very large gathering was taking place in Jallianwala Bagh and ordered a column of twenty-five rifles from each 9th Gurkhas and 59th to go with him into the city. "He told us to double through the narrow road leading to an open square and then said Gurkhas right, 59th left fire".'[4]

As in the British armoured-car attack on the crowd at Croke Park in Dublin on 'Bloody Sunday' on 21 November 1920, or the Chinese action at Tiananmen Square on 3 June 1989, the crowd was hemmed in. Jallianwallah Bagh was surrounded by walls and buildings and there were few ways to escape when the troops started firing at the densest parts of the crowd. McCallum was woken up in the mess and sent to count the empty cartridge cases, of which he counted 923. In all, some 1,650 rounds were fired.[5] The official British estimate was that 379 people, including women and children, were killed and 1,200 wounded. Some died after they had dived into a well for cover. The Indian National Congress did its own investigation and, probably unsurprisingly, came up with a higher figure of 1,000 dead. The incident created shock across the British empire. The Lieutenant Governor of the Punjab praised Dyer's action, but others criticised it.[6] Dyer was later summoned before the Hunter Inquiry, and defended himself on the grounds that he had prevented a large-scale rebellion. The inquiry censured him for his action, and he had to retire from the army, although the House of Lords exonerated him. But before that he would have the opportunity to prove that he was better at conventional warfare than at crowd control.

Amanullah could see that the British had their hands full with civil unrest, and concluded, somewhat prematurely, that British rule in India was precarious. He also assumed the British were exhausted by their efforts in the world war, and would therefore be disinclined

to fight. He was not completely wrong. A number of British regiments happened to be in India on a circuitous route home from Mesopotamia and were 'returned unwillingly to the slaughter.' John Morris, of the 2/3rd Gurkhas, whose testimony in *Hired to Kill* has proved invaluable, recalled that when he arrived in Peshawar in 1919, 'it was a common sight to see senior officers being jeered at in the streets. Troops in this state of mind were naturally little use, but their mere presence served some purpose in deceiving the Afghan agents, of whom there were known to be many in the city, as to our effective strength.'[7]

Amanullah was also having problems with factions in his own country and resorted to the age-old stratagem of a foreign adventure to relieve the pressure. He used the pretext that he wanted to prevent such disturbances spreading into Afghanistan to concentrate forces at the three main entry points across the Durand Line into the Raj: the Khyber Pass, the Kurram valley and the Khojak Pass (see Figure 5). He did not intend to invade the heartland of India itself, but hoped to gain control over the border area where British control was weak and where the people were from the same tribes as those in Afghanistan. The area is now the 'Tribal Territories' on the Pakistan–Afghan border. There were some advantages in having an 'uncontrolled space' between the British Raj and Afghanistan, but it had always been difficult to control, because the communications were so primitive. It was not until the 1920s that the British, recalling their classical education, realised that the solution was, as the Romans had done, to build roads.[8]

Meanwhile, on 3 May 1919, troops of the Afghan Army, assisted by local tribesmen, crossed the frontier at the top of the Khyber Pass and occupied the village of Bagh and the nearby springs that provided water for Landi Kotal, garrisoned by two companies of Indian infantry. The British tried to recapture Bagh on 6 May, but failed. They attacked again on 9 May with the 1st and 2nd Battalions of the recently formed 11th Gurkha Rifles and the 2nd Battalion the North Staffordshire Regiment. This time they drove the Afghan forces from the position, and the Royal Air Force bombed and strafed them as they withdrew. The British advanced through the Khyber Pass to Dacca, some miles inside Afghanistan,

and established a garrison there. Initially there was strong opposition by local tribesmen and Afghan forces, but it generally
subsided.

On 27 May the Afghans attacked the Kurram Pass, about 70 miles
(110 kilometres) west-south-west of the Khyber Pass, and besieged
the Indian army garrison at Thal (see Figure 5). The 3rd Battalion,
9th Gurkha Rifles was part of the garrison but soon ran short of
food, water and ammunition. Brigadier General Dyer quickly
assembled a relief force and on 1 June attacked the tribesmen
between him and Thal, quickly dispersing them. He took command
of the town and then prepared to attack the main Afghan force, but
they were already under orders from the Emir Amanullah to suspend hostilities, and they withdrew. An armistice was concluded on
3 June. Dyer had led brilliantly, in spite of illness and fatigue, but
then had to face the inquiry into the Amritsar massacre.

In the south, at the Khojak Pass between Afghanistan and
Baluchistan, the British pre-empted an Afghan attack. On 27 May
they attacked the Afghan fort at Spin Baldak, 6 miles (10 kilometres)
inside Afghanistan, with a force of six battalions: two British, two
Indian and two Gurkha, the 2/4th Gurkha Rifles and 2/10th
Gurkha Rifles, supported by field artillery and the RAF. The late
nineteenth-century fort was no match for modern artillery and air
attack, and the infantry seized it after some confused fighting in
which the RAF bombed one of the Indian battalions.

Amanullah had clearly miscalculated. A peace conference con-
vened at Rawalpindi the next month, in July 1919. The treaty was
signed on 8 August, at which the Afghan government was granted
the right to conduct its own foreign affairs without let or hindrance
from anyone else. The Durand Line was confirmed as the border,
and the Afghans pledged not to interfere in the political affairs of the
North-West Frontier tribes.[9] With hindsight, making the obvious
and defensible river Indus the frontier and putting what are now the
Tribal Territories of Pakistan in Afghanistan would have simplified
matters in the early twenty-first century. All the problems with Al-
Qaeda and the Taliban, now being dealt with separately by the
Afghan and Pakistan governments, would be concentrated in
Afghanistan.

It had been a mercifully short war, in which the Gurkhas were heavily involved. Charles John Morris (1895–1980), who, as John Morris, later became head of the BBC Third Programme from 1954 to 1958, had arrived back from Palestine with the 2/3rd Gurkhas as the Third Afghan War was about to start. He was sent to Shahjehanpur for internal security duties. His story, told in the still shockingly frank *Hired to Kill* (1960), is hugely revealing about events of the time and the entire lifestyle of the Indian Army, including the Gurkhas, from the end of the First World War until 1932, just before Hitler came to power in Germany the following year.

During the First World War the Indian Army was woefully short of young British officers, and in 1916 a 'curious pamphlet' was circulated, inviting junior officers in British regiments, the vast majority of whom had temporary wartime commissions, to apply for regular commissions in the Indian Army. Morris explained:

> The brochure was designed like an advertisement for foreign travel, and it gave the impression that life in India was one long holiday. There were facilities for every kind of game; even polo cost next to nothing, and it was apparently possible to shoot a tiger from the bungalow veranda as one lay sipping one's morning tea. Strangely, there was no mention of the Indian people; so far as the pamphlet was concerned they did not exist.[10]

Morris applied. Like many officers holding temporary commissions as a result of the exponential expansion of the British Army, he was looked down on by the Sandhurst-trained 'professionals', many of whom, if not dead, were now staff or senior officers. He had initially been rejected for military service because of weak eyesight – he wore glasses, then considered a terrible disability, and looked weedy. He then managed to deceive the medical for the London Scottish, and enlisted. He says he was a poor soldier but in 1915, when the army was desperately short of officers, any person with education was likely to be seized upon as a potential officer. He was sent on an officers' course and commissioned, again in the London Scottish, and served in France, where he was wounded. The same happened to my grandfather who, horror of horrors, had been to *art*

school. But my grandfather was also a big man and a PT instructor, which counted for a lot when selecting leaders.

Morris was duly interviewed by the Brigade of Gurkhas and the India Office. Asked why he was not considering a regular commission in the British Army, he said he would not be able to afford it – a common reason for officers to join the Indian Army instead, as life was so much cheaper out there. The brigadier said he was a 'bloody young fool', and accepted him. Morris was initially assigned to the 9th Gurkhas and sent to India. Then in summer 1918 he was posted to Egypt, en route for Palestine.[11] Here he was assigned to the 2nd Battalion, 3rd Gurkha Rifles, where he would spend the rest of his military career until tuberculosis cut it short in 1932.[12] After Morris had been a couple of months in Palestine, the war ended and he was shipped back to India.

With just four years' service, now as a regular British officer in the Indian Army, he found himself in temporary command of the battalion. In May 1919,

> after I had occupied this exalted position for little more than a week we were ordered to provide a junior officer for service with the Gurkha Scouts, a new unit that was being formed for special duties in the Afghan war which had just broken out. I thought that if Shahjehanpur was typical of life in peacetime India I should not for long be able to support it; better see as much as possible before I resigned. I therefore selected myself for the appointment and left for Peshawar the following night.[13]

Morris, who during this time came to realise that he was gay, found virtually intolerable the regimentation, rituals and boredom of Indian Army regimental life, as well as many of his fellow officers and, even worse, their imperious wives.[14] But there were, nevertheless, enough fellow oddballs, and enough opportunities for extraordinary adventures, to keep him on board. Among those oddballs was the Honourable Charles Granville Bruce, who, as we saw in Chapter 5, was the founder of the Gurkha Scouts in the 1890s, and now a brigadier general. For all his bear-like manner, Bruce was a fluent Nepalese speaker and a consummate authority on Nepal and the Gurkhas, as his scholarly preface to his 1928 book, *The*

Gurkhas: Their Manners, Customs and Country, reveals.[15] Morris and
Bruce hit it off, for some strange reason. Morris later came to know
him well in the 1922 Mount Everest expedition, and they remained
friends until Bruce died in 1939.

Morris knew that the Gurkha Scouts had been formed 'during
the course of the Tirah campaign'[16] – in fact, it was before – and his
experiences mirrored those of the 1890s almost exactly.

> The training of these special scouts was based on a very simple idea;
> to search out the enemy while remaining as far as possible unseen
> and unheard. These were the tactics employed by the frontier tribes-
> men themselves with success largely because regular troops, who
> were invariably hampered by their cumbrous equipment, were
> unable to move quickly in this tangled and cumbrous border
> country.
>
> The contingent formed for service in the Afghan campaign of
> 1919 was a scratch lot; and although the men were picked shots and
> young, most of them were unknown to one another and few of
> them had seen any frontier service. We had therefore to carry out
> our job while learning to do it, and the difficulty was increased
> because it was obviously inadvisable for us to be seen prowling about
> on such of the surrounding hills as remained in our hands. We car-
> ried no equipment other than a rifle, wore a combination, according
> to individual taste, of uniform and mufti without badges of rank and
> our casual appearance was the subject of amused comment by our
> more regular brethren. And since we were irregular in every sense of
> the word, it was very difficult to place us in the military hierarchy.
> We operated therefore under the direct orders of the Divisional
> Commander.[17]

Again, one of the chief problems encountered was the constant
sniping at night, and the Scouts were sent out to stalk the snipers,
although initially without success. The Scouts moved forward into
Afghan territory, reaching Dacca, on the banks of the Kabul river.
According to Morris, the 'General' – he does not say which one,
but it would probably have been Eustace or Dyer – was sceptical
about the value of the Scouts. In true special-forces fashion, Morris
and his fellow officers asked their troops what they should do. They
said that they had earmarked a particularly active sniper who had

been carefully protected by his comrades and who guarded every approach to his positions, but that the sahibs should be patient.

> A few days later, very early in the morning, I was awakened suddenly by my orderly. He was convulsed with laughter and urged me to get up at once . . . As I emerged a lance-corporal [sic; it would have been a lance naik] saluted me. In his other hand he held the trophy, a grizzled Afghan head which had been neatly severed at the neck with a Gurkha *khukri* [sic]. He carried it by its mangy beard and when he placed it at my feet, like a well-trained retriever, I noticed that it was already covered with flies. I thought how inhuman and altogether impersonal it looked; I could not believe that an hour or so ago it had formed an integral part of a thinking man.
>
> I told the corporal to take the object at once to Divisional headquarters and crawled back into my bivouac. The General sent word of his pleasure, but he would be glad if in future we refrained from sending him further exhibits until after he had dealt with his breakfast. Later that day the head was impaled outside the camp, a warning to all who cared to heed it.[18]

Displaying such 'trophies' on cairns as a deterrent was a hallmark of the Gurkha Scouts, as it had been in 1897. The general probably got the message, but the war ended very quickly and the Gurkha Scouts were again disbanded.

Although the brief Afghan incursion had been repelled, the war stimulated the tribes in Waziristan (see Figure 5) to rebel, particularly the warlike Mahsuds. In late 1919 the situation became serious and two brigades were committed to restore Indian government authority. These included four Gurkha battalions: the 4/3rd, 2/5th, 2/9th and 3/11th. After three unsuccessful assaults, they seized the Ahnai Tangi Pass by a night attack in pouring rain, which left many of the troops, who had advanced unencumbered by greatcoats and blankets, suffering from pneumonia. The force then pushed on into the main Mahsud area. Here they encountered three very strong Mahsud positions, which were overcome after heavy fighting. The British decided to occupy Waziristan and started building roads to enable them to do this.[19] But the Mahsuds remained resentful and hostile.

The tribesmen often fought each other, but would occasionally

raid British Raj territory. When this happened, a small punitive force would be sent. Morris recalled that these minor frontier campaigns 'never merited more than a line or two, if that, in the London press, but over the years a number of lives were regularly lost to them.'[20]

Communications in Waziristan remained basic for some years. There were no cross-country supply vehicles in those days, and supplies had to be carried on pack animals, often camels. These columns were extremely vulnerable to tribesmen who would hide in the hills, unseen, and emerge only to exploit any weakness that the British-Indian forces displayed. The key procedure in North-West Frontier warfare was picqueting, which meant occupying every point – usually elevated – from which the column could be shot at so that it could pass in safety. Once the column had passed, it was critical to get down from the height as fast as possible, something Gurkhas excelled at. Morris noted that although some British regiments became good at these tactics, they could 'never acquire the necessary turn of speed and eye for the peculiarities of hilly country such as are second nature to Gurkhas and others who have been bred among mountains'.[21]

In November 1921, Morris's 2/3rd Gurkhas were deployed to Dardoni, a mud-hut camp surrounded by barbed-wire entanglements in the middle of a stony plain with the hills of Waziristan standing out sharply in the distance, 'as though cut out of cardboard'. Although the tribesmen were always present, they were invisible and there was a constant battle to convince the Gurkha soldiers that they really existed. The hostile, dangerous country appeared to be uninhabited.

Two days on from Dardoni, in the middle of Mahsud country, lay the fort of Datta Khel (see Figure 5), abandoned during the Third Afghan War two years before. The 2/3rd Gurkhas were ordered to reoccupy it. When they arrived, they found it had been gutted by the tribesmen, and that they would have to remain there until it was recommissioned, which would take several weeks. All supplies had to come on pack animals from Dardoni. The area is shown in Figure 5. Companies of the 2/3rd would take turns to garrison the Mahomed Khel staging post on the plain 2 miles (3 kilometres)

before the defile – the ominously named Spinchilla Pass – leading to the fort. When a convoy passed, that company would occupy the hills on either side of the pass to ensure the convoy's safe passage. The main force at Datta Khel would take care of the last part of the route. The outlying company and the main force would often meet on the hilltop and have a picnic while watching the convoy go by. Datta Khel had been occupied without any incident and the tribesmen were still nowhere to be seen.

Then, one day, as can happen in a war zone when everything seems quiet and normal, it all went horribly wrong. Morris's company – 'A' company, with Major Paget, the second in command of the battalion in overall charge, was sent to picquet the hills on either side of the pass.[22]

'It was one of those splendid sun-filled winter mornings,' he recalled. 'The sky was unbroken by cloud, and away in the distance the snow-sprinkled mountains of Afghanistan were clearly visible. We had had an exceptionally good meal on the pass and I was feeling almost happy when I gave the signal for the retirement to begin.'[23]

As usual, the first picquets descended the slopes at breakneck speed, when Morris heard a shot. He thought it was a 'negligent discharge' – one of the men had not applied the safety catch, perhaps. Then there was a fusillade, and it was apparent that the elusive tribesmen were firing at them. He did not know it at the time but Paget had agreed that 2/69th would withdraw first and would be in a position to provide fire support until Morris's company of about eighty men was safely down on the plain. Morris thought the 2/69th had begun to retire early, rather than awaiting his signal. The 2/69th also withdrew too far, so there was a gap of about 2 miles (3 kilometres) between the Gurkhas and the Punjabis and contact was lost.[24] The tribesmen had seen it and, as they always did, seized the opportunity to cut off Morris's company. The supporting battalion must have heard the shooting, but carried on retiring.

The Gurkhas fired back, but there were no visible targets. Some of them started getting hit. 'One of the first laws in frontier warfare is that, because of the known barbarity of the tribesmen, no wounded man shall ever be left on the field. I remembered this, but

I was not unduly worried because it never occurred to me that the battalion in our rear would not come to our aid at any moment.'[25]

Morris now realised that his force was not only isolated, but also outnumbered by people they could not see. He resolved to fight his way out with as few casualties as possible. In a small ravine they found a string of camels, all loaded with ammunition boxes, but it was not the time to stop and try, probably in vain, to deny these precious resources to the enemy. At this moment,

> I observed a small party of Mahsuds rushing towards us. I had taken my loaded revolver out of its holster and now thought to use it. But the strength seemed to have drained out of my body, and although I pointed the weapon I was incapable of pulling the trigger. Also I was immotile [sic]. After what seemed an eternity but could not have been more than a few seconds my orderly grabbed me by the arm and together we turned and ran. I have often since wondered why we were not killed, but perhaps the Mahsuds' reaction was the same as mine. Later on I realised I had defecated in my trousers.'[26]

Morris and the Gurkhas with him took up a position on the plain and after a while the rifle fire stopped. 'A silence, startling in its intensity, fell over the scene.' Morris recalled that there were only about thirty men left out of a whole company – eighty or so – although some may have made it back later. They straggled back into the staging post. All the posts around its perimeter were manned and the heavy barbed-wire obstacles to close the entrances had been dragged into position, and had to be moved before they could enter.

> I went at once to report to the Colonel who was in charge of the staging post. I presumed that now he knew what had happened he would take his battalion out again to bring back our wounded. To my consternation he refused, on the grounds that his strength was insufficient to ensure against a second disaster. Probably his decision was correct, but I was in no mood to accept it. I pleaded with him on humanitarian grounds until finally he reminded me gently that I was being insubordinate and told me to go and lie down.[27]

The colonel was presumably in charge of 2/69th – the battalion that had withdrawn prematurely. Someone brought Morris a strong cup of tea laced with whisky, and he went to look out over the plain.

What follows is shocking, but in 1960 it shocked the British Army even more.

> There was no sign of any normal human being and everything was as quiet as on a normal day. But in the far distance I could discern a cloud of vultures hovering in the sky; they were waiting for the moment of death.
>
> I stood there a long time watching the shadows lengthen, thinking and yet not thinking, physically numbed and unable to move away. As dusk was falling I noticed a solitary figure, moving very slowly and apparently with great difficulty. As he came near I recognised one of my own men. He was stark naked. He had been knifed in the belly and his testicles slashed. They now hung by bleeding threads of sinew. He was unable to speak and collapsed as soon as we carried him into the camp.
>
> I knew that this would be the fate of all the others and I went once more to see the Colonel, although even I knew that night was too near for anything to be done. He spoke to me with great kindness. 'I know only too well what will happen to your men,' he said. 'You do not have to remind me. But we must wait. There is nothing more we can do until tomorrow.'
>
> Later that night, as I lay awake in my bivouac trying to work out what I might have done to prevent this disaster, Umar Sing crept in and snuggled down beside me. He did not speak, but began quietly to massage my tired and aching body. I was no longer able to keep back the tears which I had been trying desperately to control.
>
> Early next morning we went back. The dead lay scattered in small groups, and it was obvious from their postures that except for the fortunate few who had been killed instantly every man had been subjected to the most barbarous treatment when he was still alive. The bodies had been stripped and in every case the genitals had been roughly severed and stuffed into the victim's mouth. This act, the greatest insult a Moslem can offer to a Hindu or other so-called infidel, is believed by the tribesmen to deny the rewards of paradise.
>
> The string of camels had died where their drivers had abandoned them, but the boxes of ammunition had been prised open and the contents removed.[28]

The Regimental History says the Battalion lost twenty-three 'killed', including Major Paget, and nineteen wounded. The latter

would have been in other companies, or among those who made it back to the camp. However, the Mahsuds also lost heavily, including their leader, Turia, who was notorious for raiding to the east.[29]

The frank admission of homosexual relations – and it is apparent from other passages that the relationship did not just involve massaging a tired body – caused shock and denial.[30] When Morris's book was published, in 1960, homosexual relations between consenting men over the age of twenty-one were still a criminal offence, which they remained in civilian life until 1967 and, in the armed forces, until 1994. And Umar Sing was a Gurkha soldier, probably under twenty-one. Nevertheless, no one seems to have tried to prosecute the now sixty-five-year-old former head of the BBC Third Programme. The passage is important because it underlines how homosexual relations were as prevalent in the Indian Army as anywhere else, and how the establishment, as would be expected at the time, completely denied it.

Apart from Umar Sing, Morris just talks about 'his men'. In this case, naming them would have been inappropriate anyway. But what Morris calls 'the very finest type of paternal Indian Army officer' knew his men very well. General Bruce, for example, 'knew the name of every man in his regiment, together with the intimate details of their private lives'.[31]

The hideous torture and mutilation of Indian Army wounded led to calls for tough measures against the tribesmen, including the use of chemical weapons. Poison gas had first been used in 1915 and in the First World War such measures were used on a large scale. They were used quite widely in the 1920s and '30s, but not against European adversaries, and again in the 1980–8 Iran–Iraq War. In 1919, the Conference at Versailles considered requests from the Red Cross to ban them, but since the North-West Frontier tribesmen obeyed no laws of war, conditions there might be different. Churchill, the Secretary of State for War and Air in 1919, had no qualms:

I do not understand this squeamishness about the use of gas . . .
    I am strongly in favour of using poisoned gas against uncivilised tribes. The moral effect should be so good that the loss of life should

be reduced to a minimum. It is not necessary to use only the most deadly gases; gases can be used which cause great inconvenience and would spread a lively terror and yet would leave no serious permanent effects on most of those affected.[32]

Churchill also had experience of the 1897 Malakand campaign, where he had witnessed what the tribesmen did to the wounded:

we cannot in any circumstances acquiesce in the non-utilisation of any weapons which are available to procure a speedy termination of the disorder which prevails on the frontier.

If it is fair war for an Afghan to shoot down a British soldier behind a rock and cut him to pieces as he lies wounded on the ground, why is it not fair for a British artilleryman to fire a shell which makes the said native sneeze? It is really too silly.

CIGS [Chief of the Imperial General Staff] concurs.[33]

In spite of that, the Indian Army and government resisted the idea. Some gas shells and protective clothing were sent to India in 1919 with a further small shipment in 1920 for possible use on the North-West Frontier. However, the Under-Secretary of State for India blocked a further order for 10,000 respirators (gas masks). The Indian Army, including Gurkha regiments, was trained to some extent for chemical warfare but the overwhelming view was that chemical weapons would be used only in response to an Afghan Army or North-West Frontier tribal chemical attack, both of which were highly unlikely.[34]

The Russian threat had not gone away, however. In 1918, Lloyd George noted that the Turks were unlikely 'ever to be dangerous to our interests in the East while Russia, if in the future she became regenerated, might be so'.[35] The Soviet regime put great stress on chemical warfare as many regarded it as the form of future war and some, including Churchill, also thought, astonishingly, that it could be more humane. The British became concerned about the establishment of a Soviet chemical weapons school in 1927, and Indian Army preparations for chemical warfare focussed mainly on the risk of the old Russian threat returning.[36]

Had Morris undergone such an experience today, he would no doubt have had months of counselling. In those days, people were

just expected to get on with it. All Morris says is that, when he finally left Dardoni, he hoped that he 'should never again be required to set foot on the North-West Frontier of India, for the tribesmen of which I had understandably acquired a passionate hatred'.[37] He was lucky to have survived, and it is surprising that such a disaster, involving the deaths of twenty-three men, a quarter of a company, did not rate some sort of inquiry.

Morris was luckier still, however, because soon after the incident, which was not repeated, he received a telegram from Delhi offering him a completely fresh experience. He was asked to join the first attempt to climb Mount Everest, the 1922 expedition led by none other than Brigadier General the Hon. Charles Bruce, founder of the Gurkha Scouts, with whom he had corresponded but not yet met. He made his way to Darjeeling where he found Bruce's hotel.

> He had long been known to the men of his own regiment as *Bhalu*, the bear, and as he lumbered into the room, almost breaking down the door as he did so, I realised that no description could be more apt. It was typical of him that, even before shaking hands, he should address me in a stream of fluent Nepali, much of it abusive and obscene, after which he broke into roars of schoolboyish laughter. Fortunately I had the presence of mind to enter into the spirit of the occasion and answered him in the same language . . . many years later . . . he told me that he was horrified when he first set eyes on my bespectacled and unmilitary features . . . It was only my knowledge of Nepali that saved the situation.[38]

Bruce was an outstanding example of a Gurkha officer, and of that maxim, comforting to the eccentrics among us, that 'leaders stand out by being *different*'.[39]

Meanwhile, the occupation of Waziristan, and the building of roads and forts, kept large numbers of troops busy, including most of the twenty Gurkha battalions. The frontier tribes became more restive again in the 1930s and in 1935 there was a rising by the Mohmands at Peshawar. Four brigades were sent to suppress them, including one commanded by Brigadier Harold Alexander, later Earl Alexander of Tunis, and one commanded by Brigadier Claude Auchinleck, later Field Marshal Sir Claude Auchinleck. It was a hard school, but a good one.

In 1937 the Fakir of Ipi declared a holy war on the British, and a brigade was sent to occupy the remote area of Damdil, including the 2/5th, 1/6th and 2/6th Gurkhas. A picquet of eight Gurkhas – a section – was targeted for a massive attack by the Fakir's Pathans, but only two were killed and the remainder, though wounded, held them off until relieved.[40]

Because the Gurkhas were regarded as a 'third force', with a very marked neutrality between the British, on the one hand, and the Indians on the other, they did not benefit as much as the rest of the Indian Army from the reforms that took place in the inter-war period.

In June 1918, in response to burgeoning Indian nationalism, instructions were issued for the selection of Indian cadets for entry to Sandhurst, the British Royal Military College where regular infantry and cavalry officers were trained. At that time the Royal Military Academy was at Woolwich, and trained young men for the more intellectually taxing roles of artillery and engineer officers.[41] Ten Indian cadets would be taken per year, five on each of the two Sandhurst intakes.[42] It was not a radical move, the more so since the Indian cadets, rather like their British colleagues, were 'reliable, politically inert, aristocratic and conservative'.[43]

The Esher Committee of March 1919 also addressed the 'Indianisation' of the Indian officer corps. The Congress Party of India had been vocal about the entry of Indians into the commissioned ranks, and not just as Viceroy's Commissioned Officers who, as we have seen, occupied an intermediate position between warrant officers and the few British King's Commissioned Officers (see also Table 2). The lessons of the First World War (see Chapter 6) supported this idea on military grounds as well but as General Rawlinson, who headed the second Committee that reported in March 1921, observed, it would take two or three generations for Indian officers of the right kind to be produced in sufficient numbers.[44]

A more radical move was the creation of a school for Indian cadets at Indhore. The first class of thirty-three received Viceroy's Commissions on 1 December 1919 but then received King's

Commissions on 17 July 1920. Rawlinson's committee recommended that 25 per cent of the commissions granted in the Indian Army each year should be for native Indians, a figure that should rise by 2.5 per cent per year. On that basis, 50 per cent of commissions awarded would be to Indians in 1931, 75 per cent in 1941 and 100 per cent in 1951. But, given that direct-entry officers' careers typically lasted about thirty years after commissioning, the progress of Indianisation would still be very slow.

The main problem was the reluctance of British officers to serve under Indians or – although they were not yet involved – Gurkhas. In 1923 the planners came up with the 'eight units scheme', whereby two cavalry and six infantry regiments were targeted for Indianisation. This was presented as offering the Indian officers the opportunity to show how good they were, but nobody was fooled.[45]

Then in 1927 the 'Indian Sandhurst' committee recommended that 'India should have a military college of her own and thus be self-sufficient in terms of her most important national needs'.[46] It was intended that it be up and running by 1933. The Commander-in-Chief India, Field Marshal Sir William Birdwood, refused to implement the recommendation so it was shelved until he retired in 1930. In autumn 1932 the Indian Military Academy at Dehra Dun, India's Sandhurst, opened for business. Unlike the two-year course at Sandhurst, it was a three-year spell, more like a proper university, with thirty-three students per year. However, these Indian commissioned officers (ICOs) were still disadvantaged compared to their Sandhurst-trained Indian counterparts, and their commissions were still valid only in India. Once Dehra Dun opened in 1932, Indians stopped going to Sandhurst, so since the first Sandhurst intake in 1918, a maximum of 140 could have been commissioned, assuming no drop-outs.[47]

None of this applied to Gurkhas directly, although they might find themselves in future commanded by an Indian officer with similar status to a British one. For the Gurkhas, the Viceroy's Commissioned post of subedar major – adviser to the British commanding officer on all Gurkha matters, equivalent to a super-regimental sergeant major – would remain the pinnacle of

attainment. But the Gurkhas were generally unimpressed with the Indian nationalists' attempt to turn them against their British employers.

An exception was the case of Gajendra Malla, a 'line boy', the son of a Gurkha who, unlike the Gurkhas recruited directly from Nepal, therefore had the advantage of attending a Gurkha regimental school at Dehra Dun. He joined the 9th Gurkha Rifles as a clerk, but managed to get transferred to being a naik in a rifle company, and was then promoted to havildar (sergeant). His intelligence soon got him into trouble. He was arrested for alleged links with Kharagbahadur Bisht, a political activist who had been arrested in November 1930, and who had been trying to spread anti-British propaganda among Gurkhas. Gajendra admitted he knew Kharagbahadur – they had been at the Gurkha school in Dehra Dun together – but denied any conspiracy. He was released and, because he was keen and promising with an unblemished record, was promoted to the junior VCO rank of jemadar in April 1935. But he still encountered prejudice because he was a 'line boy', and this effectively debarred him from the pinnacle of Gurkha rank, subedar major, which was traditionally held by a true Gurkha hillman. And he just did not look the type.

Then, at the start of the Second World War, his opportunity came. Hill Gurkhas were not eligible for emergency King's Commissions, because they were not Indians. But Gajendra was, and got one, although he had to transfer to intelligence because emergency commissioned officers were not then allowed to serve with Gurkha regiments. After Indian independence, he found himself a full colonel in the new Indian Army and became the first recruiting officer for Indian Gorkhas. But then he was demoted to major, because the newly independent Indians found him to be too 'British'.[48] Life can be unfair.

8

The Second World War

AT THE START of the Second World War, the Indian Army numbered 194,373 officers and men in ninety-six infantry battalions, still heavily orientated towards the dry and mountainous North-West Frontier, and with little training or expertise to deal with the jungle conditions on and east of the North-East Frontier – Burma – where, apart from minor police actions, the situation had been fairly stable. On 3 September 1939 the UK declared war on Germany and the Indian Viceroy declared war the same day, although he had not consulted the Indian Congress Party, which controlled eight Indian provinces and which objected. Those Congress Party-controlled governments resigned.[1]

The Second World War started as a 'Cabinet war' between European powers and – having reintroduced a form of conscription in April 1939, which became full conscription in October, shortly after the war had started – the UK did not need massive reinforcement from the Indian Army as had happened in 1914. Initially the Indian Army, which had been starved of resources and was not trained or equipped for a European war, was not much involved. It provided a few brigades to reinforce Egypt and Malaya, although the Japanese threat, which would not be unleashed until December 1941, was fatally underrated.

The key developments affecting the Gurkhas took place in Nepal, not India. Its former ruler, Chandra Shamsher Rana, who had done so much to help the British in the First World War, had died in 1929. His brother, Bhim Shamsher, ruled for two years and then also died. He was succeeded by Judha Shamsher, the last of the Rana dynasty. Judha, like all the Ranas, was widely criticised in his own country and in the Indian press for having sold out to the

British but, fortunately for the latter, managed to have his way. In 1938, during the Munich crisis, he offered eight Nepalese battalions to help maintain Indian security in the event of war.

In 1940, at the time of the fall of France, Sir Geoffrey Betham, the British minister in Nepal, requested an interview. He found Judha surrounded by advisers, some of whom were against giving more help to Britain. Betham asked for permission to raise another ten battalions of Gurkhas. Judha asked him about the fall of France and whether Britain itself would soon be invaded. Betham said that the UK would overcome this 'serious set-back'. He was surprised when Judha agreed to his request. But Judha then allegedly asked whether he had read the 1816 Treaty of Segauli or the revised 1923 treaty, both of which used the phrase 'perpetual friendship'. Betham said he had. According to one account, Judha then asked:

'Do you let your friend down in time of need?'
'No, Sir, but there is often a difference between countries and individuals.'
'There should not be. If you win, we will win with you. If you lose, we will lose with you.'[2]

The words may not have been spoken exactly like that, but the sense is accurate. Judha would support Britain. Of course, the British were much closer to Nepal than the Germans were, and, in exchange for being allowed to recruit boys and young men of military age, Britain guaranteed Nepal's independence and the Rana regime.

The new Gurkha battalions needed Gurkha VCOs and NCOs, as well as British officers, and so experience was spread very thin. In September 1940 the 4th and 5th Indian Divisions under General Sir Archibald Wavell were deployed to meet the Italians in North Africa, but the Gurkhas were not involved in his early victories over them. It was not until 1942, after German forces under Lieutenant General Erwin Rommel arrived in North Africa in February, that the Gurkhas saw large-scale action there.

They first encountered serious opposition closer to home, and the experience was initially bad. The testimony of T. J. Phillips of the 1/9th Gurkhas from October 1941 indicates poor morale and

a total lack of initiative, with Gurkhas in the 1/9th and 1/1st refusing to do anything without direct orders from a British officer. By the time they were committed to action, they appear to have sharpened up.[3]

On 7 December 1941 the Imperial Japanese Navy attacked the US Fleet at Pearl Harbor and the Pacific war began. Having occupied French Indo-China after the fall of France in summer 1940, the Japanese now attacked the American-held Philippines, and the British possessions of Hong Kong, Malaya and the Dutch East Indies, now Indonesia. The Japanese were after their precious commodities of rubber and oil. On 19 January 1942 they attacked the British possession of Burma, with the strategic aim of severing Nationalist Chinese communications with the rest of the world and securing their hold on the rest of South-East Asia.[4] Although few realised it at the time, the Japanese were also aware of another important commodity which was under the ground in Burma. Uranium.[5] The North-East Frontier (Figure 6), had long been a theatre of war for the Indian Army, but it was now drawn further east, into Burma (Figure 8).

The first major incident involving the Gurkhas occurred in February 1942. The 48th Brigade of 17th Indian Division arrived in Rangoon on 31 January with three Gurkha battalions: the 1/3rd, 1/4th and 2/5th. The first two battalions were detached for other duties, the 1/3rd guarding supplies to the rear, while the 2/5th was brigaded with the 1/9th Jats and the 8th Burma Rifles. By the night of 19–20 February the Japanese, advancing fast through the jungle, with which the Gurkhas were, as yet, unfamiliar, had outflanked most of 17th Division including the 1/3rd, 1/4th, 2/5th, 1/7th and 3/7th Gurkhas. Behind them, to the west, was the Sittang railway bridge, an important crossing over the kilometre-wide Sittang river, which the Japanese needed to capture intact and the British needed to blow (see Figure 8). The 1/3rd and 2/5th had not eaten and were therefore allowed to stop withdrawing, while the 1/4th withdrew across the bridge, along with the headquarters of 48th Brigade and 17th Division, leaving a small force holding its eastern end. It was the only battalion that escaped before the bridge was dynamited.

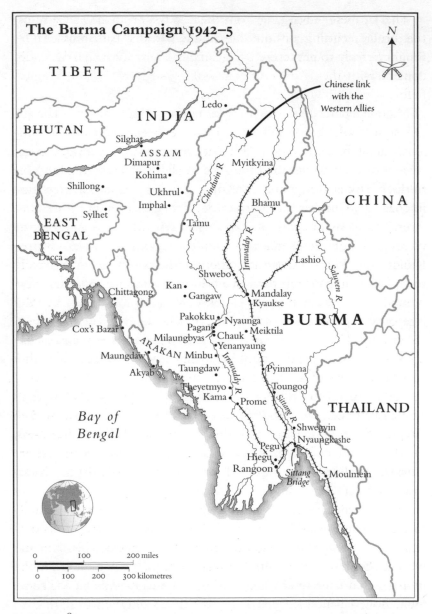

The Burma Campaign 1942–5

N

TIBET

BHUTAN

INDIA

Ledo

Silghat

ASSAM
Dimapur
Kohima

Shillong

Ukhrul

Sylhet

Imphal

EAST
BENGAL

Tamu

Dacca

Chinese link
with the
Western Allies

Myitkyina

Bhamu

CHINA

Chindwin R.

Irrawaddy R.

Lashio

Salween R.

Shwebo

Chittagong

Kan
Gangaw

Mandalay
Kyaukse

BURMA

Pakokku
Pagan
Milaungbyas
Minbu

Nyaunga
Chauk
Yenanyaung

Meiktila

Cox's Bazar

ARAKAN

Maungdaw

Akyab

Taungdaw

Thayetmyo
Kama

Irrawaddy R.

Pyinmana

Toungoo

THAILAND

Prome

Bay of
Bengal

Sittang R.

Shwegyin
Nyaungkashe

Pegu
Hlegu
Rangoon

Moulmein

Sittang
Bridge

0   100   200 miles

0   100   200   300 kilometres

FIGURE 8

216

The Japanese, advancing from the north, got to the east end of the bridge, cutting off the remaining Gurkha battalions. They fought fiercely to get to the bridge and the 1/3rd very nearly made contact with the 1/4th Gurkhas, holding the east of the bridge, before it was blown up at 0530 hours on 23 February.

Major General John Smyth VC, commanding the 17th Indian Division, took the decision to blow the reserve demolition and although it remains controversial it was probably the right one, since it delayed the Japanese advance to allow an armoured brigade to disembark at Rangoon.[6] Like the paratroops trapped at Arnhem in 1944, the Gurkhas on the east side, if they managed to reach the river, had to swim across. Given their mountain upbringing, most were afraid of the water and could not swim. Captain Bruce Kinloch and two other British officers, who could, swam the river to collect a sampan and made five crossings, rescuing about seventy wounded. Others used bamboo poles as floats from the nearby village of Mokpalin. Each of the four trapped Gurkha battalions got about a third of its men away, and left two-thirds behind. Out of 2,500 men lost in the disaster, two-thirds were Gurkhas.[7]

The remnants of the 1/3rd and 2/5th Gurkhas formed a composite battalion, as did the 1/7th and 3/7th. Of the 7th Gurkhas' 900 fatal casualties in the Second World War, some 350 died in the Sittang disaster. The 1st Battalion of 10th Gurkha Rifles also arrived in March, just before the fall of Rangoon, and joined the other Gurkha battalions as the British slowly withdrew from Burma, back towards India.

By a fortunate coincidence, in February the British had decided to create a command for Burma, I Burma Corps. The corps commander was a former lieutenant in the Warwickshire Regiment who had been with the 1/6th Gurkhas on Sari Bair ridge at Gallipoli in 1915, and later joined the Gurkhas. That officer, one William Slim, now a lieutenant general, had therefore served in both the British and the Indian armies, had served extensively with that battalion and had also commanded the 2/7th Gurkhas. But, unlike some former Gurkha officers, he never regarded his Gurkha service as a 'defining attribute' – or never admitted as much.[8] Nevertheless, the Gurkha connexion was very dominant. Slim recalled

how Major General Bruce Scott, commanding 1st Burma Division, Major General 'Punch' Cowan, commanding 17th Indian Division, and he, the corps commander, all came from the 1st Battalion, 6th Gurkhas.[9] Slim noted how those two divisional commanders 'had and held the confidence and indeed affection of their troops, British, Indian and Gurkha, to a remarkable degree.'[10]

Moreover, the news was not all bad. At Kyaukse (see Figure 8), on 28–29 April, the 48th Brigade, now entirely composed of Gurkhas, was attacked by the Japanese 18th Division. The division, which had come from Singapore – where 130,000 British and Australians had surrendered on 15 February in the worst defeat in the British empire's history – attacked a prepared position mostly held by the 7th Gurkhas. They did so by moonlight. According to the regimental history, 'The honours of the battle go to the 7th Gurkhas who bore the brunt of the attack. They broke up and handled very severely three separate attacks launched against them during the night of 28th–29th. Then, not content with that, they planned and carried out a counter-attack on the 29th that was quite brilliant and dealt great execution to the enemy.'[11]

Slim witnessed the action. After repelling the three attacks, 'at dawn on 30 April, tanks and Gurkhas sallied out and cleared a burnt-out village in front of our lines. Many Japanese in it were killed . . .The Gurkhas were particularly pleased at trapping thirty-eight of the enemy who had taken refuge in a culvert under the road.'[12]

The initial successes of the Japanese and their ability to move through the jungle, whereas British empire troops were initially wedded to the few roads, had created the impression that they were invincible. But the Gurkhas were learning that they were just as good as the Japanese, and discovering that they, too, could work in the jungle. In their counter-attack at Kyaukse they lost ten men and killed 500 Japanese. As a result of this defensive-offensive holding action, the 48th Brigade was able to withdraw smoothly across the Ava Bridge.

Soon after Kyaukse, on 10 May, Slim was visiting Shwegyin on the Sittang river and found himself in an area occupied by the 7th Gurkhas, which came under shellfire. Knowing the Gurkhas'

reputation – 'bravest of the brave' – he thought it would look bad if he ran for cover.

> So, not liking it a bit, I continued to walk forward. Then, from behind a bush that offered scant cover to his bulky figure, rose my old friend, the Subedar-Major of the 7th Gurkhas [Saharman Rai], his face creased in a huge grin which almost hid his twinkling almond eyes. He stood there and shook with laughter at me. I asked him coldly what he was laughing at, and he replied that it was very funny to see the General Sahib wandering along there by himself, *not knowing what to do*! And, by Jove, he was right; I did not!
>
> . . . A British soldier would have called out to me to take shelter and would have made room for me beside him. The average Indian sepoy would have watched anxiously, but said nothing unless I was hit, when he would have leapt forward and risked his life to get me under cover. A Sikh would have sprung up, and with the utmost gallantry, dramatically covered me with his own body, thrilled at the chance of an audience. Only a Gurkha would stand up and laugh [emphasis in original].[13]

Slim directed the withdrawal from Burma with great skill. It is not possible to detail the constant battles in which Gurkhas were involved during their time in Burma but the withdrawal of the Burma Corps across the river Chindwin illustrates their value.

On the morning of 12 May, tired after a sleepless night, the 1/10th Gurkhas reached Alon (see Figure 8) and began to dig in to hold the Japanese while the two divisions of the Burma Corps concentrated before withdrawing across the great river at Shwegyin. The all-Gurkha 48th Brigade formed the rearguard as the corps crossed the river and pulled back into Assam, India. On 10 May the 7th Gurkhas had again played an important part in stopping a re-inforced Japanese regiment. The artillery commander of the 48th Brigade, realising that they would never be able to take the ammunition back with them, had decided to fire it all at the Japanese. The result was to stop them long enough to accomplish the river crossing and continue their withdrawal back to India, crossing the border on 21 May.[14] The British did so just in time, before the onset of the monsoon, which would have made any sort of organised withdrawal impossible. It also prevented the Japanese following up. The

Burma Corps arrived back exhausted and massively depleted, but the survivors now knew how to fight the Japanese.

It was in the very final phases of the 17th Indian Division's withdrawal that the Gurkhas won their second VC of the Second World War, and their first in Burma. On 27 May 1943, after most of the division was back across the border, the 2/5th Gurkhas were holding the line on the Tiddim Road. They had been hit very hard at the Sittang bridge and in the withdrawal – having lost 543 men, including British officers, VCOs and NCOs – half their strength. If they were to continue to hold, they would have to clear the Japanese from positions overlooking their own.

Gaje Ghale had enlisted in 1936 and been in the campaign against the infamous Fakir of Ipi on the North-West Frontier. During the withdrawal, he was said to have been 'often in the forefront of the action', although the subsequent citation disputes this. As the 2/5th held the line on the Tiddim Road, he was made an acting havildar and given command of a platoon, which now comprised a number of new recruits, hastily brought in to strengthen the mauled battalion.

> it was essential to capture Basha East hill which was the key to the enemy position. Two assaults had failed but a third assault was ordered to be carried out . . . Havildar Gaje Ghale was in command of one platoon: he had never been under fire before [?] and the platoon consisted of young soldiers. The approach for this platoon to their objective was along a narrow knife-edge with precipitous sides and bare of jungle whereas the enemy positions were well concealed. In places, the approach was no more than five yards wide and was covered by a dozen machine guns besides being subjected to artillery and mortar fire . . .
>
> While preparing for the attack the platoon came under heavy mortar fire but Havildar Gaje Ghale rallied them and led them forward. Approaching to close range of the well-entrenched enemy, the platoon came under withering fire and this NCO was wounded in the arm, chest and leg by an enemy hand grenade. Without pausing to attend to his serious wounds and with no heed to the intensive fire from all sides, Havildar Gaje Ghale closed his men and led them to close grips with the enemy when a bitter hand to hand struggle ensued.

Havildar Gaje Ghale dominated the fight by his outstanding example of dauntless courage and superb leadership. Hurling hand grenades, covered in blood from his own neglected wounds, he led assault after assault encouraging his platoon by shouting the Gurkhas' battle cry. Spurred on by the irresistible will of their leader to win, the platoon stormed and carried the hill by a magnificent all out effort and inflicted very heavy casualties on the Japanese.[15]

It seems utterly extraordinary that a junior NCO who had been constantly in action throughout the withdrawal of the 48th Indian Brigade of 17th Indian Division in the face of the Japanese, from the Sittang river back to Assam, should have 'never been under fire before'. If so, it illustrates how most people's experience of war, even though in a theatre of operations, is still at one remove from actual combat. Alternatively, it illustrates how 'under fire' means a very hard definition of the same. Close combat, under intense enemy fire. 'Trigger time' . . . Either way, Havildar Gaje Ghale VC had now *most certainly* experienced the latter, to the highest degree.

The remnants of five Gurkha battalions – the 1/3rd,1/4th, 2/5th, 1/10th and the composite battalion of the 7th Gurkhas – began re-forming and were brought back up to strength. The British knew that as soon as the monsoon stopped the Japanese were likely to attack into Assam. To pre-empt this, the First Arakan Offensive was launched down the coast from July 1942, but this failed. However, the Japanese, having gained control of the main rivers in Burma and the communications along them, were content to remain on the defensive during 1942–3, while the Allies' views on the way ahead differed. The British concentrated on building up their forces in India. The Americans wanted to open up northern Burma so as to re-establish communications with Chiang Kai-shek's Nationalist Chinese who were fighting the Japanese. The British thought this impossible. Instead, they focussed on unconventional warfare options to carry the war behind Japanese lines in Burma, a development made possible by the rapidly increasing potential of Allied air power.[16]

Initially known as Long-Range Penetration (LRP) Groups, the forces placed deep in enemy territory were to keep in contact by

radio and to be supplied by air. In 1942 the Commander-in-Chief India, Field Marshal Lord Wavell, sent for Major Orde Wingate, who had made a reputation as a leader of small indigenous forces in Palestine – the Jewish Special Night Squads – and against the Italians in Abyssinia. Along with Michael Calvert, he had been sent to try to organise native resistance against the Japanese during the withdrawal from Burma.

Wingate was a gunner, trained at Woolwich, but was aloof, ascetic and distant. He therefore had a reputation for being difficult. He called his special forces Chindits, from Chinthe, a mythical creature, half lion, half flying griffin, which stands ready to ward off evil spirits at the entrance to Burmese temples. He was promoted to brigadier and given the 77th Indian Infantry Brigade to test his ideas. It comprised a British battalion, a battalion of Burma Rifles, the 3rd Battalion 2nd Gurkha Rifles and some British commandos.[17]

It is easy to see why Wingate might be either adored or abhorred, and was widely considered to be mad. He clearly did not understand the Gurkhas. Whereas some of the British participants in the enterprise were inspired by Wingate's messianic zeal, the extraordinary boldness of the enterprise, and their consequent membership of another elite, these motivational factors were lost on the Gurkhas, most of whom were young, wartime recruits.

Wingate split his brigade into seven 'columns', each based on an infantry or rifle company, of which four were based on companies of the 3/2nd Gurkhas. The British Gurkha officers, with their deep-rooted loyalty to their men, blamed problems on Wingate:

> Regardless of language difficulties, the unit was broken up, its organisation jettisoned, its sub-units mingled with British soldiers, complex tactical methods planted on it and many of the men employed as mule-drivers – an animal to which the young wartime Gurkha was little accustomed and, in any case, a noisy and vulnerable means of transport such as no experienced commander would ever have borne with for one minute in operations in such country.[18]

One of the key mistakes was mixing the Gurkhas up with men of other units at quite a low level. The regimental history of the 2nd Gurkhas reiterated that 'The Gurkha rifleman is peculiarly the

creature of his regiment and is apt to feel lost when serving in other formations.'[19]

Another Wingate innovation, which one of the Gurkhas' own officers refused to pass on, was his instruction that any wounded 'were to be left in the nearest village'. Given the Gurkhas' long and bitter experience of the North-West Frontier, as we have seen, leaving wounded was not an option, especially when fighting the Japanese who, if not always employing the sadistic and sexual ingenuity of the frontier tribesmen, would often bayonet enemy wounded to save bullets. The Japanese had not signed the 1929 Geneva Conventions, either. Colonel D. F. ('Nick') Neill recalled that 'my wounded, if we took casualties, would never be left behind: or, if they were, they would be left over my dead body . . . [It was incredible] that any commander should contemplate issuing such a morale-damaging order just as his force was on the point of being launched into the territory of an enemy as brutal and callous as the Japanese.'[20]

The first Chindit expedition, Operation Longcloth, started on 6 February 1943. The seven columns, comprising about 3,000 men, of whom 1,289 were Gurkhas, crossed the Chindwin and infiltrated 150 miles (240 kilometres) into Japanese-held territory. The attack was meant to coincide with an offensive from the north (see Figure 9) by US General 'Vinegar Joe' Stilwell, controlling a large force of Nationalist Chinese troops. Stilwell had a huge area command – the 'China–Burma–India Theatre', equivalent to Eisenhower's in Europe, later, and MacArthur's in the Pacific. His manner, judging by his nickname, was not much different to Wingate's. But while both shared disregard of conventional military protocol, Stilwell was known for much greater concern for his men. If such synergy had been achieved, the Chindits could have really disrupted any Japanese response but Stilwell's offensive was called off at the last moment. Wingate insisted that he be allowed to carry on, and Wavell let him, which was probably a mistake. Nevertheless, the Chindits cut the Mandalay–Myitkina railway supplying the Japanese northern front in Burma, where they faced the Chinese Nationalists under Stilwell's direction.

In response to the Chindit attacks the Japanese retaliated and

Wingate made a – probably bad – decision to split up his reinforced company columns into smaller groups to escape back to India.[21] As Callwell had written nearly half a century before, splitting up one's force was not in itself a cardinal sin as long as the bits were big enough to deal with anything that the enemy was likely to throw at them.[22] With the Japanese sending reinforced platoons against the fragments, however, the latter were not big enough.

Neill thought that Wingate had gone 'one river too far', as far as the Irrawaddy, where there were excellent Japanese communications, and that, if he had stopped short, he might have got out with fewer casualties. Neill described this withdrawal as a 'waking nightmare'.[23] The mules became the unacknowledged heroes of the withdrawal, and the Gurkhas came to know them.

One of the most bizarre testimonies to the Gurkhas' adaptability and to the natural bond that forms between sons of the soil and animals, however objectively the latter may have to be killed, sometimes, comes in Neill's account. The Gurkhas were struggling back under constant attacks by Japanese counter-penetration patrols, each more than a platoon in strength, and therefore superior in numbers to the withdrawing small groups of Gurkhas, who were exhausted, hungry, bitten by mosquitoes and chewed by leeches. It encapsulates the *literal* and oddly *lateral* thinking that characterised the Gurkhas, and probably still does. Neill came across one of his mule-drivers, Rifleman Prembahadur Rai, no. 107394, sitting cross-legged beneath the heads of the two mules. He was playing a bamboo flute, which Neill had seen him making some days previously. The British officer smiled at him and said, '*Bansuli kina bajaeko?*' – 'Why were you playing the flute?' Rifleman Prembahadur looked up and laughed. '"*Khachcharlai rahar lagcha, hajur!*," he replied. "*The mules like it, Sir*" [emphasis added]'[24] Prembahadur was a 10th Gurkha, seconded to the 3/2nd. He survived Operation Longcloth, but was killed at Meiktila on 13 March 1945.[25]

Although Wingate has been execrated for daring to say anything unfavourable about the Gurkhas, and although he was a rare example of a British soldier who served with them but was not won over by them, his comments have value. He fully understood the difference between the newly recruited young Gurkhas he was

given, as part of a newly raised wartime army, and the seasoned regulars who would have served on the North-West Frontier. The dependence on good British officers was also apparent. According to Wingate's report on the operation, 'only Gurkha soldiers of some years' standing, with a high proportion of experienced and Gurkhali-speaking British Officers, are fit to take part in operations of this exacting character.'[26]

As an intellectual, Wingate gave elliptical and riddle-like instructions, which, while possibly intelligible to British street kids, were unintelligible to the very literal-minded Gurkhas. That does not mean they were not intelligent, just different. Wingateisms included, 'When in doubt, don't fire' and 'The answer to noise is silence'. But Wingate was exasperated when, probably as a result, a group of Gurkhas calmly watched the enemy firing in their direction while carrying on, as they had been told to do during any free time, cleaning their rifles.[27] The Gurkhas might similarly have responded to 'Brown is the new black' by a time-consuming and nugatory effort to recolour their leather equipment, or 'Less is more' by leaving most of their ammunition behind.

Slim gives some good examples of Gurkha literal-mindedness, including one at the later Battle of Imphal–Kohima, in May 1944. Two Gurkhas had been ordered to bury Japanese bodies. It was a simple instruction, until one of the Japanese whom they picked up turned out not to be dead. One of the Gurkhas pulled out his kukri to despatch the not-quite corpse, when a passing British officer intervened. 'You mustn't do that, Johnny. Don't kill him!' The Gurkha looked at him 'in pained surprise'. 'No, *sahib*,' he protested, 'we can't bury him *alive*! [emphasis in original]'[28]

The first Chindit force struggled back in May 1943 having lost nearly 1,000 men – a third of its strength. Without Stilwell's offensive, the operation should never have been launched but it was successfully presented as a form of triumph. The key lesson was that British empire troops could take on the Japanese in the jungle and win at the tactical level. If they could win there at that level, they could certainly win at the operational and strategic. The other lessons learned included signals communications and air resupply. And Allied air power was getting stronger.

In August 1943, Churchill took Wingate with him to the Quebec Conference to sell the concept of long-range penetration to the Americans. They bought it. Plans were made for an attack on northern Burma by the 14th Army, now commanded by General Slim, from the west, by Stilwell's Chinese–American force from the north, and a Chinese force from Yunnan province to the west. Wingate, promoted to major general, would command a 'Special Force', called the 3rd Indian Division for security reasons, to complement the three-pronged attack by moving behind Japanese lines. The 'Special Force' included four Gurkha battalions – the 3/4th, 3/6th, 3/9th and 4/9th. In response to the lessons of Operation Longcloth, the Americans would provide massive air support for the Special Force. There would be B-25 Mitchell bombers, P-51 Mustang long-range fighters, C-47 Dakota transport planes and CG-4A Hadrian gliders, plus light aircraft that could land on short strips – Stinson Us and L5s, for the evacuation of wounded. This time, the forces would land by air and set up 'strongholds' – a phrase Wingate had seized on in a moment of inspiration from the Old Testament line: 'Turn you to the strong hold, ye prisoners of hope.'[29]

While the Special Force was being readied, in December 1943 the Second Arakan campaign began. The 5th Indian Division would move down the Mayu hills while the 7th Indian Division would move down the east side. The latter included the 4/1st, 4/5th, 3/6th and 4/8th Gurkhas. The British empire forces advanced southwards but from 4 February 1944 the Japanese attacked the rear of the 7th Division. The Japanese expected the British empire forces to fall back on their lines of communication but Slim did otherwise and ordered his two advanced divisions to hold firm and depend on air resupply. The 4/8th and 4/1st Gurkhas were diverted to defend the 'adminstrative box', the unglamorous title of the vital divisional resupply area where all the ammunition, fuel and food was stockpiled and the wounded were treated. The 4/1st Gurkhas were ordered to hold a hill codenamed 'Abel', and did so with enormous tenacity until close to the end of the month, when a counter-attack by other parts of the 5th and 7th Indian Divisions, the 82nd West African Division and two new divisions,

the 26th and 36th, crushed the Japanese. The 4/1st Gurkhas had lost 52 killed and 181 wounded, about a third of their strength.[30]

In spite of Wingate's reservations about the Gurkhas, which a careful analysis shows were well founded, if unsympathetically expressed, they nevertheless featured prominently in the operations of the 'Special Force'. It was their fourth 'special forces' operation, after the two incarnations of the Gurkha Scouts in the 1890s and 1919, and the first Chindit operation in 1942–3, of which they were to be an integral part. And it was a truly innovative operation – an early example of 'airland battle', a concept publicised by the Americans in the 1980s.[31]

The second Chindit operation, Operation Thursday, began with glider landings starting on 5 March 1944 (see Figure 9). The 16th Brigade entered Burma on foot from the north while the 77th under Brigadier Michael Calvert and the 111th under Brigadier 'Joe' (W. D. A.) Lentaigne were landed, initially by glider on four sites selected because they were 'all away from roads and uninhabited . . . [but] . . . there was enough flat ground to make the building of an airstrip possible in a short time, and because there was water in the immediate vicinity'.[32] Once the airstrips were built, more supplies and reinforcements would be brought in by powered transport aircraft. Calvert, known as 'Mad Mike' (1913–98), was a Cambridge-educated Royal Engineer who had been in China during the Japanese occupation and therefore knew what the Japanese could do. The thirty-one-year-old temporary brigadier (6 March was his birthday) was as tough as he looked.

The landing sites were all between 27 and 40 miles (40 and 64 kilometres) of Indaw, spreading round it from north-west to east, and were codenamed, in a clockwise direction, Aberdeen, Piccadilly, Broadway and Chowringhee. At the last moment there was panic in the British headquarters because massive logs were seen to have been placed across Piccadilly and the obvious assumption was that the Japanese had somehow found out about the plan. Slim says that the entire operation was in danger of being called off, but that he knew the Japanese were planning to launch an offensive on the Assam front, towards Kohima and Imphal, and was relying on the second Chindit operation to disrupt it, as was Stilwell with his

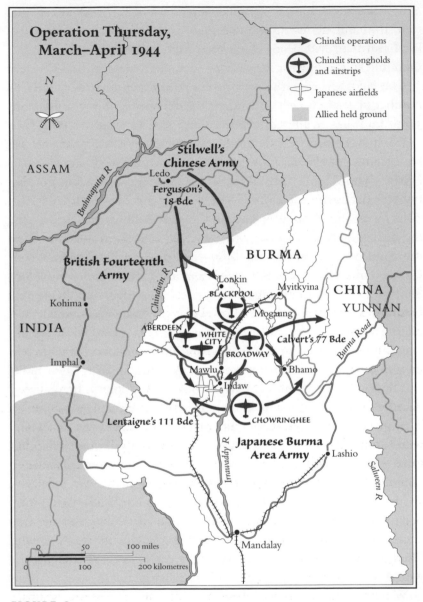

FIGURE 9

Americans and Chinese Nationalists to the north.[33] Slim therefore took the courageous decision to go ahead. It later transpired that local Burmese had been felling teak trees and had decided to lay them out in the open space to dry.[34]

The landings at Piccadilly had to be abandoned but, in spite of a number of crashes, Calvert landed at Broadway with the 3/6th and 3/9th Gurkhas, while Lentaigne landed at Chowringhee with the 3/4th and 4/9th. The latter were an independent force, known as Morrisforce, named after its commander, Lieutenant Colonel J. R. Morris, whose job was to stir up and help the loyal Kachin people fight the occupying Japanese. By the evening of 6 March, Broadway's airstrip was just about able to take a Dakota transport plane. Over the next six days a total of 9,000 men, 1,300 pack animals and 250 tonnes of weapons and stores had been landed. By 13 March, when Japanese aircraft attacked Broadway, they found that a flight of Spitfires from 221 Group Royal Air Force was also based there, the first time an operational airfield had been established behind enemy lines.[35] With the 16th Brigade, which had reached base Aberdeen after a long overland march (see Figure 9), there were now 12,000 men in the guts of the enemy.

The Japanese response to the landings was surprisingly slow, because they were building up for a major offensive towards Imphal. The Special Force fought a number of actions against the Japanese, who formed a force of about 6,000 – half the strength of the Chindit force – to deal with it. Then, on 24 March, tragedy struck. Wingate himself, the mind and soul of the audacious concept, was killed in an air crash near Imphal. Lentaigne was appointed to replace him, but there was no comparison. Slim realised that Wingate's inspirational (for some people), if eccentric, leadership was critical. 'Without his presence to animate it,' wrote Slim, 'Special Force would no longer be the same to others or to itself.'[36]

Wingate's death may have been a factor, though not the cardinal one, in the decision to divert the Chindits north to complement Stilwell's attack from that direction and to help counter the Japanese offensive against Imphal–Kohima. Special forces are a 'force multiplier' when they are used in synergy with conventional operations, and Slim knew that. Calvert's 77th Brigade was directed to capture

Mogaung (see Figure 9). Mogaung stood on a vital road and rail crossing, held by 3,500 Japanese. It was here that the Gurkhas won their second and third Burma VCs. On 11 June 1944, Oxford-educated Captain Michael Allmand, then commanding the leading platoon of B Company of the 3/6th Gurkhas, led the attack on the vital Pin Hmi road bridge on the outskirts of the town.

> The approach to the Bridge was very narrow as the road was banked up and the low-lying land on either side was swampy and densely covered in jungle. The Japanese who were dug in along the banks of the road and in the jungle with machine guns and small arms, were putting up the most desperate resistance. As the platoon came within twenty yards of the Bridge, the enemy opened heavy and accurate fire, inflicting severe casualties and forcing the men to seek cover. Captain Allmand, however, with the utmost gallantry charged on by himself, hurling grenades into the enemy gun positions and killing three Japanese himself with his kukri. Inspired by the splendid example of their platoon commander the surviving men followed him and captured their objective.[37]

Two days later Michael Allmand took over command of the company and, dashing 100 feet (30 metres) ahead of it through long grass and marshy ground, swept by machine-gun fire, personally killed a number of enemy machine-gunners and successfully led his men onto the ridge of high ground that they had been ordered to seize. His third act of gallantry, in an attack on a strong Japanese bunker position called the Red House, ten days after that, assured him the VC, but it would cost him his life.

> Once again on June 23rd in the final attack on the Railway Bridge at Mogaung, Captain Allmand, although suffering from trench-foot, which made it difficult for him to walk, moved forward alone, through deep mud and shell-holes and charged a Japanese machine gun nest single-handed, but he was mortally wounded and died shortly afterwards.
>
> The superb gallantry, outstanding leadership and protracted heroism of this very brave officer were a wonderful example to the whole Battalion.[38]

Around the time that Allmand fell, Rifleman Tulbahadur Pun, in the point section of Allmand's company, found himself the only

man left after the rest of the section, including the section commander, had all been hit in an attack on a Japanese machine-gun
post. He grabbed a Bren light machine-gun[39] from one of the
wounded

> and firing from the hip as he went, continued the charge on this
> heavily bunkered position alone, in the face of the most shattering
> concentration of automatic fire, directed straight at him. With
> the dawn coming up behind him, he presented a perfect target to the
> Japanese. He had to move for thirty yards over open ground, ankle
> deep in mud, through shell holes and over fallen trees. Despite these
> overwhelming odds, he reached the Red House and closed with the
> Japanese occupants. He killed three and put five more to flight and
> captured two light machine guns and much ammunition. He then
> gave accurate supporting fire from the bunker to the remainder of
> his platoon which enabled them to reach their objective.
>
> His outstanding courage and superb gallantry . . . were most
> inspiring to all ranks and were beyond praise.[40]

Rifleman Tulbahadur also won the VC.

Further to the south, the 3/9th Gurkhas, who had been defending Broadway, were ordered north to lend help to Stilwell's forces,
who had reached Taungni. The Japanese held a high hill called Hill
2171. The plan was a classic North-West Frontier one: 'fix' the
enemy with an attack by one company, head-on, while another
would work its way round the back, over difficult terrain, and
'strike' from the rear.

Major Frank Blaker's C Company was given the latter mission.
He was not a regular Gurkha officer, but a temporary major in the
Highland Light Infantry. Nevertheless, he had been born in India,
and was attached to the 3/9th Gurkhas during the war. His role
now, the *London Gazette* records, was to make his way over

> precipitous country, through dense jungle, to attack a strong enemy
> position on the summit of an important hill overlooking Taungni.
> Major Blaker carried out this movement with the utmost precision
> and took up a position with his Company on the extreme right flank
> of the enemy, in itself a feat of considerable military skill.
>
> Another Company, after bitter fighting, had succeeded in taking
> the forward edge of the enemy position by a frontal assault, but had

failed to reach the main crest of the hill in the face of fierce opposition. At this crucial moment Major Blaker's Company came under heavy and accurate fire at close range from medium machine gun and two light machine guns, and their advance was also completely stopped.

Major Blaker then advanced ahead of his men through very heavy fire and, in spite of being severely wounded in the arm by a grenade he located the machine guns, which were the pivot of the enemy defence, and single handed charged the position. When hit by a burst of three rounds through the body, he continued to cheer on his men while lying on the ground. His fearless leadership and outstanding courage so inspired his Company that they stormed the hill and captured the objective, while the enemy fled in terror into the jungle.[41]

Frank Blaker died of wounds while being evacuated from the battlefield. The VC citation concluded: 'His heroism and self sacrifice were beyond all praise and contributed in no small way to the defeat of the enemy and the successful outcome of the operations.'[42]

Audacious and innovative as they were, the Chindit operations – even the second, which was much bigger, better organised and successful than the first – did not win the campaign. That was the result, first of all, of Slim's successful withdrawal of the Burma Corps in 1942, and then of his resistance to the desperate Japanese attack on Kohima and Imphal, trying to get into India, from March to June 1944. As a fierce battle of attrition, with Slim's 14th Army holding and grinding down the Japanese and then counter-attacking successfully, it has something in common with the battles of Stalingrad and Kursk in Russia a year and more before. The forces were smaller than in Russia, but then the theatre and problems of resupply were much more difficult. At Kohima and Imphal, too, the Gurkhas played a disproportionate part in the action.

Two hundred miles (300 kilometres) north-west of the second Chindit operation landings, another VC was won by Rifleman 'Ganju' Lama of the 7th Gurkha Rifles, fighting against the Japanese 15th Army, which had moved into the Imphal plain to counter Slim's offensive into northern Burma. He was not a true

'Gurkha' at all, but Sikkimese, and his real name was Gyamtso Shangderpa. However, in 1942, when he enlisted, the British were not being too particular and anyone who looked like a Gurkha was quietly accepted. On the morning of 12 June, Lama was in charge of a PIAT – a projector infantry anti-tank, a Heath-Robinsonish device that propelled a shaped-charge grenade in the general direction of a tank, assuming the tank was very close. It was massively inferior to the German Panzerfaust or the American bazooka. The Japanese

put down an intense artillery barrage lasting an hour on our positions north of the village of Ningthoukhong. This heavy artillery fire knocked out several bunkers and caused heavy casualties, and was immediately followed by a very strong enemy attack supported by five medium tanks. After fierce hand to hand fighting, the perimeter was driven in in one place and the enemy infantry, supported by three medium tanks, broke through, pinning our troops to the ground with intense fire.

'B' Company, 7th Gurkha Rifles, was ordered to counter-attack and restore the situation. Shortly after passing the starting line it came under heavy enemy medium machine-gun and tank machine-gun fire at point blank range, which covered all lines of approach. Rifleman Ganju Lama, the No. 1 of the P.I.A.T. gun, on his own initiative, with great coolness and complete disregard for his own safety, crawled forward and engaged the tanks single handed. In spite of a broken left wrist and two other wounds, one in his right hand and one in his leg, . . . Rifleman Ganju Lama succeeded in bringing his gun into action within thirty yards [27 metres] of the enemy tanks and knocked out first one and then another, the third tank being destroyed by an anti-tank gun, . . . he then moved forward and engaged with grenades the tank crews . . . Not until he had killed or wounded them all, thus enabling his company to push forward, did he allow himself to be taken back to the Regimental Aid Post . . .

Throughout this action Rifleman Ganju Lama, although very seriously wounded, showed a complete disregard for his own personal safety, outstanding devotion to duty and a determination to destroy the enemy which was an example and an inspiration to all ranks.[43]

Ganju Lama had already been awarded the Military Medal for an action the previous month but, the system being as it was, and is, he heard about the VC first. He was later commissioned as a sub-edar and in 1947 joined the 11th Gurkha Rifles of the new Indian Army.

In mid-June the Japanese offensive reached its peak of ferocity, with the Japanese trying to break into the Imphal plain through the Bishenpur area to the south-west of Imphal itself.[44] Here, the Gurkhas won two VCs within 660 feet (200 metres) of each other.

There were two important geographical features, known to the British as Water Picket, or Piquet, as it was spelled at the time, and Mortar Bluff. They captured Water Picket and on 25 June attacked Mortar Bluff, which was defended by a platoon of the 2/5th Gurkhas under Subedar (Lieutenant) Netrabahadur Thapa. Owing to its commanding position the retention of Mortar Bluff was vital to the safety of other positions further down the ridge and to Bishenpur itself. The Japanese attacked, with a 3-inch (75-millimetre) field gun and a 1.5-inch (37-millimetre) anti-tank gun pouring

> shell after shell at point blank range for ten minutes into the narrow confines of the piquet, and this was followed by a determined attack by not less than one company of Japanese. A fierce fight ensued in which Subadar Netrabahadur Thapa's men, exhorted by their leader, held their ground against heavy odds and drove the enemy back with disproportionate losses . . .
>
> Still in considerable strength and as determined and ferocious as ever the enemy poured out from the jungle . . . to the piquet defences . . . both the L.M.G. [Bren light machine-gun] – and T.M.G. [Thompson sub-machine gun] of one section jammed . . . and the enemy . . . over-ran this and another section, killing or wounding 12 out of the 16 men . . . Subadar Netrabahadur Thapa himself . . . stemmed any further advance with grenades.
>
> . . . at 0400 hours a section of 8 men with grenades and small arms ammunition arrived. Their arrival inevitably drew fire and all the 8 were soon casualties . . . Subadar Netrabahadur Thapa retrieved the ammunition and . . . took the offensive . . . Whilst so doing he received a bullet wound in the mouth followed shortly

afterwards by a grenade which killed him outright. His body was found next day, kukri in hand and a dead Japanese with a cleft skull by his side.

. . . His fine example of personal bravery and his high sense of duty so inspired his men that a vital position was held to the limit of human endurance.'[45]

The limit of human endurance was not, unfortunately, enough and the Japanese took the second, vital position. The only solution for the British was to retake both. The plan was for C Company to take Mortar Bluff and then A Company to follow on and take Water Picket. The planners had reckoned without Naik (Corporal) Agansing Rai, a C Company section commander:

> Naik Agansing Rai, appreciating that more delay would inevitably result in heavier casualties, at once led his section under withering fire directly at the machine-gun and, firing as he went, charged the position himself, killing three of the crew of four. Inspired by his cool act of bravery the section surged forward across the bullet swept ground and routed the whole garrison of 'Mortar Bluff'.
>
> This position was now under intense fire from the .37 millimetre gun in the jungle and from 'Water Piquet'. Naik Agansing Rai at once advanced towards the gun, . . . killed three of the crew and his men killed the other two. The party then returned to 'Mortar Bluff' where the rest of their platoon were forming up for the final assault on 'Water Piquet'. In the subsequent advance heavy machine-gun fire and showers of grenades from an isolated bunker position caused further casualties. Once more, with indomitable courage, Naik Agansing Rai, covered by his Bren gunner, advanced alone with a grenade in one hand and his Thompson Sub-Machine gun in the other . . . and . . . killed all four occupants of the bunker. The enemy . . . now fled before the onslaught on 'Water Piquet' and this position too was captured.
>
> Naik Agansing Rai's magnificent display of initiative, outstanding bravery and gallant leadership, so inspired the rest of the Company that, in spite of heavy casualties, the result of this important action was never in doubt.'[46]

Agansing Rai gained the third VC won by Gurkhas in the fighting around Imphal in June 1944, a measure of the intensity of the

battles there. Some of the comments about Gurkhas 'lacking initiative' begin to look less persuasive when examples of the opposite, like this, are cited. Agansing Rai later told Christopher Bullock that, since his adrenalin was flowing, it seemed a good idea to take Water Picket, whether it was his company's objective or not.[47]

By 8 July 1944 the Japanese had decided to withdraw from the Imphal–Kohima cauldron and the British empire troops went on to the offensive. The campaign probably cost the Japanese 30,000 dead. By 1 February 1945 bridgeheads had been established across the great Irrawaddy river, and at the very beginning of March Slim's army took the crucial junction of Meiktila, cutting off the Japanese in Mandalay.

Not content with letting the Japanese slip away to fight another day, Slim liked to put 'hooks' behind them to stop them withdrawing and then destroy them with troops coming from the north. As the main body of the 14th Army advanced down the centre of Burma, the 25th, 26th and 82nd West African divisions advanced down the Arakan coast to the west. On 4 March 1945, the 3/2nd Gurkhas were deployed in an amphibious assault and then used to take a hill codenamed Snowdon. The Japanese had dug in on a neighbouring mountain, known as Snowdon East. Besides the usual trenches, the Japanese also made extensive use of snipers in trees. The next day, 5 March, the Gurkhas' skills as riflemen were again apparent. One of the leading sections came under sniper fire, and then, with remarkable sang-froid,

> Rifleman Bhanbhagta Gurung, being unable to fire from the lying position, stood up fully exposed to the heavy fire and calmly killed the enemy sniper with his rifle . . . The section then advanced . . . but . . . was again attacked by very heavy fire. Rifleman Bhanbhagta Gurung . . . dashed forward alone and attacked the first enemy fox-hole. Throwing two grenades, he killed the two occupants and . . . rushed on to the next enemy fox-hole and killed the Japanese in it with his bayonet.[48]

Two further enemy fox holes were still bringing fire to bear, so Gurung dashed forward alone and cleared these with his bayonet and grenades. There was almost continuous and point-blank light

machine-gun fire from a bunker on the northern tip of the objective, so Gurung leaped onto the roof of the bunker and flung two no. 77 smoke grenades into the bunker firing slit. Two Japanese rushed out of the bunker and Gurung promptly killed them both with his kukri. A Japanese soldier remaining inside the bunker was still firing the light machine-gun, so Gurung crawled inside the bunker, killed this last Japanese and captured the gun.

Showing a natural gift for command, Rifleman Gurung then 'ordered' the nearest Bren gunner and two riflemen to take up positions in the captured bunker. A Japanese counter-attack followed soon after, but the small party inside the bunker, commanded by Gurung who was showing signs of 'emergent leadership', repelled it with heavy loss to the enemy. The citation, which this account has followed very closely, concluded, with the usual understatement: 'Riflemen Bhanbhagta Gurung showed outstanding bravery and a complete disregard for his own safety. His courageous clearing of five enemy positions single-handed [!] was in itself decisive in capturing the objective.'[49] Again, Gurung's behaviour showed none of the signs of submissiveness, lack of initiative or unwillingness to assume authority that had often been levelled at the Gurkhas.

By 8 March, the 14th Army had reached the outskirts of the fabled city of Mandalay, which was largely destroyed in the fighting during the war. Slim recalled that

Mandalay Hill is a a great rock rising abruptly from the plain to nearly eight hundred feet [240 metres] and dominating the whole north-eastern quarter of the city. Its steep sides are covered with temples and pagodas, now honeycombed for machine guns, well supplied and heavily garrisoned. Throughout the day and night of 9 March, the fiercest hand-to-hand fighting went on as a Gurkha battalion [the 4/4th] stormed up the slopes and bombed and tommy-gunned their way into the concrete buildings. Next day two companies of a British battalion joined them and the bitter fighting went on. The Japanese stood to the end, until the last defenders, holding out in cellars, were destroyed by petrol rolled down in drums and ignited by tracer bullets. It was not until 11 March that the hill was entirely in our hands.[50]

Even then, the very summit of Mandalay Hill was not taken until the following morning, after the 4/4th Gurkhas had cleared the last corridors and staircases with their kukris.

The other great obstacle still held by the Japanese was Fort Dufferin, an old-fashioned rectangular fort, but one with massive earthworks behind the masonry walls, which withstood hits from medium artillery and 500-pound (230-kilogram) bombs. The RAF then switched to 2,000-pound (900-kilogram) bombs and eventually a breach was made. The 1/6th Gurkhas were involved in attacks, reminiscent of sieges throughout history, but on the morning of 20 March some Burmese appeared waving white flags and Union flags, and said the Japanese had crept away through the sewers.[51]

The final assault on Rangoon, Operation Dracula, was scheduled for 2 May. The 17th Indian Division had struggled overland to get there to meet up with the naval and air forces, British and American, sliding apparently effortlessly over the sea or flying high with total air superiority. However, Japanese submarines remained a deadly threat, as the USS *Indianapolis*, which delivered the first atomic bomb to Guam and was then sunk by one on the way home, would discover.[52] On 'D minus one', 1 May, the air forces hit all known defences on both sides of the river. Then, some hours later, a battalion of the 50th Indian Parachute Brigade dropped at Elephant Point.

According to Slim, 'A party of about thirty Japanese, either left for observation or just forgotten, offered resistance to the Gurkha paratroops. One wounded Japanese survived.'[53] These paras were Gurkhas, and the low survival rate of the Japanese should not be surprising. It was Gurkhas' first real airborne operation, and the first real confirmation of a relationship and connexion with the British paras that continues to this day.

The 50th Indian Parachute Brigade had been formed as long ago as October 1941, after the very costly success of German paratroops in capturing Crete, but parachutes and aircraft were in constant short supply – there were always other priorities, and the Gurkha parachutists were not ready for airborne operations on any scale until mid-1944. The original plan was to have three battalions –

the 151st, which would comprise British soldiers, the 152nd, Indian soldiers, and 153rd, Gurkhas. The British 151st Battalion was sent to the Middle East in December 1942 and joined the British 4th Parachute Brigade, which became part of 1st British Airborne Division. Its place was taken by a new Gurkha battalion, the 154th Gurkha Parachute Battalion, which was raised from the 3/7th Gurkhas who had been badly mauled in the retreat through Burma.

At the end of 1942 the British officers of the 3/7th had the job of getting 750 Gurkhas to volunteer for the new role. It proved easier than might be expected. There were few films about paratroops and, by mistake, the British showed one designed to train troops to *counter* paratroop attacks. This contained the message, most encouraging to the latter, but depressing for paratroops, that, if the defenders did their job, '95 percent of these men [the paratroops] should never reach the ground alive'. The subtleties of the English message were lost on the Gurkhas who just saw lots of men rolling around on the ground and thought it was terrific fun, so they all volunteered.[54]

The 153rd Gurkha Parachute Battalion provided specialised support for British empire operations at the time of the first Chindit operation. In Operation Puddle in July 1942 one British captain, J. O. M. Roberts, three Gurkha officers, four Gurkha NCOs and three British other ranks from the 153rd Gurkha Parachute Battalion were parachute-dropped about 40 miles (64 kilometres) from Myitkyna (see Figure 9), and spent six weeks reconnoitring Japanese positions. The next month, another party from the 153rd – comprising Captain G. E. C. Newland, one Gurkha NCO and four Gurkha riflemen, plus Lieutenant R. A. McLune, Royal Engineers and four British other ranks – was sent to prepare a landing strip at Fort Hertz in the very north of Burma, close to Stilwell's forces, so that an infantry company could be flown in – and out. Again, the mission was successful, but – although this is significant – more akin to a 'special forces' operation than a major airborne assault.[55]

Paratrooper-jump training at first took place at Willingdon airport, New Delhi. In October 1942, No. 3 Parachute Training

School moved to Chaklala in the Punjab. In October 1943, the 153rd Gurkha Parachute Battalion carried out a big exercise with thirty-two aircraft and dropped at Raiwala after a three-and-a-half-hour flight, and then immediately reported for training at the Jungle Warfare School that had been established there.

The first major action seen by the Indian Parachute Brigade did not involve any parachute landings, however. Between April and July 1944 they were used for defence and patrolling in the Imphal area where the great Imphal–Kohima battle was taking place. During June and July a company of the 153rd Gurkha Parachute Battalion penetrated deep into the Naga hills to obtain information on enemy routes – the long-range reconnaissance role of 'special forces', again. In March 1945 the Indian and Gurkha parachute forces were reorganised into the Indian Parachute Regiment, with two out of the three battalions provided by Gurkhas. The 153rd Gurkha Parachute Battalion became the 2nd Battalion, and the 154th became the 3rd Battalion, Indian Parachute regiment. For the first time the new Regiment adopted the distinctive airborne 'red' beret – in fact, the subtle shade of maroon selected by an officer's wife, which goes so well with the pale blue that also forms part of the paras' ensemble. The distinctive crossed kukri badges worn by the two Gurkha battalions were replaced by a badge identical to the British paras', apart from the word 'India' inscribed on the base of the parachute.

In October 1944 the powers that be had decided to form the 44th Indian Airborne Division, which would comprise two brigades, the 50th and 77th, with one British, one Indian and one Gurkha battalion in each. The choice of ethnic composition underlined the status of the Gurkhas as a kind of 'third force', between British and Indians, even though they were still part of the Indian Army. The 3rd Battalion, formerly the 154th, remained with 50th Brigade, and the 2nd Battalion, formerly the 153rd, went to the 77th.

Operation Dracula involved the movement of naval forces up the Rangoon river, but it had been mined by both the Japanese and the British. Before minesweepers could go up the river, the defences on the west bank, especially those at Elephant Point, had to be eliminated, much like the German positions on the Pointe du Hoc and

Merville Battery before the 'D-Day' landings on 6 June 1944. This time, however, Slim decided to use paratroops. The Indian Airborne Division was in the midst of reorganisation and a lot of the soldiers were on leave in Nepal. It was decided to form an improvised battalion from those who could be collected from the 2nd and 3rd Gurkha Parachute Battalions. The composite battalion again concentrated at Chaklala and was expanded into a full battalion group with the necessary additions of engineers, signals, pathfinders and medical support. It was to be dropped from forty American aircraft, whose crews had never dropped paratroops before. Two Canadian jumpmasters were included who had experience with Gurkha and Indian parachutists and could also talk to the Americans. On 14 April the battalion group moved to Midnapore where it spent ten days gathering equipment and training.

The first wave, comprising pathfinders, landing controllers and a defence platoon, took off early on 1 May, with the rest of the group following half an hour later. After four hours, Dracula's airborne cloak was over the Japanese positions, and the force landed at the dropping zone some miles from Elephant Point. They had to stop 2 miles (3 kilometres) short of the objective to allow it to be bombed one more time, and one company was mistakenly bombed and machine-gunned by Allied aircraft. When the leading company reached the Point, the Japanese platoon holding it – thirty-seven men – put up a short fight but were quickly overwhelmed.

The first Gurkha parachute operation was a complete success, although it had been a very long time coming. After the area was secured the battalion was moved into Rangoon to round up the last Japanese and to conduct anti-looting patrols.

Since 1942 a number of Gurkhas had volunteered for work with the Special Operations Executive (SOE), and its Far East branch, known as Force 136. After the Japanese withdrawal from Imphal–Kohima, a Force 136 group of forty Gurkhas was sent to find out whether the Japanese, who had dispersed into the jungle, were regrouping for another offensive. The commander was Major William Lindon-Travers, later Bill Travers, the actor, and his radio operator was James (also known as Hamish) Gow of the Royal

Signals, the son of a Scottish gamekeeper, who wrote about it in his book *From Rhunahaorine to Rangoon*.[56]

After the fall of Rangoon at the beginning of May, the British empire advance now continued, but with empire and Japanese forces interspersed all across the country. Slim recalled looking at his map, with 'blue Japanese and red British forces split haphazard all over the sheet'.[57] The British did not adopt the American convention, with blue for 'own troops', until after the war.

The Japanese were split into four main groups: in the Irrawaddy valley, on both banks of the river; in the Shan hills, east of Meiktila; east of the Sittang river and east of the mouth of the Sittang. In the former area, the Japanese, having evacuated Mandalay, withdrew south. Among the forces trying to cut them off was the 4/8th Gurkhas, who established a block to trap the Japanese at Taungdaw, west of Naung Laing, on the west bank of the Irrawaddy. The place is significant now as it is one of the places where Myanmar is suspected of mining uranium.[58] Although uranium may have been a factor in the Japanese quest to capture Burma, it is most unlikely that the Japanese land forces had any idea of the significance of the place. They were just determined to break through the block and escape.

On the night of 12–13 May 1945, Rifleman Lachhiman Gurung was on guard in an advance post when, at 0120 hours on 13 May, a force of about 200 Japanese attacked. His section bore the brunt of it. The Japanese threw 'innumerable' hand grenades at the position from close range.

One grenade fell on the lip of Rifleman Lachhiman Gurung's trench; he at once grasped it and hurled it back at the enemy. Almost immediately another grenade fell directly inside the trench. Again this Rifleman snatched it up and threw it back. A third grenade fell just in front of the trench. He attempted to throw it back, but it exploded in his hand, blowing off his fingers, shattering his right arm and severely wounding him in the face, body and right leg. His two comrades were also badly wounded and lay helpless in the bottom of the trench.

The enemy, screaming and shouting, now formed up shoulder to shoulder and attempted to rush the position by sheer weight of

numbers. Rifleman Lachhiman Gurung, regardless of his wounds, loaded and fired his rifle with his left hand, maintaining a continuous steady rate of fire. Wave after wave of fanatical attacks were thrown in by the enemy and all were repulsed with heavy casualties. For four hours after being severely wounded Rifleman Lachhiman Gurung remained alone at his post waiting with perfect calm for each attack which he met with fire at point blank range, determined not to give one inch of ground. Of the 87 enemy dead counted in the immediate vicinity of the Company locality, 31 lay in front of this Rifleman's section, the key to the whole position.[59]

Rifleman Lachhiman, miraculously, survived. By his example, according to the citation, he 'so inspired his comrades to resist the enemy to the last, that, although surrounded and cut off for three days and two nights, they held and smashed every attack'.[60] By now the reader will be familiar with citations like that, and what they mean. Two letters. VC.

The last battle in Burma was fought in July when remnants of the Japanese 28th and 33rd armies attempted to break out from the hills and cross the Mandalay–Rangoon road to join the remainder of the Japanese forces east of the Sittang river. The British, Indian and Gurkha forces, and local resistance fighters mobilised by Force 136, were all waiting for them. Much of the area was a swamp and 7th Division reported that in some places the water was 'too deep for Gurkhas to operate', since the Gurkhas are usually quite small in stature.[61] The last group to attempt to break out were 12 and 13 Naval Guard Forces, formed from the shore establishments of the Imperial Japanese Navy. There were about 400 sailors, and an Indian and a Gurkha battalion closed in on them. Only three men escaped.[62]

Of the forty-five Gurkha battalions that served in the Second World War, twenty-seven served in Burma, where 35,000 Gurkha troops fought and many died.[63] In Burma they won nine of their twenty-six Victoria Crosses, to date. In spite of some commanders' initial misgivings about the Gurkhas' suitability for certain types of warfare, they had done everything that could be expected of them. They had fought ferocious battles with tanks in conditions that could be described, if anything can, as 'conventional' war, they had adapted rapidly to jungle warfare, to airborne operations and to

coups-de-main, like Elephant Point, to special-forces operations deep in the Japanese rear for months with the Chindits; and to clandestine work with Force 136. Slim, and two of his divisional commanders, Scott, commanding the 1st Burma Division, and Cowan, commanding the 17th Indian Division, had all served in the 1/6th Gurkhas. Lieutenant General Tuker, who had served in North Africa but joined them to command IV Corps at the end, preparing to carry the war back into Malaya, was a 1/2nd Gurkha.[64] Burma was the Gurkhas' war, *par excellence*.

The Gurkhas were not initially deployed to North Africa and played no part in Wavell's early victories over the Italians. As in the First World War, they were first deployed outside India to defend the oil installations in Iraq and Persia. The 10th Indian Division, commanded by Slim, then a major general, was sent from India in May 1941 and included four Gurkha battalions – the 1/2nd, 2/4th, 2/7th and 2/10th.

The threat to the oil supplies receded as it became clear that the Soviet Union was going to survive and also provide forces to secure Persia. The 2/4th and 2/10th moved straight on to Syria (see Figure 10) where they helped defeat the Vichy French, who were nominally on the German side. Then, in March 1942, the 2/4th were sent to North Africa where Rommel's German Afrika Corps had supplanted the Italians and was proving far more formidable. The 2/4th Gurkhas, part of 10th Indian Brigade, were ordered to hold an area south-west of Tobruk codenamed 'Knightsbridge'. Digging in was very difficult because of the rocky ground. The battalion became isolated from the rest of the brigade, which was then overrun by the Germans, against whose tanks the pathetic 2-pounder (1-kg) anti-tank guns were no use. Only the 25-pounder (12-kg) field guns of the Royal Artillery were any use, and they were easily picked off. Soon after, the whole 2/4th Gurkha battalion was overrun. The Germans separated the British from the Gurkhas, and the Gurkhas from the Indians, and marched them all into captivity.

Rommel pressed on to Tobruk, where the 2/7th also went into captivity after fierce resistance. The fortress surrendered on 21 June

but the Cameron Highlanders and the 2/7th had not heard the order and kept fighting for several hours. It was the second time the 2/7th had been captured and included pretty well all of them — the first had been at Kut in 1916 (see Chapter 6).

In December 1941, Major General Francis Tuker, a 1/2nd Gurkha, had taken command of 4th Indian Division. Bernard Montgomery, who took over as commander of the 8th Army after the debacle at Tobruk, was thoroughly prejudiced against the Indian Army because when at Sandhurst he had failed to pass out high enough in his class to gain admission. Because Indian Army conditions of service were better — and less expensive — they took the higher achievers. He and Tuker had also clashed while Tuker was, unusually for an Indian Army officer, studying at the British Army Staff College at Camberley in 1925–6, and Montgomery was on the staff. Tuker's 4th Division was therefore sidelined. However, Tuker succeeded in doing what very few junior generals did, and got Montgomery to change his mind. The opportunity came at Wadi Akarit in April 1943.

Rommel's attack in March 1943 had been repelled and the Germans and Italians took up a defensive position behind the Mareth Line, running inland from the Gulf of Gabes (see Figure 10), while Rommel returned to Europe because he was ill. The Germans and Italians were then obliged to withdraw again, after being outflanked, and held a position at Wadi Akarit, 20 miles (30 kilometres) to the north. Montgomery planned to attack along the narrow coastal strip, although there were strongly fortified enemy positions in the mountains on his left (west). He planned for a small diversionary attack over some low hills but to avoid the towering Fatnassa massif further to the left, about 50 miles (80 kilometres) inland (see Figure 10).

Tuker, on the other hand, had served on the North-West Frontier and knew that a mountain like that was 'in reality very difficult to hold unless it was filled full with infantry'.[65] It was also high ground that North-West Frontier soldiers knew, from grisly experience, had to be held. Fatnassa could be out of a film based on Tolkien. It was 'a fantastic pile, like a fairy-tale mountain, split by chimneys and fissures, layered by escarpments and crowned by rock pinnacles'.[66] The corps commander, General Oliver Leese,

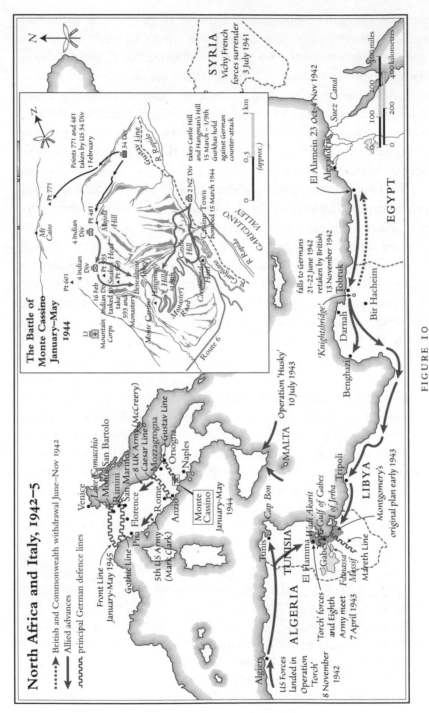

North Africa and Italy, 1942–5

••••••▶ British and Commonwealth withdrawal June–Nov 1942

⟶ Allied advances

⌇⌇⌇⌇ principal German defence lines

The Battle of
Monte Cassino
January–May
1944

FIGURE 10

put the alternative plan to Montgomery who, most unusually, accepted it.

Tuker entrusted his own former battalion, the 1/2nd Gurkhas, with the job. If anyone could scale these heights with the enemy dug in on top, they could. The mountain was considered impassable, and it was defended by Italians, but with Germans in reserve. It was a job that some armies would have assigned to specialist 'mountain' or 'Alpine' units. The Gurkhas were such a unit already – nobody needed to say so.

The four rifle companies of the 1/2nd Gurkhas moved forward just before midnight on 5 April. Kukris were useful for killing sentries silently, but one managed to shout the alarm just before he was silenced, and the defenders started firing into the night. Subedar Lalbahadur Thapa was second-in-command of D Company, attacking the Rass-ez-Zouai feature. The commander of 16 Platoon was detached with one section to secure an isolated knoll to the left. At the same time, Subedar Lalbahadur

took command of the remaining two Sections and led them forward towards the main feature on the outer ridge, in order to break through and secure the one and only passage by which the vital commanding feature could be seized to cover the penetration of the Division into the hills. On the capture of these hills the whole success of the Corps plan [XXX Corps] depended. First contact with the enemy was made at the foot of a pathway winding up a narrow cleft. This steep cleft was thickly studded with a series of enemy posts, the inner of which contained an anti-tank gun and the remainder medium machine-guns. After passing through the narrow cleft, one emerges into a small arena with very steep sides, some 200 feet [60 metres] in height, and in places sheer cliff . . .

The garrison of the outer posts were all killed by Subadar Lalbahadur Thapa and his men by kukri or bayonet in the first rush and the enemy then opened very heavy fire straight down the narrow enclosed pathway and steep arena sides. Subadar Lalbahadur Thapa led his men on and fought his way up the narrow gully straight through the enemy's fire . . .

The next machine-gun posts were dealt with, Subadar Lalbahadur Thapa personally killing two men with his kukri and two more with

his revolver . . . He and two Riflemen managed to reach the crest, where Subadar Lalbahadur Thapa killed another two men with his kukri, the Riflemen killed two more and the rest fled. Subadar Lalbahadur Thapa then secured the whole feature and covered his Company's advance up the defile.

This pathway was found to be the only practicable route up the precipitous ridge, and by securing it the Company was able to deploy and mop up all enemy opposition on their objective.

. . . The outstanding leadership, gallantry and complete disregard for his own safety shown by Subadar Lalbahadur Thapa were an example to the whole Company, and the ruthless determination of this Gurkha officer to reach his objective and kill his enemy had a decisive effect on the success of the whole operations.'[67]

In November 1942, Allied forces had landed in French Morocco and Algeria in Operation Torch, the first of an accumulating series of successful joint force landings, which culminated in Normandy in June 1944 and might have culminated in the invasion of Japan in 1946, had nuclear weapons not helped shorten the war. The American Western Task Force landed in Morocco, while the British Eastern Task Force landed in Algeria. American Torch forces, coming from the west, met the British empire 8th Army on 7 April 1943 at El Hamma, north-west of Wadi Akarit and not far from the Fatnassa mountain where Lalbahadur Thapa had won his Victoria Cross the day before. Squeezed from both sides, the German and Italian forces in North Africa surrendered in May.[68] Lalbahadur Thapa's Victoria Cross was the first of the twelve won by Gurkhas in the Second World War. With nine won in Burma, that leaves two, both of which were won in Italy, as we shall see.

With the defeat of the Axis in North Africa, the Allies pressed on into what Churchill had rather euphemistically called the 'soft underbelly' of Europe. The next stop was Italy, which was not 'soft' at all. All those who fought there remember that the fighting was extremely nasty and the rugged spine of Italy – the Apennine mountains, constantly intersected by river valleys cutting across the northward line of advance – gave the Germans

every opportunity to fight with the skill and determination for which they were and are renowned. But it was also good terrain for Gurkhas.

Operation Husky, the landings in Sicily in 1943, was a bigger operation, in terms of the number of ships and other major assets deployed, than the Normandy 'D-Day' in June 1944. With the landings in Sicily on 10 July, it coincided with the great Battle of Kursk in south-west Russia, where the Germans attacked the Russian salient on 12 July. The Allied landings led the Italians to start peace negotiations, although they did not surrender until September, leaving the Germans as occupiers. The two events together – Germany's last opportunity not to lose on the Eastern Front, which ended in a spectacular Russian victory, and the landing of massive Allied forces in Western Europe – spelled the beginning of the end for Nazi Germany.

The first Gurkha battalion in Italy was the 1/5th, which arrived in October 1943. The 1/5th Gurkhas and the 1st Battalion of the Royal Fusiliers were engaged in a fierce battle to seize the village of Mozzagrogna, level with Cassino and Anzio, on 27–8 November (see Figure 10). All the 1/5th's British officers were killed or wounded and the senior Gurkha officer took command of the remnants of three companies, which fought their way out. In December the bulk of Tuker's 4th Indian Division arrived. Initially they were assigned to attack the mountain town of Orsogna but were then ordered to move south-west across the Apennines to help with the assault on German forces holding an old Benedictine abbey on top of a mountain. It was called Monte Cassino. The terrain is shown in the inset to Figure 10. The topography, with the complex web of interlocking heights, is reminiscent of the Dargai heights, shown in Plates 21 and 22.

United States forces had taken Snake's Head, which was higher than the monastery, but could not get past German forces on Hill 593.[69] The 4th Indian Division arrived on 11 February 1944.

The quiet and retiring Tuker was a good military historian and was shocked to find that no one could tell him much about the Monte Cassino monastery. In a Naples bookshop he tracked down a book on it from 1879, from which he learned that the walls were

150 feet (45 metres) high and 10 feet (3 metres) thick. He wrote a memo to his corps commander explaining that normal 1,000 lb (454-kg) bombs would not dent the structure and that only Blockbuster demolition bombs, either the original 4,000-pound (1,814-kg) or the 12,000-pound (5,443-kg) variant, which was now available, would do any good. General Harold Alexander, the Theatre commander, authorised the bombing, but only with conventional bombs and not with Blockbusters. As a result the Germans were not dislodged.

Tuker recommended that another direct attack on the monastery would be pure folly, and recommended bypassing it, but was taken ill with ethmoiditis – an upper respiratory infection that could have been easily treated, had a specialist been available – and was removed from his command and sent back to India. Some 4,000 men of his 4th Indian Division with its three Gurkha battalions – the 1/2nd, 1/9th and 2/7th, which had been re-formed for the second time – were lost at Cassino, and Tuker called it 'the battle that should never have been fought'.[70]

While Tuker headed back to India, his 4th Indian Division was directed to attack, descending from Snake's Head (see Figure 10 inset), to capture Hill 593, to capture the monastery with its massively thick walls, and to clear the slopes above the town of Cassino, while the New Zealand forces would attack the town directly. The attack began on the night of 16–17 February with British and Indian troops attacking Hill 593 and the 1/2nd and 1/9th Gurkhas attacking the monastery. The 1/2nd Gurkhas lost 150 dead and wounded – about 20 per cent of a battalion's strength – while two of 1/9th's companies lost 94. The attack was called off.

On 15 March another attack was launched and this time C Company of the 1/9th captured Hangman's Hill, so named because a broken ski-lift pylon looked rather like a gibbet. The rest of the battalion started fighting their way towards their comrades. The Germans then counter-attacked and the 1/9th, with some British and Indian soldiers who had also reached the hill, found itself desperately trying to hold on to the key feature while running short of ammunition, water and food. Some resupply was delivered by air but, as usual in these circumstances, much of that

probably went to the Germans. The 1/9th Gurkhas' defence of Hangman's Hill is one of the famous episodes in the Battle of Monte Cassino.

Another Gurkha formation arrived in the late summer, the 43rd Gurkha Lorried Brigade, comprising the 2/6th, 2/8th, and 2/10th Gurkhas. Although their cross-country mobility was obviously second-best compared with troops in armoured personnel carriers or half-tracks, with a combination of tracks and wheels, lorried infantry was useful in a relatively developed country like Italy, with good roads, as it could keep up with tanks, and that was what they were used for, in support of the 1st Armoured Division.[71] The latter, and the 4th Indian, were both used in the battle for the little independent state of San Marino, one of two such inside Italy, along with the Vatican. The 1/9th Gurkhas were ordered to conduct a wide sweeping movement to seize the town of San Marino itself, starting on 18 September 1944. They ran into fierce German resistance and A Company became pinned down at Point 366, unable to advance or escape. Rifleman Sherbahadur Thapa was the number one Bren gunner in one of the sections. According to the *London Gazette*,

He and his section commander charged an enemy post, killing the machine gunner and putting the rest of the post to flight. Almost immediately another party of Germans attacked the two men and the section commander was badly wounded by a grenade, but, without hesitation, the Rifleman, in spite of intense fire, rushed at the attackers and reaching the crest of the ridge brought his Bren gun into action against the main body of the enemy who were counter-attacking our troops.

. . . By the intensity and accuracy of the fire which he could bring to bear only from the crest, this isolated Gurkha Bren gunner silenced several enemy machine guns and checked a number of Germans who were trying to infiltrate on to the ridge.

At the end of two hours both forward Companies had exhausted their ammunition and, as they were by then practically surrounded, they were ordered to withdraw. Rifleman Sherbahadur Thapa covered their withdrawal as they crossed the open ground to positions in the rear and himself remained alone at his post until his ammunition ran out. He then dashed forward under accurate small arms and

mortar fire and rescued two wounded men, who were lying between him and the advancing Germans.

While returning the second time he paid the price of his heroism and fell riddled by machine gun bullets fired at point blank range.[72]

Sherbahadur's mother was invited down from the hills of Nepal to receive his posthumous Victoria Cross from the Viceroy. She told the commandant of the 9th Gurkhas' depot, 'What, after all, is a medal to me? I would sooner have my son any day.'[73]

While the Allies attempted to capture the Rhine crossings, including the furthest bridge at Arnhem, in an unusually daring operation, which failed, in October 1944, the Germans continued to fight for every mountain and ridge of the Apennines. US General Mark Clark's 5th Army was advancing up the west coast of Italy and the British 8th Army – now commanded by Leese, after Montgomery had been promoted to be the land component commander for 'D-Day' and then to command 21st Army Group – was on the east side. As part of the latter, on 10 November 1944, the 1/5th Gurkhas, part of the 8th Indian Division, were close to the point where the two armies were likely to meet, the Monte San Bartolo. With the onset of severe wintry weather, fighting had already largely died down, but the 1/5th Gurkhas were ordered to move forward to see how strongly the mountain was held. Two leading Gurkhas had almost managed to reach the top of a saddle. One of them was Rifleman Thaman Gurung. Then

suddenly the second scout attracted his attention to [the] Germans . . . preparing to fire with a machine gun at the leading section. Realizing that if the enemy succeeded in opening fire, the section would certainly sustain heavy casualties, Rifleman Thaman Gurung leapt to his feet and charged them. Completely taken by surprise, the Germans surrendered without opening fire.

. . . Although the sky-line was devoid of cover and under accurate machine gun fire . . . Rifleman Thaman Gurung immediately crossed it, firing his Tommy gun, thus allowing the forward section to reach the summit, but due to heavy fire from the enemy machine guns, the platoon was ordered to withdraw. Rifleman Thaman Gurung then again crossed the sky-line alone and although . . . exposed to heavy

fire . . . put burst after burst of Tommy gun fire into the German slit trenches, until his ammunition ran out. He then threw two grenades he had with him and rejoining his section, collected two more grenades and again doubled over the bullet-swept crest of the hillock and hurled them at the remaining Germans. This diversion enabled both rear sections to withdraw without further loss.

Meanwhile, the leading section . . . was still on the summit, so Rifleman Thaman Gurung, shouting to the section to withdraw, seized a Bren Gun and a number of magazines. He then, yet again, ran to the top of the hill and, although he well knew his action meant almost certain death, stood up on the bullet-swept summit, in full view of the enemy, and opened fire at the nearest enemy positions. It was not until he had emptied two complete magazines, and the remaining section was well on its way to safety, that Rifleman Thaman Gurung was killed.[74]

His was the last Gurkha Victoria Cross of the European war, again a posthumous one. Ironically, operations had already almost ended for the winter. In April the Allies resumed their offensive, and on 2 May Field Marshal Kesselring, the German commander in Italy, asked for an armistice. That was two days after Hitler committed suicide, and the same day that the Russians completed the capture of Berlin.

This chapter has focussed on the character of the war the Gurkhas fought, on their achievements and the versatility they showed and, of course, on their courage and initiative under fire. Much has also been written on their bravery in Japanese captivity, and how they refused Japanese attempts to recruit them to use against the British, which can be found elsewhere.[75]

Outside the Ministry of Defence in London there are statues of famous British generals from the war: Montgomery, who, as we have seen, had a chip on his shoulder about not having been good enough for the Indian Army, and Field Marshal Sir Alan Brooke, the 'Master of Strategy'. But standing to the fore is the burly figure of Bill Slim, commander of the 14th Army, the 'Forgotten Army', in South-East Asia. Unlike Montgomery, who insisted on having overwhelming superiority before taking the offensive, Slim did

what he could with what he had. His forces were nowhere near as well provided, well equipped or well sustained as those who fought in North Africa and Italy. But his achievement was as great, if not greater. Perhaps that is why the civil servants in Whitehall honour his memory most of all.

At the beginning of the Second World War, Gurkhas provided 14 per cent of the combatant strength of the Indian Army, which reduced to 4.5 per cent at its end, as the combatant component of the Indian Army expanded in size ten times, from 189,000 to 1,876,999.[76] However, Gurkhas had provided about twenty per cent of the Indian Army's infantry units, and won no fewer than *ten* of the twenty-six Victoria Crosses awarded to non-British officers and other ranks of the Indian Army – 40 per cent. Most of the Gurkhas who joined were Nepalese, and not subjects of the British empire, and came from a much smaller recruiting pool, estimated at 280,000. At the start of the war, 18,000 Gurkhas were serving and up to the end of 1944 another 94,960 were recruited, giving a grand total of 112,960.[77] In 1945 there were 97,518 Gurkhas serving the British Crown.[78] The known minimum number of dead, based on the war graves, is 8,816[79] but, according to another analysis, if 1,441 missing are included it rises to 8,980.[80] The best estimate of the total casualties – killed, wounded, injured and missing – is 23,647.[81]

As we have seen, the Gurkhas performed a range of roles, many of which would be considered those of 'special' or, at least, 'specialised' forces – like paratroops, or mountain troops. Slim addressed this question in the chapter titled 'Afterthoughts' in his *Defeat into Victory*.[82] His common-sense view – that all operations of war are 'special', in one way or another, and that, apart from those carried out by very small groups, all operations by large bodies of men should be regarded as 'conventional' – is a timely and valuable corrective. 'Special forces' were better trained and better equipped for their special roles than normal troops, and yet they were deployed for much shorter periods of time, and risk increases with time. I agree with that, and hope the field marshal would not take this book's title amiss.

The war in Europe ended in the West on 8 May 1945, by which

19. Gurkhas, possibly Gurkha Scouts, 1897 or later. The men appear to be from 5th Gurkhas. The unidentified officer is also from 5th Gurkhas, possibly Lieutenant Tillard

20. Afridi or Orakzai tribesman, probably a sniper, captured by the Gurkha Scouts, 1897. They are wearing shorts, which were first worn by 5th Gurkhas in the Tirah campaign in 1897

21. The assault on Dargai, 1897. Contemporary photograph and annotation showing the flank attack of 18 October and the approach to the summit

22. The assault on Dargai, 1897. Contemporary photograph and annotation showing the key positions of Chagru Kotal, the object of the frontal attack, and Samana Suk, the commanding height above it, seized by the flanking force

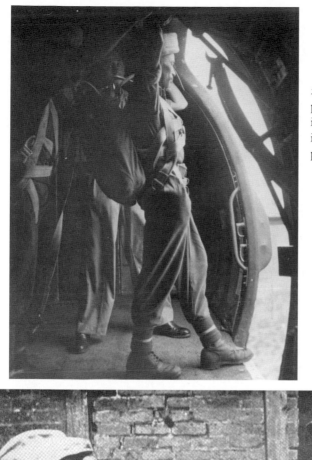

23. Early Gurkha parachutist. The helmet is of the type first issued to British paratroops after 1942

24. Brigadier Michael Calvert (*left front*) with Lieutenant Colonel Shaw (*right*) and, just visible (*left rear*), Major Lumley

25. Surrender 1945:
Japanese surrender
to Gurkhas

26. Anti-riot drills, 10th Gurkha Rifles, Malaya

27. Ambush: the Gurkha in his element. 6th Gurkha Rifles, Brunei

28. Gurkha Parachute Company, 1960s

29. Queen's Gurkha Engineers building a bridge

30. The Falklands: 7th Gurkha Rifles on the approaches to Stanley, 1982

31. Constructing an anti-tank hideout, Sierra Leone

32. Versatile as ever: a parachute-qualified Gurkha reverts to traditional transport, Afghanistan, 2006

33. Afghanistan: 2nd Battalion, Royal Gurkha Rifles on joint patrol with Afghan Security Forces, 2005

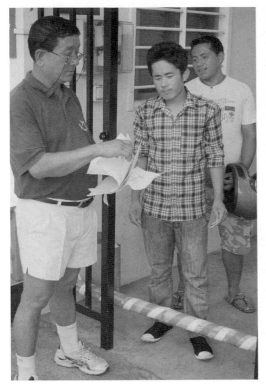

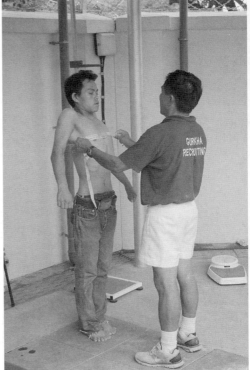

34. The first step: potential recruits begin registration at the Dharan selection centre, June 2010

35. Checking a recruit meets the physical requirements, including chest expansion. Dharan, June 2010

36. Introduction to form filling, the basis of any military career. Dharan, June 2010

time it was already 9 May in Moscow. The war against Japan lasted longer, and the Japanese surrendered to Douglas MacArthur on board USS *Missouri* in Tokyo Bay on 2 September. It was not until 12 September that Slim sat beside Mountbatten to take the formal surrender of the Japanese land, sea and air forces in South-East Asia, in Singapore. His war had been against a particularly cruel and brutal enemy.

> If I had no feeling for them, they, it seemed, had no feeling of any sort, until Itagaki, who had replaced Field Marshal Tarauchi [Terauchi], laid low by a stroke, leant forward to affix his seal to the surrender document. As he pressed heavily on the paper, a spasm of rage and despair twisted his face. Then it was gone and his mask was as expressionless as the rest. Outside, the same Union Jack that had been hauled down in surrender in 1942 flew again at the masthead.
> The war was over.[83]

9

The Paths Divide

B Y THE END of the Second World War the senior officers in the
Indian Army knew that Indian independence was only a
matter of time. The policy of 'Indianisation' had been pursued,
though not too seriously, since 1918, and it had not affected the
Gurkhas directly at all.

In late 1944 a committee had examined the organisation and
composition of the Indian Army. One of its members was the
young Enoch Powell who, like Calvert, had been made a brigadier
when he was thirty-one, and later became a prominent British pol-
itician. None of its proposals was put into effect, but it recommended that there should be only sixteen regular Gurkha battalions,
in place of the twenty that had existed before the massive wartime
expansion to forty-five.[1] There should be only eight regiments,
grouped in pairs, with two battalions per regiment. The 7th and
10th Gurkhas, as the 'junior' regiments, should be disbanded
and their soldiers from the eastern Nepali *jats* should be distributed
across the remainder, apart from the 2nd and 9th, which would
comprise Thakurs and Chhetris.[2] This did not happen and instead
most of the 3rd, 4th and sometimes 5th battalions raised during the
war were disbanded. The pre-war structure of ten regiments with
two battalions each therefore provided the material that would have
to be reworked.

In April 1945, General Claude Auchinleck (1884–1981), the
Commander-in-Chief India, wrote a paper for Lord Wavell,
the Viceroy, suggesting that the Gurkhas, whose reputation had
spread throughout all classes of British society, should be retained
for use throughout the Far East. Five months later, he wrote to
Alan Brooke, the Chief of the Imperial General Staff, saying that

Gurkhas might not be required in the future Indian Army, and that the British government should employ as many of the twenty pre-war Gurkha battalions as possible in its strategic reserve. Auchinleck valued the Gurkhas most highly, as all the British top brass did, even Montgomery, and had almost joined the 1/5th Gurkhas himself, but in the end went to the 62nd Punjabis. He was also concerned about the consequences for Nepal of abolishing the Gurkhas. The Nepalese authorities had played such an important role in encouraging young hillmen to join the Gurkhas. Others, however, felt it would be a pity to exclude the Gurkhas from the army of the independent India of the future. Tuker – now recovered from the illness that had invalided him away from Cassino, and not yet crippled by the rheumatoid arthritis that would later disable him – believed that Britain should take all twenty pre-war battalions because their outlook was British and, although he did not say it in so many words, they would not, he thought, take kindly to any Indian government of the future.[3] Having served all his life as a Gurkha, Tuker was probably less concerned than Auchinleck about splitting up the old Indian Army and keeping all the Gurkhas for the British.

It must be remembered that the problems of making the Indian subcontinent independent and splitting the Raj into two countries – India and Pakistan – were so great that the future of the Gurkhas was of relatively minor importance. In August 1946, Wavell, who had become Governor-General and Viceroy of India in September 1943, asked Jawaharlal Nehru (1889–1964), the leader of the Indian Congress Party, to form a provisional government. Nehru included two Muslims in his Cabinet but Muhammad Ali Jinnah (1876–1948), leader of the Muslim League, pressed for a 'two-state solution' and an independent Muslim state in the north-west and north-east – Pakistan.

In February 1946 there had been serious riots in Calcutta, with Hindus and Muslims murdering each other, and 5,000 people were killed. It became obvious to Tuker that 'the two states of India' – Hindu and Muslim, which would become India and Pakistan – would be at war before very long.[4]

Auchinleck and Tuker both visited Kathmandu, Auchinleck at

the end of 1945 and Tuker early in 1947. Judha – the maharajah who had supported the British war effort so faithfully, but who was about to step down and retire to a monastery in India – told Auchinleck that he was willing to allow recruitment of Gurkhas into a new Indian Army, although he was not keen. When Auchinleck suggested employing the Gurkhas as a special strategic reserve for the British government, he was much more enthusiastic.

In November 1946, Auchinleck, now a field marshal, wrote to Lord Alanbrooke, as Alan Brooke had become, who was still Chief of the Imperial General Staff, referring to the Gurkhas as a 'sort of Foreign Legion under HMG'. They could be substituted for British troops who were in short supply and they were cheaper. The War Office (as it remained until 1964) therefore made a plan to create a British Gurkha division – a true 'Foreign Legion' – which would entail converting a number of Gurkha infantry battalions into artillery, engineer and signals units and all the other arms and services that made up the complete orchestra of a division.

Slim did not like the idea, writing that 'the Gurkha is an almost ideal infantryman' and had shown himself to be that in the war. No doubt he could be trained to do other things but he would never be as good at those as he was as an infantryman. The Treasury, meanwhile, had made provision for eight battalions of Gurkhas, but the War Office also continued with plans for a Gurkha division. In 1947 it asked for twelve battalions, to include the higher-caste 9th Regiment, which it was considered would be the best to convert to artillery and engineers.[5]

The future of the Gurkhas became the subject of delicate negotiations between Britain, the provisional government of India, and Nepal. With Britain bankrupt after the war, taking the entire remaining force of Gurkhas as a British Foreign Legion ceased to be an option, and discussions focussed on splitting the 'third force' between Britain and India. Because the new state of Pakistan would be Muslim and the Gurkhas were, nominally, Hindus, Pakistan would not get any of them. An important factor was the need to use the entire recruiting area of Nepal, suggesting that the 9th and either the 7th or the 10th Gurkhas, who were recruited in the east, should be included, along with two western regiments, of which

the 2nd Gurkhas, the Sirmoor Rifles, linked to the British Rifles, was the favourite.

It was not until early 1947, just before independence, that the final decision on the fate of the Gurkhas was taken, and it was not confirmed until the Tripartite Agreement was signed by Britain, India and Nepal in Kathmandu on 9 November 1947. On 17 March 1947 the Defence Committee met at the Cabinet Office in London with the prime minister, Clement Attlee, and Lord Louis Mountbatten, the Viceroy designate who would oversee the partition. The strategic context was crucial. Churchill had made his 'iron curtain speech' in 1946 , the Gurkhas had already been involved in heavy fighting in South-East Asia, and trouble was brewing in Malaya.

The mopping-up operations at the tail end of the Second World War have received little attention. In November 1944 the 4th Indian Division had been withdrawn from Italy and sent to Greece where civil war was looming as the Germans withdrew. The three Gurkha battalions were involved in delicate operations, negotiating with and disarming the Greek communist forces, ELAS. Like all successful peace support operations, it did not often make the headlines, but it was a success and a pointer to the future.

Then, in September 1945, a brigade of the 20th Indian Division started landing in Saigon to disarm the 54,000 Japanese remaining there and to keep the peace until the French, who had been driven out after their defeat in 1940, could return. The communist Vietminh, who had been fighting the Japanese, did not like that idea at all and for about four months the 3/1st, 4/2nd, 3/8th and 4/10th Gurkhas found themselves assisted by their Japanese prisoners in fighting against the communists. It was a bizarre situation, and when the French finally collected enough troops to take over in January 1946, the Gurkhas left with a sigh of relief.

A similar situation occurred in Indonesia, the former Dutch East Indies. The Dutch were in no position to reassert control of their former colony. The 5th, 23rd and 26th Indian divisions had completed the reoccupation of Malaya, and were then deployed to the western Indonesian islands of Sumatra and Java to try to keep the peace and secure the camps where large numbers of Dutch and

other European and Asian people had been interned. The Indian divisions included six battalions of Gurkhas: the 3/3rd, 3/5th, 1/8th, 4/8th, 3/9th and 3/10th. The Indonesian nationalists, who had, again, been fighting the Japanese, did not want the colonial powers returning and there was fierce fighting. A big battle took place at Surabaya in November 1945 to secure the port and once again some of the Japanese fought on the side of the British empire, trying to rescue the remnants of the Dutch empire. Without this intervention it is likely that thousands of Dutch and other internees who had survived the horrors of Japanese incarceration might have been killed. In thirteen months, 2,136 British, Indian and Gurkha soldiers were killed and wounded. The most senior was a brigade commander who was murdered while negotiating a ceasefire on 30 October 1945.[6] The untidy end of the Second World War merged into the post-colonial conflicts of the next quarter-century.

The strategic environment was uncertain in the extreme. There were post-colonial conflicts aplenty, both Britain's own and other people's. These resulted, in part, from the spread of communist insurgency across South-East Asia, what was later called the 'domino effect'. There was also the threat of major war with the Soviet Union, as the Cold War, which became hotter with the Berlin crisis in 1948, loomed. Britain was bankrupt, the winter of 1946–7 was one of the worst on record, before or since, and there was a flu epidemic.

The cheapness of Gurkha soldiers and their versatility in all theatres of war were major factors in the decision on their future. At the time it cost £150,000 a year to maintain a Gurkha battalion in Malaya compared with £240,000 for a British one. Attlee and Mountbatten had no doubts that there was a case for retaining a substantial number of Gurkhas. The committee duly reported that British representatives negotiating with Nehru and the Nepalese would do their best to get agreement for up to 25,000 Gurkhas to be employed in the regular British Army: the equivalent of a division. There should be no suggestion of any time limit for their employment – this was not just an interim measure to paper over the cracks of partition. The instruction was immediately passed on to the War Office delegation in Delhi.[7]

The delegation was now confident that a division of British Gurkhas, or something similar, was on the cards. As for the future armed forces of independent India, the Indians seemed to be indecisive, but one thing was clear. Nehru was in charge. However, he was in a difficult position because if he agreed to let the British take some of the Gurkhas, and they were then used to enforce colonial rule and suppress national liberation movements, it would rebound on him. The Muslims, looking towards a future Pakistan, also opposed the new Indian Army getting Gurkhas as they might possibly – and did, as it turned out – have to fight them. However, they were simply outvoted.

The Indians then announced that they would give full Indian commissions to Gurkha officers in any regiments that remained in the post-independence Indian Army. The British thought this was a trick to induce the Gurkhas to stay with India. It was indeed a trick, but more subtle. Native Indian officers had had no opportunity to command Gurkhas, although they had fought side by side for 132 years. The Indians merely intended to give full Indian commissions to outstanding Gurkha VCOs, while their own officers learned the language and absorbed the *kaida* – the ethos, customs and traditions – of these foreign soldiers who had often said they despised them. Conversely, the Indians regarded the Gurkhas – who were mostly of the artisan caste, and few of whom wore the holy thread of 'warriors', never mind Brahmans – as second- or third-class people.

In May 1947, British and Indian teams headed for Kathmandu for negotiations with the new maharajah, Mohan Shamsher. Shamsher agreed to let Gurkhas serve with both armies. Then Mountbatten and a civil servant in the 'Ministry of Defence' – the small department in Storey's Gate, which, until 1964, tried to coordinate matters between the other four defence ministries – had the idea of letting Montgomery, who had taken over as Chief of the Imperial General Staff, talk to Nehru. The two men met on 23 June and, although Nehru still had serious reservations about what the British might use the Gurkhas for, they came to a gentlemen's agreement that the transfer of eight battalions to the UK should go ahead. The detail was to be worked out quietly, to avoid embarrassing Nehru in front of his own people. A plan to take the first battalions of eight

of the ten regiments, and to disband the 9th and 10th Gurkhas, had already been abandoned, and on 31 July, just two weeks before Indian independence on 15 August, the final decision was delegated to the British mission in Delhi.

There were two main drivers. The first was that the regiments selected should maximise the ability to select from the whole of Nepal, which boiled down to the 9th, either the 7th or the 10th, and two western regiments, including the 2nd. The other driver was the practical advantage of selecting regiments with battalions already serving in Burma and on standby for Malaya. Those were the 1/6th, 1/7th and 1/10th. General Neil Ritchie, now commanding in South-East Asia, and Auchinleck both assumed those battalions would be among those selected for transfer to the British Army.

So it was, for very immediate and practical reasons, as well as the need to continue to draw on the wider spread of the 'martial tribes' in Nepal, that, in the first week of August, the first two battalions of the 2nd, 6th, 7th and 10th Gurkhas were selected for transfer to the British Army. Any of the war-raised battalions still in existence would join the other regiments remaining in the new Indian Army. Thus the 4/2nd became the 5/8th and the 3/6th became the 5/5th.[8] The news reached India on 8 August.[9] Naturally, some supporters of the regiments that were to remain with India – including the senior regiment, the 1st; the much honoured 5th, with four VCs in the Second World War alone; and the higher-caste 9th – all complained. There were also complaints that 'newer' Gurkha regiments, the 7th and 10th, had in some sense 'jumped the queue', ahead of older ones, and the perhaps inevitable conspiracy theories surfaced about Slim's connexions with the 6th and 7th. Anyone who knew Slim would have known that the fact that he happened to have served with the 6th and 7th would have had no influence on his decision whatsoever.

Realistically, there was very little to choose between the regiments in terms of their professional skill, as Tuker – initially critical of what he called a 'carefree policy', even though his own 2nd Gurkhas went to the British – later acknowledged.[10] As it turned out, those who bemoaned the fact that the 1st, 3rd, 4th, 5th, 8th and 9th Gorkhas stayed in the Indian Army, which was their true home, citing

'tradition' and their record of service for the British government, were proved completely wrong. Sixty years on, the four regiments that went to the British Army had been merged into one, the Royal Gurkha Rifles, with two battalions, while the six Gorkha regiments that stayed with India all retained their historic titles and identities with five or six battalions each. However, all the Indian Gorkhas, as the Indians always write the name and which they adopted as the official spelling in February 1949, are infantry. The British Army, on the other hand, also has the Queen's Gurkha Engineers, the Queen's Gurkha Signals and the Queen's Gurkha Logistic Regiment, making it close to a true all-arms brigade. These regiments did not exist in 1947, but had been mere twinkles in the eyes of those who planned to form a British Gurkha division.

The British had simplified the task of dividing the Gurkhas as far as they could by ensuring that only the ten historic rifle regiments were involved. Shortly after the end of the war, in November 1945, all British and Gurkha units were withdrawn from the Indian Airborne Division. The Indian Parachute Regiment was disbanded along with its parachute battalions associated with existing regiments of the Indian Army. Parachute-trained personnel of the 1st and 4th (Indian) were spread through the new 'parachute' battalions, while the Gurkhas of the 2nd and 3rd battalions went to Gurkha rifle regiments stationed at Quetta. In the final organisation of the 2nd Indian Airborne Division, in January 1947, all the battalions were Indian, many of them from other 'martial races': Rajputs, Punjabis, Baluchis and Mahrattas. But the Gurkha paratroops were reintegrated with the rifle regiments.[11]

In summer 1947 the British officers serving with the Gurkhas faced an uncertain future. They had been asked to choose by 15 July 1947 whether they wanted to take redundancy and leave the Indian Army, to transfer to the British Army, or to transfer to one of the armies of the Dominions, now including India. They could not be offered the option of staying with the Gurkha regiments transferring to the British Army because before 15 July nobody knew which regiments would transfer. At this point, there were, in fact, *no* Gurkha regiments in the British Army. Eventually on 28 November 1947 the British officers were given the opportunity to opt for

continued service with the now British Gurkhas, whatever their previous choice had been.

The maharajah of Nepal had stipulated that the Nepalese Gurkhas should be consulted about their preferences: to serve with Britain overseas, to serve with India, or to leave. On 13 August 1947, thirty-six hours before independence, an announcement appeared in the *Statesman*, India's leading English-language newspaper, saying that every soldier in the ten Gurkha regiments still in the Indian Army would be invited to answer a questionnaire on his future preferences. At the time, and given the magnitude of the imminent change, few people in India probably read it.

Any Indian reservations about the status and value of Gurkhas were dispelled after 15 August. Immediately the Punjab became a disaster area as hundreds of thousands of people found themselves on the wrong side of the new border between India and Pakistan. Hindus and Sikhs in Pakistan and Muslims in India started flowing in opposite directions, accompanied by anarchy and murder, as extremist groups and simple criminals from both faiths preyed on the hapless refugees and homeless. Being 'neutral', the Gurkhas provided what little security could be offered. The remnants of the wartime 4th Indian Division, now called the Punjab Boundary Force, including the 4th and 7th Gurkhas, found the landscape stinking of corpses and strewn with mutilated dead. These included women and children, and whole families burned to death in their homes, while feral dogs fed on the remains.

Compared with this, the old North-West Frontier, now the North-West Frontier of Pakistan, was relatively quiet. When the 1/1st Gurkhas were sent eastward from there, into Jammu and Kashmir, they found hundreds of thousands of people labouring to reach the perceived safety of Hindu India or Muslim Pakistan, but so exhausted and frightened that they lacked the energy to get up from the roadside.[12] Jammu and Kashmir was one of the princely states, with a Hindu ruler and a Muslim majority. After partition it was immediately invaded by Pathan tribesmen, probably sponsored by the new Pakistan government. At the time of writing, Kashmir remains divided between India and Pakistan, and subject to competing claims. Immediately after partition, the senior officers in both the

new states' armies were still British. General Sir Rob Lockhart was still Commander-in-Chief India and Sir Frank Messervy in Pakistan. Realising that British officers could be fighting openly on different sides, the British government forbade any British officer to enter Jammu and Kashmir. John Cross, whom the author interviewed (see Introduction) was one, but he disobeyed orders and walked into and out of the border zone each morning and evening.

These events influenced the future of the Gurkhas. The Indians could see that this neutral force was extremely valuable. If the new Indian government could win the Gurkhas' loyalty, as the British had done, their value was beyond question. And the Indians were now in charge. A week after the referendum on Gurkha preferences was announced, Nehru cancelled it. Two weeks after that, on 5 September, he forwarded Auchinleck a letter he had received from Mohan Shamsher, the maharajah of Nepal. It stated that because of the agreement between India and Britain to split the Gurkhas between the two countries, and because the Gurkhas had always been part of the Indian Army, the question of a referendum was rather irrelevant. Nothing should happen until after the tripartite discussions had taken place in Kathmandu.

Informal referendums had already been held. On 8 August orders were received that the 6th Gurkha Rifles, less their third battalion, were going to become part of the British Army. That regiment held a referendum to determine who wanted to serve with it. The referendum did not have the sanction of the government. The Tripartite Agreement – the final version of which was drawn up on 7 November and which was signed on 9 November, with separate bilateral agreements between Britain and India, and between Britain and Nepal – ordered referendums to be held. But many Gurkhas did not opt to join the British.[13]

The Tripartite Agreement specified that the final apportionment of Gurkhas, either to remain with the new Indian Army or to transfer to the British Army, would be effective on 1 January 1948. It also specified that:

(i) Arrangements have been made for the continued employment of Gurkha officers and men in the Indian army . . . [The British

government] may employ Gurkha officers and soldiers . . . to maintain eight battalions . . .

(ii) All volunteers from the regular battalions of the 2nd, 6th, 7th and 10th Gurkha Rifles together with personnel from their regimental centres who opt for such service in the referendum about to be held will be transferred for service with the British Army.

(iii) Representatives of the Governments of Nepal and India will be present with the eight units earmarked for HMG while the referendum is being taken.

(iv) The Government of Nepal have agreed that Indian officers will in future serve in Gurkha units. Nepalese subjects will be eligible for Commissions in the Indian Army . . . Gurkha soldiers from regiments in the Indian Army who have completed their engagements may join [the HMG Gurkhas].[14]

There was no specific provision for the Gurkha officers in units transferred to the British Army to get full British King's Commissions. There were also three other key provisions that are still relevant more than sixty years later.

1. In all matters of promotion, welfare and other facilities the Gurkha troops should be treated on the same footing as the other units in the parent army so that the stigma of 'mercenary' may for all time be wiped out. These troops should be treated as a link between the two friendly countries.
2. The Gurkha troops . . . should be eligible to commissioned ranks with no restrictions whatsoever to the highest level to which qualified officers may be promoted.
3. The Gurkha troops should not be used against Hindu or any other unarmed mobs.[15]

These provisions, under a three-way international treaty that is still in force, applied to the Gurkhas in both the British and Indian armies. The question of commissions was particularly sensitive, and the Gurkhas were well aware of it.

The official history of the Indian 5th Gurkhas affirms that, under

266

these arrangements, Indian commissions would be granted to just three Gurkha officers in each battalion. However, that did not mean that they would have the same status as the three British officers in the original Gurkha battalions after 1815. Those roles would be taken by Indians. And, as the Indian regimental history makes clear, 'The Gurkhas did not want to serve under an Indian CO.'[16]

But the British option was even less attractive. The 'opt', as it was known, is an incredibly sensitive issue in Gurkha history, because it was handled so badly. Brigadier (later Major General) Osborne Hedley, a hugely perceptive British officer and the coordinator of the British mission to maintain Gurkha strength, was shocked by the results of the referendums.[17] His report of 30 December 1947 listed the reasons Gurkhas gave for not wanting to join the British Army, which revealed them to be well informed and worldly-wise. They thought that Malaya was a long way from Nepal. There were difficulties with the Brahman priests about travelling overseas – crossing the 'black water'. There was no precise information about the grant of King's Commissions to Gurkhas. There were doubts about married accommodation. And it was understood that if the majority of men in any unit opted to stay with India, then they would be permitted to do so. Hedley added his own postscript. He thought the two main factors affecting the results were the removal of many experienced officers from the units and their replacement by officers whom the men did not know; and the long time it had taken to formulate and confirm the option of joining a British Army Gurkha force.[18]

The latter caused a major shift in opinion. Soundings taken in July indicated that the vast majority of Gurkhas would opt to serve with the British. In the battalions destined for British service, Gurkhas could opt to transfer to Indian battalions or to leave altogether, and in those destined for the Indian Army vice versa. But feelings ran high and Gurkhas wanting to serve with the British came under some pressure.

In the 2/7th a Gurkha officer who intended to opt for British service was banned from the Gurkha officers' club. The subedar major, the senior Gurkha officer in the battalion and the CO's right-hand man, had decided he wanted to opt for India, partly

because a wartime incident had left him with some resentment against the British and partly because he was lured by the prospect of a full commission. As the top Nepalese Gurkha in the battalion, he expected the rest of the battalion to go with him.

In the referendum only 40 out of 729 soldiers opted to go to the British Army. In the 1/2nd Gurkhas, again designated for Britain, there was almost a mutiny on 3 November 1947 when the entire battalion, apart from the Gurkha officers and a few senior NCOs, refused to go on parade. The men had got the impression they were going to be sent to Malaya, even before they had been given the chance to opt one way or the other, and therefore voted unanimously to go with India. But things could go the other way just as rapidly.

General Tuker then intervened and told the men that if they joined the Indian Army the regimental truncheon bestowed on them by Queen Victoria (Plate 12) would have to be returned to her grandson, George VI. Such was the significance of the object that, when the 1/2nd re-opted in December, nearly half the battalion chose to serve with Britain. In the 2/2nd, 592 out of 834 opted to join the British Army.[19]

With the transfer of the 7th and 10th to the British Army, there was no Gurkha regiment left in the Indian Army, which recruited from eastern Nepal. For that reason, the decision to re-raise the 11th Gurkhas was made in December 1947.[20]

The large number of Gurkhas in the 2/7th who opted to remain in the Indian Army were formed into the 3rd Battalion of the revived 11th Gurkhas, with the other battalions of the revived regiment formed from 'non-optees' (non-optants – those who did not opt for British service) from the 10th Gurkhas. In the 5th Gurkhas, destined to remain in the Indian Army, the vote was again overwhelmingly in favour. The procedure went as follows:

> The day of option came and the first one to come before the committee was the Subedar-Major. His Commanding Officer asked him *'Timi HMG Gurkha ma jane manjur chha ya manjur chhaina'*('Would you like to opt for the HMG Gurkhas or would you like not to?') *'Ja ne manjur, Hazur'*('I would not like to opt for the HMG Gurkhas, Sir') came the reply . . . only three Gurkha officers and hardly a

hundred-odd GORs [Gurkha other ranks] opted for the HMG
Gurkhas. The large number of Gurkha Officers (now JCOs) and
men opting for the Indian Army involved looking after practically
the whole of the 2/6th GRs [the Gurkha Rifles] whose non-optants
were attached to the 1/5th.[21]

However, the prospect of serving under Indian officers did not
please the Gurkhas. Lieutenant Colonel Richard Pease, the last
British commanding officer of the 1/5th Gurkhas, arranged to get
some Indian officers posted to the Gurkhas immediately, to try to
ease the transition. The better Gurkha commissioned officers, formerly VCOs, were also given Indian commissions. In the 1/5th,
Padam Thapa, who had won the Military Cross, was the first officer
to join the battalion.[22]

The painful split of the British Indian Army between India and
Pakistan did have one advantage. Some excellent Indian officers had
been serving with Baluchi, North-West Frontier or Punjabi Muslim
regiments, which were now transferred to the Pakistani Army.
Hindu Indian officers could not stay with them, but they were ideal
candidates to go to the Indian Army's Gurkha regiments or Gorkha
regiments, as they became.

Lieutenant Colonel, later Major General, S. K. Korla, who had
served with the 7th Battalion of the Baluchi regiment in Burma, was
selected to take command of the 2/1st Gorkha Rifles, with Major
'Eno' Singha, another Baluchi officer, as his second-in-command.
When they arrived, the outgoing British officers gave them a frosty
reception and sent them to the Gurkha officers' club. Here, there
was nothing to eat but for two hours the Gurkhas plied them with
drink. Realising they were being tested, Korla afterwards thanked
the subedar major and said he and Eno would have to go. The subedar major called for two stretcher bearers, but Korla refused, saying
that he liked his drink but he also liked to walk home. The two
Indian officers staggered back to their tents and crashed out. The
next morning, fortunately a Sunday, they managed to make their
way to breakfast. The British officers told them that the subedar
major had said they were 'all right', and welcomed them to the regiment. Korla had been to the British Staff College and knew British

ways.[23] His Britishness, and his ability to party, made him acceptable to the Gurkhas. There were no more problems.

Reluctance to serve in Malaya, after six years of the Second World War, was one of the main reasons why many Gurkhas elected not to transfer to the British Army. The story of the 'opt' shows that by this time many Gurkhas had a very good idea of what was going on in the international and political sphere, and made their choice for good reasons. After a period of immense turmoil and dissatisfaction, those who opted for Britain accepted their new status.

For 132 years the Gurkhas had been part of the British-Indian Army, and the new Indian Army was in some ways their more natural home. In the British Army, the four Gurkha regiments that transferred were in a strange and unnatural environment. They were the British Foreign Legion. In the post-colonial and counter-insurgency campaigns of the next quarter-century, the French Foreign Legion and the Gurkhas would both play a disproportionate part in overseas operations. The Tripartite Agreement's restriction on the Gurkhas being used 'against Hindu or any other unarmed mobs', and their unusual status as a force of foreign soldiers in British pay, could make their employment politically sensitive.

In August 1948, at the start of the Malayan Emergency, the British ambassador to Nepal told the Foreign Office that it would be unwise for the BBC and other media to draw too much attention to the Gurkhas' role in anti-communist operations in Malaya, as it could embarass both Nepal and India.[24] For India, the use of Gorkha troops against Pakistan and China, for internal security and in peace support operations sanctioned by the United Nations, had no such sensitivities attached.

10

India's Gorkhas

IMMEDIATELY AFTER INDEPENDENCE, on 22 October 1947, Pakistani forces, along with tribal forces from the North-West Frontier, called lashkars, of up to a thousand men each, moved into the still independent princely state of Jammu and Kashmir. It was the start of the 1947 Indo–Pakistan War, also known as the First Kashmir War. The Pakistani units called themselves the Azad Kashmir or 'Free Kashmir' forces (AZK). The maharajah, Hari Singh, who was not a hereditary ruler but a British appointee, immediately called on Indian troops for assistance and, after having initially resisted joining India or Pakistan, joined India. Meanwhile, his state troops – which became the Jammu and Kashmir Rifles, the only state force to be incorporated in the new Indian Army as a distinct and separate regiment – held off the AZK. They lost 76 officers, 31 junior commissioned officers, the equivalent of the old VCOs, and 1,085 other ranks. Although not a 'Gorkha' regiment, 75 per cent of the Jammu and Kashmir Rifles were and are Dogras and Gorkhas, the other 25 per cent being Sikhs and Muslims.[1]

Jinnah, the Governor-General of Pakistan and founder of the modern state of Pakistan, ordered the head of his army, General Douglas Gracey, who was British, to send more troops, but Gracey refused because Jammu and Kashmir had now joined India. The British threatened to withdraw all their officers, thus crippling the Pakistani command structure, but the Pakistanis nevertheless managed to conduct operations with some success, especially in the high Himalayas.[2] The delay enabled the Indians to secure about two-thirds of the country. The territories of Gilgit and Baltistan were occupied for Pakistan by the Gilgit Scouts and forces from Chitral, another princely state whose ruler, the Mehtar of Chitral, had

acceded to Pakistan. It was the beginning of a conflict that has gone on ever since.

The main Pakistani objective was Srinagar and the Kashmir valley (see Figure 11). As soon as the state had joined India, the Indians began airlifting troops and equipment into Srinagar. The state forces held on to Punch or Poonch, close to the western border (see Figure 11) and only about 50 miles (80 kilometres) from Islamabad, and were besieged for more than a year.

The Indian Army Gurkhas were involved almost immediately. Kashmir includes the high Himalayas, and the Gurkhas' familiarity with steep slopes made them obvious candidates. The first Indian commanding officer of 1/3rd Gorkha Rifles, Lieutenant Colonel, later Lieutenant General P. O. Dunn, took over from the last British CO, Lieutenant Colonel H. V. Rose, on 29 November 1947. Lieutenant Colonel Prem Das MC took over the 2/3rd Gorkhas, and it was his battalion that gained the 3rd Gorkhas their first post-independence battle honour the next summer.

Two companies of the Pakistani 3rd Bagh Battalion, three other platoons of Pakistani troops and about a hundred Pathan tribesmen were holding the Pirkanthi feature that dominated the road between Srinagar and Domel. The Gorkhas attacked by night, without artillery preparation, and seized the feature. One of them had the presence of mind to take a photograph of members of the battalion on the summit the next day, a rare one because after the peace agreement the hill was in the Pakistan-controlled area of Kashmir, beyond the 'Line of Control' (see Figure 11).

In another action, Lieutenant Colonel Hari Chand, commanding the 1/8th Gorkha Rifles, took a handful of men on an obscure route from Kulu to Leh at an altitude of 18,000 feet (5,500 metres) and destroyed Pakistani artillery, which may have prevented Leh from falling into Pakistani hands. For this he was later awarded the Maha Vir Chakra, the new Indian decoration that was equivalent to the British Military Cross.

The Indian forces slowly got the upper hand. Poonch was relieved in November 1948 and the Indians advanced to Kargil before supply problems stopped them. At this stage Nehru asked the United Nations to intervene and a ceasefire was eventually arranged,

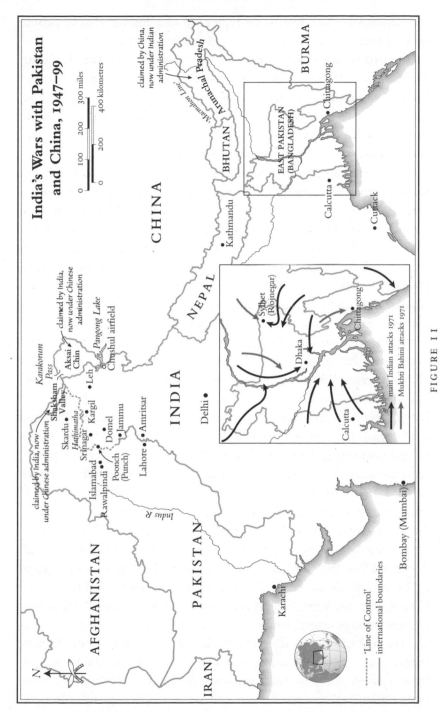

India's Wars with Pakistan and China, 1947–99

FIGURE 11

which came into effect at midnight on 1–2 January 1949. By this time the front had stabilised along the 'Line of Control'.

The 4th, 5th and 11th Gorkha Rifles were also all involved in the fighting, and have the 1947–8 war as a battle honour, with Poonch as a more specific honour for the 4th Gorkhas.

The first India–Pakistan War had been fought between two Dominions of the British Commonwealth, with senior British officials still holding positions of nominal authority. This confusing and embarrassing situation soon ended. India was declared a republic on 26 January 1950, and the new Indian Army emerged from its short and awkward adolescence into the army of a new, completely independent state. The Governor-General's bodyguard became the president's bodyguard. Non-Indian associations, particularly those connected with British royalty, were dropped. The crown in cap badges and badges of rank was replaced by the three Ashoka lions, and the four-pointed star of the Order of the Bath by a five-pointed star.

During the India–Pakistan War both sides had put people forward for gallantry awards, which had to go to the King for approval. But George VI was not prepared to have his head on awards given to people on opposite sides who had been fighting and killing each other, so no awards were made. After India became a republic, new gallantry awards were introduced for post-independence operations, which conveniently reflected their British predecessors. The new medals were established on 26 January 1950 and, as the Victoria Cross had been, they could be awarded retrospectively, back to 15 August 1947, the date of Indian independence.

The Vir Chakra, abbreviated to VrC, to avoid confusion with the VC, was the basic award, probably equating to the Queen's Gallantry Medal. The Maha Vir Chakra (MVC), the second-highest gallantry award, replaced the MC or, in certain circumstances, the DSO, and the Param Vir Chakra (PVC) replaced the VC, although it was perhaps even higher as, while some VCs were awarded to people who survived, the PVC was intended only for those who had died in combat. *Param vir* means 'bravest of the brave' and the *chakra* is the wheel on the Indian flag, which can also mean a medal or a circle.

The designs had been finalised in June 1948 but India was still, technically, a Dominion of the British Crown and the new awards could not be given until complete independence.[3] In a final move to close the chapter of British rule in India, the King's Colours were deposited at the Indian Military Academy at Dehra Dun after a solemn ceremony on 23 November 1950. The new Indian Army had come of age.

To date, India's Gorkhas have won three Param Vir Chakras. On 30 June 1960 the vast territory of the Belgian Congo, Joseph Conrad's 'heart of darkness', became independent but, unlike India thirteen years before, it was totally unprepared. Although partition of the subcontinent had brought with it mass murder and horror, the British had for generations been grooming an elite to take over, including the Indianisation of the Indian Army. In the Congo, later Zaire, now the Democratic Republic of Congo, the Belgians had done nothing to prepare the country for independence, and chaos ensued, which has continued to this day.

The province of Katanga, in the south, declared independence. In order to maintain control of the mining industry, Belgium supplied Katanga with arms and 500 mercenaries to lead its army. On 12 July 1960 the Congo government requested UN assistance to repel aggression by the recently departed colonial power. What followed was the most ambitious UN military intervention in history. It was the only time the UN had its own air force, from October 1960, although Ethiopia and Sweden supplied the jet fighters, and India supplied the Canberra bombers and their crews. It was the biggest and most complex civil-military operation by the UN until Cambodia in 1992–3. At its peak, the UN force in the Congo, known by its French acronym of ONUC, numbered 20,000 of whom 234 died in combat.[4]

With the superpowers engaged in the Cold War effectively debarred from contributing, the new Republic of India, with volunteer armed forces, was one of the ideal contributors. The Indians provided the UN force with aircraft and Indian Air Force personnel, as well as ground troops, in the form of a brigade of around 3,000 men, including Gorkhas.

In November 1961, the UN Security Council decided to stop

the hostile activities of the Katangese troops in Congo. This greatly angered Tshombe, Katanga's secessionist leader, and he intensified his 'hate the UN' campaign. There was more violence against UN personnel. On 5 December 1961, a 3/1st Gorkha Rifles Company, supported by a 3-inch (75-mm) mortar, attacked a roadblock, established by the Katangese troops, between the headquarters of the UN's Katanga command and the Elisabethville (now Lumumbashi) airfield at a strategic roundabout. The enemy roadblock was destroyed and the Gorkhas established a UN roadblock there.

Captain Gurbachan Singh Salaria (1935–61) was an Indian Gorkha officer born in Gurdaspur, Punjab. He was commissioned into the 1st Gorkha Rifles – the senior regiment, the Malaun regiment – on 9 June 1957. According to the citation, he was in charge of a platoon of the 3/1st Gorkhas that tried to link up with the adjacent Indian Gorkha company to reinforce the roadblock, when

> he met strong opposition in the old airfield area. Heavy automatic and small arms fire was brought down on his force by the enemy from a dug-in position on the right flank. The enemy held the area strongly with two armoured cars and 90 men. Captain Salaria was not deterred by the superior enemy strength and fire power. He decided to take the enemy, head-on, to achieve the objective. The Gorkhas then charged the enemy with bayonets, khukris [sic] and hand-grenades. A rocket launcher supported them in the attack. In this sharp encounter, Captain Salaria and his men killed 40 of the enemy and knocked out two enemy cars. His bold action completely demoralised the enemy who fled despite numerical superiority and well-fortified positions. However, in the engagement, Captain Salaria was wounded in the neck by a burst of enemy automatic fire, but he ignored the injury and continued to fight till he collapsed due to excessive bleeding.[5]

Salaria later died of his wounds. He had prevented the enemy from reaching to the roundabout, thereby saving the UN Headquarters in Elisabethville from encirclement. For 'extraordinary leadership and devotion to duty', Captain Salaria was awarded the highest wartime medal, the Param Vir Chakra, posthumously.[6]

In February 1963 the UN Secretary-General, U Thant, reported that the civil war had been quelled and that the foreign mercenaries

had been removed. The last UN detachment withdrew on 30 June 1964.

In the late 1950s the new Indian government had occupied some Chinese territory on its mountainous northern border with China either side of Nepal. There were two areas. One was in the west, Aksai Chin, in the north-eastern section of the Ladakh District in Jammu and Kashmir (see Figure 11). The other, also shown in Figure 11, was in the eastern sector, a region included in the British-designated North-East Frontier Agency, the disputed part of which India renamed Arunachal Pradesh and made a state. The overall area was about 34,800 square miles (90,000 square kilometres), slightly smaller than the United Kingdom, of which Aksai Chin was 12,000 square miles (33,000 square kilometres), slightly bigger than Scotland. The Chinese were, understandably, upset. In April 1960, the Chinese premier Zhou Enlai went to New Delhi to hold talks with the Indian prime minister Nehru, but no agreement was reached on the division of territory along the Himalayan border, 2,150 miles (3,225 kilometres) long. With severe internal political problems preoccupying the leadership, the Chinese People's Liberation Army attacked India on 20 October 1962.

At the time, nine divisions from the Indian eastern and western commands were deployed along the Himalayan border with China. None of these divisions was up to strength; all were short of artillery and tanks and, probably more critically, mountain clothing and other equipment for war on the high mountains. In the Ladakh province the Chinese attacked south of the Karakoram Pass at the north-west end of the Aksai Chin plateau and in the Pangong Lake area, about 100 miles (160 kilometres) to the south-east (see Figure 11). The defending Indian forces were driven from their positions on the Karakoram Pass and near Pangong Lake. However, they put up fierce resistance at Daulat Beg Oldi, near the entrance to the pass, at Chushul, south of Pangong Lake, and at the head of the supply road down to Leh, a major town and site of the Ladakh air force base.[7]

Major Dhan Singh Thapa, born on 10 April 1928 in Simla, North India, was commissioned in the 8th Gorkha Rifles on 28 August

1949, just after independence and just before the creation of the republic in 1950. His name and date and place of birth tell us that he was a 'line boy' – the son of a Gurkha soldier, who had therefore received a good education thanks to the Indian Army, and he was commissioned directly, not after service in the ranks. The Sirijap valley, north of the Pangong Lake, was vital to the defence of Chushul airfield. One of the 1/8th Gorkha outposts named Sirijap-1 was held by a platoon of C Company under the command of Major Dhan Singh when the Chinese attack came on 21 October.

At 0600 hours the Chinese directed a barrage of artillery and mortar fire over the Sirijap-1 post. The shelling continued till 0830 hours and the whole area was set on fire. Some shells fell on the command post and damaged the radio set, putting it out of action. The Chinese then attacked the outpost in overwhelming numbers. Major Thapa and his men repulsed the attack, inflicting heavy casualties on the Chinese. But the Chinese kept going and attacked again. According to the citation,

> Major Dhan Singh Thapa was in command of a forward post in Ladakh. On 20 October it was attacked by the Chinese in overwhelming strength after being subjected to intensive artillery and mortar bombardment. Under his gallant command, the greatly outnumbered [force] repulsed the attack, inflicting heavy casualties on the aggressors. The enemy attacked again in greater numbers after heavy shelling by artillery and mortar fire. Under the leadership of Major Thapa, his men repulsed this attack also with heavy losses to the enemy.
>
> The Chinese attacked for the third time, now with tanks to support the infantry. The post had already suffered large numbers of casualties in the earlier two attacks. Though considerably reduced in number it held out to the last. When it was finally overrun by overwhelming numbers of the enemy, Major Thapa got out of his trench and killed several of the enemy in hand-to-hand fighting before he was finally overpowered by Chinese soldiers.
>
> Major Thapa's cool courage, conspicuous fighting qualities and leadership were in the highest traditions of our Army.[8]

It was assumed that Major Dhan Singh had been killed, and he was awarded the Param Vir Chakra, 'posthumously'. But six months

later, he reappeared, alive. Having overwhelmed his position, the Chinese had taken him prisoner, and there was no way he could communicate the fact. He had been presumed dead and might not have got the award otherwise. But no one could take it away from him now. His 'posthumous' VC became the subject of good-humoured legend. Fortunately, his wife had not remarried, but, under Nepalese and Indian law, having returned unexpectedly, and very much alive, Dhan Singh, who had been pronounced dead, had to marry her again.[9]

Fortunately the war did not last long. The Chinese had trounced the Indians, and by 21 November had overrun all the territory they wanted to claim back. The Indians were regrouping and any attempt to press on further into the plains of Assam would have stretched Chinese lines of communication too far. The Chinese stopped where they were and pulled back 13 miles (20 kilometres) from Ladakh, although Dhan Singh's heroic stand was probably not a factor.

In 1965 another war broke out between India and Pakistan, the Second Kashmir War. It was the culmination of a series of skirmishes over disputed territory in the Jammu–Kashmir area between April and September, and the main war began with a big Pakistani attack on 1 September, which, by 6 September, had led to full-scale war between the two countries. The 4th, 5th, 8th and 11th Indian Gorkhas were all involved, but the war was most notable for the biggest tank battles since the Second World War and the Indians' successful use of air power to blunt the Pakistani assaults. Both sides captured roughly equal-sized areas of each other's territory, and the war ended after three weeks when the international community intervened on 22 September, with UN intervention and the United States embargoing military supplies to both sides. After the Indians' dismal performance against the Chinese in 1962, foreign analysts thought that Pakistan would win easily, but India's strength became apparent, and this time India got the better of the fight. Both sides agreed to return to where they had been before the war started.[10] The next war between India and Pakistan, however, would show what the Gorkhas could do.

Whereas the first two India–Pakistan wars had been about

disputes in Kashmir, the 1971 war, which was, again, mercifully brief, was precipitated by the independence movement in East Pakistan, now Bangladesh. It lasted for just thirteen days, from 3 to 16 December 1971. The Pakistani Army had responded to East Pakistani aspirations to independence by conducting genocidal pogroms against its minority Hindu population, and India opened its borders to let in up to 10 million refugees. Prime Minister Indira Gandhi expressed support for East Pakistani independence on 27 March 1971, and decided that it would be more effective to take military action, rather than simply trying to absorb those refugees who escaped. The Indian armed forces made a meticulous plan to invade East Pakistan in the winter, when the Himalayan passes would be closed, preventing any Chinese intervention.[11] During the autumn monsoon, India was also able to feed back into Bangladesh 30,000 members of the Bangladesh liberation forces, the Mukti Bahini, whom it had trained. The Pakistanis were aware of the Indian support for the Mukti Bahini, and launched what they hoped would be a pre-emptive air strike against Indian air bases in the west on 3 December. If they had hoped to emulate the Israeli success in 1967, they were mistaken. The air strikes were not nearly big enough and gave the Indians the perfect excuse to launch their well-prepared invasion of East Pakistan.

All seven Indian Gorkha Regiments claim the 1971 India–Pakistan War as a campaign honour, although the intensity of their involvement varied. The most outstanding exploits were probably those of the 4/5th Gorkhas, who carried out the Indian Army's first heliborne assault in the Battle of Sylhet in East Pakistan; the 1/3rd Gorkhas, who carried out the first amphibious assault since independence; and the 5/3rd Gorkhas who seized the Hathimatha massif on the western bank of the Shingo river in Kashmir, which not only dominated the Srinagar–Kargil–Leh highway (see Figure 11) but also the Kargil–Olthingthong–Skardu axis.

India had the advantage in that it surrounded East Pakistan on three sides and its stronger navy could dominate the sea approaches. The 4/5th Gorkhas took up position on the eastern borders of Bangladesh, in the Naga hills where Captain Ridgeway of the 44th Gurkhas, later the 8th Gurkhas, had won a VC on 22 November

1879 (see Chapter 4). The 5/5th was in the area of Shillong. On the night of 21 November 1971, well before the formal initiation of hostilities on 3 December, the 4/5th attacked Atgram, a small town in a salient surrounded by the Surma river. Two Indian officers, one Gorkha JCO and three soldiers were killed and twenty-one men wounded. In the fight, Rifleman Dil Bahadur Chhetri killed eight Pakistani soldiers with his kukri, and according to the regimental history this so affected the enemy that they never wanted to fight Gorkhas again. For his courage and 'sheer dexterity in the use of the kukri', Dil Bahadur won the MVC.[12]

If night attacks with kukris for silence were a traditional way of war, the 4/5th was to be the initiator of a new one for the Indian Army. Pakistani forces numbering about 7,000 were in the area of Sylhet, a salient of north-east Bangladesh, sticking out into Indian Assam (see Figure 11 and inset). Another battalion the 5/5th Gorkhas were heading there from the north-east. Initial reports indicated that the town of Sylhet itself was unoccupied. There was a railway bridge over the river Surma, with an airfield near by. To expedite the Indian attack, it was necessary to capture the railway bridge intact, and the Indian Army decided to try a heliborne assault.

Helicopters had first been deployed in Korea and had been used extensively in Vietnam in the 1960s, but in 1971 they were still a relatively new way of delivering an attack with air-landed troops. If things went well, they were more precise and controllable than parachutes or gliders, but they were and are vulnerable in the face of determined enemy fire. It is significant that the 4/5th Gorkhas were chosen as the force to initiate the Indian Army's use of this new way of delivering troops. The entire battalion would be landed around the key bridge.

The airlift began in the afternoon of 7 December. The first sortie of seven Russian-made Mi-8 transport helicopters, carrying men of C Company 4/5th Gorkhas, the commanding officer and his tactical headquarters, took off from Kulaura and landed twenty minutes later. The second lift brought in the rest of C Company and part of B Company. By then the Pakistanis were already firing at the landing site, initially with small arms but soon afterwards with artillery.

The second sortie was subject to small-arms fire and the third was shelled. But by this time there were two full companies right in the guts of the enemy. As the Gorkhas were digging in around the landing site – normal procedure – they saw about a hundred Pakistanis forming up to attack. Rather than wait, they immediately attacked with the cry '*Ayo Gorkhali*' – 'We are the Gorkhas' – and, in the words of the official history, 'kukris flashed in the fading light, frightening the assaulting enemy. They fled in terror, leaving behind two mutilated bodies.'[13] Realising that they had been the target of a *desant* operation – a 'vertical envelopment' – the Pakistanis kept attacking through the night. Platoons of the two companies changed their positions often, responding to threats from different directions. The official history says that '*determination, steadfastness and strict fire discipline* [emphasis in original]' kept the enemy away.[14]

Reinforcements started arriving the next morning, 8 December, from around 0400 hours, just before it got light. By 0800 hours the entire battalion was concentrated east of Sylhet, strengthening the force enough to hold off anything the Pakistanis were likely to throw at it. The battalion had enough ammunition, water and food for three days, including two 'scales of ammunition' (twice the normal amount carried by the battalion at any one time). In the evening a mountain gun and an extra platoon of the 9th Guards, an Indian regiment, arrived, and another one was helicoptered in on the morning of 9 December.

So far, the Gorkhas, who had come under attack as soon as they had landed, had not been able to secure the railway bridge over the Surma, a task that needed two companies. The Pakistani 202nd Brigade, holding Sylhet, had sent additional troops to guard the bridge. The Gorkhas sent the two companies, A and D, to man a roadblock on a road running parallel with the Surma, about 1,000 yards (a kilometre) from the bridge. The Pakistanis tried to dislodge the Gorkhas, but failed. The Gorkhas intercepted a radio message, obviously on behalf of the Pakistani commander: 'Bigger Imam wants to know why the roadblock has not been removed yet.' The reply went back: 'Have tried our best but they are sticking on stubbornly. Request send more troops.'[15]

A and D companies had had no food or sleep for four days and

began to run short of food and ammunition. Having delivered the troops four days before, the helicopters that were now needed to evacuate the wounded and bring in more supplies were nowhere to be seen, as they had been diverted to another task. The 5/5th, which was still advancing towards Sylhet and the bridge, had not yet linked up with any of 4/5th. It was decided to withdraw the two companies, which were now down to forty-five or fifty men each – about half their normal strength – back to the main battalion perimeter. Airdrops of food were organised, but helicopters were needed to take out the wounded. Forty of them were serious cases, requiring urgent surgical treatment. Captain Sengupta, the medical officer, an Indian, judging by his name, had used all his bandages and every handkerchief he could find. But still, he recalled 'there was no sign of helicopters; only bullets and shells'.[16]

The helicopters returned on day five. Immediately the surrounding Pakistani forces engaged them with fire and the first one managed to pick up only two wounded before artillery fire started coming down. Two hours later another Indian Air Force helicopter appeared and the forward air controller, Flying Officer Sharma, begged the pilot to land, explaining how bad the condition of the wounded was. The pilot did so, and took as many casualties as the helicopter could carry. Sharma got the Vir Chakra for his efforts.[17]

Finally, at about 2330 hours on 14 December, the leading elements of the 6th Rajput Regiment reached the southern bank of the Surma, the other end of the bridge, and made contact with the besieged Gorkha heliborne battalion. The 4/5th's sister regiment, the 5/5th, linked up on the 16th.[18]

The commanding officer of the 4/5th Gorkhas, Lieutenant Colonel A. B. Harolikar, had told his brigade commander that his battalion would land in the guts of the enemy and rip them apart with their kukris. It was perhaps not surprising that the Indian Army entrusted its first heliborne operation to the Gorkhas. This was the regiment – the 'frontier force', the 'Piffers' – that, in British service, had won five VCs in the Second World War and was also the heir to the Gurkha Scouts. They had landed in the middle of a Pakistani force totalling 7,000 and held their ground for eight days. Harolikar won the MVC, for a combination of courage, resilience and

professional competence. It was the kind of performance, and at the kind of level, for which a British officer might have won the DSO.

On the morning of 16 December two Pakistani officers and a few other ranks appeared carrying white flags. They asked to surrender unconditionally. All 7,000 of them. That afternoon the Indian and Pakistani brigade commanders met near the Sylhet Bridge, and there was another meeting on the morning of 17 December, by which time the war was over. But even if it had not been, it is likely that the brigade into which the 4/5th Gorkhas had been thrust would have surrendered, given the arrival of troops from outside. A total of 107 officers, including three brigadiers, plus 219 JCOs – the equivalent of the old VCOs – 6,190 other ranks and 39 non-combatants surrendered. The Pakistani soldiers wanted to be escorted to prisoner-of-war camps as soon as possible, because the people of Bangladesh, which had now achieved its independence, were not well disposed towards them. The 4/5th Gorkha Rifles were awarded Sylhet as a battle honour and East Pakistan 1971 as a theatre honour.[19] But, even more importantly, once again, a historic Gurkha – or Gorkha – regiment had been used, successfully, to try out a new way of warfare.

Although the political and military centre of the war was in and around East Pakistan, Pakistani forces also attacked in the west in the old cauldron of Kashmir. The Hathimatha massif, located on the western bank of the Shingo river, dominates the highway running from Srinagar to Kargil (see Figure 11), and was therefore a very important objective for the Indians. The 5/3rd Gorkhas were assigned to capture it.

Hathimatha stands 14,000 feet (4,270 metres) above sea level and can be scaled only by climbing up cliff-like approaches and massive rock faces. In 1971, and it was the middle of winter, the Indian Army still had relatively little experience of high-altitude operations – something that forty years' experience on the Siachen glacier has changed – and still lacked all the necessary equipment. It was a job for Gorkhas. The Indian Army captured it by 17 December 1971 in ten days of hard fighting. Lieutenant Colonel Devinder Jaggi commanded the attack, his 5/3rd Gorkhas supported by artillery.[20] The Gorkhas lost fourteen men – a relatively small number, given the

difficulty of the task. The battalion earned two Vir Chakras, one of them posthumously.

With the Pakistani pre-emptive strike in the west, the battalion was rushed from Leh to Kargil. Jaggi was ordered to concentrate his battalion on a plateau near the airfield, which was observed from enemy positions. The operation was codenamed Cactus Lily. The 5/3rd was hit by enemy observed artillery fire and there were casualties. Jaggi resolved to use the classic old North-West Frontier solution – an attack on the mountain from the rear.

Three companies of Pakistani Karakoram Scouts held well-dug-in defences, supported by artillery and mortars. They had also laid protective minefields and wire obstacles. As usual in these conditions, night attacks were preferable.

A task force under Major Shankar Prasad, the second-in-command, consisting of A Company under Major Vinod Bhanot, set off on the night of 16–17 December 1971. The Gorkhas negotiated the frozen Gangam Nullah, with enemy shells falling around them. An enemy medium machine-gun opened fire from about 660 feet (200 metres) and No. 1 Platoon assaulted Temple Post, avoiding the enemy mines by the simple expedient of stepping on the rocks and boulders as only the Gorkhas (or Gurkhas) can when rushing uphill. Once clear of the mined area, the Gorkhas were unstoppable. The official history reports how 'the snow clad mountain-tops resounded and reverberated to the repeated blood-curdling battle-cries of "Ayo Gorkhali".' All the nineteen Pakistani posts were captured, one by one. The final post, No. 25 on the summit of Hathimatha, was taken by first light on 17 December, in the nick of time, beating the deadline for cessation of hostilities. Shankar Prasad retired as a lieutenant general and became an 'armchair general' for the Indian media.[21]

With the fall of Hathimatha, the 5/3rd Gorkhas had captured the highest number of enemy posts in the sector during Operation Cactus Lily. Territory formerly held by the Pakistanis, astride the Shingo river up to Gangam Nullah junction, was in Indian hands. The Indian Army had not yet acquired the expertise in high-altitude warfare that it was later to do and, so far, the Gorkhas had proved themselves its most capable force for that kind of fighting.

India and Pakistan remained facing each other across the Line of Control in a stand-off that continues until the present day. The next major clash on the ground was in 1999, when India launched an offensive, Operation Vijay ('Victory', in Hindi), to clear Pakistani soldiers and Kashmiri militants from the Kargil area where they had been infiltrating across the Line of Control. At first Pakistan said only Kashmiri militants were involved, but captured documents and the nationality of captured prisoners of war showed that regular Pakistani soldiers were also present. The offensive, led by the 8th Indian Mountain Division, lasted from May to July, and the Indians recaptured the majority of the positions on their side of the line that had been occupied by Pakistani troops and militants. International diplomatic pressure forced the Pakistanis to withdraw from the remaining positions. It was the first major operation since India and Pakistan had both tested nuclear weapons in May 1998, and only the second direct military clash between declared nuclear-armed states, the other being the clashes between Russian and Chinese forces in the 1960s.

Once again, the Gorkhas were heavily involved. On 11 June 1999, Lieutenant Manoj Kumar Pandey, of the 1/11th Gorkha Rifles, led his men to recapture Jubar Top, a feature of great operational importance. Then, on the night of 2–3 July 1999, the battalion's progress on to its final objective at Khalubar was held up by a determined enemy firmly entrenched on commanding heights. Clearing it was critical as the battalion faced the prospect of being caught in an exposed area in daylight. Lieutenant Pandey quickly sized up the problem and led his platoon along a narrow, treacherous ridge that led to the enemy position.

According to the official account,

> While still short of the objective, the enemy fired upon the Indian soldiers effectively stalling the Indian attack. Displaying great courage, he [Pandey] surged ahead of his troops and charged at the enemy with a full throated battle cry through a hail of bullets.
>
> Although wounded in the shoulder and leg, he pressed on his solitary charge with grim determination, till he closed in on the first bunker. Then in ferocious hand-to-hand combat, he killed two of the enemy and cleared the first bunker. It was the turning point.

Inspired by their leader's spontaneous valour, the troops charged at the enemy and fell upon them. Unmindful of his grievous wounds, he rushed from bunker to bunker urging his men on. Critically bleeding, he collapsed at the final bunker and finally succumbed to his injuries, but not before the last of the enemy had been annihilated. His last words were, '*Na Chodnu*' ('*Don't Leave Them*').[22]

For his 'sustained display of the most conspicuous personal bravery and junior leadership of the highest order in the face of the enemy', Lieutenant Manoj Kumar Pandey was awarded the Param Vir Chakra, posthumously. His father, Mr Gopichand Pandey, received the award from the president of India, on behalf of his brave son.

The Gorkhas had won their first Param Vir Chakra as part of the peace support operation in the Congo, and Indian forces have been extensively employed in such operations ever since, although the definition of a 'peace support operation' can be flexible. In July 1987, after the signature of the Indo-Sri Lanka Agreement, an Indian peacekeeping force was sent to Sri Lanka where the Liberation Tamil Tigers of Elam (LTTE), known as the Tamil Tigers, were waging a sustained and sophisticated campaign against the Sri Lanka government, which ended only with their military defeat in 2009, and even that may not be the end of the story.

The 4/5th Gorkhas landed at the Palali airfield, also known as Kankesanturai, on 11 October 1987. The Gorkhas had been briefed not to fire on civilians and to treat them with all due respect, but the LTTE often dressed as civilians and, although many of the locals spoke English, they refused to converse in that language, making the Gorkhas' job as 'peacekeepers' very difficult. The Gorkhas were deployed the same night, to link up with a Sikh light infantry battalion near Kondavili. One Gorkha was killed and four men, including a company commander, were wounded by a landmine. During October and November the battalion was engaged in several fierce battles with the Tamil Tigers. During their tour in Sri Lanka, the 4/5th lost twenty-one killed and seventy wounded. The most senior was Lieutenant Colonel Bawa, the battalion commander, who was killed on the night of 11–12 October while attempting to rescue D Company, which had been surrounded by the Tamil Tigers. While radioing for mortar and air support for the

trapped company, he was hit in the chest, but carried on reporting to the brigade commander until he passed out from loss of blood. He won the Maha Vir Chakra, posthumously.[23]

The Kargil campaign of 1999 features on most of the Indian Gorkha regiments' campaign honours. Two battalions from each of the seven Indian Gorkha regiments have served on United Nations missions. The 1/11th Gorkhas, for example, served in Lebanon in 2001, and the 2/11th in the Democratic Republic of Congo in 2005.[24]

At the time of writing India still has seven Gorkha regiments – the 1st, 3rd, 4th, 5th, 8th, 9th and 11th. Each has five or six battalions, all riflemen. The 1st and 4th battalions are based at Sabatu, the 3rd and 9th at Varanasi, the 5th and 8th at Shillong and the 11th, with the regimental centre, at Lucknow. In all, there are thirty-nine battalions. That would give a total force of some 40,000. Some reports put the number higher, but if we take the conservative figure of 40,000, that makes the Gorkhas 4 per cent of India's 1 million-strong army, about the same as their proportion of the Indian Army at the end of the Second World War.[25] Some 60 per cent of the soldiers, or about 25,000, are still from Nepal. The remaining 40 per cent are either chiefly Indian Gorkhas, born in India of Gorkha families, or a minority of similar ethnic stock who live in northern parts of India. The 9th Gorkhas are Brahmans and Chhetris; the 11th, Rais and Limbus with a few Tamans; and the rest are Gurungs and Magars from the west. The Indian Army still has junior commissioned officer ranks, which evolved from the Viceroy's commissioned ranks, but Indian Gorkhas can also hold full Indian commissions, and about a hundred a year graduate from the Indian Military Academy at Dehra Dun. At the time of writing there are two brigadiers and one major general who are Nepali Gorkhas, but the most senior officers associated with Gorkha regiments are still Indians.

The most senior of all was Field Marshal Sam Manekshaw (1914–2008), who masterminded the 1971 victory. Although an adoptive 'Gorkha' because the 8th Gorkhas became his regimental home after his parent regiment, the 12th Frontier Force Regiment, went to Pakistan in 1947, Manekshaw was an Indian, of Parsi parents. He

was in the very first intake of Indian officer cadets at Dehra Dun, in 1932. The current Indian Defence Attaché in Nepal, Colonel Manmohan Singh Dhanoa, is an Indian officer who served with the 11th Gorkhas.

The Indian Army recruits its Nepali Gorkhas in much the same way as the British, but does so two or three times a year whereas the British recruit only once. There are two recruiting teams, one for the eastern *jats*, based at Darjeeling, and one for the western, based at Gorakhpur on the border, where it has been since the early nineteenth century. Whereas the British Gurkhas were recruiting 230 a year, a figure that is now down to 170 or so, the Indian Army normally recruits 2,000 to 3,000, which makes sense, given the relative size of the two countries' Gurkha or Gorkha forces. There was a surge in recruiting at the time of the Kargil operation in 1999, leaving a surplus of Gorkha manpower, so fewer men have been recruited in recent years. The Indian Gorkha criteria for selection are, on paper, the same as those for British Gurkhas, including the minimum height of 5 feet 3 inches (157 centimetres), although I have not been able to verify for myself that standards are in fact the same.

It is estimated that 10,000 ex-Indian Army Gorkhas have settled in Nepal and about 25,000 in India. The pension bill for India's Gorkhas in Nepal is 10 billion Indian rupees a year, or 16 billion Nepali, which is actually more than the Nepalese Army budget of 15 billion. Like the British, the Indian Ministry of Defence has an extensive welfare network for ex-Gorkhas in Nepal, although it is easier for the Indians to look after them than for the British as serious medical cases can be taken across the border to India.

The most recent use of Indian Army Gorkhas was in countering the Mumbai terror attacks, which began on 26 November 2008 and lasted for three days, killing 179 people, including 22 foreigners. The terrorists, who were based in Pakistan, were out to kill Westerners in particular.

The involvement of the Gorkhas – or Gurkhas –came to light only through the testimony of a British couple, Lynne and Kenneth Shaw, who alleged that the American news channel CNN had

endangered their lives by reporting where they were. The terrorists were watching CNN and were also trying to locate Westerners. The couple were in a restaurant at the Taj hotel when the terrorists struck, and hid under a marble table. When rescue came, Lynne Shaw said she thought the men were terrorists, and that she and her husband were about to be executed. She felt safe only when she '*recognised the uniforms of Gurkhas* as they were led down the stairs. "There was blood, guts, bullet cases. There was even the odd body," she said. "It was awful" [emphasis added].'[26] Other reports confirmed that the couple were then taken to the Australian Embassy for safety, '*by Gurkhas* [emphasis added]'.[27]

It is highly likely that Indian Army Gorkhas were part of the November–December 2008 security operation to rescue people and eliminate the terrorists. It is also just possible that the Gurkha contingent of the Singapore Police Force, a paramilitary unit specialising in anti-terrorist operations, could have been helping but that is unlikely. Either way, a terrified British woman was reassured only when she recognised them from their uniforms as '*Gurkhas*'.

Because they were.

I I

Britain's Gurkhas

AFTER THE TRIPARTITE Agreement between Britain, India and Nepal, the British concentrated their Gurkhas in Malaya and, as we have seen, that had been an important factor in deciding which regiments would join the British Army. The War Office intended to form a Gurkha division, which would provide its own supporting arms. The division was formed, as the 17th Gurkha Infantry Division, named after the 17th Indian Division, which had performed so heroically in Burma.

'Infantry' was and is the generic term for the troops who close with and kill the enemy, although they do many other things well. The historic distinction between 'infantry' and riflemen was, perhaps unfortunately, inappropriate. If it had been the '17th Gurkha *Rifle* Division', it would have been the only one in the British Army. The four rifle regiments were referred to, collectively, as the 'Brigade of Gurkhas', the title that the British Gurkhas still hold, but this was not a brigade in the operational-tactical sense.

Engineer and signals units, formed by attaching specialists from those arms of the British Army, were successful, but attempts to turn Gurkhas into electrical and mechanical engineers and, especially, gunners, failed. One of the problems with artillery was that the British guns were all designed to be manned by big men, which the Gurkhas were not. Four supporting-arm regiments were formed: the Gurkha Engineers, the Gurkha Signals, the Gurkha Transport and the Gurkha Military Police, the latter in 1949. The Gurkha Army Service Corps was formed in 1958.

To keep up the supply of recruits for the British Gurkhas recruiting needed to be reorganised. Until 1947, the British had recruiting centres near the Nepalese border at Kunraghat for the western *jats*

and at Darjeeling for the eastern. After Indian independence, these British recruiting centres were relocated, but remained inside India and in 1953 the Indian government objected to the British continuing to recruit inside India, and the British came to an agreement with the Nepalese government. Two recruiting centres were set up in the Terai, at Dharan in the east and at Paklihawa in the west. The latter was later moved north to Pokhara, where it still is, along with Dharan, today.

During the Second World War the British had sponsored the Malay People's Anti-Japanese Army (MPAJA), which was officially disbanded in December 1945.[1] Like the people in Vietnam and Indonesia, however, many Malays did not relish a return to colonial rule and were attracted by the promises of communism. Many of them retained their weapons. Chin Peng, the Secretary-General of the Malayan Communist Party, who had been honoured for his services with Force 136, began to plan an armed insurrection. The Malayan Emergency was declared on 17 June 1948. The timing of the Gurkhas' move to Malaya, where all recruit training was concentrated at Sungei Patani in the north-west, was perfect (see Figure 12). John Cross, who served there in 1948–9, said that 'had the Gurkhas not been there at the critical moment when trouble broke out, it would have taken far longer than it did to have beaten the communists. It is even possible that they would have won.'[2]

But it very nearly did not happen. When the author interviewed him, John Cross said that on 27 November 1947 he had gone to Delhi to see Brigadier Hedley, who masterminded the split of the Gurkhas between Britain and India. Hedley said he had just been approached by a senior Indian – an Indian communist, as it happened – and asked if he would allow all the units that had been earmarked for Malaya and Hong Kong to stay in India for an extra year while their accommodation was sorted out. With hindsight, the motives of the 'senior Indian' were clear. Had Hedley agreed to his request, the insurrectionists in Malaya would have had a free hand.[3]

As it was, Malaya became the home for six of the eight Gurkha battalions. Two battalions were detached, one for Singapore and

one to go to Hong Kong where, after the communist victory in the Chinese Civil War, in 1949, the new China was expected to swallow the British colony.

By this time Chin Peng had about 5,000 fighters under arms, and an extensive network of supporters, whether out of choice or out of fear. In counter-revolutionary warfare doctrine, this is called the 'passive phase'. The active phase began in June 1948, with small-scale military actions, intimidation and sabotage. The guerrillas targeted the rubber production that was so vital for the country's economy.[4] Most of the old soldiers in the Gurkha battalions had fought in North Africa and Italy, and were not yet experienced in jungle warfare. There were also many new recruits, who were not experienced at anything. The Gurkhas suffered their first casualties in January 1949 when Chin Peng's communist guerrillas, whom the British referred to at the time as CTs – communist terrorists – ambushed a platoon of A Company 1/6th Gurkhas, killing the company commander, his Gurkha officer, now a QGO, and nine others.[5] For the next twelve years the Gurkhas would be heavily committed in Malaya.

In 1950 a specialised Jungle Warfare School was set up by Colonel Walter Walker at Kota Tinggi on the east coast (see Figure 12). The Gurkhas provided many of the instructors, the demonstration platoon, which demonstrated how drills and tactical manoeuvres were meant to performed, and also the 'enemy'. They would do the same job at the British Royal Military Academy at Sandhurst, where I first encountered them in 1973.

The Gurkha Engineers were a success in Malaya and elsewhere, as Ochterlony, who had noted the fort-building skills of the Nepalese, would have expected. In Malaya they built the first operational bridge, and the bridge on the Rompin–Gamas road, in 1948 (see Figure 12). They also carried out engineering work at the Thirra Pass in Aden, and built border fencing to protect Hong Kong against the tide of would-be Chinese immigrants from the end of the Chinese Civil War in 1949.[6] Although bridge-building, which was essential in the Malayan jungle, harnessed a natural aptitude, the Gurkhas also proved that they were good signallers. The Gurkha Signals provided the 'rear link' communications from each battalion

back to the brigade headquarters, and later provided the whole signals network for the 48th Gurkha Infantry Brigade (1957–76).

By 1955 the laborious process of defeating the communist insurrection was showing results. John Cross recalled:

> The guerrillas were moving in smaller parties in deeper jungle, contacts were becoming more scarce, helicopters more frequent. Gone were the early days of pitched battles and casualties. Now we were more dependent than ever on tracking, on reading signs, on a real knowledge of jungle lore. It was realised all too little that, in addition to luck, the fewer the numbers of the enemy, the better the standard of soldiering required to deal with them.[7]

The twelve years in Malaya were formative for the British Gurkhas. It was a discrete, specialised environment where their skills as light infantry, and the necessary engineer and signals support, were utilised to the maximum. Most of the British Army was facing in a different direction, east, across the north German plain, against the Russians. Whether the Gurkhas could have adapted to such a role was never put to the test. The fact is, issues in Malaya, Singapore, Hong Kong and Brunei meant that they did not have to.

The Malayan Emergency was the only time a European colonial power defeated a communist insurrection. On 31 August 1957, Malaya achieved independence, becoming the Federation of Malaya. Guerrilla forces still operated against the new, elected government, and the British continued to help the Malaysian Federal Forces, as they were now called. The emergency officially ended on 1 August 1960, but, in 1961, John Cross was sent back to Malaya after two years with the 1/7th Gurkha Rifles in Hong Kong. The 1/7th was put under command of the Malaysian 2nd Federal Brigade, the only non-Federation troops to be deployed, apart from occasional detachments of the 22nd SAS Regiment. The latter were officially there for 'training', but in fact took part in operations.

A body of about thirty-five Chinese guerrillas, opposed to the Malayan Federal government, was operating in the Thai–Malayan border area, where the 'aboriginal' – native – population led what some would call a 'primitive' lifestyle, although their culture was as developed in its own way as any. The Gurkhas' job, with Cross in

charge, was to win over the native population from supporting the Chinese guerrillas, whom they liked, to supporting the Malayan government, which, at that point, they did not.

Operation Bamboo had been under way for three years. The Gurkhas were deployed to win over the 'hearts and minds' of the indigenous tribes. Only when that had been done, and the Chinese guerrillas isolated, could the latter be destroyed.[8] For two years the 1/7th Gurkhas worked with the Malayan government, the Malayan Police and the tribesmen on Operation Bamboo, until they were redeployed to Brunei.[9]

The Gurkhas provided a quarter of the riflemen and half the engineers deployed in Malaya during the 1948–60 emergency, as well as what were effectively special-operations units after Malayan independence.[10] Because the Gurkhas were so successful, the Malayan campaign has been studied exhaustively. However, the Gurkhas were about to become victims of their own success.

The achievement of the 17th Gurkha Infantry Division owed a great deal to the energy and determination of Brigadier Walter Walker, who in 1958 was commanding the 99th Brigade and who masterminded Operation Tiger to eliminate ninety-six guerrillas known to be still operating in the area adjacent to Singapore. He ordered the 2/2nd Gurkhas to set an ambush, but after twenty-seven days there had been no sign of the enemy, and the soldiers, who had been lying a swamp, were getting extremely uncomfortable. Walker refused to lift the ambush, and the next day three guerrillas walked into the trap. Only then was Walker satisfied. The Gurkhas had, once again, showed 'unbelievable stamina, excellent marksmanship and superb fieldcraft'.[11] Walker was promoted to major general and the commander of the 17th Gurkha Infantry Division, as well as the complementary office of major general, Brigade of Gurkhas.

Walker was summoned to see General Sir Richard Hull, commanding Far East Land Forces, in Singapore. Britain was planning to pull out of the Far East. Hull was about to leave to become the last Chief of the Imperial General Staff, an office he held from 1961 to 1964.[12] Hull told Walker that with the withdrawals from overseas

the British Army would have to economise and that if it came to a choice between British or Gurkha infantry, the latter would have to take the hit. The Whitehall mandarins were planning to cut the Gurkhas to a single infantry brigade group of about 4,000 men. At that time the Brigade of Gurkhas was 15,000 strong. In October 1962 *The Times* got hold of the story that the Ministry of Defence, which was still a very small department which only coordinated all the different service ministries, was planning to reduce the Brigade of Gurkhas from eight battalions to four, resulting in a reduction to 8,450 or 9,000 men available in British service.[13]

As the major general, Brigade of Gurkhas, Walker had to make an annual report to the king of Nepal. After making his formal report, he used the opportunity to tell King Mahendra about the plans, and ask whether the king had been consulted, which, of course, he had not. Then Walker and a very embarrassed British ambassador left. Walker also leaked the plans to the American ambassador, who saw the Gurkhas as a stabilising factor in Nepal's unstable politics. In spite of the Gurkhas' outstanding role in Malaya, it was to be a case of the old 'equal misery for all'.[14] Walker was later recalled from Borneo and nearly court-martialled, and the fact that the Secretary of State for War, John Profumo, who was outraged, was sleeping with the same woman as the Soviet Naval Attaché, did not save him. Field Marshal Lord Slim was brought out of retirement and sent on a comical 'undercover' mission to explain the British decision to King Mahendra. Personally, Slim thought that anyone who cut the numbers of Gurkhas, with the world situation as it was, was 'crackers'.[15] He was right.

In May 1961 the Federation of Malaya announced plans for a new state, Malaysia, comprising the old Malaya and the two adjacent territories of Brunei and Singapore, plus the British-controlled areas of Borneo – north Borneo, known as Sabah, and Sarawak (see Figure 12).

The British liked the idea but it ran directly counter to those of President Sukarno of Indonesia, who had a grandiose plan for uniting all the Malay peoples in a 'regional association', which in fact meant a superstate, called Maphilindo – Malaya, the Philippines and Indonesia, also sometimes referred to as Malaya Irredenta – 'Greater

Malaya'. Even if this proved unachievable, a more modest extension of Indonesian control over the whole of Borneo, including Sarawak, Brunei and Sabah, might be. The mainly Chinese population of Singapore did not want to be ruled by Malays and neither did the sultan of Brunei, while to the Malays the prospect of Malaya Irredenta dominated by Indonesia was even more horrific.[16]

On 8 December 1962 there was a rebellion against the sultan of Brunei, which targeted the usual key points in any developing country: the sultan's palace, the prime minister's residence, police stations and power stations. Insurgents also occupied the oilfields in Seria (see Figure 12). The British immediately scrambled forces to help, under a prepared plan, but the unit designated to help, the Queen's Own Highlanders, was unavailable, having been deployed against pirates on the Borneo coast, so the nearest unit, the 1/2nd Gurkhas in Singapore, went instead.[17] Reinforced by the Queen's Own Highlanders, two other British battalions and a company of 42 Commando Royal Marines, they quickly brought the situation under control.[18]

At this stage Walker was still commanding the 17th Gurkha Infantry Division and, in spite of the clouds looming as a result of his frankness with the king of Nepal, was made Commander British Forces Borneo. His aim was to clear any remaining rebels out of Brunei before Malaysia was created in August 1963. Sukarno, seeking to disrupt these plans, was sponsoring cross-border raids from Indonesia into Borneo. Malaysia eventually came into being on 16 September 1963, but without Brunei, and two years later Singapore opted out of the union. Meanwhile, Indonesia was clearly embarked on a policy of 'confrontation' (konfrontasi) with the Federation of Malaya, a phrase publicised by the Indonesian Foreign Minister, Dr Subandrio. At first it was assumed to mean political, economic and low-level military pressure just short of war.[19] The latter focussed on the 1,200-mile (1,920-kilometre) land border between the Indonesian, formerly Dutch, province of Kalimantan and the future Malaysian provinces of Sarawak and Sabah, known as North Borneo until Malaysia was formally established (see Figure 12).

Having failed to prevent the creation of Malaysia, Sukarno broke trade and diplomatic links with the country and began cross-border

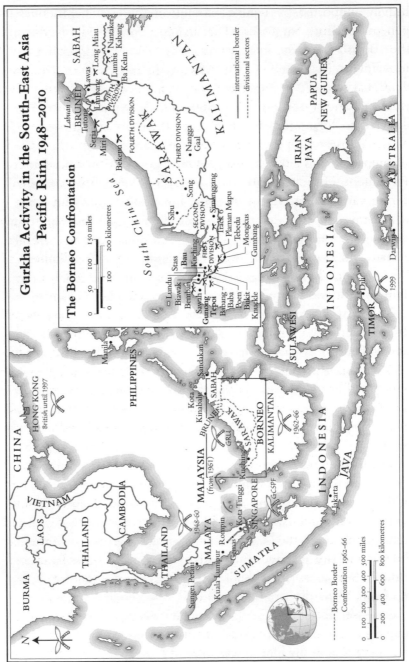

FIGURE 12

raids by the so-called North Kalimantan National Army or TNKU, heavily supported by regular Indonesian forces. The Indonesian penetrations into Sarawak and Sabah were conducted covertly and the British needed information about Indonesian plans and movements. Major John Cross, still of the 7th Gurkhas – an 'unconventional soldier', if ever there was, who spoke numerous native languages and at one point headed the Jungle Warfare School – was directed to form Border Scouts from the Borneo tribesmen. He worked closely with the SAS, whom he did not like much, but was accompanied and aided by his 7th Gurkhas, another 'special forces' assignment. His job was to create a team of Scouts from the bewildering variety of tribes in the area, including Dyaks and Ibans – which means 'person' in their respective languages, but the names stuck – as well as Malays, Muuruts, Kelabits, Kyans, Kenyahs, Punans and Dusuns. The Ibans were known as the 'headhunters of Borneo' and although their habit of chopping heads off had been dying out, it was rekindled during the Japanese occupation.[20]

The first open clash took place on 12 April 1963 when 'Indonesian-based border terrorists' – IBTs – attacked a police station at Tebedu in south-west Sarawak.[21] By this time Cross and the SAS had implemented a successful 'hearts and minds' programme, which had brought many of the tribespeople on side by providing simple medical support, which cured many of the local people's ailments very quickly, and electricity, including a small hydroelectric plant.[22]

The Borneo tribesmen were very different from the Gurkhas and Cross agonised about how to train them, using the customs and lore of the jungle in which they lived. The very name, 'Border Scouts', which was inspired by renowned bodies of crack shots and intrepid fighters, including the Gurkha Scouts on the North-West Frontier, did not translate at all well into Malay or any of the other languages. 'Bodoh Sekat', as they tended to pronounce it, meant 'stupid hindrance' – hardly an inspiring title.[23]

Cross set about producing guidelines on how to move in the jungle and avoid being tracked, which was the cause of most casualties. Very few of the locals were good at reporting detail, a key part of scouting and reconnaissance. It was one of Cross's Gurkha

instructors who had the brainwave. Cross recalled that the Ibans were 'attractive people, with poise and immense natural dignity, so I was never conscious that they were almost naked'.[24] But one of the Gurkha instructors clearly was. The younger women would often congregate at waterholes, to collect water. The Gurkha instructor 'hit on the idea of lying up in places frequented by bare-breasted maidens and, on [their] return, the Scouts were asked to give particulars of the colours of their skirts, the contents of any back-basket and a description of their anatomy. This method stimulated considerable interest and amusement.'[25] A British soldier might have come up with the same idea, but this came from a Gurkha.

While the British forces were restricted to their side of the border, the military initiative would lie with the Indonesians. The SAS started carrying out covert patrols across the border in December 1963. In 1964, General Walker got clearance to mount larger raids in platoon or company strength, a top-secret operation codenamed 'Claret', which began in May 1964. Initially there was a limit of 9,900 feet (3,000 metres) from the border, beyond which penetration was prohibited but this was later extended to 13 miles (20 kilometres). The aim was to use minimum force, but nevertheless to disrupt and deter Indonesian cross-border attacks. The first such attack was against the Indonesian garrison at Natakor south of Pensiangan (see the inset to Figure 12). The troops were A Company, 1/2nd Gurkhas, commanded by Major Dig Willoughby. The Indonesian commander and five of his men were killed and the camp destroyed. Four Gurkhas were wounded.[26]

'Claret' operations were carried out by Gurkhas, in cooperation with the SAS and Border Scouts, by the Parachute Regiment, the Royal Marines and the British, Australian and New Zealand SAS, but the Gurkhas bore the brunt of the 'Claret' raids.[27] During 1965 it became clear that the Indonesians were losing the fight, but, in retaliation, attacks on Malaysian territory by Indonesian forces became more aggressive. Detecting confused political signals from Jakarta, the British reduced the number of their own cross-border raids, a policy that the British soldiers, concise as ever, summarised as 'Be kind to Indos'.[28] All it did was to give the Indonesians the opportunity to regroup for a final fling.

On 20 November 1965 a 'Claret' operation, 'Time Keeper', was launched. It was a company-sized incursion by C Company 2/10th Gurkha Rifles, reinforced by the Reconnaissance and Assault Pioneer platoons of the Headquarters Company – a company group. The target was an entrenched camp, still under construction, at Gunong Tepoi about 3 miles (5 kilometres) across the border. It stood at the apex of three ridges that converged to form an isolated hill. The two eastern ridges and the valleys between were covered with thick secondary jungle, which could be almost as difficult to negotiate as barbed wire.

On the morning of 21 November the company group got to about 2,640 feet (800 metres) from the target, and paused for a quick bite to eat. Then the Assault Pioneer Platoon was left to secure the patrol base while nos 7, 8 and 9 platoons and the Reconnaissance Platoon moved forward. The company commander, Captain Maunsell, and three Gurkhas cut a 1,320-foot (400-metre) tunnel through the secondary jungle, using gardeners' secateurs for silence. Kukris would have made more noise. By 1330 hours they were just 66 feet (20 metres) from the Indonesians. Only two felled trees, laid across the ridge top, were in their way. Then they were spotted. The Indonesian who sent up the alarm was shot, but the Indonesians immediately started firing.

The Gurkhas immediately attacked, running three abreast along the ridge. No. 7 Platoon swung left and no. 8 to the right. Captain Maunsell recovered a wounded Gurkha and on the right Lieutenant (QGO) Bahadur Rai, the 8 Platoon commander, led a rush that reached the enemy trenches. On the right, Lance Corporal Rambahadur Limbu of 7 Platoon was leading the support group – the Bren gun team – of his section. What happened is described below, but the account contains a deliberate mistake.

> On 21st November 1965 in the Bau District of Sarawak Lance Corporal Rambahadur Limbu was with his Company when they discovered and attacked a strong enemy force located in the border area. The enemy were strongly entrenched in platoon strength, on top of a sheer sided hill, the only approach to which was along a knife edge ridge allowing only three men to move abreast. Leading his support group in the van of the attack he could see the nearest

trench and in it a sentry manning a machine gun. Determined to gain first blood he inched himself forward until . . . he was seen and the sentry opened fire, immediately wounding a man to his right. Rushing forward he reached the enemy trench . . . and killed the sentry, thereby gaining for the attacking force a foothold on the objective . . . Appreciating that he could not carry out his task of supporting his platoon from this position, he courageously left the comparative safety of his trench and, with a complete disregard for the hail of fire he got together and led his fire group to a better fire position . . .

. . . he saw both men of his own group seriously wounded . . . and . . . immediately commenced . . . to rescue his comrades . . . he crawled forward, in full view of at least two enemy machine gun posts who concentrated their fire on him . . . but . . . was driven back by the accurate and intense . . . fire . . . After a pause he started again . . .

Rushing forward he hurled himself on the ground beside one of the wounded and calling for support from two light machine guns . . . he picked up the man and carried him to safety . . . Without hesitation he immediately returned . . . [for the other] wounded man [and] carried him back . . . through the hail of enemy bullets. It had taken twenty minutes to complete this gallant action and the events leading up to it. For all but a few seconds this Non-Commissioned Officer had been moving alone in full view of the enemy and under the continuous aimed fire of their automatic weapons . . . His outstanding personal bravery, selfless conduct, complete contempt of the enemy and determination to save the lives of the men of his fire group set an incomparable example and inspired all who saw him

Finally . . . Lance Corporal Rambahadur was . . . responsible for killing four more enemy as they attempted to escape.[29]

Lance Corporal Rambahadur Limbu won the VC, the last one awarded to a Gurkha up to the time of writing, and the only VC awarded to a surviving recipient until Johnson Beharry of the Princess of Wales's Royal Regiment won one for actions in Iraq in May and June 2004. The deliberate mistake is the location. 'Claret' operations, across the border into Indonesia, were secret. Therefore, it was transposed into the Bau district of Sarawak on the other side

of the border. Anyone reading the citation might have thought it showed that the Indonesians were penetrating into Malaysia in some strength and establishing a fortified post there. In fact, they had been pushed onto the defensive by the 'Claret' operations.

By March 1966 the confrontation had ended and an agreement, signed in Bangkok on 1 June, was ratified in Jakarta on 11 August 1966. The confrontation had cost the rest of the British armed forces nineteen killed and forty-four wounded and the Gurkhas, who had borne the brunt of the top-secret 'Claret' operations, forty killed and eighty-three wounded.[30]

Once again, the Gurkhas had been prominent in covert, 'special forces'-style actions.

By 1971 all Gurkhas had been withdrawn from Malaysia. Singapore, which had achieved partial independence in 1949 and full independence in 1955, retained a Gurkha police contingent, and still does. In the 1950s and 60s there were race riots in Singapore between Chinese, Malays and Indians, and the Gurkhas were perceived as neutral. The Gurkha Contingent Singapore Police is a paramilitary force that now comprises about 1,850 officers – 13 per cent of the total police in Singapore – with units specialising in hostage situations, public order and maritime operations. They are trained in basic police procedures, including preservation of evidence, road accident and traffic management, but their main focus is public order, counter-terrorism and jungle operations. One third of their nine months' training is for jungle operations.[31] In Brunei the Gurkha battalion remained at the sultan's expense, and he also set up his own Gurkha Reserve Unit, employing former Gurkhas.

As soon as the confrontation in Malaysia was over, the pressure to cut the Gurkhas returned. In 1966 a 'rundown' started. The plan was to reduce the Brigade of Gurkhas from 14,500 to 10,000 over three years, to be completed by the end of 1969. The first phase had only just begun when the decision to withdraw from 'East of Suez' precipitated another reduction, planned to take the Gurkhas down to 6,000.

But then events intervened. The sultan of Brunei's willingness to pay for a Gurkha battalion postponed the planned amalgamation of

the two battalions of the 2nd Gurkhas in 1971. Most significantly, in August 1969 the British Army had been deployed in Northern Ireland and in 1972, the worst year of the 'Troubles', up to 30,000 troops were deployed there. That left gaps elsewhere and in 1971 the 7th Gurkha Rifles were posted to Church Crookham in the UK, the first time a Gurkha battalion had been based in Britain. The new Conservative government announced that the Brigade of Gurkhas would not be run down below 6,700. For that reprieve, the Gurkhas could thank a number of people, including, in large measure, the Provisional IRA.

There was never any possibility of the Gurkhas being deployed to Northern Ireland. To do so would have invited criticisms that the British were intent on maintaining the province for 'imperial' reasons and were using 'imperial troops to do it', but, with the equivalent of a British Army division there already, the Gurkhas could be used to do other things. Then, in 1974 there was a crisis in Cyprus and the 10th Gurkhas, which had just taken over from the 7th, were sent to guard the British sovereign base at Dhekelia. This role evolved into the UN operation to police the 'Green Line' between the Greek area and the Turkish Republic of North Cyprus, which was created in the wake of the Turkish invasion, and the Gurkhas stayed on.

Then, in 1976, Mao Zhedong, the Chinese communist dictator, died and there was a crisis in the Kwantung province adjoining Hong Kong, creating a flood of refugees. The Queen's Gurkha Engineers formed boat troops to deal with refugees attempting to reach Hong Kong by water. In 1982 the 2nd Battalion, 7th Gurkha Rifles was re-raised to help deal with the crisis – the third time in its history, after Kut and Tobruk.

That same year the 1/7th Gurkha Rifles had once again arrived in Church Crookham for their tour of duty in the UK. They were made part of 5th Infantry Brigade, a light brigade with an 'out of area' – outside the Nato area, which meant anywhere in the world apart from Western Europe – role. Then, while the plans for using 5th Infantry Brigade were still being developed, there was a totally unexpected bolt from the blue. On 2 April, Argentina invaded the British possession of the Falkland Islands (Malvinas). After the

Falklands War the 5 Brigade was converted to the 5th Airborne Brigade, but it was not called that at the time.

The Foreign Office opposed sending the Gurkhas with the rest of the 5th Brigade because it might offend 'Third World' (developing) countries. The Chief of Defence Staff, responsible for all three armed services, Field Marshal Sir Edwin Bramall, was the regimental colonel of the 2nd Gurkha Rifles and, although it might have seemed unlikely, the Secretary of State for Defence, the very unmilitary-looking John Nott, had done national service with the 2nd Gurkhas in the 1950s. The army thought the Gurkhas would be ideal for the cold and miserable conditions in the Falklands, which were approaching the middle of winter in the southern hemisphere. In a sudden and totally unexpected turn of events, the 1/7th Gurkhas soon found themselves on board the great Cunard ocean liner *QE2* – which had been designed with a subsidiary role as a high-performance troopship able to outrun submarines – en route for the Falklands, 8,000 miles(12,000 kilometres) away.[32] The last 'purification' ceremony for Gurkhas who crossed the 'black water' had taken place in the 1960s and, given that the Gurkhas had already crossed it to get to the UK, it was not an issue.

The Gurkhas were stunned by the size and luxury of the ship. Rifleman Baliprasad Rai recalled that he had never before 'slept in such beautiful surroundings or in such a big, soft bed, or perhaps I never will'. But, he figured, 'if I was going to war, then there was no better way to go.'[33]

The Gurkhas' reputation preceded them. The British media, quite deliberately, published pictures of the Gurkhas sharpening their kukris. The Argentine media took the bait. The fact that the Amritsar massacre had also just featured in Richard Attenborough's acclaimed film *Gandhi* added to the Argentine appetite for gruesome stories about Gurkha cruelty.

The reality was very different. The *QE2* moored at South Georgia (see Figure 13) and the Gurkhas were trans-shipped to a smaller vessel, the P & O ferry *Norland*. There were still 800 nautical miles (1,600 kilometres) to go, and the weather in the South Atlantic was atrocious.

Dhanbahadur Rai was with the 1/7th as a signals corporal in the

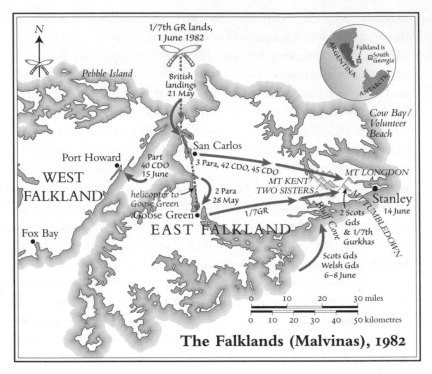

The Falklands (Malvinas), 1982

FIGURE 13

battalion tactical headquarters, responsible for signalling to its five companies. He had joined the Gurkhas in 1973 and served in Hong Kong, Brunei and the UK. I found him working for the Gurkha Welfare Service in Damak, in the Terai of eastern Nepal. He had left the British Army in June 1988 and spent nine years with the sultan of Brunei's Gurkha Reserve Unit, providing security for the sultan. He had then spent two years working for a shipping company and returned to Nepal where he joined the Gurkha Welfare Service in 2005. His account of the Falklands has not been published before. 'We went on the *QE2* to South Georgia,' he recalled. 'We were then transferred to a small boat [the *Norland*] carrying the battalion. We were on board for four days and four nights. It was terrible. We reached the land at about 0300 hours. We landed and dug shell scrapes and waited for dawn.'[34]

About halfway to the Falklands, Mike Seear, the operations and training officer who had recently joined the Gurkhas from the light

infantry, recalled, 'The Gurkhas were puking like crazy. Vomit everywhere.'[35] Once one person starts vomiting in a confined space, the smell makes others do the same. After their four days being tossed by the waves, the Gurkhas finally arrived at San Carlos Water and transferred to a landing craft utility, which was designed to carry two tanks or 140 men. They were packed on board 200 at a time, and then chugged towards the shore as dawn came up, landing at a rickety jetty. Dhanbahadur's account merges together the time on the *Norland* and on the LCU. All told, they had spent twenty days on a liner, a ferry and a landing craft. Accounts of the Gurkhas coming ashore stress their zeal. It was probably nothing to do with zeal to fight the Argentinians, but relief in getting off the ship on which they had spent four days and nights, on occasion being buffeted by 70-foot (21-metre) waves.[36]

Then the battalion headquarters, and the rest of the battalion – consisting of four rifle companies, A to D, and the support company, which held the heavier weapons and other specialists – walked for about five hours. Their move across East Falkland is shown in Figure 13. They were picked up by helicopters and taken to Goose Green, which had been captured by 2nd Battalion, the Parachute Regiment, in an extraordinary action in which the Paras' commanding officer, Lieutenant Colonel 'H' Jones, won a posthumous VC. 'We were guarding prisoners. But they were young – some of them were fifteen, sixteen – schoolboys. "What's your age," we would ask. "I'm sixteen, I'm seventeen." Then, after Goose Green we moved forward and we met a Scots Guard [to guide them to the rendezvous with that battalion], and that was our first incident. We got a shell. It landed near our area – the battalion headquarters. We just heard it.'[37] They kept moving until nightfall, stopped and dug shell scrapes, and the same happened the following day. There were only about six hours of daylight, so far south at that time of year. Then, the day after that, B Company came under Argentinian artillery fire. 'Not heavily – no casualties. Then we moved, heading to Tumbledown hill.' In all the official and media accounts of the Falklands War, it is Tumbledown *mountain* (see Figure 13). But to Dhanbahadur, a Gurkha, it was a *hill*. That says something.

The Scots Guards were to attack Tumbledown, with the Gurkhas following behind. We were supposed to finish the attack and they would give us covering fire from Tumbledown so our battalion task was to attack Two Sisters hill. Unfortunately the Scots Guards delayed the attack. During the night we followed the Scots Guards and then our CO [Lieutenant Colonel David Morgan] told us to stop. The ground was like a valley when we stopped and afterwards the shelling started. The one shell landed near by and at the same time one guy is shouting 'I'm still okay. I'm not dying,' and he came to me.

I touched him and then I felt him in the shoulder. I felt something but I could not see because it was night. Then, after the shelling stopped, we felt that he was wounded by a shell fragment. In the left shoulder. I didn't actually feel the fragment. It was liquid. The head-quarters and A Company had twelve wounded. We got all the wounded people and called a helicopter and sent it to the hospital ship, which was SS *Uganda*.

The next morning we started to move. The CO sahib and the anti-tank Milan Platoon commander [the Milan was our anti-tank missile carried by infantry] and the FOO [forward observation officer – the artillery observer] were just going up and they got a rifle shot. Our commanding sahib was shouting. He said, 'Look, Goli Ayo!' 'Get down! Someone fired!'

The artillery observer, Captain Keith Swinton,[38] did not speak Gurkhali and for a critical second did not understand.

Then the FOO was standing and looking and the second shot hit him in the chest. We treated and casevaced [evacuated] him. He came to meet us in Church Crookham after he was recovered.

Everyone looked to find out who was firing and where the fire had come from, but it was instantly apparent he was a Scots Guards soldier. They [the people firing] were where the Scots Guards were.

It was a 'friendly fire' incident. Dhanbahadur thought the Scots Guard had occupied a position where there had previously been an enemy sniper. 'Then we moved about three to four hours ahead. Maybe the time was about two o'clock.' This would have been right, as dawn came only at about 1000 hours. 'And then we heard on the radio that the war is over. Then we saw by bino [binoculars] that all the Argentinians were carrying white flags and heading to Stanley.'[39]

After all the training, the waiting, the terrible seasickness and the long traipse across the Falklands, the 1/7th had seen very little action. Their only death was after the end of the war, when a lance corporal was killed by a grenade that he struck with a spade. They had suffered fourteen casualties, taken a handful of prisoners and not reached the capital, Port Stanley. Dhanbahadur was philosophical. 'One soldier died after the war, clearing trenches. Nobody killed in the war, just wounded. We were very relieved by that.' The commanding officer, David Morgan, was equally so. 'If we can win wars by our reputation,' he said, 'who wants to kill people?'[40]

After about a week, Dhanbahadur discovered that he, too had become a casualty. 'I felt the pain in my toe. I went to the medic and he told me, "You have frostbite, but it's not serious. It's normal."' Dhanbahadur had succumbed during the long march towards Port Stanley. He was told to massage his foot and to keep it warm but not go near the fire. After about six months, it was cured. He recalled, 'The worst thing was the food, because we didn't get any resupply all the time. The next worst thing was the weather, and frost on the feet.'[41]

The Gurkhas returned from the Falklands relieved, and not a little embarrassed by the heroes' welcome they received.

Four years later they were in the news again, but for less meritorious reasons. The Support Company had been sent to Hawaii on a training exercise with the Americans. There were a number of complaints about the food and their British officer, who had been seconded from another British regiment, had failed to get his men's trust. Things came to a head at the party to celebrate the end of the exercise when the officer had tried to stop the men drinking. Since they had paid for the booze, they refused, and beat up the company commander and a Gurkha captain. It was a serious matter but could have been dealt with by sending a trusted British officer to carry out an inquiry and find the guilty men. Instead the whole company – about 120 of them, including the Gurkha captain who had himself been knocked out – were herded into cages and kept there for two days to make them identify the ringleaders. They closed ranks and refused.

Then 111 Gurkhas – the entire Support Company, less the officers – were discharged for mutiny and sent back to Nepal. According to John Cross, matters were made worse because the British alerted the Nepali customs, police and administration to the fact that a 'bolshie' bunch of Gurkhas were returning in disgrace. The British ambassador went to see the king, but his attitude reflected the fact that the British Gurkhas are less highly regarded in Nepal than in Britain – or Argentina. According to John Cross, the reaction of the Nepali authorities was: 'You say they're Rais and Limbus – well, if you recruit people like that, what do you expect? A hundred and eleven? Have another hundred and eleven . . .'[42]

John Cross spoke to Indian Gorkhas at the time, who were astonished at the public humiliation meted out to the Hawaii 111 by the British authorities in the glare of the British media. The Indians had had four comparable incidents, but dealt with them quietly. 'Why do you advertise it?' Cross was told.[43] The harsh response could be interpreted as a relic of colonial times, because it threatened the mystical, unquestioning loyalty that the Gurkhas had had for their British officers. Most British soldiers would quietly admit that soldiers in British regiments occasionally got drunk and beat up officers, but only when off duty.

The following ten years would be critical for the Gurkhas. Britain was due to hand Hong Kong back to China in 1997, and Hong Kong had become the Gurkhas' main home. There was a real possibility that the entire brigade, then about 8,000 strong, might be disbanded. In 1988 a paper on their future was circulated. All the options were thought through, but complete disbandment was thought improbable. It was agreed that there would be a military role for the Gurkhas after 1997, but the question was: for how many?

On 22 May 1989 the Defence Secretary, George Younger, made an announcement, which was described as the most significant for the Gurkhas since 1947. Their proposed strength was again reduced by half, to about 4,000, in four battalions, plus the Queen's Gurkha Engineers, the Queen's Gurkha Signals and the Gurkha Transport Regiment (later the Queen's Own Gurkha Logistic Regiment).[44]

But at least the Gurkhas' survival into the twenty-first century was assured.

Some in the British Army had argued that the Gurkhas should go before a single British regiment was touched. This attitude could be seen as a last manifestation of the old rivalry and hostility between the British and Indian armies. The Gurkhas' own world now centred on Hong Kong, while the rest of the British Army focussed on Northern Ireland and the north German plain. There were still big cultural and conceptual differences between the two. Two years later the next Defence Secretary, Tom King, announced a further cut, to 2,500, as part of the review entitled, very imprecisely, *Options for Change*.

Then, again, events intervened. The end of the Cold War resulted, not in a 'peace dividend', but in a profusion of interventions in other people's wars, which had boiled to the surface after the lid of superpower confrontation was removed. The Iraqi invasion of Kuwait and the Gulf War of 1990–1 saw the return of a kind of warfare unseen since the Second World War and made more perfect by satellite navigation systems and precision weapons.

The British eventually deployed an armoured division to the Gulf, which meant that the Gurkha infantry who were not trained for mechanised warfare were not involved, but 28 Ambulance Squadron of the Gurkha Transport Regiment was part of the British support in the force maintenance area, making it the only Gurkha unit deployed in the desert.

Very soon, however, a fundamental shift in the pattern of international relations precipitated a whole series of peace support operations in 'weak' or 'failed' states. For 350 years, since the Peace of Westphalia, although wars between nations were regular, frequent and extremely violent, nations had usually avoided interference in other nations' internal affairs. By 1991, the Cold War superpower confrontation, with the risk of local problems triggering superpower conflict, had definitely ended. That gave the Secretary-General of the United Nations, Boutros Boutros-Ghali, the opportunity to legitimise the international community's intervention in a string of 'failed states', which in part resulted, again, from the end of the Cold War.[45]

The British Army and the Gurkhas, with their tradition of over-seas operations, were ideally suited for such interventions. Gurkha battalions were soon deployed in Bosnia, Kosovo, Sierra Leone and East Timor. It soon became apparent, as Callwell had noted nearly 100 years before, that in such operations – where the focus was, first, during the initial response to an emergency, on supplying local people with their needs and then on rebuilding the infrastructure – there was more need for engineers, transport and other logistical troops than for infantry. A relatively small number of infantry were needed to provide security for an effort that was more 'tail' than 'teeth'. The Queen's Gurkha Engineers, as they had become in 1977, and the Queen's Own Gurkha Transport Regiment, from 1992, which became the Queen's Own Gurkha Logistic Regiment in 2001, would be heavily involved in peace support and post-conflict operations in the new world order.

By October 1995 the British infantry was facing a crisis as the number of fit young men who could make the grade as combat infantry was inadequate, and this was a particular problem for the British regiment with the highest physical requirements of all, the 'gold-standard' regiment, the Paras. It was another result of the recurring complaint, which has been made over many generations, that British youngsters, in this case the 'couch-potato' generation, are not as 'robust' or as fit as they had been. The authorised infantry strength was 24,000 soldiers but the army was 1,200 short. An obvious solution was to bring in the Gurkhas. As one newspaper put it: 'But the Paras may not like the solution – because the wiry Nepalese are tougher than they are and do better in the punishing "P" Company tests, as their physique is ideal for carrying heavy loads for long distances at speed, and they have a good head for heights.'[46]

Platoons or companies of Gurkhas were drafted in, an approach that is still operating. The Gurkhas had provided two battalions of Indian Army paratroops in the Second World War, and the Independent Gurkha Parachute Company had operated as part of the Parachute Regiment from 1960 to 1970, with John Cross in command for some of the time. There is a Gurkha Reinforcement Company with the 1st Battalion the Mercian Regiment at the time

of writing. Rifleman Remand Kulung, killed in Afghanistan on 12 August 2010, was from that Gurkha Reinforcement Company.[47]

To help stem the manpower crisis, a company from the 2nd Gurkhas was attached to the 2nd Battalion the Parachute Regiment. They were trained as paratroops in case a parachute operation at battalion level was ever needed, but remained members of the 2nd Gurkha Rifles, subordinated to the 5th Airborne Brigade. As such, they wore the maroon beret, but with the Gurkhas' crossed-kukri badge.

When researching in Nepal, I met a serving Gurkha officer who, as a warrant officer, had passed the 'P' Company selection at Catterick, North Yorkshire, in 1996. He had joined the Gurkhas in 1984, and was thirty-one at the time. 'There were five Gurkhas on that [intake],' he said. 'All of us passed.'[48] Following that, the group of Gurkhas completed the normal eight jumps, including a night jump, at RAF Weston-on-the-Green, to earn their wings and red beret.

However, he confirmed that the Gurkha Reinforcement Company had also trained for tactical air-landing operations – TALO, in which the airborne force would be landed by Hercules transport planes and then drive at breakneck speed at the enemy, as in the Israeli raid on Entebbe.[49] Sometimes that is a better way of putting troops on the ground, and enables them to be landed in a much more concentrated and precise fashion. But, as Brigadier John Holmes, commanding the 5th Airborne Brigade, as it was renamed after the Falklands, told me in the 1990s, 'There has to be an airfield at the other end.'[50] There may not be, which is why the British Army retains the ability to drop a battalion of paratroops if necessary.

The strong connexion between the Gurkhas and the Paras continues, with the 170 or so successful Gurkha recruits each year joining the 2nd Infantry Training Battalion. They form a company, along with a Guards company and a Parachute Regiment company.

'The Gurkhas are the best company there – there is no doubt,' the Gurkha officer added. Given the fact that there are 11,000 applications for in the region of 200 places in the British Army Gurkhas – there were 230 places until the early 2000s and is currently around 170 – and the rigour of the selection procedure, that should not be

surprising. Successful recruits do their initial training at Pokhara before being taken to Kathmandu and flown to Manchester to join the Training Battalion. 'When they arrive they look very good, and they hit the ground running.'[51]

As the handover of Hong Kong approached, a further rundown of the Gurkhas began. In 1994 the four regiments that had joined the British Army on 1 January 1948 were merged into a single regiment, the Royal Gurkha Rifles (RGR: see the 'family tree' in Figure 4). The British Gurkha on the jacket of this book is from the 6th Gurkha Rifles. The regiment was reorganised, initially with three battalions: the 1st Royal Gurkha Rifles (1 RGR), comprising the old 2nd and 6th Gurkhas; 2 RGR, comprising the old 7th Gurkha Rifles; and 3 RGR, comprising the 10th Gurkhas. Soon afterwards, however, in 1996, as part of the imminent British withdrawal from Hong Kong in 1997, 2 and 3 RGR were also merged to form 2 RGR, comprising the old 7th and 10th Gurkhas. There was a final logic and symmetry to the organisation, which reflected the choice of Gurkha regiments for the British Army in 1947. The new 1 RGR was recruited from the western *jats*; the new 2 RGR from the eastern.

Meanwhile, in 1992, Brigadier Philip Trousdell had taken over as commander of 48th Gurkha Brigade in Hong Kong. It was a total surprise – he had been expecting to go to a staff job, as a colonel, and was not a Gurkha, but a Royal Irish Ranger. He told me he telephoned the mess to order a dozen bottles of champagne. Nevertheless, when he arrived he immediately realised the implications of the handover of Hong Kong five years hence and of moving all the Gurkhas back to the UK.

Ever since their transfer to the British Army in 1948 the Gurkhas had been 'in the British Army, but not of it'. As their story has demonstrated, they inhabited their own world to some extent, hermetically isolated, first in Malaya, and then in Hong Kong and Brunei. Although battalions rotated through Church Crookham from 1971, the UK was still not their real home. On arriving in Hong Kong, Brigadier Trousdell found the understandable pride of some of the British Gurkha officers tinged with a certain arrogance. 'They were certainly a creation of the British Army,' he told me, 'but with a strong flavour of the immediate post-war years rather

than of the post–Cold War era. Now they are in the first echelon of operational infantry.'[52]

The move back to the UK would be a culture shock, personally and professionally, and Brigadier Trousdell tried to impress this on the British Gurkha officers, but found some of them unconcerned. He was immensely impressed with the Gurkha soldiers.

'Everybody wants a Gurkha driver,' he recalled. 'The vehicle is properly maintained, first paraded [a series of standard checks carried out every morning, without fail], oil, tyres . . . '

'Don't the Brits do it?'

'No. And, the driver can get out and fight as well as any infantryman.

'The Brits were asking, "How can we train our people as well as the Gurkhas?" You can't, you can't. Okay?'[53]

It was the senior Gurkha major in Hong Kong who impressed Brigadier Trousdell most. The Gurkha major went to the commander and said, 'We're going to be in the UK.' They were going to be 'light-roled infantry', and that would probably involve air–land operations, with which the Gurkhas had more than a passing acquaintance. The Gurkha major suggested holding a study day on attack helicopters. General Trousdell recalled the Gurkha major's 'incredible vision', and the response from some of the British officers. 'Attack helicopters? Gurkhas don't *do* attack helicopters.' In fact, the Gurkhas were already coming to terms with air–land battle. The first Gurkha helicopter pilot, Pim Bahadur, qualified in 1993.[54]

Brigadier Trousdell developed the classic relationship with the senior Gurkha major in his brigade, the fount of all knowledge on Gurkha matters. One day, he asked him whether he should learn Nepalese.

'No, sahib.'

'Why not?'

'Because you'll say something to the boys – they'll smile, then go away and tell their mates they didn't understand what you said. *As brigade commander you need to address the long-term interests of the Gurkhas. Conduct all training in English. Because they'll soon be back in UK.*'[55]

So Brigadier Trousdell did.

His next posting was as Director of Public Relations for the British Army. He soon came across the defence correspondents, a dying breed, including myself.

It was in that capacity that I had my only encounter with the Gurkhas while they were on operations. The Gurkha 28 Transport Squadron was part of the British Logistics Battalion in the United Nations Protection Force (UNPROFOR), but the biggest deployment of the British Gurkhas in Bosnia was after the ceasefire and the signing of the November 1995 Dayton Agreement, which brought the Bosnian 'Civil War', with big input from the neighbouring states of Croatia and Serbia, to an end. UNPROFOR had done the difficult job, trying to save lives without the force or mandate to do as its commanders would have wished. The successor force, the Nato Peace Implementation Force (IFOR), had more teeth. One third of it was British. The Royal Gurkha Rifles, so renamed the year before (1994), the Queen's Gurkha Engineers and a squadron of the Queen's Gurkha Signals were all deployed. The Gurkha 'corps' regiments – engineers, signals and logistics – were so named because they were also part of, and officered by specialists in, the Corps of Royal Engineers, the Royal Corps of Signals and the Royal Logistic Corps, the latter having been created in 1993.[56] The key point about the Gurkhas – all of them – is that the supporting arms – engineers, signals and logistics – were trained to exactly the same consummate standard of skill-at-arms and minor tactics as the professional infantry, before those who had better qualifications in maths, science and computing were deployed to the 'corps' units.

In January 1995 the headquarters of the 13,000 British IFOR contingent, still arriving in Bosnia as UNPROFOR left, was at Gornji Vakuf, on the old fault line between Bosnian Croats and Muslims. I arrived after a flight into Split with the Royal Air Force, where the arrival briefing by a sergeant major was professional and witty. In four weeks there had been eighty-seven road accidents. The biggest danger was not snipers, but road accidents as IFOR arrived and UNPROFOR left. At Gornji Vakuf I found a room to rent and headed for the the British headquarters, which was guarded by Gurkhas. I showed my IFOR ID, and the guard saluted smartly. The next day I returned for breakfast, a breakfast only the British

Army could provide. I showed my ID again, and the Gurkha guard smiled.

'Oh, Chris, it's you. Sahib talk about you.'

Impressive. They had seen me once before, and knew me by name. Obviously, my arrival had attracted interest.

In the senior ranks' bit of the cookhouse the reason why the sahibs had been talking became apparent.

'Nice article, Chris. Pity about the headline.'

Journalists do not write the headlines. Sub-editors do. 'Squaddies are warned: the real enemy is the Bosnian roads.' British soldiers do *not* like being called 'squaddies'. All was explained, and forgiven, and I tucked into the 'BT' breakfast. Breakfast with the Gurkhas is always 'BT' – 'British-trained', meaning British food, as opposed to other meals, which may be 'GT' – Gurkha-trained'.[57] That morning the relaxed professionalism of the Gurkha soldiers had made an instantaneous impression on me.

In 1999, 1 RGR and the Queen's Gurkha Engineers were deployed in Kosovo, the latter clearing the main roads of mines. Shortly afterwards, in September, 2 RGR, based in Brunei, were deployed to East Timor. The Sultan was paying for them, but he agreed to their deployment as part of the international intervention force, INTERFET.

In 2000, British forces were sent to Sierra Leone, after the UN temporarily lost control, to stabilise the country. A company of 2 RGR formed a company group to train the Sierra Leone Army, which had disintegrated in yet another 'failed state'. 'We had to do the absolute basics in recruit training,' a former Gurkha colour sergeant said. The company commander acted as the chief instructor as well as commanding the group. The Headquarters Platoon provided the instructors while the Gurkha riflemen provided security and did all the administration, including the cooking. The company ran two six-month courses to instruct the future leaders of the putative Sierra Leone Army in the rudiments of military skills and procedures.[58]

Although the Gurkhas had not played a major part in the Gulf War of 1991, they were much more prominent in the invasion of Iraq in

March 2003. The 1st Battalion of the Royal Irish Regiment also had a Gurkha reinforcement company, which was about to disband when the battalion was deployed as part of what the British called Operation Telic.

Gurkha infantry were back where they had been in 1916, and the objectives were very similar. They helped to secure the key oilfields at Rumailah, and to maintain control in and around Basra, where they worked with the local police. The 69th Squadron of the Queen's Gurkha Engineers was used to build bombproof protection at the Kuwaiti port of Shaiba, a 200-bed hospital, a rifle range and prisoner-of-war holding areas, because there were many Iraqi prisoners. The Queen's Own Gurkha Logistics Regiment was constantly used to provide transport along routes vulnerable to disruption by insurgents, and the Queen's Gurkha Signals was made responsible for providing secure communications for the British military headquarters in Baghdad.

The most intense fighting, however, would be in Afghanistan. The Gurkhas had been prominent in the first three Afghan Wars, and would be in the fourth. The initial western intervention in Afghanistan in October 2001, in retaliation for the attacks on the United States on 11 September, were mainly handled by special forces – acting in concert with the Northern Alliance against the Taliban government, which had unwisely acted as a 'safe haven' for Al-Qaeda – and by air power. The Taliban government was removed, and for a while it seemed as if Afghanistan would be rebuilt after thirty years of war along lines acceptable to the West. But, just like the rulers sponsored by the British in the first two Afghan Wars, the Western-sponsored government soon faced a resurgence of opposition. Distracted by Iraq, the West took its eye off the ball in Afghanistan, and the Taliban regrouped and took control of large areas of southern and eastern Afghanistan, operating across the Durand Line border, as porous as ever, with Pakistan.

In late 2003, 2 RGR, which had just returned to Brunei from the UK, was sent to Afghanistan. They had three tasks. The first would have been familiar to their predecessors, the Sirmoor Rifles, in 1840 when volunteers were requested to work with Shah Shuja's

bodyguard. They were to train the National Afghan Army. The second was to provide security around Kabul, and the third was to provide a provisional reconstruction team to help build confidence in the new Afghan government.

Operations intensified in 2006 and a composite company, D (Tamandu) Company, formed from both Gurkha battalions, was sent to reinforce the 16th Air Assault Brigade. The company was named after the place where Bhanbhagta Gurung, of the 2nd Gurkhas, won his VC on 5 March 1945. In keeping with the frequent association with the Paras, it was initially subordinated to the 7th (Parachute) Regiment Royal Horse Artillery and also worked with the 3rd Battalion, the Parachute Regiment. The company was in Afghanistan from January to October 2006 and witnessed a significant increase in Taliban activity. In August and September it provided riflemen as part of mobile outreach groups, not dissimilar to the role of Gurkha Scouts on the North-West Frontier or the 'Claret' operations in Borneo. The groups aimed to disrupt Taliban preparations and movements in northern Helmand province and to reassure the local population. By taking the war to them, the mobile outreach groups disrupted Taliban attacks on the administrative and population centres. The composite company probably saw more continuous action than any Gurkha unit since 1945.[59]

The first full Gurkha battalion to be deployed in the Fourth Afghan War was a battle group, called Tiger Force, based on the 1st battalion, the Royal Gurkha Rifles (1 RGR), reinforced by 69 Squadron Queen's Gurkha Engineers, a Queen's Gurkha Signals detachment, to communicate with higher levels of command, and Queen's Own Gurkha Logistics Regiment drivers, cooks and other supporting staff. It was there from September 2007 to April 2008, and saw fierce fighting, in which its people won five Military Crosses, one OBE, three Mentions in Despatches, one Queen's Commendation for Valuable Service and nine Joint Force Commander's Commendations.

During this tour, 1 RGR suffered one fatality and fourteen or fifteen wounded. During the move back to Kandahar after the first major battle on the river Helmand between Gereshk and Sangin, in the fighting at the end, Major Alexis Roberts was killed by an

improvised explosive device (IED) on 4 October 2007. He was, like so many of those killed in the latest Afghan conflict, a talented and popular officer who would have gone far in the service. He had been attached to 1 RGR from 2 RGR, and had previously been an instructor at Sandhurst where the son of the heir to the throne Prince William had been an officer cadet in his platoon.[60]

A Gurkha officer who was a watchkeeper for the battalion group told me that the Taliban quickly knew they were up against Gurkhas.

> Mostly we monitored – intercepting Taliban radio. They would say, 'The Gurkhas are coming – run.' They knew they were Gurkhas after the first battle.
>
> The most panicking moment was when the first [man] was killed [Major Roberts]. That was a hit for all. After that, the boys became confident and so angry. It made them more determined. Even in the hospitals – when we go and see the casualties it was, 'I want to recover quickly and go and fight the Taliban.' We were not scared, exactly, but feeling we were on proper operations.[61]

Afghan memories are long. Afghans will tell you how they beat the British at Maiwand in 1880, and the fact that the Gurkhas were back 127 years later would not have been lost on them.

Major Roberts's parent regiment, 2 RGR, followed 1 RGR, fighting in Afghanistan from September 2008 to April 2009. They, too, had one death, Rifleman Yubraj Rai, on 4 November 2008. In their attempt to save him, two Gurkha soldiers showed the same disregard for enemy bullets as previous generations of Gurkhas, a story recounted in the prologue.

At the time of writing, 1 RGR is again serving in Afghanistan, until September 2010, and 2 RGR is due to return for six months in April 2011.[62] Since they were formed in 1815, the Gurkhas have constantly been drawn back to that stark, dusty land, and faced ferocious and cunning adversaries who seem to emerge from nowhere, and return whence they came. Afghanistan has been central to the story of the Indian and British Gurkhas, and it is where we end their story to date.

12

The Gurkhas Now, and the Future

O N 1 JUNE 2001 the Crown Prince of Nepal went mad and killed himself, beginning a period of turbulence in the country. His uncle took over as King Gyanendra, but was not popular. Gyanendra concentrated power in himself and had strong direct links with the Nepalese security forces. This fanned the flames of discontent and the Maoists, who formed the 'left wing' in Nepal, were drawn into confrontation with the security forces. There was a Maoist insurrection in the hills, which had the effect of forcing all the able-bodied young men down into the Terai, which is why a large number of Gurkha recruits now come from there. The security forces acted with restraint, but it became apparent that they were not going to win.

In 2008 the king was deposed and Nepal became a republic. The long relationship that the British government and the Nepalese monarchy had enjoyed, and which had underpinned British and Indian Gurkha recruitment since the 1880s, was no more. The 2008 election was not conclusive and an interim government was formed with twenty-two parties. The prime minister, Prichandra, was a hard-line Maoist and tried to sack the army chief, General Katawal. Katawal said he reported to the president, not the Maoist prime minister, and the president backed him. Prichandra then resigned, taking all the Maoists with him. That made things difficult, as the Maoists were the largest party.

Under the interim government it was planned to integrate 3,000 to 4,000 Maoist insurgent soldiers into the Nepalese security forces. The security forces were not unwilling, but said they took orders from the government, and it was impossible to get twenty-two parties to agree.

Meanwhile, the main regional players, India and China, would have no truck with the Nepalese Maoists. India has no desire to have a Maoist state on its border. China is not bothered by events in Nepal, as the latter has not succoured Tibetan separatists, and has quietly continued to spread its influence in Nepal, as it has in Burma and throughout Africa, by building roads and other infrastructure projects.

At the time of writing the unstable political situation in Nepal has not affected Gurkha recruiting, either British or Indian. In 2008, Prichandra said he was going to stop Gurkha recruiting but as soon as he became prime minister nothing more was heard. The Maoists did not interfere with the British Gurkha operation in Nepal in any way, apart from a rather comical incident when Lieutenant Colonel Adrian Griffiths, based at British Gurkhas Pokhara, was kidnapped. Adrian, originally a 6th Gurkha, is a great expert on Gurkha history and shared his knowledge with me. His 'kidnap' was a mistake and the Maoist guerrillas eventually sent him home in a taxi.

Once Prichandra became prime minister he learned the value of the Gurkhas, British and Indian, to the Nepali economy, and opposition to Gurkha recruitment promptly ceased. The only potential problem with Gurkha recruitment would be consistently heavy Gurkha casualties in Afghanistan, but that has not happened so far. Of the seven members of the Gurkha Brigade killed in the latest Afghan War up to the time of writing, three have been British officers.

British Gurkhas Nepal is responsible for recruiting Gurkhas and also for looking after Gurkhas who have retired and returned home. To this end the Defence Attaché (DA) in Nepal, who was a Gurkha Engineer when I researched this book, wears three 'hats'.[1] As DA Nepal he is the ambassador's link with the Nepalese security forces, and is involved in helping modernise them and make them more democratic and accountable, a process called 'security sector reform'. As commander of British Gurkhas Nepal, he is responsible for recruiting and selection. At the moment the British Army selects 176 a year out of about 11,000 applicants, and the Gurkha Contingent Singapore Police Force recruits 80. India runs a similar operation, recruiting about 2,000, but the numbers vary according

to need. His third 'hat' is as head of Gurkha Welfare Services, which employs a considerable number of ex-Gurkha warrant officers and NCOs in nineteen Gurkha wefare centres across Nepal and one in Darjeeling, India. The welfare centres, tidy, well-maintained islands in the exotic chaos that is Nepal, are bases for the distribution of pensions and also offer medical help and advice. Many of the older ex-Gurkhas living in the hills do not have bank accounts, so distributing pensions to ex-Gurkhas, or their dependants if they have died, is a big commitment.

The first stage of selection takes place at Dharan in the east and Pokhara in the west. The children of Gurkhas can also apply in Kathmandu, but no one else can. 'Otherwise, we'd be overwhelmed.' The very start of the selection process can be seen in Plates 34 to 36. I saw the potential 2011 intake being registered at Dharan and Pokhara. They had to be between seventeen and a half and twenty-one years old on 1 January 2011. The recruiting officers, ex-Gurkhas who still look frighteningly fit in their 'Gurkha Recruiting' T-shirts, checked each applicant's height – minimum 5 feet 3 inches (1.6 metres) – and weight – minimum 110 pounds (50 kilograms) – and chest expansion – not less than 2 inches (5 centimetres). Anyone with glasses, contact lenses or tattoos, or who cannot manage eight heaves – pull-ups, done in the correct fashion – is rejected immediately. To avoid accusations of unfairness, recruits are divided into groups of six so that they can witness each other's performance. Outside the selection centres at Dharan and Pokhara, vendors offer unauthorised books and CDs purporting to help hopefuls pass the selection, but the official CD gives any applicant all the information they need. Recruits' documents and educational qualifications are rigorously checked.

The education standard required has recently been increased, and is now fairly comparable with five good GCSEs in the UK. That means that the Gurkha recruits who arrive at Catterick nowadays are educationally a lot better qualified than most of the British recruits, although that used not to be the case. Those who satisfy the registration requirements are invited to attend one of a number of regional selection processes run over a two-week period in August and September, and are shown a video on how to prepare for it, and

how to train for the exercises they will have to perform. Those who pass regional selection are invited to one of the central selection courses at Pokhara, run over a four-week period in November and December, and if successful are enlisted and given some basic training before being sent to Catterick for recruit training with the Guards and Paras. The selection includes many more physical and mental tests, including the *doko* race. A *doko* is a Nepali basket carried on the back. To pass, candidates have to cover 3 miles (5 kilometres) in forty-eight minutes carrying 55 pounds (25 kilograms), and there is a 1,300-foot (400-metre) vertical climb over the course of the route.

British officers joining the Gurkha Rifles from Sandhurst and the Platoon Commanders' course at Brecon undergo seven weeks' familiarisation in Nepal before joining their unit. This includes a week's attachment to an area welfare centre, a three-week language course and a ten- to fifteen-day trek to a Gurkha welfare service project in the hills, and then reporting on the progress of that project. The Gurkha welfare service operates in the areas whence Gurkhas are recruited, and so the project achieves several aims, including instilling an understanding of language, culture and environment from which the Gurkhas come.

British officers and NCOs posted to the Queen's Gurkha engineers, signals and logistic regiments do a shorter familiarisation spell, again including a trek into the hills. When the Gurkhas were based in Hong Kong all officers and senior ranks posted to the brigade had to attend a language course in Hong Kong, and pass. It is no longer compulsory, but most do attend a language course. Otherwise, there could be problems, as the 7th Gurkha Rifles' forward observation officer found in the Falklands.

In August 2007 the selection centre at Pokhara ran a 'female capability assessment' to try to establish comparable standards for women. The same tests were included, but modified – reducing the load and the distance to be carried and covered in the *doko* race, for example. The team were confident that they could run a selection process for female Gurkhas if required, but the prospect is fraught with difficulty.[2] Women can join all arms of the British Army apart from infantry and armour. The physical standards required for

troops in the other arms, which include women, are therefore lower than those for the infantry, in terms of muscular strength. The Gurkha supporting arms – engineers, signals and logistics – have always been trained to exactly the same high standards as the rifle battalions. That means that they can, if necessary, become riflemen in an instant. If women are to be admitted to the Gurkha engineers, signals and logistics regiments, then those will have to accept a lower standard of training than the rifle battalions. Thus, the prized flexibility of the Brigade of Gurkhas would be compromised.[3]

Some Gurkha girls have found a way round the problem. The head of one of the Gurkha area welfare centres told me that his daughter had gone to the UK, joined the Royal Logistic Corps, trained as a chef and, not surprisingly, got herself posted to the Queen's Own Gurkha Logistic Regiment. She then spent five months with them in Afghanistan. However, that option would be open only to the daughters of Gurkhas or ex-Gurkhas, not to any young woman from Nepal.[4]

It is nearly 200 years since the fighting skills, discipline and engineering acumen of the Nepali Gurkhas attracted the attention of British soldiers. The East India Company, a commercially minded organisation, also liked them because they were cheap. They formed a 'third force' in British India, neither British nor Indian, and that also made them useful. After they had proved their loyalty in the Indian Mutiny, circumstances combined to bring about a massive expansion in the Gurkhas. The threat to the North-West Frontier and pseudo-scientific theories of 'martial races', plus improved relations with Nepal, all helped ensure that the number of Gurkha regiments rose from three to ten.

During their history, the Gurkhas have been a very 'special force' in various ways. Their role as a 'third force' in India is one. But their physical hardihood and innate aptitude for appraising and negotiating mountainous terrain, plus their marksmanship, led to the creation of the Gurkha Scouts, in the 1890s and again in 1919. These were used for roles similar to 'special forces' today. They accompanied cloak-and-dagger missions during the Great Game, and were selected for long-range desert missions with Lawrence of

Arabia. They fought in all the British empire theatres in the First World War, and in all but north-west Europe in the Second. They were key to victory in Burma and as Chindits and paratroops again acted as 'special forces'. In Borneo, they were again in a 'special force' role, and bore the brunt of the secret 'Claret' missions into Indonesian territory. These were so secret that even the last Gurkha VC citation had the location of the action misplaced.

It was clearly a role to which the Gurkhas were, and are, suited and for which the British Army was happy to use them. One of the reasons, perhaps, although it has never been mentioned, is that the Gurkhas, unlike their more garrulous British colleagues, are most unlikely to see their mission as such. And to talk about it.

Until 1947 the Gurkhas, while they had certain idiosyncrasies, were broadly similar to other units of the Indian Army, although they had become less similar because the process of 'Indianisation' from 1918 was not applied to them. With the transfer of four regiments to the British Army on 1 January 1948 their position changed. For the British Army, which was not their home, they were a very different, a very special corps. Keeping them apart, almost in their own world, in Malaya, Brunei and Hong Kong, hid the dysfunction. But when Hong Kong was given back to China in 1997, Britain became their home. They do feel that their identity is under threat.[5] But, paradoxically, their absorption into the British Army has made reservations about employing them, such as those expressed in 1982, evaporate.

India's Gorkhas have not undergone the same pressures. They remained in their natural home. While the four regiments that went to the British Army have been amalgamated into one, with two battalions, the six that stayed in the Indian Army, plus the revived 11th Gorkhas, have retained their individual identities and each has five or six battalions. A genealogist looking at the family tree in Figure 4 might think that the Indian line would continue for a long time, but that the British one might come to an end. That would be a tragedy, and very bad for British security.

In the 1990s the British Army was under-recruited and the Gurkhas, who have never had a recruiting problem, were used to plug the gap. As this book reaches its end, the British Army does not

have a shortage of recruits, but that could change very quickly when the economy picks up. The British Army and other security forces need a constant stream of fit recruits, and with changing lifestyles their availability cannot be guaranteed. Fighting is not something that people want to do all their lives. With a 10 per cent chance of being killed or wounded on a tour in parts of Afghanistan, British officers whom I have taught, who are coming up for their third tour, are doing the sums and leaving. It is not inconceivable that the British Gurkhas could be expanded, although it is unlikely. In order to increase the number of 'ethnic minorities' in the armed services, the preferred solution is to absorb them into existing regiments rather than create new 'ethnic' units. An imaginative future history of the greatly expanded Gurkhas in AD 2300 can be found on the internet.[6]

As we have seen, since Indian independence in 1947 and the transfer of four Gurkha regiments to the British Army on 1 January 1948, the British Gurkhas' position has been an uncertain one. Chapter 11 catalogues a series of close calls for the Brigade of Gurkhas. In May 2010 a new British government, the first coalition since the Second World War, was formed. The new coalition government had to make massive spending cuts and, once again, the Gurkhas looked vulnerable. Speaking to the *Observer* newspaper on 29 August 2010, Patrick Mercer, a Tory MP and a former army officer, said: 'The first people to go will be the Brigade of Gurkhas, probably in their entirety. In the past, the Gurkhas' existence was guaranteed by the fact they are cheaper to run than British troops, and that there was a shortage of British troops. Recent changes mean they are now just as expensive, and recruitment is extremely healthy at the moment. I am afraid the writing is on the wall.'[7]

In some quarters, elements of the old tension between the British and Indian armies resurfaced. Why should any more British regiments be scrapped or amalgamated and the Gurkhas retained? Ironically, the successful campaign to win Gurkha soldiers equal pay, pensions and other rights with British soldiers had made them expensive and therefore more vulnerable.[8] But when the results of the so-called 'Defence Review' were announced on 19 October 2010 the Prime Minister David Cameron said that there would be

no losses of infantry regiments as a result of the 'review', and that any reductions in manpower for the army would be made away from the front line. He added that 'there is no cut whatsoever in the support for our forces in Afghanistan'.[9]

With British troops heavily committed in Afghanistan it would have been political suicide to announce cuts to the infantry in autumn 2010. On 19 October it was announced that the British Army would be reduced by 7,000, from 102,000 to 95,000. The main reductions were to be made by streamlining headquarters and other staff, and by mothballing the ironmongery for large-scale conventional war — tanks and artillery. Even so, the planned cuts of 7,000 would be difficult to achieve and the instant reaction of some — that the Gurkhas were 'safe' — may have been premature. It is likely to be spring 2012 before the scale of reductions in force levels in Afghanistan becomes clear, and what the implications are for the rest of the British standing army, of which the Gurkhas are a part. The Gurkhas will be subject to reductions in line with the rest of the Army. There are a couple of special points about the Gurkhas, however. With two infantry battalions and their integrated engineer, signals and logistics units, they are the nearest the British Army has to a 'regimental combat team', and while the currrent high levels of recruitment for the British Army as a whole may subside with the end of recession and withdrawal from Afghanistan, Gurkha recruitment is unlikely to dry up. With the commitment to pay pensions and look after the welfare of ex-Gurkhas in Nepal, the British Ministry of Defence will remain committed to a substantial operation in that country, and might as well continue recruiting at the same time. The Gurkhas have also survived, in part, because of their reputation for endurance and bravery. It must be said, however, that every British unit that has served in Helmand Province in Afghanistan could produce tales of equal worth.

In an uncertain world, where security operations need to be undertaken swiftly and force has to be delivered precisely, a highly professional and politically neutral force is what you need. To anyone who suggests that the time has now come to disband the Gurkhas, I would simply say this. The British government is now committed, rightly, to paying pensions and benefits to thousands of

Gurkhas and their dependants. With the world as it is, to dispense with the young Gurkhas actually serving as a consummate fighting force, and to stop the recruitment of young men supremely suited to military service, would not just be throwing the baby out with the bathwater. It would be throwing the baby out while being obliged to keep the bathwater at the right temperature for another fifty years.

The Gurkhas are a uniquely adaptable, professional and apolitical force, perfectly suited to twenty-first-century security operations, from disaster relief to full-scale war. The Gurkhas are involved in the latter right now.

It works. Don't fix it.

Notes

PREFACE AND ACKNOWLEDGEMENTS

1. http://www.guardian.co.uk/world/2009/may/21/gurkha-uk-settle-rights-lumley. Accessed 20 June 2010.
2. The *Protocol Additional to the Geneva Conventions of 12 August 1949, and Relating to the Protection of Victims of International Armed Conflicts* (Protocol 1), 8 June 1977, states:

Article 47. Mercenaries

1. A mercenary shall not have the right to be a combatant or a prisoner of war.
2. A mercenary is any person who:
    (a) is especially recruited locally or abroad in order to fight in an armed conflict;
    (b) does, in fact, take a direct part in the hostilities;
    (c) is motivated to take part in the hostilities essentially by the desire for private gain and, in fact, is promised, by or on behalf of a Party to the conflict, material compensation substantially in excess of that promised or paid to combatants of similar ranks and functions in the armed forces of that Party;
    (d) is neither a national of a Party to the conflict nor a resident of territory controlled by a Party to the conflict;
    (e) is not a member of the armed forces of a Party to the conflict; and
    (f) has not been sent by a State which is not a Party to the conflict on official duty as a member of its armed forces.

Indian and British Gurkhas certainly do not meet criteria (c), (e) or (f). Nor are they recruited for any specific conflict (a), but for service in the British or Indian armies generally. If not British nationals they have nevertheless 'resided', for the duration of their service, in Indian or British-controlled territory – for example, Hong Kong.

3. Lt Gen Sir George MacMunn KCB KCSI DSO, *Martial Races of India* (Sampson, Low, Marston, London, 1933), p. 195.

4. I am grateful to my friend and colleague, Dr Peter Caddick-Adams, who has lectured on board the Cunard liner *Queen Mary 2*, for this interesting snippet.

5. R. Haycock, 'British Arms in India', in G. Jordan, (ed.), *British Military History: A Supplement to Robin Higham's Guide to the Sources* (Garland, New York, 1988), p. 216.

6. John Chapple, *Bibliography of Gurkha Regiments and Related Subjects* (Gurkha Museum Publication No. 4, Winchester, 1980).

7. 'The Highlandmen of Nepal', *The Navy and Army Illustrated*, vol. 11 (1900), pp. 337–9, cited in A. P. Coleman, *A Special Corps: The Beginnings of Gorkha* [sic] *Service with the British* (Pentland Press, Edinburgh, Cambridge, Durham, USA, 1999), Foreword by Rodney Needham, p. xxiii. Coleman's book is the definitive work on the beginnings of the Brigade of Gurkhas.

8. Lionel Caplan, *Warrior Gentlemen: 'Gurkhas' in the Western Imagination*, (Himal Books, Classics, Kathmandu, 2009; first published by Berghahn Books, Oxford, UK, and Providence, RI, USA, 1995), p. 17. (Hereafter referred to as Caplan, 2009.) See also Lionel Caplan. '"Bravest of the brave": Representation of "the gurkha" in British military writings', *Modern Asian Studies*, vol. 25, no. 3, (1991), pp. 571–97, (hereafter referred to as Caplan, 1991); and 'Martial Gurkhas: the persistence of a British military discourse on "race"'. In Peter Robb (ed.), *The Concept of Race in South Asia* (Oxford University Press, New Delhi, 1995), pp. 260–81 (hereafter referred to as Caplan, 1995).

9. Caplan, 2009, p. 10, citing extracts from 'Who are the Gurkhas', *The Empire Annual for Boys* (Danvers Dawson, 1917), pp. 119–21.

10. Basanta Thapa and Mohan Mainali (eds), *Lahure ko Katha (Story of the Lahurés)*, (Himal Books, Kathmandu, 2002), cited in Harka Gurung, Foreword to Caplan, 2009, p. ix.

11. Ralph Lilley Turner MC MA, *A Comparative and Etymological Dictionary of the Nepali Language with indexes of all words quoted from other Indo-Aryan Languages compiled by Dorothy Rivers Turner,*

M.A. (London, Kegan Paul, Trench, Trubner & Co., Ltd, 1931), p. ix.

12. Interview with serving Gurkha officer, on condition of anonymity, Damak, 6 June 2010.

13. Clare Balding, 'Ramblings', BBC Radio 4, 0600 hours, 20 June 2010, walking along the South Downs Way, 'with *the Gurkhas*'.

14. Conversations with Lt Col (retd) John Cross, Pokhara, and a serving Nepalese Gurkha officer, Damak, 10 and 6 June 2010.

15. John P. Cross, *'A Face Like a Chicken's Backside': An Unconventional Soldier in Malaya & Borneo, 1948–1971* (Cultured Lotus, Singapore, 2003), (first published by Greenhill Books, Lionel Leventhal, London, 1996).

16. John Cross and Gurkha, interviews, Damak, 10 and 6 June 2010.

17. Christopher Bullock, *Britain's Gurkhas, with a Foreword by the Colonel Commandant Brigade of Gurkhas, General Sir David Richards KCB, CBE, DSO, ADC Gen* (Third Millennium, London, 2009).

18. Byron Farwell, *The Gurkhas* (Allen Lane, London, 1984), p. 14, cited in Caplan, 2009, p. 12.

19. Caplan 2009, p. 6.

20. Tony Gould, *Imperial Warriors: Britain and the Gurkhas* (Granta, London, 1999).

21. A. P. Coleman, *A Special Corps: The Beginnings of Gorkha Service with the British* (Pentland Press, Edinburgh, Cambridge, Durham, USA, 1999).

22. The Gurkha Museum, *The Lineages and Composition of Gurkha Regiments in British Service* (Gurkha Museum, Winchester, March 2010).

23. Caplan, 2009, pp. 12–13, referring to the work of C. Geertz, *Works and Lives: The Anthropologist as Author* (Polity Press, Cambridge, 1989), pp. 4–5.

PROLOGUE

1. 'In pictures: Gurkhas fight for security in Musa Qaleh', in http://www.mod.uk/defenceinternet/pictureviewers/gallerygurkhasfightforsecurityinmusaqaleh.htm, Notice 6 November 2008, retrieved 1 September 2010. Rifleman Yubraj Rai, sadly killed that day, is known by his first name, Yubraj. In a British regiment he

would be Rifleman Smith, or Rifleman Jones. But Rai is the name of his *jat*, one of the ethnic groups or clans of Nepal, and since Gurkhas are usually recruited from a few of those *jats*, the convention is to identify people by their first names. Another soldier killed, on 13 August, was Ishwor Gurung, of 69 Gurkha Field Squadron, Queen's Gurkha Engineers. The Gurungs are the most recruited of the *jats*. Again, he was described as Sapper Ishwor.

2. http://www.mod.uk./DefenceInternet/DefenceNews/ MilitaryOperation/ColourSergeantKrishnabahadurDuraKilledin Afghanistan.htm. Notice 17 November 2008, retrieved 14 October 2010.

CHAPTER 1: WHENCE 'THE GURKHAS'?

1. Ralph Lilley Turner MC MA, *A Comparative and Etymological Dictionary of the Nepali Language with indexes of all words quoted from other Indo-Aryan Languages compiled by Dorothy Rivers Turner, M.A.* (London, Kegan Paul, Trench, Trubner & Co., Ltd, 1931), pp. 149–50.
2. Ibid., p. 149.
3. Ibid., p. 149.
4. Mike Chappell, *The Gurkhas* (Osprey, London, Auckland, Melbourne, Singapore and Toronto, 1993), pp. 12–26.
5. See, for example, Bighan Golay, 'Rethinking Gorkha identity: outside the imperium of discourse, hegemony, and history', *Peace and Democracy in South Asia*, vol. 2, nos. 1 & 2 (2006), pp. 23–49.
6. Ministry of Defence (Colonel R. G. Leonard, late 5th Gurkhas), *Nepal and the Gurkhas* (HMSO, London, 1965), pp. 23–4. This excellent and indispensable book was the result of a process of development begun by Major E. R. Elles, Royal Artillery, with *A Report on Nepal*, published in 1883 and republished with additions, by Major Newham Davis of the Buffs and Captain Eden Vansittart of 5th Gurkhas, in 1896. The next edition, by Col. B. U. Nicolay, 4th Gurkhas, was *The Handbook on Gurkhas*, published in 1915 and republished in 1918. The following edition was edited by Major C. J. Morris, 3rd Gurkhas, and published in 1933, 1936, and 1942. Morris was an intellectual, rare in the Indian Army, and his story is told in Chapter 7. The 1965 edition drew on Morris's work and benefited

from notes on the eastern tribes by Lt Col A. V. A. Mercer of 7th Gurkhas. Given the strong family traditions present in the British and Indian armies and in the Gurkhas, this Mercer was probably a descendant of the Mercer who served with 4th Gurkhas and then 7th in the Second Afghan War (see plates). There has not been room in the present book to explore in great detail the early history of Nepal and its associated geography and ethnicity. *Nepal and the Gurkhas* is essential reading for anyone who wants more.

7. Pictures of all the kings of Gorkha and information about them are on display in the Gurkha Musem in Winchester, visited by the author on 9 June 2010.

8. Some older sources say he was born in 1730, which would have meant acceding at the age of twelve, but his date of birth is now generally acknowledged as 1723. See the official commentary on his portrait, Prithvi Narayan Shah, the Great, unifier of Nepal, in the Nepal National Art Gallery, visited by the author on Sunday 13 June 2010, or also on http://www.pbase.com/image89713554, retrieved 30 May 2010.

9. *Nepal and the Gurkhas*, pp. 21, 24–6.

10. MacMunn, *Martial Races of India*, p. 199.

11. In 1768 only Great Britain (England and Scotland), France, Spain, Portugal, the Netherlands, Denmark, Norway, Sweden and Switzerland would have been recognisable within their modern boundaries and natural borders. Belgium, Italy and Germany were nineteenth-century creations, and most of the European states, with far less obvious borders than Nepal, are twentieth century.

12. *Nepal and the Gurkhas*, pp. 1–3.

13. Gurkha officer to the author, with tongue in cheek, on arrival in Nepal, 3 June 2010.

14. http://www.travax.nhs.uk/registered/countries/malariamaps/malaria_in_nepal.asp, retrieved 26 May 2010.

15. *Nepal and the Gurkhas*, pp. 2, 8–9; current temperatures from James McConnaichie and David Reed, *The Rough Guide to Nepal* (6th edition, Rough Guides, Penguin, October 2009), p. 11.

16. *Nepal and the Gurkhas*, p. 4.

17. http://www.travax.nhs.uk/registered/countries/malariamaps/malaria_in_nepal.asp, retrieved 26 May 2010.

18. *Nepal and the Gurkhas*, pp. 3–4, 16–17. Legends of this kind often have their roots in distant human memory. The Great Flood, in the

Bible and the *Epic of Gilgamesh*, for example, may well be a distant folk memory reflecting the breakthrough of the Mediterranean, through the Dardanelles, to swamp a low-lying inland freshwater lake and create what is now the Black Sea, around 5500 BC. The cataclysm was so intense that the memory could well have survived in oral tradition until the appearance of the first writing more than two thousand years later.

19. *The Rough Guide to Nepal*, p. 429; Tessa Feller, *Culture Smart! Nepal – the Essential Guide to Customs and Culture* (Kuperard, London, 2008), p. 19.

20. *Nepal and the Gurkhas*, p. 52. Abolition of the requirement from 1967: interview with Hon. Major Chandraparsad Limbu MBE, Area Welfare Officer, Dharan, 4 June 2010.

21. Interview with serving Gurkha officer, on condition of anonymity, Damak, 6 June 2010.

22. Interview with Hon. Major Chandraparsad Limbu MBE, Area Welfare Officer, Dharan, 4 June 2010.

23. Interview with Dhanbahadur Rai, formerly of 7th Gurkha Rifles (1973–88), Hotel Kalash, Damak, 6 June 2010.

24. *Nepal and the Gurkhas*, pp. 45–6, 88–132. In 1965 (p. 46), the official manual listed them as follows:

'True Gurkha martial tribes'	Thakur, Chhetri, Gurung, Magar, Rai, Limbu, Sunwar, Tamang
'Enlisted at times'	Lepcha, Newar, Thakali, Punyal, Sherpa, Manjhi, Kumhal, Nagarkoti, Bhujel
Not enlisted *as such* [emphasis added]	Tharu, Bhote (i.e. Tibetan), Bajanghi, Dotiyal, Kisundo, Chepang, Thami
Tradesmen	Sarki, Kamai, Damai, Sunar
Others	Gaini, Argi, Bhanra, Chunara, Drai, Kasai, Pore

25. Major A.C. Lovatt, Major-General George MacMunn DSO, with a Foreword by Field Marshal Earl Roberts VC KG, *The Armies of India* (Charles Black, London, 1911), cited in Caplan, 1991, p. 580. MacMunn, later a lieutenant general, wrote the words, while Lovatt painted the excellent pictures. MacMunn was a prolific and fascinating

writer about all aspects of India, and was also a first-rate military historian who wrote books on Gustavus Adolphus and Prince Eugene.

26. Caplan, 2009, p. 261.

27. Conversation with my colleague, Dr Laura Cleary, Cranfield University, who has spent a good deal of time with the Nepali military teaching defence management and good governance, and also Gurkha officers in Nepal.

28. *Nepal and the Gurkhas*, pp. 88–92, cover the Gurungs; pp. 93–6, Magars; pp. 97–106, Limbus; p. 110, Rais; pp. 111–13, Tamangs; pp. 114–16, Sunwars; pp. 117–18 , Thakurs; pp. 119–23, Chhetris, and pp. 124–32 'Lepchas, Newars and other tribes not normally enlisted'.

29. H. H. Risley, *Tribes and Castes of Bengal* (Calcutta, 1891), cited in *Nepal and the Gurkhas*, p. 107.

30. The Church of England resulted from Henry VIII's adoption of Protestantism because the Pope would not give him a divorce, as well as its reimposition as the state religion by Elizabeth I who, nevertheless, did not 'wish to make windows into men's souls'.

31. *Nepal and the Gurkhas*, pp. 38, 114–15.

32. *Nepal and the Gurkhas*, pp. 119–23. Unfortunately the source does not provide any detail of his subsequent service in the Nepalese Army. He could not have reached the rank of full colonel in the British-Indian Army at that time.

33. Sylvain Levi, *Le Nepal* (3 vols, Paris, 1897), cited in *Nepal and the Gurkhas*, p. 125.

34. Statistics on display on the noticeboards at Gurkha recruiting centres East (Dharan) and West (Pokhara), visited by the author June 2010.

35. Ibid.

36. *Nepal and the Gurkhas*, pp. 46, 117, 119.

37. Ibid., pp. 46, 124–32.

38. Dr Laura Cleary, conversations with Nepali military, February 2010. On the use of the kukri as a machete, conversation with Second Lieutenant Mark Willis, 7th Gurkha Rifles, then a fellow University Cadet at Oxford University, Sennybridge, March 1974.

39. Captain F.N. Raper, 10th Native Infantry, *Memoir of Gurwall and Kamaon*, Forward by G.H. Fagan, Adjutant-General, in *Papers Relating to the Nepaul War. Printed in Conformity with the Resolution of the Constitution of Proprietors of the East India Stock of the 3 March 1824* (London, 1824, 2 vols, reprinted by BIMLA, New Delhi, 1985) [hereafter referred to as *PRNW*], pp. 143–9, this, p. 146.

40. Covering note in *PRNW*, p. 143.

41. Revd Wood, *Travels in India and Nepal* (1891), section cited in full in R. J. Marrion and D. S. V. Fosten, *The Tradition Book of Gurkhas* (Belmont Maitland, London, ?1965). The date of this excellent short book is not given, but from the price it is pre-decimalisation (1971). Parts of the same passage are used to publicise kukris for sale in http://www.nepaliexporter.com/files_british_gurkha_knife.htm, retrieved 30 May 2010.

CHAPTER 2: COLLISION, CONFLICT AND COOPERATION WITH THE BRITISH

1. A. P. Coleman, *A Special Corps: The Beginnings of Gorkha Service with the British* (Pentland Press, Edinburgh, Cambridge, Durham, USA, 1999, Foreword by Rodney Needham), p. 5.

2. *Nepal and the Gurkhas*, pp. 24–5.

3. Ibid., p. 25.

4. http://www.britannica.com/EBchecked/topic/176643/East-India-Company, retrieved 29 May 2010. The two best books on the East India Company are Philip Lawson, *The East India Company: A History* (*Studies in Modern History*), (Longman, 1993); and John Keay, *The Honourable Company: A History of the English East India Company* (Macmillan, New York, 1994). The East India Company's army played an important role in extending its influence across India from the 1770s. See 'Role of army in British East India Company, British India', http://www.indianetzone.com/39/role_army_british_east_india_company .htm.

5. *Nepal and the Gurkhas*, pp. 25–6; Coleman, *A Special Corps*, p. 6.

6. The exact dates vary but in 2009 Indra Jatra was celebrated from 1 September. In *Encyclopædia Britannica*, retrieved 29 May 2010, from: http://www.britannica.com/EBchecked/topic/286650/Indra-Jatra

7. Machendra Jatra (2010). In *Encyclopædia Britannica*, retrieved 29 May 2010, from: http://www.britannica.com/EBchecked/topic/354565/Machendra-Jatra.

8. *Nepal and the Gurkhas*, p. 27.

9. The parallels are striking. The Normans were Scandinavians who had settled in northern France where they absorbed French culture and language and the Christian religion, which they seem to have practised in a more extreme form than the English, whose country they

conquered in 1066. The Anglo-Saxon and Danish aristocracy and monarchy disappeared, and the Normans ruled with a mixture of terror and economic exploitation, assuaged by priestly forgiveness.

10. The letter is reproduced in *The Indian History Sourcebook* at http://www.fordham.edu/halsall/india/1617englandindies.gtml, retrieved 30 May 2010. The 1617 letter, from the Great Mogul Jahangir to King James, translated into the English of the Bible that bears his name, and of Shakespeare, reads:

> I have given my general command to all the kingdoms and ports of my dominions to receive all the merchants of the English nation as the subjects of my friend; that in what place soever they choose to live, they may have free liberty without any restraint; and at what port soever they shall arrive, that neither Portugal nor any other shall dare to molest their quiet; and in what city soever they shall have residence, I have commanded all my governors and captains to give them freedom answerable to their own desires; to sell, buy, and to transport into their country at their pleasure . . .

11. The official website of the Indian Army is the best source on the early days of the East India Company forces. However, the website warns that any information relating to the period after 1948 is classified. See http://indianarmy.nic.in/Site/FormTemplete/frmtemp12P21C.aspx?MnId=qXAT5Eowt3c=&ParentID=a2GSpnDbrul=, retrieved 30 May 2010.

12. Ibid.

13. For the role of the army in the British East India Company, British India, see http://www.indianetzone.com/39/role_army_british_east_india_company.htm.

14. http://indianarmy.nic.in/Site/FormTemplete/frmtemp12P21C.aspx?MnId=qXAT5Eowt3c=&ParentID=a2GSpnDbrul=, retrieved 30 May 2010.

15. For the role of the army in the British East India Company, British India, see http://www.indianetzone.com/39/role_army_british_east_india_company.htm.

16. W. Kirkpatrick, *An Account of the Kingdom of Nepaul, being the substance of observations being made during a mission to that country in the year 1793* (London, 1811), p. 215, cited in Coleman, *A Special Corps*, pp. 12–13. The publication date suggests Ochterlony probably read it.

17. Ibid., pp. 13, 56.

18. On Arthur, and also Richard, Wellesley, see Richard Holmes, *Wellington: The Iron Duke* (HarperCollins, London, 2002).

19. Sir William Wilson Hunter, *Life of Brian Houghton Hodgson, British Resident at the Court of Nepal* (John Murray, London, 1896), p. 39.

20. Ibid., p. 40.

21. Hunter, *Life of Brian Houghton Hodgson*, p. 60; Coleman, *A Special Corps*, p. 16.

22. Coleman, ibid., citing Francis Buchanan Hamilton, *An Account of the King of Nepaul and of the Territories annexed to this Domain by the House of Gorkha* (Edinburgh, 1819), p. 110.

23. *Nepal and the Gurkhas*, pp. 27–9.

24. Coleman, *A Special Corps*, pp. 60–8.

25. Christopher Bullock, *Britain's Gurkhas*, pp. 21–2; *Nepal and the Gurkhas*, pp. 28–30.

26. Coleman, *A Special Corps*, p. xxv.

27. Moira's plan is analysed in Chandra B. Khanduri, *Marching Off with Colours: A Re-discovered History of Gorkhas* (Gyan Sagar, Delhi, 1997). See also Bullock, p. 22.

28. Khanduri, *Marching Off with Colours*, p. 96.

29. Bullock, p. 22.

30. MacMunn, *The Martial Races of India*, p. 188, gives 3,500 altogether. For a more detailed breakdown, see http://meerutup.tripod.com/may2sep06.htm, accessed 3 July 2010.

31. MacMunn, *The Martial Races of India*, p. 189.

32. Bullock, p. 22.

33. Tony Gould, *Imperial Warriors: Britain and the Gurkhas* (Granta, London, 1997), p. 65.

34. John Shipp, *Memoirs of the Extraordinary Military Career of John Shipp, Late a Lieutenant in HM's 87th Regiment* (London, 1829). Republished as *The Path of Glory, being the Memoirs of the Extraordinary Career of John Shipp: Written by Himself*, ed. C. J. Stranks (Chatto and Windus, London, 1969).

35. Shipp, 1829 edition, pp. 81–2, cited in Gould, p. 63. The Stranks edition (1969), p. 116, has edited out the hyperbole – a shame. It leaves: 'But the people who inhabit this paradise are proverbial for their cruelty, cold-hearted and cunning, powerful in war, and active as the goats that live on their mountains.'

36. Shipp, ed. Stranks (1969), pp. 118–19.

37. Alexander Fraser to his father, 20 January 1815, Fraser Papers, vol. 34, Scottish Record Office, Edinburgh, pp. 191, 192.

38. Alexander Fraser to his father, 1 January 1815, Fraser Papers, vol. 34, p. 166.

39. Alexander Fraser to his mother, 3 April 1815, Fraser Papers, vol. 34, p. 342. Although solid shot was still in widespread use, exploding shells with a burning fuse were also common and particularly useful for lobbing over fortifications to wreak havoc inside.

40. Colonel Charles E. Callwell, *Small Wars* (3rd edition, 1906 [1st edition 1896; 2nd 1899], HMSO, London, 1906, republished by University of Nebraska Press with an Introduction by Douglas Porch, Bison Books, 1996), p. 363.

41. Letter from Lieutenant Ross to Captain Birch (20 April 1815), in the Ramsay Papers (Papers of the Ochterlony Family owned by Ean Ramsay, direct descendant of Major General Sir David Ochterlony, Bart., GCB), reproduced in Coleman, Appendix E, pp. 253–4, with diagram.

42. Ibid.

43. NAM, *6511–54*, Letter from Colonel L. L. Showers DSO, 6 August 1965, covering transcription of memorial to his great-great-grandfather. If this Nepalese 'chief' was called Bhim Sen, it was a very different Bhim Sen. Lieutenant Ross's account (Coleman, p. 254) describes the Nepali as 'a sirdar'.

44. Ross to Birch, 20 April 1815, reproduced in Coleman, p. 254.

45. 'Convention or Agreement entered into between Kajee Ummer Sing Thapa and Major-General Ochterlony, on the 15th May 1815', *PRNW*, pp. 607–8, reproduced in Coleman as Appendix F, pp. 255–6. See also MacMunn, p. 190; Bullock, p. 25.

46. Coleman, ibid.

47. MacMunn, p. 190.

48. Coleman, p. 129.

49. On the Russian threat to India see C. D. Bellamy, 'British views of Russia: Russian views of Britain', in Philip Towle (ed.), *Estimating Foreign Military Power* (Croom Helm, Beckenham, 1982), pp. 37–76, esp. pp. 40–2.

50. Shipp, ed. Stranks (1969), pp. 109–10.

51. Shipp, ed. Stranks (1969), p. 106.

52. Ochterlony despatch dated 19 February 1816, *PRNW*, pp. 933–4, cited in Coleman pp. 137, 291, and map 8 in Coleman, p. 138 (source: Gurkha Museum, OPS/008 map 1816).

53. Shipp, ed Stranks (1969), p. 113.

54. Callwell, *Small Wars*, p. 491.

55. Shipp, ed. Stranks (1969), p. 102.

56. 'The Treaty of Segauli (4 March 1816) and translation of a related engagement', *PRNW*, pp. 835–6, reproduced as Appendix G to Coleman, pp. 257–9.

57. Adam to Edward Gardner, 16 March 1816, *PRNW*, p. 968.

58. MacMunn, *The Martial Races of India*, pp. 187–8.

59. Bengal secret letter, 27 December 1814, covering G. H. Fagan to Colonel Ochterlony, comd 3 div Fd Army, 21 November 1814 (Bumrowly), in *PRNW*, pp. 230–1.

60. Raper, Memoir of Gurwall and Kamaon, *PRNW*, pp. 143–9; this, p. 146.

61. Cited in Coleman, p. 92.

62. Letter from William Fraser, 24 February 1815, Fraser Papers, cited in Coleman, pp. 95–6.

63. Coleman, pp. 96–7, and the 'Descriptive detail of men engaged in the Affair of the 21st instant with the loss sustained by subsequent desertions', as Appendix A, p. 243; Gould, p. 46. Both historians agree the story is almost certainly apocryphal.

64. Fraser Papers, vol. 8, p. 400, cited in Coleman, p. 101.

65. Coleman, p. 115, and the full document, with Ochterlony's comments on the original proposals, in Appendix D, 'Memorandum of four Propositions. . .', pp. 251–2.

66. Coleman, pp. 116–17.

67. Ibid. Tony Gould, p. 59, finds Coleman's conclusion that the Nasiris were 'Ochterlony's Own' 'the most plausible, as well as agreeable, explanation'. So does the present author.

68. India Office Records, Military Department Records (IOR, MDR), British Library, L/Mil/5/391, f. 275, cited in Coleman, pp. 122, 289.

69. Lawtie to Ochterlony, apparently 10 April 1815 – a mis-transcription of 18 April – cited in Coleman, pp. 122, 289.

70. Coleman, pp. 122–3, 289.

71. Ibid., pp. 125, 289.

72. Coleman, Appendix F, p. 255.

73. Coleman, pp. 150–3.

74. Coleman, p. 155. Figures based on returns from Ochterlony and Young, dated 1 July 1815.

75. Gould, p. 66, citing William Fraser to John Adam on 27 April 1815. Fraser wrote to Adam: 'the Rajah of Lahore who obtained, at the

period that Umr Singh besieged Kangarh [1806–9], a considerable number [of Gorkhas], found them to be excellent.'

76. Coleman, p. 155.
77. IOR, MDR, L/Mil./17/2/272, ff. 141a, cited in Coleman, pp. 158, 254, reference 620.
78. Coleman, p. 294, n. 620. F. L. Petre, author of *The 1st King George's Own Gurkha Rifles* (London, 1925), p. 5, refers to this order as 'not now traceable at Simla'.
79. Khandari, *Marching off with Colours*, p. 223; Gould, p. 61.
80. Coleman, p. 294, n. 620.
81. Coleman, p. 159.
82. Gould, pp. 61–2.
83. *PRNW*, p. 760.
84. Coleman, p. 160.

CHAPTER 3: PROVING COMPETENCE AND LOYALTY

1. Gould, p. 68.
2. Ibid., pp. 59, 68.
3. See Sir William Wilson Hunter, *The Life of Brian Houghton Hodgson, British Resident at the Court of Nepal* (John Murray, London, 1896).
4. Hodgson Papers, vol. 10, in British Library, Oriental and India Office Collections, cited in Gould, pp. 72, 433.
5. Coleman, pp. 163–4.
6. Ibid., pp. 164–5.
7. Ibid., p. 176.
8. Ibid., pp. 165–6.
9. Phrase used by the British Army in Afghanistan, 2008–10, to refer to contact with enemy forces.
10. Coleman, p. 171.
11. Byron Farwell, *The Gurkhas* (W. W. Norton, New York and London, 1984), pp. 35–6.
12. Ibid.; Coleman, p. 171; Bullock, p. 29, with a near-contemporary picture of the action.
13. Young to adjutant general, 29 December 1829, cited in Coleman, pp. 174, 296.
14. Ibid., pp. 474, 296.

15. Military letter from Bengal to the Court of Directors, India Office, L/Mil/3/32, no. 52 of 6 November 1830, cited in Coleman, pp. 178, 296.
16. Coleman, pp. 174–5.
17. Ibid., pp. 174–5.
18. Ibid., p. 176.
19. Military letter from Bengal, 6 November 1830, cited in Coleman, pp. 178, 296.
20. Cited in F. Loraine Petre, *The 1st King George's Own Gurkha Rifles (The Malaun Regiment)*, (London, 1925), p. 47.
21. The Peace of Westphalia (1648) is often regarded as the origin of the modern nation state and gives the state a monopoly on (mass) organised violence.
22. NA (Kew), WO 43/420, Relative Ranks, Calcutta, 24 October 1827.
23. Ibid., folios 86–239, 290, 306 (8 October 1840), referring to the General Order of 27 June 1837. It was now *Her* Majesty's forces, as Victoria acceded on 20 June.
24. Michael Simkins and Ron Embleton, *The Roman Army from Caesar to Trajan* (Osprey, London, 1984), pp. 10, 12, 36 and Plate G; Coleman, pp. 178–9.
25. B. H. Hodgson, 'On the origin and classification of the military tribes of Bengal', *Selections from the Records of the Government of Bengal*, xxvii (Calcutta, 1857), pp. 657, 658, cited in Coleman, pp. 189, 298.
26. Coleman, p. 183, citing Bengal General Order no. 251 of 4 December 1829; Bengal General Orders dated 15 February and 12 March 1830 show that ninety-five men transferred to the Indian line infantry. *The Tradition Book of Gurkhas*, which is excellent, says (p. 8): 'The 2nd Battalion was absorbed by the 1st in 1826', but unlike Coleman is not able to cite contemporary references. It could be that 1829 (the date of the original order) has been wrongly transcribed as 1826. These things happen.
27. Coleman, pp. 182–5.
28. Parliamentary Papers, House of Commons, 1831–2, xiv, v (Military), Appendix (A), no. 55, paras 2265, 2268, 2278, 2282, 2283, 2284.
29. Lord Colchester (ed.), *A Political Diary 1828–30 by Edward Law, Lord Ellenborough*, 2 vols (London, 1881), ii, pp. 92–3, 3 September 1829.
30. Coleman, p. 199.
31. Fane Collection, Lincolnshire Archives, 6/6/4, cited in Coleman, pp. 200–1, 299.

32. Fane Collection, 6/6/7, cited in Coleman, pp. 202–4, 299.

33. Ibid. Report in Coleman as Appendix I, pp. 261–3. Fane concludes by saying that the available force (15,000) could be trebled in a short time (to 45,000), 'on the principle of the Landueler'. This may be a reference to the German mobilisation system – Landwehr.

34. See the author's 'British views of Russia' in Towle (ed.), *Estimating Foreign Military Power*, pp. 37–76; this, pp. 54–5. The Royal United Services Institute, founded in London at the instigation of the Duke of Wellington in 1831, was one of a number of institutes dedicated to the more scientific and rigorous analysis of military affairs.

35. Coleman, p. 205.

36. Gould, pp. 73–4.

37. Peter Hopkirk, *The Great Game: On Secret Service in High Asia* (John Murray, London, 1990, and subsequent editions (Oxford University Press)), is the definitive work on British-Russian rivalry and its consequences.

38. Ibid.

39. The war is excellently covered in Gregory Fremont-Barnes, *The Anglo-Afghan Wars, 1839–1919* (Osprey, Oxford, 2009). For the First Afghan War, pp. 14–42, this, pp. 24–7.

40. Field Marshal Sir John Chapple, *The Lineages and Composition of Gorkha Regiments in British Service* (Gurkha Museum, Winchester, 1984), p. 10; 2010 edition, p. 20.

41. Ibid., Coleman, pp. 206–7, 299.

42. David Willets, Defence Correpondent, 'Caring Heroes Killed by a Traitor', *Sun*, 15 July 2010, accessed on http://www.thesun.co.uk/sol/homepage/news/campaigns/our_boys/3054927/Gurkha-officers-killed-by-a-rogue-Afghan-soldier-were-befriending-locals-before-attack.html; sky.com/skynews/Home/World-News/Afghanistan-Three-British-Soldiers-From-Royal-Gurkha-Rifles-Killed-In-Attack-By-Rogue-Afghan/Article/201007215664356. Both accessed 19 July 2010. The excellent *Sun* report said that 'four other Gurkha *warriors* were injured'. Josh (James) Bowman, a company commander, was the second most senior British officer to be killed in the Fourth Afghan War up to that point, after Lt Col Rupert Thorneloe, commanding officer of the Welsh Guards (1 July 2009), a former student of the author. The three Gurkhas – two British officers and an NCO – were repatriated to the UK on 20 July 2010, along with

Marine Matthew Harrison of 40 Commando, Royal Marines. Like all the bodies of those killed in Afghanistan, they were flown into RAF Lyneham and then taken through Wootton Basset and thence by road past the Defence Academy of the UK at Shrivenham to the John Radcliffe Hospital in Oxford for the inquest.

43. *Punch* Magazine, vol. 6 (18 May 1844), p. 209. The telegraph was not in use in India until the 1850s and it would not be possible to telegraph the UK until the late 1860s. An Irishman, Napier would no doubt have been familiar with the wording to be used to priests: 'Pater, peccavi': 'Father, I have sinned,' the traditional beginning of a Roman Catholic confession. The story began with a linguistically talented 17-year-old young lady, Catherine Winkworth, who had written to *Punch* saying that the dispatch should have read *Peccavi* – a clever wrist-slap. Ms Winkworth later became famous for translating German hymns into English.

44. Letter dated 25 May 1845, cited in H. B. Edwardes and H. Merrivale, *Life of Sir Henry Lawrence* (London, 1870), p. 482, cited in Coleman, pp. 211–13, 300.

45. Farwell, p. 38.

46. Bullock, p. 33.

47. Farwell, p. 39. He gives Fisher's rank as a lieutenant colonel, which, although that rank commands a battalion today, is incorrect. The very few British officers commanded at much higher levels than their equivalents today.

48. Despatch to the adjutant general of the army, dated 30 January 1846; Viscount Hardinge, *The War in India: Despatches of Hardinge and Others* (London, 1846), pp. 76, 102, cited in Coleman, pp. 214, 300. Bullock, p. 33, dates the despatch 13 February, but it would have been copied repeatedly.

49. Charles Viscount Hardinge, *Viscount Hardinge: By his Son and Private Secretary in India* (Oxford, 1891), p. 20, cited in Coleman, pp. 215, 300.

50. Hunter, *Life of Brian Houghton Hodgson*, p. 105.

51. Coleman, pp. 215–16.

52. See Hopkirk, *The Great Game*. General Chernyayev, the 'Lion of Tashkent', captured the Central Asian city in 1865 in direct defiance of specific orders from the Foreign Ministry in Moscow, which did not want to acquire more potentially unmanageable territory.

53. Coleman, p. 216.

54. Lt Gen W. Napier (ed.), *Defects Civil and Military of the Indian Government by Lt.-General Sir Charles James Napier, GCB* (2nd edition, London, 1853), pp. 24, 25, cited in Coleman, pp. 221, 300.

55. NA (Kew) PRO, 30/64/8. Letter from Borough of Portsmouth, 16 March 1849; letter from Lord Mayor, 15 March 1849.

56. Coleman, p. 222.

57. Coleman, p. 226, citing Napier: 'In India peace is never certain for a single day'; and Dalhousie that 'in India one is always sitting on a volcano'.

58. Lt Gen W. Napier (ed.), *Defects Civil and Military of the Indian Government*, pp. 28–31.

59. Gould, p. 110.

60. Coleman, pp. 229–31.

61. Ibid., p. 233.

62. Ibid., pp. 235–37.

63. First report of the Select Committee of the House of Lords 1852–3, Parliamentary Papers, 1852–3, p. xxxi.

64. Gould, pp. 136–7, explains this most clearly.

65. J. B. R. Nicholson, illustrated by Michael Roffe, *The Gurkha Rifles* (Osprey, London, 1974), pp. 4–9, Plates A and B; Mike Chappell, *The Gurkhas* (Osprey, London, 1994), pp. 12–13, Plates A and B. Chappell gives the acquisition of the 66th's identity – and red coats – as 1849, but Napier's first order is clearly from February 1850. The 3rd Gurkhas officially adopted khaki in the field in 1878, but it is widely believed the Kumaon Battalion wore some form of brown or khaki during the Indian Mutiny.

66. Christopher Hibbert, *The Great Mutiny: India 1857* (Penguin, London, 1980), p. 55. This is probably the best single-volume history of the mutiny.

67. Farwell, *The Gurkhas*, p. 41; Gould, pp. 110–11. On p. 111 he also refers to the same sentiment, but in a different incident.

68. Gould, p. 112, citing Field Marshal Lord Roberts of Kandahar, *Forty-One Years in India* (one-volume edition, London, 1898), p. 54; Roberts VC, *London Gazette*, no. 22212, p. 5516, 24 December 1858.

69. Farwell, p. 41.

70. Ibid., p. 42.

71. http://www.britishempire.co.uk/forces/armycampaigns/indiancampaigns/mutiny/delhi.htm. This is an excellent account of the 'siege' of Delhi, with good contemporary maps.

72. Major Charles Reid, *1857–1957 Centenary of the Siege of Delhi. The Defence of the Main Piquet at Hindoo Rao's House and other Posts on the Ridge as recorded by Major Reid Commanding the Sirmoor Battalion, 2d K E VII's Own Gurkha Rifles (The Sirmoor Rifles). Extracts from Letters and Notes Written during the Siege of Delhi in 1857 by General Sir Charles Reid GCB* (Gurkha Museum, Winchester), p.13.

73. Gould, p. 113; Farwell, pp. 43–4.

74. Reid, *1857–1957 Centenary of the Siege of Delhi*, p. 14.

75. http://www.britishempire.co.uk/forces/armycampaigns/ indiancampaigns/mutiny/delhi.htm, accessed 21 July 2010.

76. Reid, *1857–1957 Centenary of the Siege of Delhi*, p. 15.

77. Ibid., p. 16.

78. Ibid., p. 16.

79. Farwell, p. 46.

80. Reid, *1857–1957 Centenary of the Siege of Delhi*, p. 28.

81. James Hare to his father, 24 June 1857, cited in Gould, p. 114.

82. Interview with Gavin Edgerley-Harris, Gurkha Museum, 21 April 2010.

83. Field Marshal Roberts (1898) gives slightly different figures to the official history, saying that the Gurkhas started with 450 men and then received reinforcements of a further 90, making 540. Gould, p. 116.

84. Gould, pp. 115–16.

85. Gould, p. 116; Farwell, p. 46; Bullock, pp. 38–9; http://www. britishempire.co.uk/forces/armycampaigns/indiancampaigns/ mutiny/delhi.htm, accessed 21 July 2010.

86. NA (Kew), WO 32/7311, Victoria Cross (India) Recommendations approved by the Queen, extract from General Orders, 17 July 1857. The file was closed for fifty years until 1909.

87. Ibid., 13 August 1857.

88. http://www.britishempire.co.uk/forces/armyunits/corpsofguides/ corpsofguides.htm provides an excellent account of the Guides. Accessed 20 July 2010.

89. Ibid.

90. NA (Kew) WO 32/7311, 16 September 1857. Despatch from Major General Wilson, commanding Delhi Field Force.

91. Ibid., 22 September 1857. Major General Wilson to adjutant general of the army.

92. Ibid., 4 December 1857.

93. UK Ministry of Defence, Defence Internet, Honours and Awards, accessed 21 July 2010. The most recent award to a living recipient at

the time of writing was to Private Johnson Beharry of the Princess of Wales's Royal Regiment in March 2005 for an action in Iraq in May 2004. I am grateful for this advice to my friend Professor Richard Holmes, who, as a retired brigadier, was regimental colonel of the Princess of Wales's Regiment at the time, and therefore very knowledgeable on the matter.

94. WO 32/7311, letter, 17 March 1858, minute of 9 March, to Sir Henry Storks, then employed (from 1857 to 1859) by the War Office as Secretary for Military Correspondence.

95. Ibid., letter of 27 March 1858 with recommendations for ten VCs.

96. Ibid., letter dated 16 April 1858, Minute to Sir Henry Storks dated 12 April.

97. Tytler died of pneumonia aged fifty-four. He is buried at Kohat, in the North-West Frontier province of Pakistan. See http://www.findagrave.com/cgi-bin/fg.cgi?page=gr&GRid=11390718, accessed 20 July 2010.

98. Hibbert, p. 367.

99. Ibid., p. 382.

100. Gould, p. 117; Marrion and Fosten, pp. 19, 31. The regimental historian of the 8th expressed concern that they were not honoured for the Sylhets' role in 1857.

101. See 'The Indian Revolt', *New York Daily Tribune*, 16 September 1857 (despatch from London, 4 September 1857). Marx does not use the term.

102. Hibbert, pp. 390, 432.

103. Gould, p. 116.

CHAPTER 4: RIFLEMEN, AND AFGHANISTAN'S PLAINS . . .

1. Rudyard Kipling, 'The Young British Soldier', in Rudyard Kipling, ed. R. T. Jones, *The Collected Poems of Rudyard Kipling* (Wordsworth Poetry Library, Ware, Hertfordshire, 1994), pp. 439–40.

2. The fictitious character in Bernard Cornwell's historical novels, dramatised as a TV series in the 1990s.

3. As in *motostrelkovye voyska* – 'motor-rifle forces'. In the 1941–5 war large numbers of regiments, divisions and corps were designated 'rifle', as opposed to 'infantry'. A rifle is a *vintovka*, from *vint*, a screw.

4. The breakthrough was the ingeniously simple Minié rifle, which had a cup in the base of a cylindro-conical bullet (as opposed to the traditional ball), which could still be dropped down the barrel quickly. However, when the rifle was fired, the gases pushed out the edge of the cup, expanding the base of the bullet to engage the rifling, thus imparting the spin necessary to carry it accurately towards a distant target. The British used it with terrible effect against the less well-armed Russians in the 1854–6 Crimean War, and the figure of 200,000 battle dead in the 1861–5 American Civil War owed much to it. After the Indian Mutiny, there were some who still opposed giving rifles, as opposed to smooth-bore muskets, to 'native' troops.

5. 'The truncheon stands just under 6 ft. high, is chiefly of bronze, and is surmounted by the Royal Crown in silver supported by three Gurkha riflemen in bronze. On a ring of silver below the figures are inscribed the words "Main Picquet, Hindoo Rao's House, Delhi, 1857". Below this ring is a representation in bronze of one of the minarets on the Delhi Gate of the Palace of the Moguls and in the minaret hang two silver crossed kukris, the national weapon of the Gurkha. Below this again comes another silver ring on which is inscribed on three sides "Sirmoor Rifles". On a third ring just above the upper end of the staff, the words "Main Picquet, Hindoo Rao's House, Delhi, 1857" are again inscribed, this time in the "nagri" script.' Marrion and Fosten, pp. 11–12.

6. Conversation with Gavin Edgerley-Harris, Archivist, Gurkha Museum, Winchester, 21 April 2010; Marrion and Fosten, pp. 11–12.

7. Marrion and Fosten, pp. 8, 11, 17, 19, 21. It will be remembered that the British Army standardised spelling of 'Gurkha' was introduced in 1891.

8. 'Frontier Force – British Raj', http://www.globalsecurity.org/military/world/pakistan/rgt-ff-1.htm, retrieved 19 August 2010.

9. Gould, pp. 136–7.

10. Ibid., p. 118. Peel was involved in the arguments over the award of VCs – WO, 32/7311, 9 March 1858 and 17 March 1858.

11. Gould, p. 118.

12. Sir Henry Lawrence, 'Military Defence of Our Indian Empire' (1844), reprinted in *Essays, Military and Political, Written in India* (London, 1859), p. 57.

13. Gould, p. 120.

14. Sources: Farwell, pp. 293–4; Gould, pp. 12, 171, 173, 293–4, 325,

339, 386, 402, 417; Gurkha Terms and Conditions of Service Review, http://www.arrse.co.uk/gurkhas/48491-gurkha-terms-conditions-service-review.html, accessed 22 July 2010; Bullock, pp. 263-4. The humorously named website (ARmy Rumour SErvice) is used by serving personnel of the British Army and is a major source of current information on it.

15. http://www.bharat-rakshak.com/LAND-FORCES/Heraldry/Ranks/23-Rank-Insignias.html, retrieved 22 July 2010.

16. Gould, pp. 75–91.

17. Gould, p. 101.

18. Key ingredients of the nineteenth-century 'revolution in warfare' – the railway, the telegraph and photography – also led to a media revolution. Trains meant newspapers could be distributed far more widely, so more could be sold. And while people were waiting for them, they were a captive market for newspapers. The telegraph meant that correspondents could file their copy soon after the event, and photography led to a completely new form of journalism.

19. William Howard Russell, *My Diary in India, in the Year 1858–9* (London, 1860), pp. 197–209.

20. Gould, pp. 104–5.

21. Ibid., p. 105, citing Leo E. Rose, *Nepal: Strategy for Survival* (Berkeley, California, 1971), p. 133.

22. Gould, p. 105.

23. Ibid., p. 106.

24. Major General Sir John Mitchell, *Thoughts on Tactics and Military Organisation together with an Enquiry into the Power and Position of Russia* (London, 1838). For views of Russia, see Irving H. Smith, 'An English view of Russia in the early eighteenth century', *Canadian Slavic Studies*, vol. 1, no. 2 (Summer 1967), pp. 276–83; and the author's 'British views of Russia', in Towle (ed.), pp. 37–76.

25. Smith, p. 277.

26. Interestingly, Abraham Lincoln, the US president who freed the slaves, said on 24 August 1855: 'When it comes to this, I should prefer emigrating to some country where they make no pretense of loving liberty – to Russia, for instance, where despotism can be taken pure, and without the base alloy of hypocracy.' Accessed on http://www.carrothers.com/lincoln.htm, retrieved 26 July 2010.

27. *Sbornik geograficheskikh, topograficheskikh i statisticheskikh materialov po Azii*, vols XLI, XLIV, XLIX. Available in the British Library.

28. Sir George Clarke, 'Note on threatened invasions of India and their effect on British policy', in *Memoranda and Notes by Sir George Clarke while Secretary of the Committee of Imperial Defence 1904–07*, document no. 41, 3 April 1905, p. 5.

29. NA (Kew), CAB XCIA 632, *General Kouropatkine's scheme for a Russian Advance upon India, with Notes thereon by Lord Roberts*, August 1891, printed for the Committee of Imperial Defence, March 1903, pp. 1–5.

30. M. I. Ivanin, *Opisaniye Zimnyago Pokhoda (Description of the Winter Expedition* [the Expedition to Khiva, 1839–40]), (St Petersburg, 1874), p. 4.

31. Sir Colin MacGregor, *The Defence of India: A Strategical Study* (Simla, 1884), p. 142.

32. Ibid., pp. 9, 41, 48, 51 (quotation from the last).

33. WO 33/337, *Reports of British Observers*, cited in Philip Towle, 'The Influence of the Russo-Japanese War on British Naval and Military Thought 1905-14', PhD thesis, London University, 1973, p. 297.

34. Nirad Chaudhuri, 'The "Martial Races" of India', Parts I–IV, *The Modern Review* (Calcutta, July 1930–February 1931). This, part IV, February 1931, p. 218.

35. Ibid., Part II, September 1930, p. 306.

36. Marrion and Fosten, pp. 25–7, 31–5, 37.

37. Ian Heath and Michael Perry, *The North-East Frontier 1837–1901* (Osprey, Oxford, 1999), p. 3. This is an excellent and almost unique study of an almost forgotten theatre.

38. Ibid., pp. 8, 15.

39. R. G. Woodthorpe, Lieutenant Royal Engineers, *The Lushai Expedition, 1871 1872* (Hurst and Blackett Publishers, London, 1873), accessed through http://www.archive.org/stream/ lushaiexpedition00woodrich/lushaiexpedition00woodrich_djvu.txt (full text), retrieved 25 July 2010; Reprinted as Lieut. R. G. Woodthorpe RE, *The Lushai Expedition, 1871 1872* (Naval and Military Press, London, 2004).

40. Woodthorpe, pp. 39–41; Heath and Perry, *The North-East Frontier*, p. 8.

41. Woodthorpe, p. 115.

42. Ibid., pp. 115–16.

43. Ibid., p. 143.

44. Defining what was of chief value to the enemy – what is now known as axiological targeting (from the Greek *axios* – 'worth') – was, and is,

always a problem in asymmetric conflict against actors who are not conventional, developed nation states. As Callwell observed, 'But when there is no king to conquer, no capital to seize, no organized army to overthrow, and when there are no celebrated strongholds to capture, and no great centres of population to occupy, the objective is not so easy to select.' He cites Lord Wolseley: 'your first object should be the capture of whatever they prize most.' And then, 'If the enemy cannot be touched through his patriotism or his honour, then he can be touched through his pocket.' Callwell, *Small Wars* (1906 edition, ed. Porch, 1996), p. 40.

45. Source: http://www.armynavyairforce.co.uk/indian_army.htm. An excellent site. Retrieved 25 July 2010. Citation: http://www.army.mod.uk/gurkhas/14281.aspx, Honours and Awards, Victoria Cross. Retrieved 25 July 2010.

46. Source: http://www.victoriacross.co.uk/descrip_m.html, retrieved 25 July 2010. Citation: in *London Gazette*, no. 23902, p. 4489, 27 September 1872. Major General MacIntyre's obituary appeared in *The Times*, 17 April 1903.

47. Heath and Perry, *The North-East Frontier*, p. 8.

48. Harold E. Raugh, Jr, 'Storming the Rebel Strongholds: The Perak War, 1875-1876', *Soldiers of the Queen*, Journal of the Victorian Military Society (England), vol. 102 (September 2000), pp. 7–12.

49. Citation in http://www.army.mod.uk/gurkhas/14281.aspx, Honours and Awards, Victoria Cross. Retrieved 25 July 2010.

50. Heath and Perry, *The North-East Frontier*, pp. 8–9.

51. Citation in http://www.army.mod.uk/gurkhas/14281.aspx, Honours and Awards, Victoria Cross. Retrieved 25 July 2010.

52. Pierre Louis Napoleon Cavagnari was the descendant of an old noble Italian family from Palma who served the Bonaparte family and therefore entered French service. He was therefore the son of a French general by his marriage with an Irish lady, and was born in France on 4 July 1841. He was naturalised as a UK citizen and joined the military service of the East India Company. He passed through the East India Company military college at Addiscombe, and served through the Oudh campaign against the mutineers in 1858 and 1859.

53. See David Loyn, BBC correspondent, whom the author was privileged to invite to address his students in 2009, *Butcher and Bolt: Two Hundred Years of Foreign Involvement in Afghanistan* (Hutchinson, London, 2008).

54. Brian Robson, *The Road to Kabul: The Second Afghan War, 1878–1881* (Spellmount, Staplehurst, UK, 2003), is a good recent account. Also Fremont-Barnes, *The Anglo-Afghan Wars*, pp. 43–78.

55. Farwell, p. 57.

56. See, for example, Bullock, p. 54. A Google search will find that Kipling never said that, exactly, but he meant it by what he said in the last verse of 'The Young British Soldier'.

57. Rudyard Kipling, 'The Young British Soldier', in Rudyard Kipling, ed. R. T. Jones, *The Collected Poems of Rudyard Kipling* (Wordsworth Poetry Library, Ware, Hertfordshire, 1994), pp. 439–40.

58. There are numerous accounts of the treatment of British and Indian prisoners and wounded from the 1880s until 1947, and of Soviet prisoners and wounded from the 1980s. The bodies of Soviet soldiers recovered after falling to the Mujaheddin were sometimes repatriated in steel coffins welded shut, so the relatives could not see what had been done to them. For a British report, see the ground-breaking account by John Morris, a gay officer who served on the North-West Frontier, and was later Controller of the BBC Third Programme, in *Hired to Kill: Some Chapters of Autobiography* (Rupert Hart-Davis, in association with The Cresset Press, London, 1960), pp. 131–3, cited in Chapter 7.

59. *Rescuing the wounded under fire in Afghanistan* is a painting depicting an action in the 1890s on display in the atrium in the UK Joint Services' Command and Staff College, Shrivenham.

60. This is the rifle made famous in the Cy Endfield film *Zulu* (1963), depicting the defence of Rorke's Drift in Natal, South Africa, at the same time – 1879. The Martini-Henry was an excellent weapon, but could overheat and jam after firing about twenty-four rounds very quickly. Specimen (decommissioned) in the author's possession, courtesy of Robert Shaw, who brought it back from Afghanistan.

61. Callwell, *Small Wars* (1906, republished with Porch introduction, 1996), Chapter IX, pp. 108–9. The force that invaded Zululand in January 1879 comprised three columns, each quite big enough to hold off the entire Zulu army. The problem came when Lord Chelmsford split no. 3 column further, leaving part of it at Isandhlwana – permanently.

62. Sam Browne had lost an arm in the Indian Mutiny and therefore had a belt specially designed to allow him to draw his sword with only one hand, while still keeping the scabbard stable. It has a robust

waist-belt and one or two cross-straps, designed to hold steady the scabbard and 'frog' into which it fits. It was subsequently adopted as the standard accoutrement of officers and senior warrant officers throughout much of the British Army, except for cavalry, artillery (later), and rifles (including the Gurkhas), who wore cross-belts. It is also worn with formal uniform by officers of British Commonwealth armies, and by the Russians.

63. Fremont-Barnes, *The Anglo-Afghan Wars*, pp. 56–8.

64. Citation in http://www.army.mod.uk/gurkhas/14281.aspx, Honours and Awards, Victoria Cross. Retrieved 25 July 2010.

65. http://www.britishbattles.com/second-afghan-war/peiwar-kotal.htm. Retrieved 19 July 2010.

66. Fremont-Barnes, *The Anglo-Afghan Wars*, pp. 62–3.

67. The force also comprised 3rd Sikh Infantry (53rd Sikhs), 23rd Bengal Native Infantry (Pioneers), 29th Bengal Native Infantry and 5th Punjab Infantry, Punjab Frontier Force.

68. http://www.britishbattles.com/second-afghan-war/charasiab.htm. Retrieved 19 July 2010.

69. Baronet in 1881, baron in 1892, earl in 1900; Bullock, p. 51.

70. After relinquishing his Indian command in 1893, Lord Roberts returned to his homeland two years later as commander-in-chief of British forces in Ireland, becoming field marshal in 1895. Four years years after that he returned to South Africa to replace General Sir Redvers Buller, who had not done well in the opening phases of the Boer War. He turned the situation round and was in turn succeeded in command by Kitchener. See Brian Hodgson (2008); 'Roberts, Frederick Sleigh, First Earl Roberts, 1832–1914', *Oxford Dictionary of National Biography*, Oxford University Press, doi:10.1093/ref:odnb/35768.

71. For example, javelin throwing, archery, fencing, riding and shooting, or skiing and shooting – the biathlon.

72. Cited in http://www.garenewing.co.uk/angloafghanwar/marchtokandahar/regiments_march.php, retrieved 19 July 2010. Roberts's explanation, 1897.

73. Bruce Collins, 'Fighting the Afghans in the 19th century', *History Today*, vol. 51, no. 12 (December 2001), pp. 12–19, accessed on http://www.historytoday.com/MainArticle. aspx?m=17795&amid=17795, retrieved 19 July 2010.

74. Bullock, p. 51.

75. NAM, C. A. M. (C. A. Mercer), *Afghanistan 1878–79–80, Book of 2nd Afghan War*, 6903–8.
76. These details are helpfully given in http://www.garenewing.co.uk/angloafghanwar/marchtokandahar/regiments_march.php. Retrieved 19 July 2010.
77. http://www.britishbattles.com/second-afghan-war/kandahar.htm, retrieved 26 July 2010. This website incorrectly suggests that George White of the 92nd, won his VC at Kandahar: he had already won it at Charasiab.
78. http://www.sgwmfb.co.uk/sirgeorgewhite.htm, retrieved 26 July 2010.
79. Brevet Major E. R. Elles RA, *Report on Nepal* (Calcutta, 1884), pp. 44–5, cited in Gould, pp. 128, 437.
80. Ibid.
81. Gould, pp. 129, 437, citing Purushottam Banskota, *The Gurkha Connection: A History of the Gurkha Recruitment in the British Indian Army* (Jaipur, 1994).
82. Gould, pp. 130, 437.
83. Gurkha Museum, recruitment report by Captain C. A. Mercer, July/August 1886, cited in Gould, pp. 131, 437.
84. Gould, pp. 131–2.
85. Ibid., pp. 132–3.
86. Frederick Hamilton-Temple-Blackwood, 1st Marquess of Dufferin and Ava (21 June 1826–12 February 1902). He was Viceroy from 1884 to 1896. See 'Dufferin and Ava, Marquess of', *Encyclopaedia Britannica*, 11th edition, 1911.
87. Gould, pp. 134–5.

CHAPTER 5: GURKHAS IN THE 'GREAT GAME'

1. Transliteration from the Russian is an inexact science. Sometimes spelled Grombtchevski, or Grombachevsky. The author uses the Nato system for the Russian, which accurately mirrors the Polish pronunciation, Grombchevskiy.
2. Patrick French, *Younghusband: The Last Great Imperial Adventurer* (HarperCollins, London, 1994), pp. 67–8. This award-winning book is recommended.

3. Ibid., p. 69, citing Francis Younghusband, *The Heart of a Continent* (John Murray, London, 1896) p. 229.

4. Ibid., p. 72, citing Younghusband, *The Heart of a Continent*, p. 261.

5. Ibid., pp. 72–3, citing Francis Younghusband, *Report on a Mission to the Northern Frontier of Kashmir in 1889* (Calcutta, 1890, reprinted as *The Northern Frontier of Kashmir*, New Delhi, 1973), p. 52 of the latter.

6. Ibid., p. 75, citing Younghusband, *The Heart of a Continent* (1896), p. 268.

7. Ibid., pp. 75–6.

8. Ibid., p. 76, citing Younghusband, *The Heart of a Continent* (1896), pp. 268–72.

9. Ibid., p. 76; photograph, double page halfway between pp. 120 and 121.

10. Ibid., p. 76, citing Younghusband, *The Heart of a Continent* (1896), p. 272.

11. Ibid., p. 80, citing Younghusband, *Wonders of the Himalaya* (London, 1924), pp. 199–200.

12. Ibid., pp. 96–7.

13. Colonel Algernon Durand CB CIE, British agent at Gilgit 1889–94, Military Secretary to the Viceroy of India 1894–9, *The Making of a Frontier: Five Years' Experiences and Adventures in Gilgit, Hunza, Nagar, Chitral and the Eastern Hindu-Kush* (Thomas Nelson, London, Edinburgh, Dublin and New York, 1899), scanned in full at http://www.tertullian.org/rpearse/scanned/durand.htm, retrieved 28 July 2010. E. F. Knight, *Where Three Empires Meet: Travel in Kashmir, Tibet and Gilgit* (London, 1893), republished by Saujanya Books, Srinagar, 2007. In the 1890s the Russians introduced an excellent new magazine rifle, the 0.3-inch (7.62-mm) Mosin model 1891, which, in slightly modified form, was in service throughout the Second World War and, with a telescopic sight, made an excellent sniper rifle.

14. Knight, *Where Three Empires Meet*.

15. *London Gazette*, 12 July 1872, accessed at http://www.army.mod.uk/gurkhas/14281.aspx, Honours and Awards, Victoria Cross. Retrieved 25 July 2010.

16. NAM 2005-10-57, Letters of Algernon Durand to Lord Roberts 1891–1898, transcribed by D. Anderson for subsequent article, 'The Friends at Gilgit 1888–1895: Algernon Durand and George Scott

Robertson', *Journal of the Society for Army Historical Research* (2004). Letter 1, p. 2 of the archival transcription.

17. Aylmer: http://en.wikipedia.org/wiki/List_of_Victoria_Cross_recipients_by_campaign, retrieved 22 July 2010. Although scholars are normally discouraged from using Wikipedia, this list is reliable. According to the citation in http://www.victoriacross.co.uk/descrip_a.html, Aylmer 'forced open the inner gate with gun-cotton which he had placed and ignited, and although severely wounded, fired 19 shots with his revolver, killing several of the enemy, and remained fighting until, fainting from loss of blood, he was carried out of action'.

18. *London Gazette*, 12 July 1872, accessed at http://www.army.mod.uk/gurkhas/14281.aspx, Honours and Awards, Victoria Cross. Retrieved 25 July 2010.

19. An excellent account is Robert Johnson, *The 1897 Revolt and Tirah Valley Operations from the Pashtun Perspective* (Tribal Analysis Center, Williamsburg, VA, 2007), accessed at http://www.tribalanalysiscenter.com/PDF-TAC/The%201897%20Revolt%20and%20Tirah%20Valley%20Operations. Retrieved 25 July 2010. This, p. 6.

20. Ibid., pp. 8–9; Colonel H. D. Hutchinson, *The Campaign in Tirah, 1897–98* (London, 1898), p. 129.

21. Major General Nigel Woodyatt, Colonel 7th Gurkhas (ed.), *The Regimental History of the 3rd Queen Alexandra's Own Gurkha Rifles from April 1815 to December 1927*, (Philip Allan, London, 1929), pp. 69–70.

22. Cited in T. R. Moreman, *The Army in India and the Development of Frontier Warfare, 1849–1947* (Macmillan, London, 1998), p. 55.

23. Woodyatt (ed.), *The Regimental History of the 3rd . . . Gurkhas*, p. 70.

24. Ibid.

25. Ibid.

26. *History of the 5th Royal Gurkha Rifles (Frontier Force) 1858 to 1928* (for private circulation only), (printed and published for the Regimental Committee by Gale and Polden, Aldershot, London and Portsmouth, 1929), p. 139.

27. [Charles] John Morris, *Hired to Kill: Some Chapters of Autobiography* (Rupert Hart-Davis in association with The Cresset Press, London, 1960), p. 141. Morris served with 2nd Battalion, 3rd Gurkhas and accompanied Bruce on two Everest expeditions.

28. Woodyatt (ed.), *The Regimental History of the 3rd . . . Gurkhas*, p. 75; *History of the 5th Royal Gurkha Rifles*, p. 153.

29. Courtesy of the Gurkha Museum. Photographs courtesy of Carl Schultze, defence journalist.

30. Callwell, *Small Wars*, p. 472.

31. Johnson, *The 1897 Revolt*, p. 1. See also Hutchinson, *The Campaign in Tirah, 1897–98*.

32. Woodyatt (ed.), *The Regimental History of the 3rd . . . Gurkhas*, p. 68.

33. Ibid.

34. Johnson, *The 1897 Revolt*, p. 13

35. Bullock, p. 52 (painting), pp. 54–5.

36. Johnson, *The 1897 Revolt*, p. 13; Woodyatt (ed.), *The Regimental History of the 3rd . . . Gurkhas*, p. 68.

37. If you must enquire further, http://www.colonialwargaming.co.uk/ Inspiration/Poetry/McGonagall/Dargai.htm. Retrieved 26 July 2010.

38. *History of the 5th Royal Gurkha Rifles*, pp. 142–3.

39. Ibid., p. 143.

40. Ibid., p. 152.

41. Ibid.

42. Ibid.

43. Ibid., p. 151.

44. Ibid.

45. The Lee-Metford was still in widespread use in the 1899–1902 Boer War. The Lee-Enfield, first introduced in 1895, and which remained in regular British Army service until the 1950s, was of almost identical design, but adapted for the use of cordite, which necessitated deeper rifling.

46. *History of the 5th Royal Gurkha Rifles*, p. 152.

47. Morris, *Hired to Kill*, p. 68.

48. http://www.army.mod.uk/gurkhas/14281.aspx, Honours and Awards, Victoria Cross. Retrieved 25 July 2010.

49. Gould, pp. 169–70; French, *Younghusband*, pp. 202–72.

50. French, *Younghusband*, p. 237.

51. http://www.army.mod.uk/gurkhas/14281.aspx, Honours and Awards, Victoria Cross. Retrieved 25 July 2010.

52. Ibid.

53. Marrion and Fosten, pp. 25–37.

54. Byron Farwell, *Armies of the Raj, from The Great Indian Mutiny to Independence 1858–1947* (W.W. Norton and Company, London, 1991), pp. 205–6.

55. A spectacular extract from the film can be viewed on http://
talkieking.blogspot.com/2010/03/color-in-movies-part-1-
kinemacolor.html, accessed 30 July 2010.

CHAPTER 6: THE GREAT WAR FOR CIVILISATION, 1914–19

1. The inscription on the back of the medal issued to all British empire
participants. Although the Armistice came on 11 November 1918,
the war did not formally end until the Treaty of Versailles in 1919.
2. Farwell, *Armies of the Raj*, pp. 204–15. See also http://
www.indianetzone.com/35/curzon_kitchener_conflict_1902-1905_
british_india.htm, retrieved 30 July 2010.
3. Army Department Order no. 981, dated 26 October 1894.
4. Farwell, *Armies of the Raj*, p. 216.
5. Ibid.
6. Ibid, pp. 215–16. Whether the staff course addled the officers' brains
is unclear, but the slang phrase 'doolally' apparently originates from
psychological problems encountered by some people while stationed
there. The Pakistani Staff College now educates captains and majors
with ten to twelve years' service.
7. Gould, pp. 175–6.
8. Gould, pp. 165–6.
9. Information in displays on these senior Nepalese regiments in the
museum at Gorkha, Nepal. Author's visit 9 June 2010.
10. Lieutenant Hamish Reid to Colonel and Mrs Reid, 11 September
1914, in BL Asia-Pacific and African Collection, formerly Oriental
and India Office Collections (OIOCC) – OIOCC: MSS Eur.
F206/315–16, cited in Gould p. 177.
11. Bullock, p. 57.
12. Reid, 11 September 1914, cited in Gould, p. 177.
13. Gould, p. 178.
14. F. S. Poynder, *The 9th Gurkha Rifles, 1817–1936* (London, 1937),
p. 81. The 9th became the 9th Gurkhas in 1894, but the regiment
traces its origins to the Fategarh Levy of 1817.
15. Cited in Gould, p. 178. Kismet means 'fate' in Turkish. It may be the
origin of Nelson's enigmatic last words, 'Kiss me Hardy' – '*Kismet,
Hardy.*'

16. Farwell, p. 249.

17. General Sir James Willcocks, *With the Indians in France* (London 1920), pp. 82–7.

18. Gould, pp. 179–80.

19. Cited in Charles Chenevix-Trench, *The Indian Army and the King's Enemies 1900–1947* (London, 1988), p. 37.

20. NAM, Bagot-Chester War Diary, 31 December 1914.

21. Ibid., 5 February 1915.

22. http://www.tribuneindia.com/2000/20001104/windows/main1. htm 4 November 2000, retrieved 20 July 2010; Farwell, *Armies of the Raj*, pp. 249–50.

23. Gould, p. 184.

24. An excellent account of the battle and its place in Allied planning is http://www.1914-1918.net/bat13.htm, retrieved 30 July 2010.

25. *London Gazette*, 18 November 1915; http://www.army.mod.uk/ gurkhas/14281.aspx, retrieved 30 July 2010.

26. The Gurkha Museum, *The Allanson Diary: Gallipoli 1915*, Introduction by Lieutenant Colonel M. J. F. Wardroper, CO 6th Queen Elizabeth's Own Gurkha Rifles, January 1977, p. 8.

27. Gould, pp. 188–9. He makes good points.

28. Ibid., p. 188.

29. Geoffrey Miller, 'Turkey Enters the War and British Actions', http://www.gwpda.org/naval/turkmill.htm, retrieved 30 July 2010.

30. Cited in Bullock, p. 67.

31. Major Cecil Allanson, writing of Bruce after visiting him in hospital on 16 July 1915, cited in Gould, p. 190.

32. The Gurkha Museum, *The Allanson Diary: Gallipoli 1915*, p. 2. Allanson himself had attended the Indian Staff College when it opened at Deolali in 1905. See the CV on pp. 62–4.

33. The best account, and an exemplary piece of readable military history, is Alan Moorehead, *Gallipoli* (Hamish Hamilton, London, 1956). Also Philip J. Haythornthwaite, *Gallipoli 1915: Frontal Assault on Turkey* (Osprey, Oxford and New York, 1991). Both contain outstanding graphics, which are utterly indispensable to any understanding of what went on.

34. Gould, p. 190.

35. John Parker, *The Gurkhas: The Inside Story of the World's Most Feared Soldiers* (Headline Books, London, 1999), p. 118. Although a popular

account, the treatment of Gallipoli is one of the most detailed available in that genre.

36. Ibid.

37. Cited in Parker, pp. 119–20.

38. For a list of all the place names to be encountered in the complex Gallipoli landscape, see http://www.anzac.govt.nz/gallipoliguide/gallipolinames.html, retrieved 31 July 2010.

39. Bullock, pp. 68–9.

40. *The Allanson Diary*, p. 20.

41. Moorehead, *Gallipoli*, pp. 282–3.

42. Several slightly differing versions are cited. This full citation is reproduced verbatim from the Gurkha Museum's copy of *The Allanson Diary: Gallipoli 1915*, pp. 26–7. A faithful reproduction of this part is in Moorehead, p. 285, and Parker, p. 122. Some versions omit the phrase 'blood was flying about like spray from a hairwash bottle'. Also http://www.6thgurkhas.org/website/regiment-battles/gallipoli-campaign.

43. *The Allanson Diary*, pp. 26–7. The segment '*when I saw a flash in the bay*' (emphasis added), referring to the navy firing, is often omitted. It does not appear in Moorehead, p. 285 and Parker, p. 122.

44. Haythornthwaite, p. 73.

45. I am grateful to Andy Mullen, a former student of mine on the Cranfield Global Security MSc, now a security consultant, who has conducted battlefield tours of Gallipoli, for his insights into the mystery based on detailed reconnaissance and knowledge of the ground.

46. 'Predicted fire' – fire from the map alone, without adjustment, was developed in response to the requirements of trench warfare on the Western Front, and depended on precise maps and meteorological data. It would have been a very risky business in 1915.

47. Gould, p. 191.

48. Allanson to Cox, 0630 hours, 9 August 1915 in Indian Brigade War Diary, cited in Robin Prior, *Gallipoli: The End of the Myth* (Yale University Press, New Haven and London, 2009), p. 182.

49. Prior, ibid.

50. Gould, p. 191.

51. *The Allanson Diary*, p. 65. Ab. 3338, HQ New Zealand and Australian Division 17.8.[1]5, To Australian and New Zealand Army Corps (Sir William Birdwood).

52. *The Allanson Diary*, p. 28.

53. Ibid., pp. 33–4; Haythornthwaite, p. 73; Gould, p. 192; Bullock, p. 72.

54. Cited in Gould, p. 192, Parker p. 125.

55. Parker, p. 126.

56. Moorehead, pp. 334–55, for a stupendous account.

57. Cited in http://www.6thgurkhas.org/website/regiment-battles/gallipoli-campaign, retrieved 31 July 2010.

58. Cited in Gould, p. 190.

59. Gould, p. 193, Farwell, *The Gurkhas*, p. 107.

60. NA HO 45/10838/331607/3: 1917–18; *Report of the Commission appointed by Act of Parliament to enquire into the Operations of War in Mesopotamia, Together with a Separate Report by Commander J. Wedgwood, D.S.O., M.P., and Appendices*, Cmnd 8610; Crown copyright.

61. Lieutenant General Sir Aylmer Haldane, *The Insurrection in Mesopotamia 1920* (William Blackwood, Edinburgh and London, 1920), p. 8.

62. Gould, pp. 192–3, citing Allanson's diary, with scepticism, also; Parker, p. 128.

63. Gould, pp. 193–4.

64. Norman Dixon, *On the Psychology of Military Incompetence* (Cape, London, 1976), p. 105.

65. Colonel J. N. Mackay, *History of the 7th Duke of Edinburgh's Own Gurkha Rifles* (Edinburgh, 1962), p. 56.

66. Ibid.

67. Bullock, pp. 75–7.

68. Ibid., p. 77.

69. *Nepal and the Gurkhas*, pp. 117, 119, 132.

70. *London Gazette*, 8 June 1917, cited in http://www.army.mod.uk/gurkhas/14281.aspx.

71. Bullock, p. 80.

72. http://www.firstworldwar.com/battles/ramadi.htm, retrieved 31 July 2010.

73. Bullock, p. 81.

74. Ibid., p. 82.

75. http://www.firstworldwar.com/battles/sharqat.htm, retrieved 31 July 2010; Bullock, p. 83.

76. Gould, p. 196.

77. *London Gazette*, 21 April 1918, cited in http://www.army.mod.uk/gurkhas/14281.aspx.

78. The best coverage by far is James Nicholson, *The Hejaz Railway*

(Stacey International, London and al Turah, Riyadh, 2005). See also James Nicholson, 'The Hejaz Railway', *Asian Affairs*, vol. XXXVII, no. III, November 2006.

79. 'Pheon', 'A Gurkha with Lawrence', *Journal of the United Service Institution of India*, vol. 72, no. 307 (1942), pp. 124–9.
80. T. E. Lawrence, *Seven Pillars of Wisdom* (Penguin, in association with Jonathan Cape, London, 1962), introductory chapter, p. 22.
81. 'Pheon', 'A Gurkha with Lawrence', pp. 125–6.
82. Ibid., p. 127.
83. Ibid., p. 128.
84. Conversation with Gavin Edgerley-Harris, curator, Gurkha Museum, who found the article, 30 July 2010.
85. 'Pheon', 'A Gurkha with Lawrence', p. 129.
86. The Gurkha Museum, *The Lineages and Composition of the Gurkha Regiments in British Service* (2010 edition), p. 125.
87. Lawrence, *Seven Pillars of Wisdom* (1962), introductory chapter, p. 22.

CHAPTER 7: EMPIRE UNDER THREAT

1. NA WO 32/13087, *Report of the Committee on the Lessons of the Great War*, October 1932, p. 29. There is an earlier version, 8 July 1932, in the Liddell Hart Military Archive at King's College London (LHCMA) LH 10/1932/111, 8 July 1932.
2. Gary Sheffield, *Forgotten Victory: The First World War: Myths and Realities* (Headline, London, 2001).
3. The Gurkha Museum, *The Second Afghan War 1878–1880 and the Third Afghan War 1919* (The Gurkha Museum, August 2009), p. 16; Fremont-Barnes, *The Anglo-Afghan Wars*, pp. 80–4.
4. Gould, p. 205, citing article by Brig McCallum of 1975.
5. Ibid.
6. Bullock, pp. 85–6.
7. Morris, *Hired to Kill*, p. 65
8. Ibid.
9. Fremont-Barnes, p. 85.
10. Morris, *Hired to Kill*, p. 47.
11. Ibid., p. 48. The other reason my grandfather was commissioned was probably a discarded copy of *The Times* that he picked up on the

endless train journey to the commissioning board. Bored, he read it over and over again. At the board, the first question was 'What was the leader in *The Times* this morning, Sergeant Buckland?' He replied, 'It was about cricket, sir. Actually, I'm rather a keen cricketer myself . . .' He passed.

12. (Charles) John Morris, *Traveller from Tokyo* (Cresset Press, London, 1943, p.10, cited in William Snell, 'John Morris at Keio University 1938-1942', from an unidentified journal pp. 29-59, quote on p.30, reproduced in http://koara.lib.keio.ac.jp/xoonips/modules/xoonips/download.php?file_id=14440, retrieved 24 October 2010.

13. Morris, *Hired to Kill*, p. 65.

14. For a good account of life in the Indian Army between the world wars, see Gould's chapter, 'Twilight of the Raj', in *Imperial Warriors*, pp. 203–34.

15. Major W. Brook Northey MC, late 1st KGO Gurkha Rifles and Captain C. S. Morris, 3rd QAO Gurkha Rifles with a foreword by Brigadier-General the Hon. C. G. Bruce, CB, MV/O, late 5th Royal Gurkha Rifles and 6th Gurkha Rifles, *The Gurkhas: Their Manners, Customs and Country* (John Lane, the Bodley Head, London, 1928). Chapter 4, 'The people and their languages', pp. 63–73, is by Professor [later Sir] Ralph Turner.

16. Morris, *Hired to Kill*, p. 67.

17. Ibid., pp. 67–8.

18. Ibid., p. 69.

19. Bullock, p. 89.

20. Morris, *Hired to Kill*, p. 126.

21. Ibid., p. 127.

22. Maj-Gen Nigell Woodyatt, CB, CIE, *3rd Queen Alexandra's Own Gurkha Rifles From April 1915 to December 1927*, (Philip Allan & Co., London, 1929), pp. 293–94.

23. Morris, p. 130.

24. Ibid., p. 131.

25. Ibid., p. 132.

26. Ibid.

27. Ibid.

28. Ibid., pp. 132–3.

29. Woodyatt, *3rd Gurkhas*, p. 295.

30. Gould, p. 222.

31. Morris, *Hired to Kill*, p. 147.

32. Edward M. Spiers, 'Gas and the North-West Frontier', *Journal of Strategic Studies*, vol. 6, issue 4 (1983), pp. 94–112, this, p. 96, citing Churchill, minute, 12 May 1919, NA WO 32/5184.

33. Ibid., p. 97, citing Churchill, minute, 22 May 1919, NA WO 32/5185.

34. Ibid., p. 98 onwards.

35. NA War Cabinet minutes, CAB/23/6, cited in John Silverlight, *The Victor's Dilemma* (Barrie and Jenkins, London, 1970), p. 97.

36. Spiers, p. 98 onwards.

37. Morris, *Hired to Kill*, p. 187.

38. Ibid., p. 141.

39. From a Bulmer's Cider management training pamphlet, cited by Police Commissioner Geoffrey Dear, now Lord Dear, at a lecture on leadership in the 1980s, remembered by the author.

40. Major General (retd) Ian Cardozo (ed.), *The Indian Army: A Brief History* (Centre for Armed Forces Historical Research, United Service Institution of India, New Delhi, 2005), pp. 37–9.

41. After the Second World War the two were amalgamated to form (confusingly) the Royal Military Academy at Sandhurst. During the 1920s it was said that it was more difficult to get into Woolwich than Cambridge. In 1946, the Military College of Science, also at Woolwich, became the Royal Military College of Science at Shrivenham.

42. Cardozo, p. 40.

43. Gould, p. 215, citing Stephen P. Cohen, *The Indian Army: Its Contribution to the Development of a Nation* (New Delhi, 1971 and 1990), p. 119.

44. Gould, p. 215.

45. Ibid.

46. Ibid.

47. Cardozo, p. 40.

48. Gould, pp. 210–14.

CHAPTER 8: THE SECOND WORLD WAR

1. Cardozo, p. 41.

2. Account by Lieutenant General Sir Francis Tuker, in *Gorkha: The Story of the Gurkhas of Nepal* (London, 1957), p. 213, cited in Gould,

p. 233. Gould warns that this source is 'challenging', which presumably means that it may be exaggerated.

3. Gould, p. 237.

4. 'Burma, Dec. 1941–May 1942', *The Times Atlas of the Second World War* (Times Books, London, 1989), pp. 76–7.

5. I am grateful to my PhD student Annie Kemp, researching disaster management in South-East Asia, for alerting me to this. The Japanese, like the US, UK, Germany and USSR, were now aware of the possibilities of nuclear fission, and Burma was a key source of uranium.

6. Gould, p. 239–40.

7. Bullock, p. 140.

8. Gould, p. 241.

9. Field Marshal Viscount Slim, GCB, GCMG, GCVO, GBE, DSO, MC, *Defeat into Victory* (Cassell and Company, London, 1956, reprinted in the Pan Military Classics series by Pan Books, London, 2009), p. 29. Slim's book was hailed by the London *Evening Standard* as 'the best general's book of World War II', and that is probably true of books by British generals, although George S. Patton's *War as I Knew It* (US) and Konstantin Rokossovskiy's *A Soldier's Duty* (Russia) are also special. Slim is an important source on the Gurkhas, and his 'Afterthoughts' on the future of military forces are still valuable today. The best recent books on Slim are Robert Lyman, *Slim, Master of War: Burma and the Birth of Modern Warfare* (Constable and Robinson, London, 2004) and John Latimer, *Burma: The Forgotten War* (John Murray, London, 2004).

10. Slim, *Defeat into Victory* (Pan, London, 2009), p. 44.

11. Colonel J. N. Mackay, *History of the 7th Duke of Edinburgh's Own Gurkha Rifles* (Edinburgh, 1962), p. 111.

12. Slim, *Defeat into Victory* (Pan, London 2009), p. 98.

13. Ibid., p. 117.

14. Bullock, p. 143.

15. *London Gazette*, 30 September 1943, cited in http://www.army.mod. uk/gurkhas/14281.aspx, Honours and Awards, Victoria Cross. Retrieved 25 August 2010.

16. 'Burma 1942–1945', *The Times Atlas*, pp. 162–3.

17. The Gurkha Museum, *The Gurkhas in World War II: Chindits* (The Gurkha Museum, 2009), cover, p. 2.

18. Tuker, *Gorkha*, pp. 220–1.

19. Lieutenant Colonel G. R. Stevens, *A History of the 2nd King Edward*

VIII's Own Goorkha Rifles (The Sirmoor Rifles), vol. III, 1921–48 (Aldershot, 1952), p. 200.

20. From an unpublished paper in the Gurkha Museum, N1, *One More River*, cited in Gould, p. 253.

21. Gurkha Museum, *The Gurkhas in World War II*, p. 3.

22. Callwell, *Small Wars* (1906 edition, republished 1996), Ch. IX, p. 108.

23. Neill's paper, pp. 28–30, cited in Gould, p. 255.

24. Ibid., p. 19, cited in Gould, p. 254, paraphrased by the author.

25. Gould, p. 254.

26. Brigadier Orde C. Wingate, *Report on Operations of 77th Indian Infantry Brigade in Burma, Feb–June 1943* (New Delhi, 1943), p. 4.

27. Ibid., p. 41.

28. Slim, *Defeat into Victory* (Pan, 2009), p. 386. The same story is repeated about the 1/5th Gurkhas ordered to bury nine Germans at Mozzagrogna in Italy late in 1943. The latter, Bullock, p. 115. No doubt it happened on several occasions.

29. Zechariah, chapter 9, verse 12.

30. Bullock, pp. 148–9.

31. See the chapter of that title in the author's *The Evolution of Modern Land Warfare: Theory and Practice* (Routledge, London, 1990).

32. Slim, *Defeat into Victory* (Pan, 2009), p. 296.

33. Ibid., pp. 299–300.

34. Ibid., p. 303.

35. Ibid. pp. 303, 305; Gurkha Museum, *The Gurkhas in World War II: Chindits*, p. 6. *The Times Atlas*, p. 163, map 3, is good but unfortunately the date is wrong: the second Chindit operation took place in 1944, not 1943.

36. Slim, *Defeat into Victory* (Pan, 2009), p. 308.

37. *London Gazette*, 26 October 1944, cited in http://www.army.mod.uk/gurkhas/14281.aspx, Honours and Awards, Victoria Cross. Retrieved 25 August 2010 .

38. Ibid.

39. The outstanding British light support weapon (light machine-gun) of the Second World War and the savage wars of peace that followed it, normally deployed one per section. The Bren was still used by the Royal Navy relatively recently to shoot at mines because it was more accurate than the general purpose machine-gun, which succeeded it. The name comes from a combination of Brno, the Czech arms

manufacturing establishment where it was developed before the war, and Enfield, where the British took up production.

40. *London Gazette*, 9 November 1944, cited in http://www.army.mod.uk/gurkhas/14281.aspx, Honours and Awards, Victoria Cross. Retrieved 25 August 2010.

41. *London Gazette*, 26 September 1944, cited in http://www.army.mod.uk/gurkhas/14281.aspx, Honours and Awards, Victoria Cross. Retrieved 25 August 2010.

42. Ibid.

43. *London Gazette*, 7 September 1944, cited in http://www.army.mod.uk/gurkhas/14281.aspx, Honours and Awards, Victoria Cross. Retrieved 25 August 2010.

44. See the maps in Slim, *Defeat into Victory* (Pan, 2009), pp. 325, 326.

45. *London Gazette*, 12 October 1944, cited in http://www.army.mod.uk/gurkhas/14281.aspx, Honours and Awards, Victoria Cross. Retrieved 25 August 2010.

46. *London Gazette*, 5 October 1944, cited in http://www.army.mod.uk/gurkhas/14281.aspx, Honours and Awards, Victoria Cross. Retrieved 25 August 2010.

47. Bullock, pp. 161–2.

48. *London Gazette*, 5 June 1945, cited in http://www.army.mod.uk/gurkhas/14281.aspx, Honours and Awards, Victoria Cross. Retrieved 25 August 2010.

49. Ibid.

50. Slim, *Defeat into Victory* (2009), p. 535.

51. Ibid., pp. 536–7; Bullock, p. 163.

52. The subject of an excellent TV film, *Mission of the Shark: The Saga of the USS Indianapolis* (1991).

53. Slim, *Defeat into Victory* (2009), p. 579.

54. The Gurkha Museum, *The Gurkha Parachutist* (The Gurkha Museum, 2009), pp. 1–2, film on the latter, citing the regimental history of the 7th Gurkhas.

55. Gurkha Museum, *The Gurkha Parachutist*, p. 3.

56. See the excellent website http://www.burmastar.org.uk/force. Retrieved 27 August 2010. Gow's book is occasionally cited, but appears to have been published privately.

57. Slim, *Defeat into Victory* (2009), p. 181.

58. Desmond Ball, 'Burma's Nuclear Programs: the Defector's Story', *Security Challenges*, vol. 5, no. 4, (Summer 2009), pp. 119–31.

59. *London Gazette*, 27 July 1945, cited in http://www.army.mod.uk/ gurkhas/14281.aspx, Honours and Awards, Victoria Cross. Retrieved 25 August 2010; Gould, p. 268.

60. Ibid.

61. Slim, *Defeat into Victory* (2009), p. 601.

62. Ibid., p. 603.

63. Bullock, p. 164.

64. Slim, *Defeat into Victory* (2009), pp. 29, 599–602.

65. Gould, p. 245, citing Lieutenant General Sir Francis Tuker, *Approach to Battle* (London, 1963), p. 318.

66. Gould, p. 245, citing Chenevix-Trench, *The Indian Army*, p. 225. Google Earth provides a good picture.

67. Extracts from *London Gazette*, 15 June 1943, cited in http://www. army.mod.uk/gurkhas/14281.aspx, Honours and Awards, Victoria Cross. Retrieved 25 August 2010; also http://www.ww2talk.com/ forum/unit-documents/19802-all-victoria-crosses-world-war-two-8.html, which has the complete citation.

68. 'North Africa Nov 1942–May 1943', in *The Times Atlas of the Second World War*, pp. 116–17.

69. 'Italy January–August 1944' in *The Times Atlas of the Second World War*, pp. 132–3. The three-dimensional graphic of the Monte Cassino area (Map 1) is particularly good. There is also Google Earth.

70. Tuker, *Gorkha*, p. 227.

71. Bullock, pp. 118–19.

72. *London Gazette*, 28 December 1944, cited in http://www.army.mod. uk/gurkhas/14281.aspx, Honours and Awards, Victoria Cross. Retrieved 25 August 2010.

73. Gould, p. 225.

74. *London Gazette*, 22 February 1945, cited in http://www.army.mod. uk/gurkhas/14281.aspx, Honours and Awards, Victoria Cross. Retrieved 25 August 2010.

75. See the excellent chapter in Bullock on 'Malaya and Singapore', pp. 126–35: and Gould, pp. 269–77.

76. The Gurkha Museum, *Lineages and Composition of the Gurkha Regiments* (March 2010 edn), p. 118.

77. Ibid., p. 104.

78. Ibid., p. 124.

79. Ibid., p. 125.

80. Ibid., p. 116. 4,300 known killed, 1,011 died of wounds, 1,893 died of disease, 335 accidental deaths, giving 7,539 total deaths, plus 14,082 wounded, 1,441 missing, 319 injured and 266 'POD'.
81. Ibid.
82. Slim, *Defeat into Victory* (2009), pp. 612–30; Special Force, p. 625 onwards.
83. Ibid., pp. 610–11.

CHAPTER 9: THE PATHS DIVIDE

1. Gurkha Museum, *The Lineages and Composition* (March 2010), pp. 104, 119; Bullock, p. 164. The 1st, 2nd, and 9th Gurkhas who had lost battalions in Singapore, and the 7th, which lost a battalion at Tobruk, were authorised to raise fifth battalions: the remaining six Gurkha regiments all raised third and fourth battalions. That makes forty-four. Then there were the two parachute battalions. One of those was converted from the 3/7th Gurkhas; the other one was a new one, making forty-five.
2. Gurkha Museum, *Lineages and Composition* (March 2010), p. 119.
3. Gould, pp. 286–7.
4. Ibid., p. 288.
5. Ibid., p. 289.
6. Bullock, pp. 125, 167–8. The author is grateful to Brigadier Bullock for alerting him to these important but unpublicised footnotes to the Second World War.
7. Gould, p. 292.
8. Gurkha Museum, *Lineages and Composition* (March 2010), p. 119.
9. Colonel R. D. Palsokar MC (retd), *History of the 5th Gorkha Rifles (Frontier Force)*, vol. III, 1858–1991 (Bombay 1991), p. 99. This is an Indian official history of the regiment seen from the point of view of forty-four years' service with the independent Indian Army.
10. Ibid, pp. 296–9.
11. Richard A. Rinaldi, Indian Army Airborne/Special Forces Units, accessed at http://www.orbat.com/site/cimh/regiments/Indian%20Army%20AirborneSF.pdf, retrieved 29 August 2010.
12. Author's interview with Lieutenant Colonel (retd) (then Captain)

John Cross, formerly of the 1/1st Gurkhas, at his home, Pokhara, Nepal, Thursday 10 June 2010.

13. Palsokar, *History of the 5th Gorkha Rifles* (1991), p. 100.

14. Ibid., pp. 100–1.

15. Gould, pp. 306–7, citing the British Library, Oriental and Indian Collection, L/P&S/12/3093, Annexure III, *Tripartite Agreement*, 7 November 1947.

16. Palsokar, *History of the 5th Gorkha Rifles* (1991), p. 102.

17. Gould, pp. 9, 310, 315, 317, 322. Hedley, as major general, had interviewed Gould for the Gurkhas and, in spite of the fact that the young national-serviceman had slipped on the polished floor and inadvertently prostrated himself in front of the general, passed him as a potential officer.

18. Gould, p. 315, citing WO 32/13252, Hedley to Major General C. H. Boucher, 30 December 1947.

19. Gould, pp. 309–16.

20. http://www.bharat-rakshak.com/LAND-FORCES/Units/Infantry/388-11-Gorkha-Rifles.html, retrieved 29 August 2010.

21. Palsokar, *History of the 5th Gorkha Rifles* (1991), p. 101.

22. Ibid., p. 102.

23. Gould, pp. 318–19.

24. Ibid., p. 320.

CHAPTER 10: INDIA'S GORKHAS

1. http://indianarmy.nic.in/Site/FormTemplete/frmTemp1P2C_1.aspx?MnId=uWUCFPglwNc=&ParentID=VE+Qz4Hs3YO=, retrieved 25 August 2010.

2. http://www.globalsecurity.org/military/world/war/indo-pak_1947.html, retrieved 26 August 2010.

3. http://www.bharat-rakshak.com/IAF/Awards/Gallantry/302-MVC.html, retrieved 27 August 2010.

4. CDB, 'Congo, UN operations', in Richard Holmes (ed.), *The Oxford Companion to Military History* (Oxford University Press, Oxford, 2001), pp. 221–3.

5. http://www.bharat-rakshak.com/HEROISM/Salaria.html, retrieved 28 August 2010.

6. Ibid.

7. http://www.globalsecurity.org/military/world/war/indo-prc_1962. htm, retrieved 29 August 2010.

8. Cited in http://www.statemaster.com/encyclopedia/Dhan-Singh-Thapa, retrieved 29 August 2010.

9. Conversation with Honorary Major Judbahadur Gurung, late QGE, now the curator of the Gurkha Museum, Pokhara, outside the British base, 10 June 2010.

10. DJJ, 'India-Pakistan Wars', in Holmes (ed.), *Oxford Companion to Military History* (2001), p. 439.

11. Ibid.

12. Palsokar, *History of the 5th Gorkha Rifles (Frontier Force)*, vol. III, pp. 201–2.

13. Ibid, pp. 204–5, quotation on the latter.

14. Ibid., p. 205.

15. Ibid., p. 206.

16. Ibid.

17. Ibid., p. 207.

18. Ibid., pp. 207–8.

19. Ibid., pp. 208–9.

20. 'More Glory & Battle Honours for the 3rd Gorkha Rifles: Pirkanthi & Hathimatha', in http://frontierindia.net/more-glory-battle-honours-for-the-3rd-gorkha-rifles-pirkanthi-hathimatha, retrieved 29 August 2010. Brigadier Jaggi's book, *Kargil and the Kanchi: A Saga of Faith and Fortitude* (?1999), is reviewed in this article but no fuller publishing details are given and the author has been unable to track down a copy.

21. Ibid.

22. http://www.bharat-rakshak.com/HEROISM/Pandey.html, retrieved 30 August 2010.

23. Palsokar, *History of the 5th Gorkha Rifles*, pp. 269–76.

24. Conversation with a senior Indian Army officer speaking on condition of anonymity, Kathmandu, 3 June 2010.

25. International Institute for Strategic Studies, *The Military Balance 2008* (IISS/Routledge, 2008), pp. 341–6.

26. 'Mumbai Hotel Terrorist Massacre, Loose Lips Sink Ships,' in http://scaredmonkeys.com/2008/12/01/mumbai-hotel-terrorist-massacre-loose-lips-sink-ships-british-couple-claims-cnn-endangered-their-lives-be-reporting-location/, retrieved 30 August 2010.

27. Ibid.

CHAPTER 11: BRITAIN'S GURKHAS

1. Bullock, pp. 170–9, is a full and comprehensive account of the main events of the twelve-year campaign.
2. John P. Cross, *A Face Like a Chicken's Backside: An Unconventional Soldier in Malaya and Borneo, 1948–1971* (1996; this edition Cultured Lotus, Singapore, 2003), p. 19. Also the author's interview with him, Pokhara, Thursday 10 June 2010.
3. Interview with John Cross, 10 June 2010.
4. Cross, *A Face Like a Chicken's Backside*, pp. 19, 23.
5. Bullock, p. 173.
6. Visit to the Gurkha Museum, Pokhara, 8 June 2010.
7. Cross, *A Face . . .*, p. 34.
8. Ibid., pp. 50–1.
9. For a full account of this fascinating operation, see Cross, *A Face . . .*, pp. 47–136.
10. Bullock, p. 179.
11. Gould, p. 343, citing Cross, *In Gurkha Company*, p. 82.
12. Hull held the office as a general. All his predecessors since 1940 had been field marshals.
13. Gould, p. 346.
14. Ibid., pp. 344–5.
15. Ibid., pp. 347–8.
16. Will Fowler and Kevin Lyles, *Britain's Secret War: The Indonesian Confrontation 1962–66* (Osprey, London, 2006), p. 3.
17. Gould, p. 349.
18. Fowler and Lyles, pp. 4–6.
19. Ibid., p. 4.
20. Cross, *A Face . . .*, p. 145–6.
21. Ibid., p. 11.
22. Fowler and Lyles, p. 9.
23. Cross, *A Face . . .*, p. 150.
24. Ibid., p. 146.
25. Ibid., p. 150.
26. Fowler and Lyles, p. 24.
27. Ibid., p. 42.
28. Ibid., p. 38.
29. *London Gazette*, 22 April 1966, cited in http://www.army.mod.uk/gurkhas/14281.aspx, Honours and Awards, Victoria Cross. Retrieved 30 August 2010.

30. Fowler and Lyles, p. 42.

31. Interview with a Singapore Police inspector, Kathmandu, 4 June 2010.

32. The same is true of its successor, the *QM2*. Its latent performance is far higher than publicly displayed.

33. Cited in Gould, p. 367.

34. Interview with Dhanbahadur Rai, former sergeant in 7th Gurkha Rifles, Hotel Kalash, Damak, now an Assistant Gurkha Welfare Officer, 6 June 2010.

35. A complete and detailed account of the 1/7th, in the period immediately before the Falklands War and during the campaign by one of their officers, is Mike Seear, *With the Gurkhas in the Falklands: A War Journal* (Leo Cooper, Barnsley, 2003). This, p. 124.

36. Bullock, p. 212. The landing is described in Seear, pp. 136–7.

37. Interview with Dhanbahadur Rai, 6 June 2010.

38. Seear, pp. 271, confirms what happened, and that it was 'friendly fire'.

39. Interview with Dhanbahadur Rai, 6 June 2010.

40. Cited in Gould, p. 370.

41. Interview with Dhanbahadur Rai, 6 June 2010.

42. Interview with John Cross, 10 June 2010.

43. Ibid.

44. Gould, pp. 376–7.

45. See the author's *Knights in White Armour: The New Art of War and Peace* (Hutchinson, London, 1996, and Pimlico, London, 1997).

46. 'Gurkhas on alert to bolster Paras' depleted infantry', *Independent*, Saturday 14 October 1995, p. 11. 'Shortage of fighting fit young recruits may force Army chiefs to bring in legendary colonial regiment.'

47. http://icasualties.org/oef/Nationality.aspx?hndQry=UK, retrieved 1 September 2010.

48. Interview with a serving Gurkha captain from one of the western *jats*, speaking on condition of anonymity, 11 June 2010.

49. Ibid.

50. Interview with Brigadier John Holmes while the author was defence correspondent at the *Independent*, 1996.

51. Interview with Gurkha captain, 11 June 2010.

52. Interview with Lieutenant General Sir Philip Trousdell (retd), formerly Chairman of the Gurkha Welfare Trust, Moondance Restaurant, Pokhara, 8 June 2010.

53. Ibid.
54. Pointed out by Hon. Major Judbahadur Gurung, MBE, curator of the Gurkha Museum, Pokhara, 8 June 2010.
55. Interview with General Philip Trousdell, 8 June 2010.
56. Created from the Royal Corps of Transport, Royal Army Ordnance Corps, Royal Pioneer Corps, Army Catering Corps and the postal and courier section of the Royal Engineers.
57. 'Squaddies are warned: the real enemy is the Bosnian roads', *Independent*, Saturday 20 January 1996, p. 11.
58. Interview with serving Gurkha officer speaking on condition of anonymity, Dharan, 5 June 2010.
59. Bullock, pp. 258–61.
60. http://casualties.org/oef/Nationality.aspx?hndQry=UK, accessed 31 August 2010.
61. Interview with a serving Gurkha officer speaking on condition of anonymity, Pokhara, 8 June 2010.
62. Interview with a Gurkha welfare officer, responsible for dealing with the families of serving Gurkhas in the event of problems and casualties, Kathmandu, 3 June 2010.

CHAPTER 12: THE GURKHAS NOW, AND THE FUTURE

1. My thanks, again, to Colonel Andrew Mills, for facilitating a wonderful trip.
2. Display on the 'female capability assessment', noticeboard, British Gurkhas, Pokhara, June 2010.
3. Matthew Hicky, 'Hiring Gurkha girls will weaken British Army, warns top brass', *Daily Mail*, 24 October 2008.
4. Interview, GWC Gorkha, 9 June 2010.
5. Interview with a Nepali Gurkha officer, 6 June 2010.
6. 'British Army 2300 AD: The Brigade of Gurkhas, on http://www.users.globalnet.co.uk/~dheb/2300/Europe/UK/Gurkha/Gurkha.htm, retrieved 1 September 2010.
7. 'Gurkha regiment faces axe as Liam Fox insists on £20 bn Trident replacement', *Observer*, 29 August 2010. http://www.guardian.co.uk/world/2010/aug/29/british-army-gurkhas-spending Retrieved 24 October 2010.

8. John Ingham, Defence Editor, 'Gurkhas fear the axe for regiment', *Daily Express*, 1 September 2010, in http://www.express.co.uk/posts/view/196804/Gurkhas-fear-the-axe-for-regiment   Retrieved 24 October 2010.

9. *Gurkhas safe in the Strategic Defence Review*, http://www.damiancollins.com/2010/10/gurkhas-safe-in-the-strategic-defence-review/Retrieved 19 October 2010.

Bibliography

PRIMARY SOURCES: INTERVIEWS

Cleary, Dr Laura, Cranfield University, various conversations on her experiences of Security Sector Reform in Nepal, April–May 2010.

Cross, Lieutenant Colonel (retd) John, at his home, Pokhara, 10 June 2010.

Edgerley-Harris, Gavin, curator of the Gurkha Museum, Winchester, 21 and 27 April, 30 July, 27 August 2010.

Griffiths, Lieutenant Colonel Adrian, Pokhara, 8 June 2010.

Gurung, Hon. Major Judbahadur MBE, curator of the Gurkha Museum, Pokhara, 8 June 2010.

Limbu, Hon. Major Chandraparsad MBE, Area Welfare Officer, Dharan, 4 June 2010.

Mills, Colonel Andrew, DA Nepal, British Embassy, Kathmandu, 3 June 2010.

Rai, Sergeant (retd) Dhanbahadur, Kadash Hotel, Damak, 6 June 2010.

Trousdell, Lieutenant General (retd) Sir Philip, Moondance Restaurant, Pokhara, 8 June 2010.

Inspector, Gurkha Contingent Singapore Police Force, speaking on condition of anonymity, Kathmandu, 4 June 2010.

Retired Gurkha NCOs/WOs speaking on condition of anonymity: British Gurkhas Nepal, Kathmandu, 3 June 2010; Area Welfare Centre, Dharan, 4 June 2010; Area Welfare Centre, Terathum, 5 June 2010; Area Welfare Centre, Damak, 6 June 2010; Area Welfare Centre, Gorkha, 9 June 2010.

Serving Gurkha officers speaking on condition of anonymity: Dharan, 4 June 2010; Damak, 6 June 2010; Pokhara, 8 June 2010; Kathmandu, 9 June 2010.

377

PRIMARY SOURCES: ARCHIVES

UK National Archives, Kew (NA)

CAB XCIA 632, General Kouropatkine's scheme for a Russian Advance upon India, with Notes thereon by Lord Roberts . . . , August 1891, printed for the Committee of Imperial Defence, March 1903.

CAB/23/6, War Cabinet minutes.

HO 45/10838/331607/3: 1917–18, Report of the Commission appointed by Act of Parliament to enquire into the Operations of War in Mesopotamia, Together with a Separate Report by Commander J. Wedgwood, D.S.O., M.P., and Appendices, Cmnd 8610.

Parliamentary Papers, House of Commons, 1831–2, xiv, v (Military), Appendix (A), no. 55.

Parliamentary Papers, House of Lords, 1852–3, xxxi, 1st report of the Select Committee of the House of Lords, 1852–3.

PRO 30/64, Lt Gen Sir Charles Napier Papers.

WO 32/7311, Victoria Cross (India): Recommendations approved by the Queen.

WO 32/13087, Report of the Committee on the Lessons of the Great War, October 1932 (The Kirke Report).

WO 33/337, Reports of British Observers attached to Russian and Japanese Forces in the Field [1904–05].

WO 43/420, Relative Ranks [of East India Company and King's/Queen's Regiments' officers].

The British Library, Asia-Pacific and African Collection (formerly Oriental and India Office Collection):

L/P&S/12/3093, Annexure III, Tripartite Agreement, 7 November 1947.

Military Department Records (IOR, MDR), British Library, L/Mil/5/391, f. 275, IOR, MDR L/Mil./17/2/272. Ff. 141a.

PRNW: Papers Relating to the Nepaul War. Printed in Conformity with the Resolution of the Constitution of Proprietors of the East India Stock of the 3 March 1824 (2 vols, London, 1824). British Library, St Pancras, Oriental and Indian Collection.

Raper, Captain F. N., 10th Native Infantry, Memoir of Gurwall and Kamaon, in PRNW, pp. 143–9.

National Army Museum, Templer Study Centre (NAM) (see also diaries):

Bagot-Chester War Diary, 31 December 1914.

C. A. M. (C. A. Mercer), *Afghanistan 1878–79–80, Book of 2nd Afghan War*, 6903–8.

National Army Museum, Chelsea (NAM), NAM 6511–54, Letter from Col. L. L. Showers DSO, 6 August 1965.

2005-10-57, Letters of Algernon Durand to Lord Roberts, 1891–1898, transcribed by D. Anderson for subsequent article, 'The Friends at Gilgit 1888–1895: Algernon Durand and George Scott Robertson', *Journal of the Society for Army Historical Research* (2004).

Gurkha Museum, Winchester (GM) (see also diaries and books published by the GM):

Extracts from the Letter Book of the 2nd King Edward VII's Own Gurkha Rifles (Sirmoor Rifles), 1853–1889.

N1, 'One More River', unpublished paper.

OPS/008, map 1816.

Liddell Hart Centre for Military Archives (LHCMA), King's College, London:

LH 10/1932/111 1932, 8 July. *Report of the Committee on the Lessons of the Great War*, October 1932 (the Kirke Report); (pre-publication version).

PRIMARY SOURCES: OFFICIAL ORDERS, DOCUMENTS AND REPORTS

Callwell, Colonel Charles E., *Small Wars* (3rd edition, 1906 [1st edition 1896, 2nd 1899], His Majesty's Stationery Office, London, 1906, republished by University of Nebraska Press with an Introduction by Douglas Porch (Bison Books, 1996), p. 363.

Clarke, Sir George, 'Note on Threatened Invasions of India and their

Effect on British Policy', in *Memoranda and Notes by Sir George Clarke while Secretary of the Committee of Imperial Defence 1904–07*, Document no. 41, 3 April 1905.

Elles, Brevet Major E. R., RA, *Report on Nepal* (Calcutta, 1884).

Lawrence, Sir Henry, 'Military Defence of Our Indian Empire' (1844), reprinted in *Essays, Military and Political, Written in India* (London, 1859).

London Gazette, The, Published by Authority: no. 22176, p. 3903, 24 August 1858. Tytler VC; no. 23902, p. 4489, 27 September 1872. Macintyre VC; no. 24314, p. 2476, 14 April 1876. Channer VC; no. 24697, p. 2241, 18 March 1879 . Cook VC; no. 24843, p. 2968, 11 May 1880. Ridgeway VC; no. 26165, p. 2805, 26 May 1891. Grant VC; no. 26306, p. 4006, 12 July 1892. Boisragon, Manners-Smith VCs; no. 27584, p. 4976, 7 August 1903. Walker VC; no. 27636, p. 331, 15 January 1904. Walker VC; no. 27758, p. 574, 24 January 1905. Grant VC; (Supplement) no. 29371, p. 11450, 16 November 1915. Kulbir Thapa VC; (Supplement) no. 30122, p. 5702, 8 June 1917. Wheeler VC; (Supplement) no. 30757, p. 7307, 18 June 1918. Karanbahadur Rana VC; (Supplement) no. 36053, p. 2719, 11 June 1943. Lalbahadur Thapa VC; (Supplement) no. 36190, p. 4347, 28 September 1943. Gaje Ghale VC; (Supplement) no. 36690, p. 4157, 5 September 1944. Ganju Lama VC; (Supplement) no. 36715, p. 4423, 26 September 1944. Blaker VC; (Supplement) no. 36730, p. 4569, 3 October 1944. Agansing Rai VC; (Supplement) no. 36742, p. 4673, 10 October 1944. Netrabahadur Thapa V.C; (Supplement) no. 36764, p. 4900, 26 October 1944. Allmand VC; (Supplement) no. 36785, p. 5129, 7 November 1944. Tulbahadur Pun VC; (Supplement) no. 36860, p. 5933, 26 December 1944. Sherbahadur Thapa VC; (Supplement) no. 36950, p. 1039, 20 February 1945. Thaman Gurung VC; (Supplement) no. 37107, p. 2831, 1 June 1945. Bhanbagta Gurung VC; (Supplement) no. 37195, p. 3861, 24 July 1945. Lachhiman Gurung VC; (Supplement) no. 43959, p. 4947, 21 April 1966. Rambahadur Limbu VC.

MacGregor, Sir Colin, *The Defence of India: A Strategical Study* (Simla, 1884).

Ministry of Defence (Colonel R. G. Leonard, late 5th Gurkhas), *Nepal and the Gurkhas* (HMSO, London, 1965).

Napier, Lt Gen Sir Charles (ed.), *Defects Civil and Military of the Indian Government by Lt.-General Sir Charles James Napier, GCB* (London, 1853).

PRNW: Papers Relating to the Nepaul War. Printed in Conformity with the

Resolution of the Constitution of Proprietors of the East India Stock of the 3 March 1824 (London, 1824, 2 vols, reprinted by BIMLA, New Delhi, 1985).

Protocol Additional to the Geneva Conventions of 12 August 1949, and Relating to the Protection of Victims of International Armed Conflicts (Protocol 1), 8 June 1977.

PRIMARY SOURCES: MEMOIRS AND DIARIES

Allanson, Major Cecil, The Gurkha Museum, *The Allanson Diary: Gallipoli 1915*, Introduction by Lt Col M. J. F. Wardroper, CO 6th Queen Elizabeth's Own Gurkha Rifles, January 1977.

Colchester, Lord (ed.), *A Political Diary 1828–30 by Edward Law, Lord Ellenborough*, 2 vols (London, 1881).

Cross, Lt Col John P., *'A Face Like a Chicken's Backside': An Unconventional Soldier in Malaya & Borneo, 1948–1971* (Cultured Lotus, Singapore, 2003). (First published by Greenhill Books, Lionel Leventhal, London, 1996.)

Durand, Colonel Algernon CB CIE, British Agent at Gilgit 1889–1894, Military Secretary to the Viceroy of India 1894–1899, *The Making of a Frontier: Five Years' Experiences and Adventures in Gilgit, Hunza, Nagar, Chitral and the Eastern Hindu-Kush* (Thomas Nelson, London, Edinburgh, Dublin and New York, 1899), scanned in full as http://www.tertullian.org/rpearse/scanned/durand.htm, retrieved 28 July 2010.

Haldane, Lt Gen Sir Aylmer, *The Insurrection in Mesopotamia 1920* (William Blackwood, Edinburgh and London, 1920).

Ivanin, Mikhail I., *Opisaniye Zimnyago Pokhoda (Description of the Winter Expedition* [the Expedition to Khiva, 1839–40]), (St Petersburg, 1874).

Kirkpatrick, W., *An Account of the Kingdom of Nepaul, being the substance of observations being made during a mission to that country in the year 1793* (London, 1811).

Knight, E. F., *Where Three Empires Meet: Travel in Kashmir, Tibet and Gilgit* (London, 1893). Republished by Saujanya Books, Srinagar, 2007.

Lawrence, T. E. (Thomas Edward), *Seven Pillars of Wisdom: A Triumph* (Penguin, in association with Jonathan Cape, London, 1962).

Mercer, Captain C. A., Recruitment Report, July/August 1886, Gurkha Museum, Winchester.

Morris, (Charles) John, *Traveller from Tokyo* (Cresset Press, London, 1943).

Morris, (Charles) John, *Hired to Kill: Some Chapters of Autobiography* (Rupert Hart-Davis, in association with The Cresset Press, London, 1960).

Reid, Major Charles, *1857–1957 Centenary of the Siege of Delhi. The Defence of the Main Piquet at Hindoo Rao's House and other Posts on the Ridge as recorded by Major Reid Commanding the Sirmoor Battalion, 2d K E VII's Own Gurkha Rifles (The Sirmoor Rifles). Extracts from Letters and Notes Written during the Siege of Delhi in 1857 by General Sir Charles Reid GCB* (Gurkha Museum, Winchester).

Roberts, Field Marshal Lord Frederick of Kandahar, *Forty-One Years in India* (1-volume edition, London, 1898).

Russell, William Howard, *My Diary in India, in the Year 1858–9* (Routledge, Warne and Routledge, London, 1860).

Seear, Major Mike, *With the Gurkhas in the Falklands: A War Journal* (Leo Cooper, Barnsley, 2003).

Shipp, John, *Memoirs of the Extraordinary Military Career of John Shipp, Late a Lieutenant in HM's 87th Regiment* (3 vols, London, 1829). Republished as *The Path of Glory: being the memoirs of the extraordinary military career of John Shipp written by Himself*, ed. C. J. Stranks (Chatto and Windus, London, 1969).

Slim, Field Marshal Viscount, GCB, GCMG, GCVO, GBE, DSO, MC, *Defeat into Victory* (Cassell and Company, London, 1956, reprinted in the Pan Military Classics series by Pan Books, London, 2009).

Tuker, Lt-Gen Sir Francis, *Approach to Battle: A commentary. Eighth Army, November 1941 to May 1943*, (Cassell, London, 1963).

Willcocks, Gen. Sir James, *With the Indians in France* (Constable & Co., London, 1920).

Wingate, Brigadier Orde C., *Report on Operations of 77th Indian Infantry Brigade in Burma, Feb–June 1943* (New Delhi, 1943).

Woodthorpe, Lieutenant R. G. Royal Engineers, *The Lushai Expedition, 1871, 1872* (Hurst and Blackett Publishers, London, 1873), accessed through http://www.archive.org/stream/lushaiexpedition00woodrich/lushaiexpedition00woodrich_djvu.txt (full text), retrieved 25 July 2010; reprinted as Lieut. R. G. Woodthorpe RE, *The Lushai Expedition, 1871, 1872* (Naval and Military Press, London, 2004).

Younghusband, Capt. Francis, *Report on a Mission to the Northern Frontier of Kashmir in 1889* (printed by the Superintendent of Government

Printing, India. Calcutta, 1890; reprinted as *The Northern Frontier of Kashmir*, New Delhi, 1973).

Younghusband, Capt. Francis, *The Heart of a Continent* (John Murray, London, 1896).

Younghusband, Lt Col Francis, *Wonders of the Himalaya* (John Murray, London, 1924).

PRIMARY SOURCES: DICTIONARIES AND ATLASES

Darby, H. C., and Fullard, Harold (ed.) *The New Cambridge Modern History* vol. xiv. *Atlas* (Cambridge University Press, 1970).

Keegan, John (ed.), *The Times Atlas of the Second World War* (Times Books, London, 1989).

Turner, Professor Ralph Lilley, M.C., M.A., *A Comparative and Etymological Dictionary of the Nepali Language with indexes of all words quoted from other Indo-Aryan Languages compiled by Dorothy Rivers Turner, M.A.* (London, Kegan Paul, Trench, Trubner & Co., Ltd, 1931).

PRIMARY SOURCES: REGIMENTAL, FORMATION AND ARMY HISTORIES

Bullock, Brigadier (retd) Christopher, *Britain's Gurkhas, with a Foreword by the Colonel Commandant Brigade of Gurkhas, General Sir David Richards KCB, CBE, DSO, ADC Gen* (Third Millennium, London, 2009).

Cardozo, Major General Ian (retd) (ed.), *The Indian Army: A Brief History* (Centre for Armed Forces Historical Research, United Service Institution of India, New Delhi, 2005).

History of the 5th Royal Gurkha Rifles (Frontier Force) 1858 to 1928 (for Private Circulation Only), (printed and published for the Regimental Committee by Gale and Polden, Aldershot, London and Portsmouth, 1929).

Mackay, Colonel J. N., (James Noble), *History of the 7th Duke of Edinburgh's Own Gurkha Rifles* (William Blackwood & Sons, Edinburgh, 1962).

Palsokar, Colonel R. D. MC (retd), *History of the 5th Gorkha Rifles (Frontier Force)*, vol. III, 1858–1991, (Published by The Commandant, 58

Gorkha Training Centre, P.O. Happy Valley, Shillong, 793 001, printed in Bombay, 1991).

Petre, F. Loraine, *The 1st King George's Own Gurkha Rifles (The Malaun Regiment), 1815–1921* (Royal United Services Institute, London, 1925).

Poynder, F. S., (Frederick Sinclair), *The 9th Gurkha Rifles, 1817–1936* (Royal United Services Institute, London, 1937).

Steven, Lt-Col G. R., *A History of the 2nd King Edward VIII's Own Goorkha Rifles (The Sirmoor Rifles)*, vol. III, 1921–1948 (Gale & Polden, Aldershot, 1952).

Tuker, Lt Gen Sir Francis, *Gorkha: The Story of the Gurkhas of Nepal* (Constable & Co., London, 1957).

Woodyatt, Maj Gen Nigel, Colonel 7th Gurkhas (ed.), *The Regimental History of the 3rd Queen Alexandra's Own Gurkha Rifles from April 1815 to December 1927* (Philip Allan, London, 1929).

SECONDARY SOURCES: BOOKS

Banskota, Purushottam, *The Gurkha Connection: A History of the Gurkha Recruitment in the British Indian Army* (Nirala Publications, Jaipur, 1994).

Bellamy, C. D., 'British Views of Russia: Russian Views of Britain', in Philip Towle (ed.), *Estimating Foreign Military Power* (Croom Helm, Beckenham, 1982), pp. 37–76.

Bellamy, Christopher, *The Evolution of Modern Land Warfare: Theory and Practice* (Routledge, London, 1990).

Bellamy, Christopher, *Knights in White Armour: The New Art of War and Peace* (Hutchinson, London, 1996; and Pimlico, London, 1997).

Brook Northey, Major W., MC, late 1st K.G.O. Gurkha Rifles, and Morris, Captain C. J., 3rd Q.A.O. Gurkha Rifles, with a Foreword by Brigadier General the Hon. C. G. Bruce, C.B., M.V/O, late 5th Royal Gurkha Rifles and 6th Gurkha Rifles, *The Gurkhas: Their Manners, Customs and Country* (John Lane, the Bodley Head, London, 1928).

Caplan, Lionel, *Warrior Gentlemen: 'Gurkhas' in the Western Imagination* (Himal Books, Classics, Kathmandu, 2009). (First published by Berghahn Books, Oxford, UK, and Providence, RI, USA, 1995.)

Chappell, Mike, *The Gurkhas* (Osprey, London, Auckland, Melbourne, Singapore and Toronto, 1993).

Chapple, Brigadier (later Field Marshal Sir) John, *Bibliography of Gurkha*

Regiments and Related Subjects (Gurkha Museum Publication no. 4, Winchester, 1980).

Chenevix-Trench, Charles, *The Indian Army and the King's Enemies 1900–1947* (London, 1988).

Cohen, Stephen P., *The Indian Army: Its Contribution to the Development of a Nation* (New Delhi, 1971 and 1990).

Coleman, A. P., *A Special Corps: The Beginnings of Gorkha* [sic] *Service with the British* (Pentland Press, Edinburgh, Cambridge, Durham, USA, 1999), with a Foreword by Rodney Needham.

Dixon, Norman, *On the Psychology of Military Incompetence* (Cape, London, 1976).

Farwell, Byron, *The Gurkhas* (W. W. Norton, New York, and Allen Lane, London, 1984).

Farwell, Byron, *Armies of the Raj: From the Great Indian Mutiny to Independence*, (W. W. Norton and Company, London, 1991).

Feller, Tessa, *Culture Smart! Nepal – the Essential Guide to Customs and Culture* (Kuperard, London, 2008).

Fisk, Robert, *The Great War for Civilisation: The Conquest of the Middle East* (HarperCollins, London, 2005).

Fowler, Will, and Lyles, Kevin, *Britain's Secret War: The Indonesian Confrontation 1962–66* (Osprey, London, 2006).

Fremont-Barnes, Gregory, *The Anglo-Afghan Wars, 1839–1919* (Osprey, Oxford, 2009).

French, Patrick, *Younghusband: The Last Great Imperial Adventurer* (HarperCollins, London, 1994), pp. 67–8.

Geertz, C., *Works and Lives: The Anthropologist as Author* (Polity Press, Cambridge, 1989).

Gillard, David, *The Struggle for Asia 1828–1914: A Study in British and Russian Imperialism* (Methuen, London, 1977).

Gould, Tony, *Imperial Warriors: Britain and the Gurkhas* (Granta, London, 1999).

Gurkha Museum, *The Gurkha Parachutist* (Gurkha Museum, Winchester, 2009).

Gurkha Museum, *The Gurkhas in World War II: Chindits* (Gurkha Museum, Winchester, 2009).

Gurkha Museum, *The Second Afghan War 1878–1880 and the Third Afghan War 1919* (Gurkha Museum, Winchester, August 2009).

Gurkha Museum, *The Lineages and Composition of Gurkha Regiments in British Service* (Gurkha Museum, Winchester, March 2010).

Hamilton, Francis Buchanan, *An Account of the King of Nepaul and of the Territories annexed to this Domain by the House of Gorkha* (Edinburgh, 1819).

Haythornthwaite, Philip J., *Gallipoli 1915: Frontal Assault on Turkey* (Osprey, Oxford and New York, 1991).

Heath, Ian, and Perry, Michael, *The North-East Frontier 1837–1901* (Osprey, Oxford, 1999).

Hibbert, Christopher, *The Great Mutiny: India 1857* (Penguin, London, 1980).

Holmes, Richard, *Wellington, the Iron Duke* (HarperCollins, London, 2002).

Holmes, Richard, *Sahib: The British Soldier in India, 1750–1914* (Harper Perennial, London, 2006).

Holmes, Richard (ed.), *The Oxford Companion to Military History* (Oxford University Press, Oxford, 2001).

Hopkirk, Peter, *The Great Game: On Secret Service in High Asia* (John Murray, London, 1990), and subsequent editions (Oxford University Press, Kodansha International, New York, Tokyo, London, 1994).

Hunter, Sir William Wilson, *Life of Brian Houghton Hodgson, British Resident at the Court of Nepal* (John Murray, London, 1896).

Hutchinson, Colonel H. D., *The Campaign in Tirah, 1897–98* (London, 1898).

International Institute for Strategic Studies, *The Military Balance 2008*, (IISS/Routledge, London, 2008).

Johnson, Robert, *The 1897 Revolt and Tirah Valley Operations from the Pashtun Perspective* (Tribal Analysis Center, Williamsburg, VA, 2007), accessed at http://www.tribalanalysiscenter.com/PDF-TAC/The%201897%20Revolt%20and%20Tirah%20Valley%20Operations. Retrieved 25 July 2010.

Jordan, G., (ed.), *British Military History: A Supplement to Robin Higham's Guide to the Sources* (Garland, New York, 1988).

Keay, John, *The Honourable Company: A History of the English East India Company* (Macmillan, New York, 1994).

Khanduri, Chandra B., *Marching off with Colours A Re-discovered History of Gorkhas* (Gyan Sagar, Delhi, 1997).

Kipling, Rudyard, in Jones, R. T., (ed.), *The Collected Poems of Rudyard Kipling* (Wordsworth Poetry Library, Ware, Hertfordshire, 1994), pp. 439–40.

Latimer, John, *Burma: The Forgotten War* (John Murray, London, 2004).

Lawson, Philip, *The East India Company: A History (Studies in Modern History)*, (Longman, London, 1993).

Lovatt, Major A. C., and MacMunn, Major General George DSO, with a Foreword by Field Marshal Earl Roberts VC, KG, *The Armies of India* (Charles Black, London, 1911).

Loyn, David, *Butcher and Bolt: Two Hundred Years of Foreign Involvement in Afghanistan* (Hutchinson, London, 2008).

Lyman, Robert, *Slim, Master of War: Burma and the Birth of Modern Warfare* (Constable and Robinson, London, 2004).

McConnaichie, James, and Reed, David, *The Rough Guide to Nepal* (6th edition, Rough Guides, Penguin, October 2009).

MacMunn, Lt Gen Sir George, KCB KCSI DSO, *The Martial Races of India* (Sampson, Low, Marston, London, 1933).

Marrion, R. J. and Fosten, D. S. V., *The Tradition Book of the Gurkhas* (Belmont-Maitland, London, 1960s, reprinted by the National Army Museum, available in 2010, date unknown).

Mitchell, Major General Sir John, *Thoughts on Tactics and Military Organisation together with an Enquiry into the Power and Position of Russia* (London, 1838).

Moreman, T. R., *The Army in India and the Development of Frontier Warfare, 1849–1947* (Macmillan, London, 1998).

Moorehead, Alan, *Gallipoli* (Hamish Hamilton, London, 1956).

Nicholson, James, *The Hejaz Railway* (Stacey International, London and al Turah, Riyadh, 2005).

Nicholson, J. B. R., illustrated by Michael Roffe, *The Gurkha Rifles* (Osprey, London, 1974).

Parker, John, *The Gurkhas: The Inside Story of the World's Most Feared Soldiers* (Headline Books, London, 1999).

Prior, Robin, *Gallipoli: The End of the Myth* (Yale University Press, New Haven and London, 2009).

Risley, H. H., *Tribes and Castes of Bengal* (Calcutta, 1891).

Robson, Brian, *The Road to Kabul: The Second Afghan War, 1878–1881* (Spellmount, Staplehurst, UK, 2003).

Rose, Leo E., *Nepal: Strategy for Survival* (University of California Press, Berkeley, California, 1971).

Sheffield, Gary, *Forgotten Victory: The First World War: Myths and Realities* (Headline, London, 2001).

Silverlight, John, *The Victor's Dilemma* (Barrie and Jenkins, London, 1970).

Simkins, Michael, and Embleton, Ron, *The Roman Army from Caesar to Trajan* (Osprey, London, 1984).

Thapa, Basanta, and Mainali, Mohan (eds), *Lahure ko Katha (Story of the Lahurés)*, (Himal Books, Kathmandu, 2002).

Wood, Revd [no first name given], *Travels in India and Nepal* (London, 1891).

SECONDARY SOURCES: ARTICLES AND JOURNALS

Anderson, D., 'The friends at Gilgit 1888–1895: Algernon Durand and George Scott Robertson', *Journal of the Society for Army Historical Research* (2004).

Anon., 'The Highlandmen of Nepal', *The Navy and Army Illustrated*, vol. 11 (1900), pp. 337–9.

Ball, Desmond, 'Burma's nuclear programs: the defector's story', *Security Challenges*, vol. 5, no. 4 (Summer 2009), pp. 119–31.

Bellamy, Christopher, 'Gurkhas on alert to bolster Paras' depleted infantry', *Independent*, Saturday 14 October 1995, p. 11.

Bellamy, Christopher, 'Squaddies are warned: the real enemy is the Bosnian roads', *Independent*, Saturday 20 January 1996, p. 11.

Caplan, Lionel, '"Bravest of the brave": representation of "the Gurkha" in British military writings', *Modern Asian Studies*, vol. 25, no. 3 (1991), pp. 571–97.

Caplan, Lionel, 'Martial Gurkhas: the persistence of a British military discourse on "race"', in Peter Robb (ed.), *The Concept of Race in South Asia* (Oxford University Press, New Delhi, 1995), pp. 260–81.

Chaudhuri, Nirad, 'The "martial races" of India', Parts I–IV, *The Modern Review* (Calcutta, July 1930 – February 1931).

Collins, Bruce, 'Fighting the Afghans in the 19th century', *History Today*, vol. 51, no. 12 (December 2001), pp. 12–19, accessed on http://www.historytoday.com/MainArticle.aspx?m=17795&amid=17795, retrieved 19 July 2010.

'Foreign Affairs', *Punch, or the London Charivari*, Vol. VI (1844), Saturday, 18 May 1844, p. 209. 'The despatch of Sir Charles Napier, after the capture of Scinde'(spoof).

Golay, Bighan, 'Rethinking Gorkha identity: outside the imperium of discourse, hegemony, and history', *Peace and Democracy in South Asia*, vol. 2, nos. 1 & 2 (2006), pp. 23–49.

Hicky, Matthew, 'Hiring Gurkha girls will weaken British Army, warns top brass', *Daily Mail*, 24 October 2008.

Nicholson, James, 'The Hejaz Railway', *Asian Affairs*, vol. 37, no. 3, November 2006.

'Pheon', 'A Gurkha with Lawrence', *Journal of the United Service Institution of India*, vol. 72, no. 307 (1942), pp. 124–9.

Raugh, Harold E., Jr, 'Storming the rebel strongholds: the Perak War, 1875–1876', *Soldiers of the Queen*, Journal of the Victorian Military Society (England), vol. 102 (September 2000), pp. 7–12.

Sbornik geograficheskikh, topograficheskikh i statisticheskikh materialov po Azii (Collection of Geographical, Topographical and Statistical Materials on Asia), *Vyp.* (Editions) 24, 32, 38, 50, St Petersburg 1886–92, British Library Pre–1975 catalogue No. 285, Russia, Departments of State and Public Institutions, p. 28 Shelfmark 10059.b.19.

Smith, Irving H., 'An English view of Russia in the early eighteenth century', *Canadian Slavic Studies*, vol. 1, no. 2 (Summer 1967), pp. 276–83.

Spiers, Edward M., 'Gas and the North-West Frontier', *Journal of Strategic Studies*, vol. 6, issue 4 (1983), pp. 94–112.

THESES

Towle, Philip, 'The Influence of the Russo-Japanese War on British Naval and Military Thought 1905–14' (PhD, London University, 1973).

OFFICIAL WEBSITES

anzac.govt.nz/gallipoliguide/gallipolinames.html, retrieved 31 July 2010.

army.mod.uk/gurkhas/14281.aspx, Honours and Awards, Victoria Cross.

indianarmy.nic.in/Site/FormTemplete/frmtemp12P21C.aspx?MnId= qXAT5Eowt3c=&ParentID=a2GSpnDbrul= retrieved 30 May 2010.

indianarmy.nic.in/Site/FormTemplete/frmTemp1P2C_1.aspx?MnId= uWUCFPglwNc=&ParentID=VE+Qz4Hs3YO=, retrieved 25 August 2010.

indianetzone.com/39/role_army_british_east_india_company.htm

mod.uk/defenceinternet/pictureviewers/
gallerygurkhasfightforsecurityinmusaqaleh.htm 'In pictures: Gurkhas
fight for security in Musa Qaleh', retrieved 1 September 2010.

victoriacross.co.uk/descrip_m.html, retrieved 25 July 2010.

OTHER INTERNET SITES, INCLUDING NEWSPAPER ARTICLES

doi:10.1093/ref:odnb/35768, *Oxford Dictionary of National Biography*,
Oxford University Press, retrieved 19 July 2010.

frontierindia.net/more-glory-battle honours for the 3rd-gorkha-riflesd-
pirkanthi-hathimatha, More Glory & Battle Honours for The 3rd
Gorkha Rifles: Pirkanthi & Hathimatha', retrieved 29 August 2010.

icasualties.org/oef/Nationality.aspx?hndQry=UK, retrieved 1 September
2010.

scaredmonkeys.com/2008/12/01/mumbai-hotel-terrorist-massacre-loose-
lips-sink-ships--british-couple-claims-cnn-endangered-their-lives-be-
reporting-location/, retrieved 30 August 2010.

1914-1918.net/bat13.htm, retrieved 30 July 2010.

6thgurkhas.org/website/regiment-battles/gallipoli-campaign, retrieved 31
July 2010.

armynavyairforce.co.uk/indian_army.htm, retrieved 25 July 2010.

arrse.co.uk/gurkhas/48491-gurkha-terms-conditions-service-review.
html. 'Gurkha Terms and Conditions of Service Review', retrieved 22
July 2010.

bharat-rakshak.com/LAND-FORCES/Heraldry/Ranks/23-Rank-
Insignias.html, retrieved 22 July 2010.

bharat-rakshak.com LAND-FORCES/Units/Infantry/388-11-Gorkha-
Rifles.html, retrieved 31 August 2010.

bharat-rakshak.comIAF/Awards/Gallantry/302-MVC.html, retrieved 27
August 2010.

bharat-rakshak.com/HEROISM/Salaria.html, retrieved 28 August 2010.

bharat-rakshak.com/HEROISM/Pandey.html, retrieved 30 August 2010.

britannica.com/EBchecked/topic/286650/Indra-Jatra, retrieved 29 May
2010.

britannica.com/EBchecked/topic/354565/Machendra-Jatra, retrieved 29
May 2010.

britannica.com/EBchecked/topic/176643/East-India-Company, retrieved 29 May 2010.

britishbattles.com/second-afghan-war/peiwar-kotal.htm, retrieved 19 July 2010.

britishbattles.com/second-afghan-war/charasiab.htm, retrieved 19 July 2010.

britishbattles.com/second-afghan-war/kandahar.htm, retrieved 26 July 2010.

britishempire.co.uk/forces/armycampaigns/indiancampaigns/mutiny/delhi.htm, retrieved 21 July 2010.

britishempire.co.uk/forces/armyunits/corpsofguides/corpsofguides.htm, retrieved 20 July 2010.

colonialwargaming.co.uk/Inspiration/Poetry/McGonagall/Dargai.htm, retrieved 26 July 2010.

findagrave.com/cgi-bin/fg.cgi?page=gr&GRid=11390718, retrieved 20 July 2010.

firstworldwar.com/battles/ramadi.htm, retrieved 31 July 2010.

firstworldwar.com/battles/sharqat.htm, retrieved 31 July 2010.

fordham.edu/halsall/india/1617englandindies.gtml, retrieved 30 May 2010.

garenewing.co.uk/angloafghanwar/marchtokandahar/regiments_march.php, retrieved 19 July 2010.

globalsecurity.org/military/world/pakistan/rgt-ff-1.htm, 'Frontier Force – British Raj', retrieved 19 August 2010.

globalsecurity.org/military/world/war/indo-pak_1947.html, retrieved 26 August 2010.

globalsecurity.org/military/world/war/indo-prc_1962.htm, retrieved 29 August 2010.

guardian.co.uk/world/2009/may/21/gurkha-uk-settle-rights-lumley, retrieved 20 June 2010.

gwpda.org/naval/turkmill.htm, Geoffrey Miller, 'Turkey Enters the War and British Actions', retrieved 30 July 2010.

indianetzone.com/35/curzon_kitchener_conflict_1902-1905_british_india.htm, retrieved 30 July 2010.

meerutup.tripod.com/may2sep06.htm, *The Indian History Sourcebook*, retrieved 3 July 2010.

nepaliexporter.com/files_british_gurkha_knife.htm, retrieved 30 May 2010.

orbat.com/site/cimh/regiments/Indian%20Army%20AirborneSF.pdf,

Richard A. Rinaldi, Indian Army Airborne/Special Forces Units, retrieved 29 August 2010.

pbase.com/image89713554, retrieved 30 May 2010.

sgwmfb.co.uk/sirgeorgewhite.htm, retrieved 26 July 2010.

statemaster.com/encyclopedia/Dhan-Singh-Thapa, retrieved 29 August 2010.

talkieking.blogspot.com/2010/03/color-in-movies-part-1-kinemacolor. html, accessed 30 July 2010.

thesun.co.uk/sol/homepage/news/campaigns/our_boys/3054927/ Gurkha-officers-killed-by-a-rogue-Afghan-soldier-were-befriending-locals-before-attack.html, retrieved 19 July 2010.

travax.nhs.uk/registered/countries/malariamaps/malaria_in_nepal.asp, retrieved 26 May 2010.

tribuneindia.com/2000/20001104/windows/main1.htm 4 November 2000, retrieved 20 July 2010.

users.globalnet.co.uk/~dheb/2300/Europe/UK/Gurkha/Gurkha.htm, British Army 2300 AD: The Brigade of Gurkhas, retrieved 1 September 2010.

ww2talk.com/forum/unit-documents/19802-all-victoria-crosses-world-war-two-8.htm, retrieved 25 August 2010.

sky.com/skynews/Home/World-News/Afghanistan-Three-British-Soldiers-From-Royal-Gurkha-Rifles-Killed-In-Attack-By-Rogue-Afghan/Article/201007215664356, retrieved 26 May 2010.

guardian.co.uk/world/2010/aug/29/british-army-gurkhas-spending, retrieved 24 October 2010.

express.co.uk/posts/view/196804/Gurkhas-fear-the-axe-for-regiment(1 September 2010) retrieved 24 October 2010.

damiancollins.com/2010/10/gurkhas-safe-in-the-strategic-defence-review, retrieved 19 October 2010.

Illustration credits

ILLUSTRATIONS

Author's collection: 1–6, 34–36, text page 21. © The Gurkha Museum Winchester: 8–14, 19, 21–22, 24–33. © Courtesy of the Council of the National Army Museum, London: 15–18. © National Galleries of Scotland: 7. Carl Schultz via The Gurkha Museum Winchester: 20, 23.

MAPS

Figure 3: Lieutenant Ross's report: Ramsay Papers reproduced in Coleman, *A Special Corps.* Figure 6: The North-East Frontier and the India-Burma Border: Brigadier E. D. Smith, *Battle for Burma* (Batsford, London, 1979). Figure 7 (inset): Gallipoli: Alan Moorehead, *Gallipoli.* Figure 9: Operation Thursday March–April 1944: Brigadier E. D. Smith, *Battle for Burma.* Figure 12 (inset): Borneo Confrontation: Will Fowler and Kevin Lyles, *Britain's Secret War: The Indonesian Confrontation 1962–66.*

Index